Geographies of Globalisation
A Demanding World

Living in a Globalised World

Geographies of Globalisation: A Demanding World

Edited by Clive Barnett, Jennifer Robinson and Gillian Rose

Material Geographies: A World in the Making

Edited by Nigel Clark, Doreen Massey and Phillip Sarre

These publications form part of an Open University course DD205 *Living in a Globalised World*. Details of this and other Open University courses can be obtained from the Student Registration and Enquiry Service, The Open University, PO Box 197, Milton Keynes, MK7 6BJ, United Kingdom: tel. +44 (0)845 300 60 90, email general-enquiries@open.ac.uk

Alternatively, you may visit the Open University website at www.open.ac.uk where you can learn more about the wide range of courses and packs offered at all levels by The Open University.

To purchase a selection of Open University course materials visit www.ouw.co.uk or contact Open University Worldwide, Michael Young Building, Walton Hall, Milton Keynes, MK7 6AA, United Kingdom for a brochure. Tel. +44 (0)1908 858793; fax +44 (0)1908 858787; email ouw-customer-services@open.ac.uk

Geographies of Globalisation
A Demanding World

Edited by Clive Barnett, Jennifer Robinson and Gillian Rose

SAGE Publications Ltd
1 Oliver's Yard
55 City Road
London EC1Y 1SP

SAGE Publications India Pvt Ltd
B 1/I 1 Mohan Cooperative Industrial Area
Mathura Road
New Delhi 110 044

SAGE Publications Inc.
2455 Teller Road
Thousand Oaks, California 91320

SAGE Publications Asia-Pacific Pte Ltd
33 Pekin Street #02-01
Far East Square
Singapore 048763

in association with
The Open University
Walton Hall, Milton Keynes
MK7 6AA
United Kingdom

Contents

Notes on Contributors

John Allen is Professor of Economic Geography at The Open University. He has written widely on issues of power and spatiality, and his recent publications include *Lost Geographies of Power* (Blackwell, 2003).

Clive Barnett is Reader in Human Geography at The Open University. His research focuses on the geographies of democracy and public life. He is author of *Culture and Democracy* (Edinburgh University Press, 2003) and co-editor of *Spaces of Democracy* (Sage, 2004).

David Lambert is Reader in Historical Geography at Royal Holloway, University of London. He is the author of *White Creole Culture, Politics and Identity During the Age of Abolition* (Cambridge University Press, 2005) and a co-editor of *Colonial Lives Across the British Empire* (Cambridge University Press, 2006).

Karim Murji is a Senior Lecturer in Sociology at The Open University. His research interests are in the intersections between culture, ethnicity and racism. He recently co-edited *Racialization: Studies in Theory and Practice* (Oxford University Press, 2005).

Steve Pile is Professor of Human Geography at The Open University. He recently published *Real Cities* (Sage, 2005), which looked at the place of fantasy and emotions in everyday city life. His work, more broadly, examines the issues of space, psychoanalysis and the politics of identity.

Jennifer Robinson is Professor of Urban Geography at The Open University. She has published widely on South African cities, especially on the spatiality and politics of apartheid and post-apartheid cities. Her most recent book, *Ordinary Cities* (Routledge, 2006), offers a post-colonial critique of urban studies.

Gillian Rose is Professor of Cultural Geography at The Open University. Her most recent book is *Visual Methodologies* (Sage, 2007), and she is currently researching the ways family photographs make domestic, national and global spaces.

Roger Silverstone was Professor of Media and Communications at the LSE from 1998 until his untimely death in 2006. His publications include *Television and Everyday Life* (Routledge, 1994) and *Media and Morality: On the Rise of the Mediapolis* (Polity Press, 2006).

Preface

This book and its companion volume, *Material Geographies: A World in the Making* (Clark et al., 2008) are part of the Open University course *Living in a Globalised World*. Both books explore key characteristics of globalisation today.

That the world is now globalised seems an incontrovertible fact. There are thousands of books analysing what globalisation is and hundreds of thousands of newspaper articles reporting its various aspects. There are commissions on the state of the world economy, scares over the state of the planet's climate and campaigns against certain forms of globalisation; resources and commodities travel thousands of kilometres and television pictures can show almost any part of the world instantaneously. Why then two more books on the phenomenon?

Globalisation today has a paradoxical form. On the one hand, it seems to saturate our everyday lives in ways it never has before. Many ordinary, seemingly trivial aspects of people's lives now involve some kind of connection with places far away. The clothes we buy, the food we eat, the music we listen to and the television we watch (not to mention the set we use to watch it on), these are more and more likely to come from distant places. More people are migrating now than ever before in human history. Everyday life has gone global for many people around the world. But on the other hand, that greater involvement in some of the processes bringing distant parts of the world together does not always seem to lead to a greater understanding of globalisation. Indeed, globalisation can seem rather baffling. Moreover, it seems clear that even among those people who do claim some understanding of contemporary forms of globalisation there are debates and arguments about the implications of various globalising processes. Globalisation is at once deeply familiar and hotly contested.

These two books concentrate on this paradox of contemporary globalisation. In doing so, they examine both how global processes are now so pervasive and why globalisation is so debated.

Both books examine the four things that most commentators agree are fundamental to the way globalisation has become part of everyday life. They both examine the global economy, looking at patterns of trade, work and finance; they both look at various global political institutions and campaigns; they both examine the way new technologies are increasingly networking the world; and they both explore migration as a particularly important globalising process. In exploring these four processes, both books suggest that the geography of globalisation – the pattern of where things are and why – is crucial to understanding how it now works. Thinking geographically is a necessary part of understanding globalisation.

To understand some of the key debates about that rich and surprising global geography, *Geographies of Globalisation: A Demanding World* and *Material*

Geographies: A World in the Making focus on three things that are especially important to globalisation today. The first of these aspects is the importance to globalisation not only of the connections that make the world globalised, but also of the *disconnections* that characterise the contemporary world. Not even global capital flows everywhere; there are borders and boundaries that limit flows and movements of all kinds. There are also places seemingly left out of the globalisation club; places with only a few connections to the internet, places with no resources to sell, places ignored by the big global players, places kept distant from elsewhere. Both books explore this very uneven geography of globalisation. Secondly, *Material Geographies: A World in the Making* especially looks at the importance of the *non-human* to globalisation today (and indeed to globalisation in the distant past). One reason that globalisation is challenging is that its non-human, or natural, events and processes seem often to disrupt or to challenge human ways of going global. New viruses, climate change, volcanoes, earthquakes and tsunamis are a reminder that humans are not the only actors on the planet: planet earth itself is also active. Taking that action seriously is a necessary part of understanding contemporary globalisation. Finally, the two books examine how globalisation is made and remade in all sorts of different ways by the *different sorts of actions* of political organisations, institutions and campaigns. This is a particular theme of *Geographies of Globalisation: A Demanding World*, which explores a range of demands to take responsibility for global issues.

Together, we think that these two books can help us to understand a great deal about the paradoxical nature of living in a globalised world. After reading one or both of them, we hope you will agree.

The Open University course *Living in a Globalised World* was produced as a collaborative effort by a large team of people. In relation to these two books in particular, some of them deserve special thanks. Professor Peter Jackson from Sheffield University was an extremely helpful External Assessor, providing us with very good advice at all stages of the course. Following preliminary work by Fiona Harris, Stephen Clift coordinated the editing and production of these volumes. Diane Mole was responsible for the lovely design, and Janis Gilbert and Howie Twiner produced the maps and other figures. Karen Bridge was a great Media Project Manager and Michele Marsh an excellent course team secretary. Finally, coordinating the authors and much more besides was our wonderful Course Manager Caitlin Harvey. Caitlin worked extremely hard with unfailing goodwill, extraordinary efficiency and sound advice, and without her the quality of these books, and the course, would have been greatly diminished.

Gillian Rose, Chair of Production
Chris Brook, Chair of Presentation

Clark, N., Massey, D. and Sarre, P. (2008) *Material Geographies: A World in the Making*, London, Sage/Milton Keynes, The Open University.

Introduction

Jennifer Robinson, Gillian Rose and Clive Barnett

We are often told that all sorts of things – people, ideas, diseases, commodities, information, images – travel around the world today faster and more frequently than they have ever done before. Moreover, although some global journeys happened a very long time ago – from the journeys of Polynesians across the Pacific thousands of years ago to the upheavals of the Atlantic slave trade from the sixteenth to the nineteenth centuries – many connections between different parts of the world are much more recent, drawing on new technologies such as the internet and communications satellites. It is easy to take for granted that we live in a globalised world, one in which different places, thousands of kilometres apart, are closely linked together.

Yet are these different places so closely linked? With all the potential for instant communication now, some parts of the world remain quite unconnected; the spread of the internet, for example, is very uneven. Even where connections exist, they may not be utilised; phone calls may be too costly to make or information about events in distant places may simply be ignored. What are the processes that actually bring distant people and places closer together or, in fact, keep them quite far apart? To address this question, this book takes a detailed look at one aspect of the relationships between people and places in a globalised world: the demands for action and interaction that can now circulate around the world. The potential for communication and other kinds of interaction across the globe has opened up opportunities for the demands of those living in quite distant places to be brought to our attention, and for our demands to be addressed to others, whether they be relatively close by or quite far away.

Let us take a moment to think about this. In many countries it is unusual to open a newspaper, listen to the radio or walk down a local shopping street without encountering a demand to pay attention to something happening far away. We might be asked to think about a tragedy on a different continent, to donate money to alleviate poverty, to protest against climate change or to buy fair trade coffee or chocolate. All of these demands bring us into contact, even if only fleetingly, with people and places far away. They are an intrinsic, everyday part of making a globalised world.

Distant places are brought close to our lives by demands that come to us through various forms of the mass media, such as television or newspapers; through political actions such as protest marches or a charity's campaign; or perhaps through personal relationships – our families and friends might live far away and yet be a regular source of demands! Taking a closer look at these demands will help us to see how globalisation can indeed lead to distant people and places becoming more closely connected. We explore in some detail in Chapter 1, for example, how various political campaigns can make conditions in faraway factories appear very near. Chapter 2 considers how communications technologies can seem to open up opportunities to interact with anyone, anywhere, in more or less real time. And Chapter 5 examines how vivid images of distant people and places can make them very present in our lives. Demands to address working conditions in factories, to be in touch, or to be concerned about the fate of people far away all help us to appreciate how quite distant places are being brought closer together.

Demands also help us to understand why, although there are myriad opportunities for interaction and connection in a globalised world, some people and places remain quite distant from our lives, and may even be pushed further away.

Think again about those demands you encounter on a day-to-day basis. In the newspaper, on the radio, on the street: do you always respond to them? Do you even notice them? You would not be unusual if you did not; all of us find it impossible to respond to every demand that comes our way in a world that can seem saturated with information and debate. How is it, then, that in a globalised world some people and places remain far away from our lives as connections are not made, interactions are not pursued, and even basic knowledge and understanding may be absent?

This book seeks to address these questions in order to understand more about living in a globalised world. By exploring the demands that circulate across the globe, we learn more about how globalisation works, how it is produced, some of its consequences, and how it affects relationships and interactions among different people in different parts of the world.

It becomes quickly apparent that there is a complex geography to the globalised world. Far from being a seamless web of flows and interactions, we suggest that globalisation has created a world in which distances still matter, and in which some places are perhaps as far apart as they have ever been. Nonetheless, the interactions enabled by communications technologies, as well as by other kinds of connections, have created opportunities for very close links between other places. If we are to understand the nature of life in a globalised world, we need to keep both these possible outcomes in mind.

Most importantly, the simple fact of more global connections does not explain the nature of the globalised world. Certainly, in some instances, these connections can be used to make distant places seem very close together: when you chat to your friends on the internet, they may be in the next room or on the other side of the planet. However, in other cases, people and places can be pushed away, kept at a distance, as we switch off the TV, switch on the answering machine, disconnect the computer. The technologies that seem central to producing a globalised world enable both proximities and distances – some processes draw distant places closer together, others keep them apart.

By examining the circulation of demands in a globalised world we are able to learn more about these changing geographies of globalisation. In Chapter 3, we consider how citizens demanding action on pollution reach out to influence the distant headquarters of transnational firms operating in their neighbourhoods. We discuss, in Chapter 7, how political organisations demanding reparations for slavery can bring the consequences of slavery in Africa close to the concerns of those European nations responsible for the slave trade. In Chapter 4, we think about ways in which demands to maintain close personal ties can keep migrants attached to distant countries even as they find ways to belong and settle in their new homes. These examples all illustrate how the globalised world is shaped through the production of new kinds of proximities, bringing distant people and places closer together.

Demands also help us to understand how globalisation is shaped by the production of new kinds of distances, however, in simple personal ways, as we change TV channel or walk on the other side of the road from people wanting donations for charity, but also in the wider political world, as wealthy countries refuse to respond to demands to save lives in poor countries or to help to prevent atrocities and suffering in situations of conflict or genocide (Chapter 8). Chapter 2 looks at how the very global media that enable more interactions across the world also provide the opportunities to distance ourselves from demands. We also consider, in Chapter 6, how past connections that continue to shape demands for action in the globalised world today can be forgotten or put out of mind as easily as the statues commemorating them which we might walk past every day and never notice.

We see how new kinds of distances emerge in a globalised world, for example, as demands provoke people to push distant events and people far from their everyday concerns. In some circumstances this can be positive; if we were unable to put some distance between ourselves and the rest of the world, we might feel overwhelmed by demands (Chapters 2 and 5 explore this). Consequently, managing information and media flows can be an important skill for life in a globalised world, but many of the demands in a globalised world – such as demands for action by states or other organisations – require people to keep their distance. We do not all need to go to the seat of government to make our political opinions known – signing a petition, for example, is a way of acting at a distance, as we will see in Chapter 5. Much of life in a globalised world happens at a distance.

To understand what it means to live in a globalised world, the making of proximities and distances needs to be discussed further. We are not suggesting that the pure physical facts of being close by or far away are unimportant, but the processes that make up a globalised world – including the circulation of demands – are constantly remaking proximities and distances. Processes of globalisation are in fact producing new kinds of proximity and distance, determining who is drawn closer to our everyday experiences and who is kept at a distance, who may become vividly present at certain moments and who made absent from our concerns.

An important part of the making of these new geographies of globalisation is how people respond to the demands that are made of them. As we will explore, especially in Chapters 5–8, a wide range of responses is made to the demands that circulate in a globalised world. This might involve simply not paying attention, ignoring information, genuinely not noticing or actively contesting that a particular issue has anything to do with you; it might also entail a whole range of more positive responses. How we respond to demands determines whether people and places are drawn closer or pushed further away; whether they are allowed to have a presence in our lives or whether we insist on their absence.

The circulation of demands in a globalised world presents a considerable personal and political challenge for us as individuals. To what extent are we in some way part of events in distant places? What might we be responsible for, possibly without even knowing it? Should we even care what happens on the other side of the world? Perhaps our responsibility extends only to our neighbourhood, or to the region or country we live in. Importantly, demands are addressed to different kinds of organisations and institutions, and this raises other questions. Should the government of one country intervene in the affairs of another, for instance? Is the current government of a country still responsible for what its predecessors did hundreds of years ago?

In this book, you will come across cases where people refuse responsibility, for example for the consequences of past globalisations such as slavery (Chapter 7) or for disasters in distant places (Chapter 8).

Sometimes individuals or organisations can feel defeated by the complexity of the problem they have become aware of. Responding to conflict situations, for instance, can be incredibly complicated and in Chapter 8 we see how even those with the best of intentions can cause harmful outcomes. In other cases, you will find that people take responsibility for distant events, perhaps because they feel in some way connected to them, as in the case of sweatshops, which are discussed in Chapter 1, or because they feel moved to concern by the plight of others, as Chapter 5 investigates.

There is much to think about here, but we suggest that both taking and refusing responsibility play a part in remaking the relationships of proximity and distance that shape the globalised world in which we live.

This book examines a wide range of demands – demands for justice, solidarity, communication, redress and belonging. It considers how and why these demands are made, how people respond to them, and what happens when they are ignored. In general terms, we are eager to discover how, whenever demands are posed and responded to in the context of a globalised world, new kinds of geographies are being made. Places are pushed further away; people are brought close together. As proximities and distances are reconfigured, the globalised world is being reshaped; new opportunities for interaction are created, even as some potential connections are refused and closed off. The challenges and possibilities of living in a demanding world can be understood if we explore how new kinds of geographies and new kinds of relationships are being made, and are being made possible.

Chapter 1

Claiming connections: a distant world of sweatshops?

John Allen

Contents

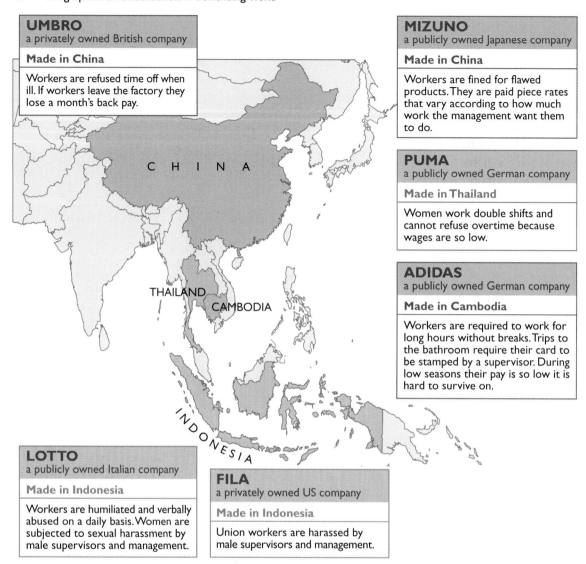

UMBRO
a privately owned British company

Made in China

Workers are refused time off when ill. If workers leave the factory they lose a month's back pay.

MIZUNO
a publicly owned Japanese company

Made in China

Workers are fined for flawed products. They are paid piece rates that vary according to how much work the management want them to do.

PUMA
a publicly owned German company

Made in Thailand

Women work double shifts and cannot refuse overtime because wages are so low.

ADIDAS
a publicly owned German company

Made in Cambodia

Workers are required to work for long hours without breaks. Trips to the bathroom require their card to be stamped by a supervisor. During low seasons their pay is so low it is hard to survive on.

LOTTO
a publicly owned Italian company

Made in Indonesia

Workers are humiliated and verbally abused on a daily basis. Women are subjected to sexual harassment by male supervisors and management.

FILA
a privately owned US company

Made in Indonesia

Union workers are harassed by male supervisors and management.

Figure 1.1   Sweatshop conditions reported by workers in factories supplying leading brands. 'Publicly owned' means that the company has shareholders and 'privately owned' means that it does not
Source: adapted from Oxfam (based on interviews with workers in factories), 2004

1   Introduction

Many of the smaller branded goods on sale to consumers in Europe and North America – the latest in clothing and footwear or the smart toys and electronic gadgets on offer – are made in factory 'sweatshops'. Found in the backstreets of modern, Western cities, but more often than not a feature of the poorer parts of the world, factory sweatshops are an integral part of today's global economy. Increasingly, as you can see from Figure 1.1, they are to be found in East Asia, in parts of China, Indonesia, Cambodia and Thailand, but they are just as likely to be located in Mexico and Central America, and on the Indian subcontinent. Goods that require little in the way of technology or expensive investment, are suitable candidates for sweatshop production: a term which takes its name from the working conditions under which such goods are produced. As these are primarily places of small-scale, flexible manufacturing, sweatshop workers – mainly women, sometimes children – are commonly subjected to long working hours, forced overtime and a relentless pattern of shift work. Wages are often below subsistence level and the working environment is frequently unhealthy, dangerous and sometimes intimidatory. Job security is largely non-existent and those who protest their exploitation or organise in response to it are likely to lose their jobs, often without warning. Similar things have been said about work in call centres in some countries, although not to the same degree or extent. Workers in factory sweatshops often have to endure poor working conditions and few commentators go out of their way to deny such a state of affairs.

A question that is worth asking, then, is given that many people in Europe, North America and other wealthy contexts benefit from the lower prices afforded by sweatshop exploitation in faraway places, should we involve ourselves with the fate of such distant workers? Or are we, quite simply, too far away to care?

Campaign groups, such as Oxfam, the Clean Clothes Campaign and various trade union organisations, have long argued that consumers should be involved and they have achieved considerable success in recent years in making the link between sweatshops 'abroad' and the benefits reaped by consumers 'at home'. Through a mix of highly charged media campaigns, boycotts and protests, such groups have used the labels of the big 'brands' – companies such as Nike, Gap, Puma, Adidas and Wal-Mart – to make their geographical point: that the daily hardships suffered by sweatshop workers in places such as Cambodia and Indonesia to produce goods for the already privileged should concern us. In a globalised world, they argue, there is a connection between what we wear every day and the poverty wages behind the label.

Activity 1.1

You have already glanced at Figure 1.1 and some of the working conditions highlighted by Oxfam in one of their campaigns. Now consider the images in Figures 1.2–1.5, which have all been used by campaigning groups at various times to convey the message that it is consumer demand for cheap clothing and other basic goods which perpetuates sweatshop conditions.

Figure 1.2 gives you a sense of the scale of the factory workshops and together with the other images provides an insight into sweatshop working conditions.

Do such images connect with your life? Are you moved in any way? Or are they simply too remote to register in any meaningful manner?

Figure 1.2   Workers assemble shoes at a Nike factory in Vietnam

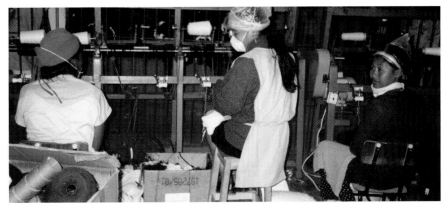

Figure 1.3   Working at the bottom of the global supply chain in Cambodia
(used by the Clean Clothes Campaign)

Figure 1.4   Line workers fix and shape shoe mouldings in a footwear factory in Vietnam

Figure 1.5   A sewing station in a Chinese factory (used by the Clean Clothes
Campaign)

The difficulty perhaps is that things which happen at some distance from the everyday routine of our lives are often hard to place or connect with. Moreover, it has to be said that not everyone views factory sweatshops in quite the same way as groups such as Oxfam, or indeed endorses their negative claims about the use of cheap labour in places such as East Asia. For that is what the statements of such groups are: *claims*. And they are far from uncontroversial.

In fact, it is possible to mount a quite different claim which insists that the location of poorly paid sweatshops in developing parts of the world is not only a positive phenomenon, but also the key to a poorer nation's economic development. For some economists and pro-market thinkers, factory sweatshops represent a way out of poverty: the price of an entry ticket into global markets. Previous low-wage economies such as Hong Kong and South Korea, we are told, turned their countries around economically by exploiting their low-cost advantages in global markets. Best to leave well alone, is their message to the antisweatshop campaigners, and let the markets do their work.

Broadly speaking, for our purposes, the claims and counter-claims around sweatshops, as sketched here, underpin two contrasting *demands*: one to be involved in matters of economic inequality and injustice, no matter how remote; the other to leave such matters well alone, to remain distant from but not necessarily indifferent to the plight of others elsewhere. The aim of this chapter is to explore both positions in order to examine the idea that we should assume some *responsibility for elsewhere*, and how this is understood to work in the arguments of the antisweatshop movement and its more pro-market opponents.

Arising out of this, a major concern of the chapter will be to show how – *in both demands* – what we take to be near to us and what we experience as far away is less rigid than may at first appear. In the case of the antisweatshop movement, a critical part of its campaign has been to try to bring exploitation and injustice in some parts of the world to the attention of people in other, richer parts. Through a series of well-orchestrated campaigns, a distant world of sweatshops has been deliberately drawn closer in an attempt to make present to those in the affluent parts of the world what life is really like elsewhere. Conversely, those who view the use of cheap labour in parts of Asia as the beginning of something better, economically, have tended to distance consumers from what is happening there by insisting on the complex, fragmented nature of the marketplace. In a world where physical distance is measured in miles and kilometres, such concerns may seem odd at first glance, but the intention is merely to ask you to think carefully about how, in the context of globalisation, some demands can lead to issues being brought close to us, while others can make them appear increasingly distant.

In the next two sections, I spell out in more detail the claims and the counter-claims which have been made around factory sweatshops. Following that, in Section 4 I look more closely at how these claims are translated into demands to take responsibility at-a-distance for conditions in sweatshops, considering both those who take a benign view of the global marketplace and those who see it as an institution which effectively obscures our geographical responsibilities. For the moment, though, I focus on the highly charged issue of the virtues and the vices of global factories overseas.

Chapter aims

◆ To examine the extent to which consumption of cheap branded goods makes consumers responsible for the conditions under which they are made.

◆ To consider the arguments for and against overseas sweatshop exploitation.

◆ To explore how consumers are distanced from overseas sweatshop exploitation and, conversely, how the antisweatshop movement has attempted to make the issue live and proximate.

2   From global factories over there …

Looking back over the 1970s, it is perhaps hard now to appreciate just how dramatic were the changes to the global map of industry taking place at that time. As more and more of the world's industry shifted from the affluent nations to the poorer, less developed countries in search of a cheaper labour force, the global economic map had to be redrawn to take account of the borders crossed and the distances traversed by firms from wealthier countries seeking to generate higher profits by relocating their manufacturing and assembly operations elsewhere.

Among the many factors which heralded this global upheaval was the ability of firms to separate out routine industrial tasks from the rest of their business: to be able to divide the simple, low-paid work from the activities of research, marketing, administration, management, and so on. Much debated at the time among academics and politicians, this geographical separation of tasks was a real departure from what had gone before, where the economies of North America and Europe had

Defining developed and developing countries

At the end of the colonial era, as many new nations gained independence, relative levels of economic development became an important criterion by which to distinguish between countries. The former colonial powers and wealthier parts of the world generally became known as advanced industrial, or *developed*, countries, while former colonies and poorer nations became known as *less developed*, or more positively, *developing* countries. Critics of the uneven distribution of wealth across the globe highlighted the role which wealth creation in some places had played in impoverishing poorer nations and, rather, described them as actively *underdeveloped*. The question as to whether economic change is developing or underdeveloping countries remains a vital issue, as the debate over sweatshops highlights.

manufactured almost everything, and the rest of the world, or what seemed like it, exported raw materials and foodstuffs to the industrial countries. Where before goods were made in one country, components were now increasingly drawn from across the globe before final assembly. To put a pair of trainers together, for example, may well have involved sourcing the rubber from one country, the air soles from a second, and the dyes from a third, with the finished article finally stitched together in factories elsewhere. Driven by North American and European firms, cheaper locations such as Hong Kong, Singapore, South Korea, Taiwan and Mexico became host, for the first time, to global factories: factories which produced goods, not for sale in their own local markets, but, and this is the main point, for *re-export to the West*.

Perhaps not surprisingly, curiosity about these 'global factories' revolved largely around questions of geography. Why over there rather than over here? Why cross such distances to produce what could be made at 'home'? The advantages of a cheap labour force recruited and trained to produce what turned out to be a rather narrow range of consumer goods with limited technology or investment topped the list of responses. Low-cost locations, or more accurately low wages, offered a competitive edge in global markets much sought after by North American and European firms. Such an edge heralded the beginning of 'offshore' production and what, nowadays, has become known as global 'outsourcing'.

2.1   Offshore fragments of industry

The rise of global factories in the 1970s owed much to the rapid improvement in transport and communications technologies which took place at that time and which made it possible to keep in touch with, and control, production processes in different parts of the world. Just as significant was the fragmentation of industrial production whereby *parts* of the manufacturing process could be relocated over vast distances. Sewing in garment and footwear production, for instance, was among the first activities to be relocated to East Asian destinations, as was the assembly work in electronics and toys. Production in both these cases could easily be transferred offshore, in contrast to, say, those tasks which required complex and specialist technologies or expensive capital investment to set up a factory outlet. Interestingly, it would have taken little in the way of investigative zeal to piece together the emerging geography of this new low-cost landscape. A quick glance at the label inside a pair of sports trainers or at the side of a glossy Matchbox toy would have revealed the whereabouts of its offshore production. Japan figured prominently in those days, as did Taiwan and South Korea, and a map of offshore locations targeted by Western firms could have been quickly drawn on such a basis. Such a map would have revealed what became known at the time as the new international division of labour (see Figure 1.6).

Defining the new international division of labour

The new international division of labour (NIDL) took its name from the fact that, in contrast to what had gone before, firms from the Western, industrialised countries, especially the USA and in Europe, started to invest directly in the 'Third World', as it was then called. Whereas poorer, 'Third World' countries had previously mostly exported raw materials and minerals, now they became involved in exporting manufactured products. Through a process of foreign direct investment, Western firms established increasing numbers of branch plants in the poorer economies of the global 'periphery'. At the same time, factories in the core, industrial nations closed and workers were laid off, resulting in a process known as 'deindustrialisation'. The loss of manufacturing jobs in the 'core' economies, however, was mirrored by the growth of manufacturing jobs at the global 'periphery' (although the two were not always directly related) – in economies which subsequently became known as the Newly Industrialising Countries (NICs). The 'Asian Tigers', namely Hong Kong, Taiwan, Singapore and South Korea, were a significant part of the NICs, as were Mexico and Brazil. Figure 1.6 shows the changing distribution of world manufacturing between the 'core' and the 'periphery' from the 1950s on. Note how the proportion of manufacturing in the developing countries increased from the 1970s through to the end of the twentieth century.

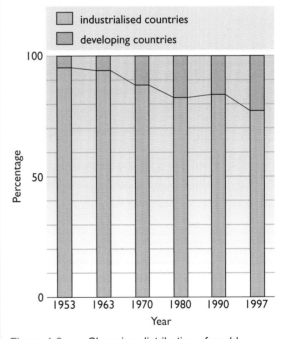

Figure 1.6   Changing distribution of world manufacturing production (UN estimate) between industrialised and developing countries, 1953–97. Source: Dicken, 2003, p. 38, Figure 3.4

What such a map would have failed to reveal, however, was the changing nature of the *connections* put in place by Western firms as they shifted work around the globe. It is often assumed that when Western firms, or any firm for that matter, reach out across borders to establish a factory outlet here, an assembly plant there or a subsidiary in some far-off location, they do so through *directly* investing and thereby wholly owning such facilities. In the 1970s and 1980s, among the low-cost manufacturing overseas operations, this was indeed often the case, but increasingly Western firms started to conduct their business at-a-distance through a variety of *indirect* means, of which subcontracting became the principle arrangement. Subcontracting is a way of putting out work to partner firms on a defined, contractual basis, where the tasks involved are specified precisely, as are the turnaround times and the quality of the finished goods. As a business arrangement, it is more flexible than owning factories overseas and more enforceable than a straightforward market exchange relationship.

Activity 1.2

Before you read on, I would like you to dwell for just a moment on the significance of this shift from direct investment by Western firms to the establishment of subcontracting ties with overseas partners. Aside from outside firms being able to pass on to the subcontractor the economic risk of supplying a particular good, this relatively new global arrangement made it easier for firms to change subcontractor should they fail to meet their production demands and prices.

How, then, would you begin to draw up the lines of responsibility for, say, the production of a pair of sports trainers in a small independent factory in Thailand contracted to a global 'brand' name such as Nike? Is Nike ultimately responsible? Is it solely down to the factory owner? Read on to the end of this subsection before you make up your mind.

Nike Inc., the US sportswear firm, did in fact take the lead in organising its overseas manufacturing business on a subcontracting basis (Donaghu and Barff, 1990). Early on in the 1970s, it established a web of contractual relationships (or partnerships, as it preferred to call them), with factories in Taiwan and South Korea, to produce its branded footwear. Of these factories, the big-volume producers among them were also contracted to other Western firms to produce a range of footwear. Nike maintained an arm's length relationship with most such producers, but with others it established closer ties to produce its 'top-of-the-range' footwear. These factories, in turn, often subcontracted the majority of their routine and standardised work, as well as their material-sourcing requirements. A decade or so later, Nike also developed subcontracting links with factories in China, Thailand and Indonesia in an effort to further diversify its assembly operations. These factories, as before, formed part of a more extensive network of subcontracting operations through which component and subassembly work was outsourced.

So, by the end of the 1990s, Nike had an estimated 800 contracted suppliers worldwide, with approximately half that figure located in Asia, and many thousands of manufacturers tied indirectly into its business operation. Between them, this network of partners, volume producers, component and subassembly firms manufactured for Nike around 175 million pairs of shoes each year (Hartman and Wokutch, 2003). Far from unusual, this complex, fragmented supply network, conducted largely at arm's length on a contract basis, became something of the norm for the global factory business. Gap Inc., the high street clothing chain, for instance, which subcontracts its garment production worldwide, has ties with around 2000 factories in Asia where workers sew and assemble its products (Gap Inc., 2004). Like Nike, it has a complex set of sourcing arrangements whereby it selects and places orders with manufacturers around the globe who, in turn, subcontract their basic, routine and material operations. Realistically, then, the merchandise that it sells in its retail stores in the West and beyond may have passed through dozens of hands, factories and firms and across any number of international borders before reaching the shopping mall.

A shirt on sale in one of Gap's many European stores may have been cut, trimmed and sewn by factory hands, or even by home-based workers, in, say, Cambodia or the Philippines, with little more than scissors and a sewing machine; yet we would be hard pressed to know precisely how this set of events came to pass or, indeed, whether the lines of responsibility are known. In between, a chain of buyers and suppliers, trading companies and sourcing agents, place their orders, purchase materials, coordinate production schedules and conduct their contractual business in a way that fragments responsibility into such small measures that it could be argued that no one can reasonably be held to account. The market *alone* seems responsible for how things come together, how something like a shirt's design, sourcing, production, assembly and export are pieced together through a series of commercial contracts.

This might help to explain why the harsh realities of life in what appear to be remote factories initially failed to register at the headquarters of the big Western firms (Hartman et al., 2003). Along with the fragmented geography of manufacturing production, it is possible to find a parallel fragmentation of responsibility, as the global marketplace makes it just that much more difficult to know who, if anyone, should be held to account for, say, the corners cut in producing goods on time or the safety measures compromised to get an order out that week. In that sense, the workings of the global market not only tangle and complicate the economic relationships involved, they also enable the actions of those overseas to be perceived as *distant* and *beyond the control* of Western companies, no matter how well intentioned their management may be. By distant here, I mean that the contractual arrangements of the marketplace made everyday life in global factories seem not just far away to many boardroom executives, but too remote to do anything about anyway. Besides which, why should they feel responsible for factories that they did not own in the first place?

Even the use of the term 'offshore production', to describe the relocation of industry, is not entirely innocent in this respect, with its connotations of faraway locations, rather than those which might be merely on the other side of an international border, as is the case with US firms outsourcing production to nearby factories in Mexico.

Figure 1.7   Land available to build maquiladoras, foreign-owned factories, in Mexico, close to the US/Mexico border

From a pro-market standpoint, global market forces and the competitive pressures that they generate leave businesses with no choice but to take advantage of lower labour costs elsewhere. In the textile business or the toy business, lower wage costs are the key to profitability; if your competitors find a cheaper labour source, you either follow their example or go out of business. It is not, so the argument runs, because managers lack integrity or compassion that there are now more manufacturing jobs in the developing than the developed world as a result of the geographical relocation of industry; rather, it is because 'the market' dictates such a change.

Defining global markets

Global markets for manufactured goods, as opposed to, say, primary commodities such as oil and timber, arose largely in the second half of the twentieth century as trade between countries intensified. The lowering of transport costs and the relative fall in trade barriers enabled firms in one country to compete with a domestic rival in another. The supply of manufactured goods across the globe as a result of worldwide demand, principally from the affluent economies, thus heightened competition between firms across, rather than within, national borders. The ability to access global markets through a firm's cross-border activities on a subcontract basis, in that sense, represents an extension of the global trading system. As part of the new international division of labour there is now a global market for material and component parts as well as finished goods. In each case, the uneven geography of labour costs in manufacturing forms part of a firm's decision about where to source these different elements. Table 1.1 gives an indication of the variations in labour costs across a range of countries.

Table 1.1   Labour costs per worker in manufacturing, 2000: selected countries

Country	Labour force (million)	Labour cost per worker in manufacturing (US$ per year)	Value added[1] per worker in manufacturing (US$ per year)
China	756.8	729	2885
India	450.8	1192	3118
USA	144.7	28,907	81,353
Indonesia	101.8	3054	5139
Brazil	79.7	14,134	61,595
Russian Federation	77.7	1528	n.d.
Bangladesh	69.2	671	1711
Japan	68.3	31,687	92,582
Germany	40.9	33,226	79,616
Mexico	40.4	7607	25,931
Thailand	36.8	3868	19,946
Philippines	31.9	2450	10,781
Turkey	31.3	7958	32,961
UK	29.9	23,843	55,060
Ethiopia	27.6	1596	7094
France	26.7	n.d.	61,019
Italy	25.7	34,859	50,760

Note: n.d. = no data.

[1]Value added measures the estimated monetary value added to goods by the labour of each worker over a year.

Source: adapted from Castree et al., 2004, p.10, Table 1.1, based on World Bank data

Those very same global market forces are also held responsible for why firms such as Nike and Gap have continuously shifted their assembly work from one country to the next since the 1970s. Faced with price competition in their own retail markets, the big retailers responded to rising wages in places such as Hong Kong, Taiwan and South Korea by switching production to the Philippines, Malaysia and Thailand and, later, to China, Vietnam and Cambodia, in their quest to reduce operating costs. The failure to meet the turnaround times specified in a contract or to adjust to the fluctuation in orders demanded by a contractor, or simply rising wage costs, could all equally trigger the search for a new, more competitive location. While some work in the footwear and electronics industries required a level of expertise not easily maintained by constantly switching suppliers, the basic nature of much clothing and textile production made it particularly vulnerable to the threat of relocation on the basis of cost. In response to clear market signals, many multinational firms simply took advantage of the uneven geography of economic development, as it was at the time. But they were not alone in doing so.

By the end of the 1990s, these multinational firms had been joined by successful Hong Kong and Taiwanese trading companies and sourcing agents who themselves moved work and contracts 'offshore' to mainland China, Cambodia and other parts of East Asia to lower costs. Of the 3000 clothing factories currently operating in Guangdong Province, a region just across what was until 1997 the international border between China and Hong Kong, it is estimated that around half are run by Hong Kong manufacturers (Liu, 2003). For firms, whether big or small, wherever they originate, the process of moving jobs around the globe in this way is now claimed as a run-of-the-mill aspect of globalisation. The process of outsourcing may have started with shirts and shoes, calculators and cuddly toys, but it now encompasses anything from microwaves, software design, computer programming, accountancy and insurance underwriting to clinical pathology services. So, what started out as a movement offshore of Western industrial jobs has, it would seem, turned into a global demand from countries such as India and China to act as outsourcing centres for manufacturing and service work of all kinds, from many different countries, including just about anything that can be sent down a wire (see HSBC, 2003; Indian Chamber of Commerce, 2004).

On this account, urban locations such as Hyderabad, Bangalore and Mumbai in India and Guangzhou, Shanghai and Shenzhen in China are not merely the offshore targets of Western outsourcing demands; rather, firms from these countries are accelerating the process by exploiting their own comparative, geographical advantages. If work moves from Singapore, the UK or the USA to India and China because the know-how, skills and human resources are available there for a fraction of the cost back 'home', that is precisely because Asian entrepreneurs are actively seeking to capture the work from abroad. They may still be largely producing goods and services for distant users, but they do so as part of a global contractual business that *fragments* both production and responsibility across borders, between Asian and non-Asian firms alike.

It is difficult to know for sure what this movement of work so far and, in some cases, so quickly, will mean for the livelihoods of workers in the poorer regions of Asia. One *claim*, however, is that the exploitation of their cheap labour resources offers developing economies the chance to move on to the first rung of the development ladder *and* the possibility of moving beyond factory and, indeed, office sweatshops to a more sustained form of wealth creation.

2.2   In praise of cheap offshore labour?

Claims over the benefits of globalisation and the exploitation of cheap offshore labour generate strong feelings and, not surprisingly, divide opinion between those who favour the global marketplace and its detractors. The issue turns on whether the constant search for ever-cheaper manufacturing and service locations is seen as a good *or* a bad thing. It may appear odd, at first, to suggest that exploiting the poor of another country can, on any measure, be regarded as a good thing, but Paul Krugman (1997), the well-known US trade economist, and Martin Wolf (2004), the chief economic commentator of the *Financial Times*, argue that it is short-sighted not to believe so. In an article entitled 'In praise of cheap labour: bad jobs at bad wages are better than no jobs at all', Paul Krugman set out the broad argument:

> The only reason developing countries have been able to compete with the [developed world] is their ability to offer employers cheap labour. Deny them that ability, and you might well deny them the prospect of continuing industrial growth, even reverse the growth that has been achieved. And since export-orientated growth, for all its injustice, has been a huge boon for all workers in those nations, anything that curtails that growth is very much against their interests. A policy of good jobs in principle, but no jobs in practice, might assuage our consciences, but it is no favour to its alleged beneficiaries.
>
> (Krugman, 1997, p.4)

Krugman accepts that workers in poor countries who produce goods for the already privileged of this world are paid very little. But he argues that, wherever these re-export industries have taken hold, there has been an identifiable improvement in the lives of ordinary people. In part, this is because the outside firms seeking to source their operations at a lower cost almost invariably pay more than local companies. They do so, he points out, not because they are of a more generous nature, but simply to entice workers to move to their factories, from the surrounding rural areas or wherever. An Indonesian woman, for instance, perhaps one of those in Figure 1.8, leaves her family and the countryside to sew clothes for Nike to earn the higher wages and is better off financially than the members of her family that she left behind. As more firms move work to the area – this time, say, a Taiwanese or a Hong Kong firm – factories start to compete with one another for workers, and wages are bid up as the pool of available labour is absorbed. Krugman describes this as a 'ripple effect' through the economy as wages rise steadily and the country moves out of abject poverty to something that, while far from wonderful, is certainly a measurable improvement on livelihoods that were available before.

There are two points which are central to this line of thinking. One, according to Wolf (2004), is that the whole process, as odd as it may sound, is about *mutual* exploitation. Outside firms do indeed exploit the poor by taking advantage of the profitable opportunities that a pool of cheap labour represents. But Indonesian or Chinese workers, for instance, could

Figure 1.8   Women workers leaving a Nike factory in Indonesia

be said to exploit the incoming firms by extracting higher pay from them and taking advantage of opportunities that previously were unavailable to these workers. In this way, both sides stand to gain from the arrangement. And, leading directly on from this, this mutual exploitation is said to represent the price of an *entry* ticket into the global marketplace. Today's affluent Asian economies such as Hong Kong, Taiwan, South Korea and Singapore all started out this way, by exploiting their low-cost resource base, and, as we can see from Figure 1.9, their growth rates since the 1960s over a 30-year period have been impressive. Compared with other less developed parts of the globe, export-led growth has been a huge boon to the workforce of these Asian countries.

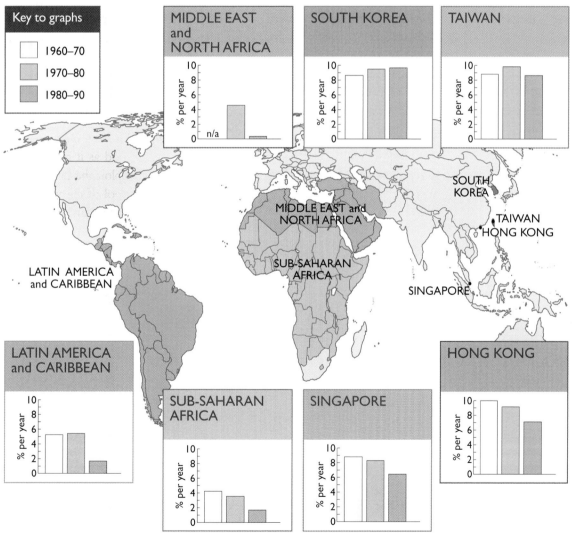

Figure 1.9   Economic growth rates in the Asian NICs and other developing regions, 1960–90
Source: adapted from Broham, 196, p. 107, Table 1, based on World Bank GDP data

On the basis of this type of evidence, it is concluded by Wolf and others that what is needed for today's poor countries is more of the same: greater opportunities to exploit their low-cost resources, not fewer; more global exploitation, not less. After all, they point out, you would be hard pressed to find a sweatshop in Hong Kong or Singapore nowadays, precisely because they have moved onwards and upwards in a kind of virtuous circle of economic growth to better jobs, higher living standards and much improved working conditions. Indeed, some of the biggest companies moving work around the East Asia region in the present day are based in these countries, as well as Taiwan and South Korea. One of the largest, the Pou Chen Group, a Taiwanese-owned company, has factories in China, Indonesia and Vietnam. Other firms such as the Hong Kong-based Li & Fung or the Taiwanese-based Nien Hsing Textile Company, are at the centre of subcontracting networks which span much of East Asia, sourcing materials from one place, dyes from another, zips from somewhere else and assembling the outfits in yet another location (see Figure 1.10).

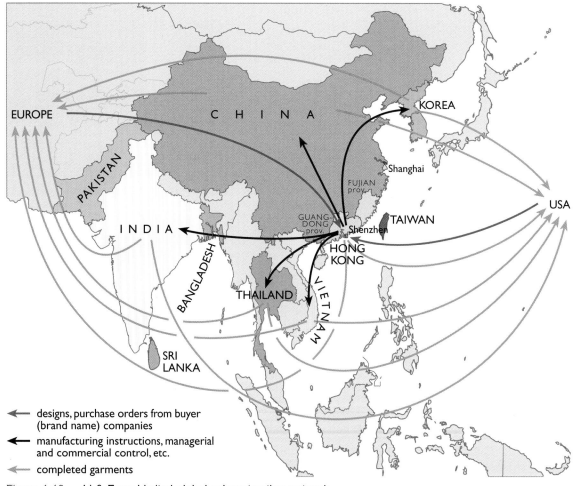

Figure 1.10   Li & Fung Limited global subcontracting network
Source: Oxfam International, 2004; Oxfam Hong Kong, 2004

By the 1990s, powerful companies like these, many of which started out as low-cost offshore manufacturers, were a small but significant part of a Taiwanese or a Hong Kong economy that had gone increasingly 'high tech', moving up the value chain by making the shift from cheap labour industries to better paid, more highly skilled work. More to the point, both Krugman (1997) and Wolf (2004) argue that the route out of poverty which these countries took is precisely the one that today's poorer countries, such as Bangladesh, Cambodia, Indonesia, Vietnam and parts of India and China, wish to follow. And, we are told, it is the exploitation of their abundant cheap labour which holds the key to that development process.

Significantly, no one from the pro-market lobby is actually denying that sweatshops exist, or trying to cover up the fact that workers in such places have to endure bad working conditions. But, as the subtitle of Krugman's (1997) article suggests: 'bad jobs at bad wages are better than no jobs at all'. Low as the wages are in the offshore T-shirt or microwave factories compared with those in more developed economies, they tend to be higher than those of other workers around them. The human side to globalisation, on this view, is that thousands of people, mainly women, take these jobs because that is the best hope that they have. Of course, Western, and indeed non-Western, firms will shift their business from one low-cost country to the next, as Nike and others did before them, but not without first leaving behind the spoils of globalisation: the dollars in circulation, the improved trading facilities, the better communications and, above all, the prospect of moving beyond the global factory business. In short, it is in the broad interests of those working in sweatshop industries to ensure that the cheapness of their labour is capitalised upon – that it is put to use – by overseas firms. Any other set of actions, by all concerned, it is argued, would be irresponsible.

Not everyone, however, primarily those in the antisweatshop movement, would agree with this claim. For them, the logic of unfolding events is deeply contestable. In fact, they would argue that it is because we are so used to thinking that the market is a law unto itself, that we allow ourselves to be deluded by its simple logic. As we shall see in the next section, far from being a good thing, those in the antisweatshop movement claim that the constant search by the clothing giants and other multinationals for ever-cheaper offshore locations seals the fate of the poorer nations. Economic globalisation, of the kind that exploits the difference in wage levels between countries, they declare, is not part of the solution for the poor of this world: it is at the heart of the problem. The human side to globalisation for them is not about using poverty as an economic asset, it is about sharing in a more equitable manner the benefits that globalisation can bring. This is the message that the antisweatshop campaigners have tried forcefully to 'bring home' to consumers in the West and beyond.

Summary

- The shift of the world's manufacturing base from developed to developing economies in the 1970s heralded the beginning of a new global division of labour and the rise of global factories to produce for Western markets. The search for ever-cheaper labour sources undertaken by multinational firms established a new geography of low-cost manufacturing operations which, to this day, remains controversial.

- The rise of subcontracting as the most flexible arrangement between international firms and their offshore producers in places such as East Asia steadily became something of the norm for the global factory business. One consequence was to further *fragment* offshore production, giving rise to a greater sense of *distance* between retailers and the working lives of those who endure poor conditions and minimal wages to produce the goods they sell.

- For Krugman and Wolf, the exploitation of poorer countries' cheap labour sources is hailed as a positive outcome, even when undertaken in sweatshop conditions. They *claim* that it gives the poorer countries a competitive edge which, over time, can lift their people out of poverty and move them further along the path of economic development and wealth creation.

3   ... to sweatshops closer to home

Holding up the East Asian success story as the way forward has, as I indicated above, little appeal for the antisweatshop movement. For its members, a different image comes to mind of thousands of workers eking out a living from the numerous sweatshops which dot that part of the world: one that involves the perpetuation of poverty wage levels, the use and abuse of poor communities, and the constant taking advantage of what is ready to hand, followed by withdrawal and abandonment. What they see is a vicious circle of decline, a 'race to the bottom', as they graphically describe it.

Figure 1.11   Clean Clothes Campaign rally, Amsterdam, 1999. The graffiti on the inflated shoe box says 'living wage' and 'do it' in Dutch
Source: Clean Clothes Campaign, exhibit 27

The comparatively small economies of Hong Kong, Singapore and Taiwan, as well as South Korea, may have fared well since the 1970s, but, as the antisweatshop movement sees it, few others can follow their example. Campaigners have not been slow to point out that the global economy nowadays is far more competitive and unequally structured, making it much more difficult for countries such as Bangladesh or Indonesia simply to mirror the achievements of the 'Asian Tigers'. The world economy is not a level playing field where all countries start out from the same economic position; the gap between rich and poor countries is wider than ever before and the uneven economic legacies are too great for those at the bottom to overcome. History, and indeed geography, sweatshop campaigners argue, is not on their side. Figure 1.12 shows how, over the last century, the richest countries increased their share of income fourfold while the poorest countries' income share remained fairly constant throughout.

This, you may well agree, is not the easiest or most straightforward message to get across, especially to audiences removed from the daily hardships that workers in Asian sweatshops have to endure. With the likely impression that little, if anything, can be done about market forces on the far side of the globe, the fragmented nature of

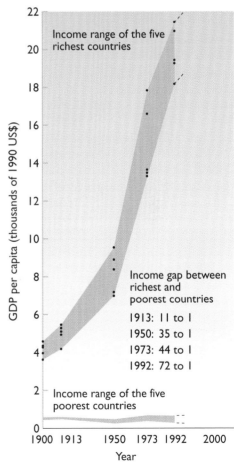

Figure 1.12   The widening income gap between countries, 1900–2000: the five richest countries in contrast to the five poorest
Source: Dicken, 2003, p.513, Figure 15.1

much of what goes on in the world economy can make such hardships appear very remote. The challenge, then, that the antisweatshop movement faced in the 1980s and into the 1990s was how to bring to the attention of consumers and retailers, mainly in Europe and North America, the distant exploitation and injustice that, it claimed, underpinned these consumers' lifestyles.

Umbrella organisations such as the Clean Clothes Campaign with its network of groups in Europe and beyond, as well as large non-governmental organisations (NGOs) such as Christian Aid and Oxfam in the UK, and the more recent university-based movement in the USA, set themselves the task of trying to *connect* the bits and pieces of the market machinery that comprise the global clothes industry. Where the market fragmented responsibility or sought to erase it, campaigning groups, often through rallies such as the one shown in Figure 1.11, tried to render the connections visible, by tracking the lines of so-called responsibility between those who actually bought and wore the socks, shirts, vests and trainers and those who laboured to produce them in far-off locations. What they set out to do was *collapse* the economic distance created by the market which separated the producer from the consumer.

Defining non-governmental organisations

Non-governmental organisations (NGOs), as the term implies, act alongside, or even in opposition to, official government bodies (although they often draw on government funding), with many different ambitions. Some work to promote development, others to meet local community needs or to encourage environmental change. Some groups are also interested in bringing about wider political changes, often at the international level, in relation to the areas in which they work. In recent years, NGOs have become a critical force in raising public awareness about issues that hitherto may not have reached a great many people outside of established interest groups and governments. Acting as pressure or advocacy groups, they frequently lobby on a single-issue basis – such as the environment, human rights or sweatshop exploitation – to achieve clearly defined goals. Although not necessarily democratically accountable, and often with limited resources, their willingness to pursue direct political action alongside traditional lobbying tactics gives them an influence that repeatedly outweighs their membership and size.

In practice, the attempt to bring the far-off within reach often touched upon a range of emotions that tried to give remote sweatshops a heightened sense of presence for distant consumers. Such is Lern's story, given in Extract 1.1.

3.1   Bringing remote sweatshops within reach

Activity 1.3

You can judge for yourself how effective campaigning groups have been in revealing the connections between producers and consumers by reading Extract 1.1, 'Nike in Thailand: Lern's story'. Posted on the Oxfam website in 2003, it represents one among many ways in which antisweatshop campaigners have attempted to make Asian sweatshops known to a wider global audience of buyers and consumers. Read it carefully and make up your own mind as to the basis of the appeal. What, if anything, is it saying about our involvement in Lern's predicament? How does it try to draw us closer to events elsewhere?

Extract 1.1

'Nike in Thailand: Lern's story'

This is Lern's story, based on an interview [by Tim Connor] conducted with her on 30 November 2002. Lern is not her real name. She asked to use a different name so that she wouldn't be victimised for giving this interview. Lern's description of working conditions at her factory fits closely with descriptions that other workers from the factory have given in interviews with staff of the Thai Labour Campaign.

Lern grew up in a rural area in northern Thailand. It was hard to find work there, and the work available was very badly paid, so in 1998 she moved to the city to look for work.

She soon found a job working on the stitching line in a factory owned by the Bed and Bath Prestige Company, which produced clothes for children and adults. During her time working at the factory it produced for many companies, including Reebok, Adidas, Levi's Haddad and a number of US Universities.

Nike was one of the largest customers. The factory was producing for Nike when Lern started there in 1998, and continued to produce for Nike right up until October 2002, when the factory closed. Lern has a card from Nike with a summary of the company's code of conduct on it. Like other workers at the factory she was required to wear this card on a piece of string around her neck whenever she was working.

Working hours at the factory were so long that work completely dominated Lern's life. Her shift started at 8.30am. Theoretically it finished at 5.30pm but most nights she worked overtime until 10pm and three or four days a week she worked until 2am. During the high season, in the lead up to Christmas, she would work past 2am. In really busy periods she would work right through the night.

Lern was supposed to get one day off a week, on Sunday. In reality, this depended entirely on the level of orders. When orders were low she got Sunday off. During busy times she would sometimes work a whole month with no days off. Depending on the level of orders, Lern worked between 70 and 110 hours per week.

Lern and other workers were willing to work this many hours in order to earn enough to save and to be able to send some money home to their families. The legal daily minimum wage in the Bangkok area is 160 Baht ($US3.70), too low to meet workers' most basic physical needs.

At the Bed and Bath factory, as in many clothing factories in Thailand and other countries, workers were paid according to a target system. On those few occasions when there was no overtime and they only worked from 8.30am to 5.30pm, their income for the day could be less than 100 Baht ($US2.30), or could be as high as 200 Baht ($US4.60), depending on how complicated the garment was to produce. When they worked overtime until 10pm they could earn between 200 and 300 Baht ($US4.60–$US6.90) in the day. When they worked overtime until 2am their daily income was between 300 and 700 Baht ($US6.90–$US16.20).

Lern had a permanent job at the factory, but the factory also employed contract workers during busy periods. These workers were only paid for 50 hours of overtime per month. They were required to work much longer hours but were not paid for the additional hours. ...

Nike, Levi's, Reebok, Adidas and other companies that placed orders at the factory all have codes of conduct. These codes were put up on the walls of the factory and workers wore a summary of the Nike code around their neck. The only person who ever explained the codes to Lern and the other workers at the factory was their employer. According to Lern he explained to them how to lie to company representatives whenever they visited the factory. Before someone from Nike, Reebok, Adidas, Levi's or another customer visited the factory, workers had to clean all the machines and prepare the factory. All workers were given cloth masks for the day. Mr. Chaiyapat instructed them to only speak positively and to say that they always finished work at 8pm.

When the company representatives arrived they would identify which workers they wanted to speak to. Factory personnel would then take those workers to a room in the factory for the meeting. On the way to the meeting workers would be reminded that they should only say positive things about the factory and warned that they would be punished if the factory received a negative report.

To the best of Lern's knowledge no-one from any of the brand name companies ever tried to meet with workers in a completely confidential setting, away from the factory. No-one ever provided workers at Bed and

Bath with education about their union rights, or with an explanation of how companies like Nike had made a commitment to ensure that these rights were respected.

In April 2001 the factory relocated. The new site was close to a factory owned by the Topline company, which had a union. From that point on Mr. Chaiyapat worked hard to make sure the workers would not form a union. He frequently made speeches to workers over the loudspeaker in which he warned that any worker who tried to form a union should 'say good-bye to your parents'. Workers took this threat seriously. According to Lern, Mr. Chaiyapat was constantly surrounded by six bodyguards and workers regarded him as akin to a mafia leader. They did not doubt that he was capable of arranging violence against them. Security guards would constantly monitor workers during breaks and if five or more workers were talking together the guards would approach them and ask them what they were talking about.

In October, the factory closed and Mr. Chaiyapat disappeared, owing workers back pay and severance pay. Lern and 350 other workers have been camped at the offices of the Ministry of Labour for the last month, demanding that the Thai government and Nike, Adidas, Levi's and the other brands give workers the money they are owed.

(In conducting the interview for this case study [Tim Connor] was assisted by Pramjai Jaikla, a staff member of the Thai Labour Campaign, who acted as interpreter.)

(Connor, 2002a, pp.1–2)

In one sense, we are being asked to identify with Lern's predicament, to care about what happens to her and others like her. But there is also a sense in which, by using the retail brand names in the e-campaign, a link is being demonstrated between what people might wear and the working lives of those who suffer 'behind the label'. In many of the campaigns waged by the antisweatshop movement – whether it be a demonstration on the high street, the boycott of a major retailer, the lobbying of politicians or an email campaign – there is an attempt to collapse the economic distance between 'us' and 'them'. This increases the presence of distant sweatshops in the hearts and minds of those who perhaps shop without giving a second thought to the conditions under which their latest purchase – a pair of trainers or socks perhaps – was produced. Among the many issues highlighted by the antisweatshop movement in such campaigns have been the proven use of child labour in Cambodian factories; the use of forced or prison labour on the Indian subcontinent; and the verbal and physical abuse of workers in China; together with violations over unsafe machinery, blocked exits, environmental hazards, appalling sanitary conditions and, as in Lern's case, excessive working hours, forced overtime and the payment of minimal wages.

The message of the often quite diverse campaigns tends to be direct, intense and carefully targeted. Figure 1.1, if you glance back at it, is much the same in both its directness and tone. There would appear to be little that is ambivalent about the political aims of the antisweatshop movement. Exploitation and injury at the workplace, it claims, is the same whether near or far. The barriers of distance that are often spoken about make no difference to a sense of injustice that, in practice, is just as relevant 'here' as it is 'there', in distant sweatshops overseas (Castree et al., 2004). Part of the campaigners' message, it would seem, is that we cannot escape our involvement in what is a seamless economic process that spans the globe. Once we pull on a T-shirt or a tracksuit made by exploited labour overseas, we are caught up in a grossly unfair system that benefits us at the expense of distant others.

At times, though, it is hard to know exactly what to make of all this, of such seemingly uncomplicated claims. Are they part of a political appeal to an assumed, almost innate sense of social justice that resides within us in the hope that we will respond positively to such gestures? Or are stories such as Lern's simply an emotional demand to care for the well-being of workers in remote, sometimes unheard of locations? Perhaps we are being made to feel guilty of perpetuating such dreadful working conditions by our often unthinking spending habits or, worse still, perhaps we are really to blame for them? I will return to these and other similar questions in Section 4, but for now I want to remain with the manifest claims of the antisweatshop movement and how it has challenged the sense in which market forces can erase or, at least, distance us from responsibilities to others elsewhere.

There are, to my knowledge, at least two ways in which this challenge has been mounted. The first, which I have already touched upon, gathered momentum in the 1990s when, to great effect, different elements within the growing antisweatshop movement *sidestepped* the tangled arrangements of the market by targeting the most visible icons of global trade, the big retail 'brands': Adidas, Nike, Gap, Umbro, Puma, Reebok, Fila, French Connection, Mattel, Disney, and so on. The antisweatshop movement, through campaigns such as 'No Sweat', fixed on brand-based multinationals as a direct and immediate political entry point into what had become a rather confusing economic landscape. In a diffuse and fragmented economic world where no one appears to be directly accountable for the bad conditions in faraway factories, the company logos offered an accessible way into the issues.

Figure 1.13   Logo artwork from the No Sweat Campaign

The voice of Naomi Klein, journalist and political activist, has been one of the strongest, in this respect. Company logos, she argues

> have become the closest thing we have to an international language, recognised and understood in many more places than English. Activists are now free to swing off this web of logos like spy/ spiders – trading information about labor practices, chemical spills, animal cruelty and unethical marketing around the world.

(Klein, 2000, p.xx)

Klein's critique of the duplicitous nature of the branded corporations' actions, in her popular book *No Logo* (2000), captured neatly the confusion among many shoppers. If the big retail labels are powerful enough to dominate what is bought and sold in the West and to fix price levels between them, then surely they have the power and influence to demand improvements in sweatshop conditions elsewhere?

In support of her case, Klein documented the ways in which the clothing and footwear majors took full advantage of the unequal geography of East Asia and beyond by moving production around to locations where workers were least protected and wages were at their lowest as part of 'a race to the bottom'. By linking the actions of the branded retailers directly to the abuse of poor communities, she managed, at a stroke, to cut out everything in between. In doing so, she was able to draw closer politically what was happening elsewhere.

Actually, I say draw closer politically, but that needs elaborating a little. It is not that the hardships which took place in poorer locations distant in miles and kilometres moved in any physical sense, but rather that such hardships were brought directly to the attention of many of the world's most affluent buyers and consumers. The collapse of the distance created by the market separation of producer and consumer placed responsibility for what was previously seen as faraway back in the hands of North American and European corporate boardrooms, city governments and consumer groups. This was not, however, to be the only way in which the antisweatshop movement bridged the gap between 'near' and 'far'.

Another claim made by the movement is that we are all in some way *connected* to a market system which effectively allows sweatshops to exist in the first place. This is about more than targeting the big brand names and linking them directly to exploitation abroad; rather, it is about piecing together the global market machinery that ties the corporate buyer, the boardroom executive, the factory owner and the consumer into a system which establishes particular lines of responsibility (Hartwick, 2000; Young, 2003; Oxfam, 2004). On this view, the specific connection to those who, for instance, actually sew, assemble and pack garments on a remote factory floor may either be through the act of retailing the clothes, or subcontracting their assembly, or plainly and simply through the act of wearing them. In each case, it is *how* individuals, groups and institutions are tied into the market system that matters and that draws them closer to the lives of distant others.

Few people are really in a position to do much about, for example, Lern's predicament directly, but, it is argued, no matter how mediated the tie, everyone can do something within the limits of their power, position and relative influence. Choosing to buy one brand and not another is one option for a consumer, as is organising a boycott of a clothing label, but neither is particularly far-reaching in its impact on the everyday working lives of those labouring in sweatshops. For that, others connected in a more immediate way, such as the factory manager or sourcing agent would be targeted. In this more practical way, the movement has attempted to track the lines of responsibility across the globe to counter the claim that market forces are virtually untraceable, given their often taken-for-granted complexity and fragmentation.

It is debatable whether the lines of connection drawn by the movement have really done justice to the market fragmentation recounted in Section 2, especially given the myriad number of economic interactions involved and their often shadowy nature. But in many ways that is beside the point. Politically, the connections drawn have already served their purpose, which is to *make present* to those who buy and sell the clothes the conditions under which they have been produced. In fact, it was the tide of criticism which followed this insight which, for the big corporate retailers of the 1990s, made it just that much more difficult for them to plead impotence in the face of what, at times, really are complex market forces.

3.2   Corporate connections

As I mentioned in Section 2, what was happening in the factories of overseas contractors was said to have appeared remote to most, if not all, the chief executive officers of the clothing multinationals in the 1980s. Overseas contractors were selected on the basis of market price, quality and reliability, not on whether forced or child labour happened to be employed to stitch the product together. However, all that changed in the early 1990s when the geographical ties between the big retailers and their overseas suppliers were made known to a wider global audience. By mapping out the *connections* between the subcontracting practices of leading international clothes retailers and sweatshop conditions elsewhere, activists within the movement claimed that the leading firms could be seen to benefit *directly* from the misfortune of others in the poorest parts of the world. The image proved to be a dogged one and, as indicated, firms such as Nike, Gap and Levi Strauss found themselves under intense public pressure to account for their connection to sweatshop conditions.

A major response, as you may have gleaned from Lern's story in Extract 1.1, was the development of *corporate codes of conduct*. The codes themselves amounted to an explicit acceptance by the big retailers that they bore some responsibility for the distant factories which laboured indirectly under their name. Usually voluntary in practice, many of the codes cover conventions on the minimum age of employment, acceptable working conditions, health and safety measures, hours of work and pay, and operate on the understanding that they should be displayed openly on the factory floor so that all contracted workers are fully aware of their rights and entitlements. Levi Strauss was the first big corporation to develop its code of conduct, *(Business Partner) Terms of Engagement*, in 1991 after it was accused of taking advantage of Chinese prison labour at one of its overseas suppliers, followed by Nike in 1992 after negative publicity about labour malpractices among its Indonesian subcontractors (Jenkins et al., 2002).

Nike's code of conduct is reproduced in Extract 1.2 in a shortened form and consists of a checklist of standards and practices which its overseas contractors are expected to meet.

Activity 1.4

Nike drew up its code of conduct, as I have indicated, to meet its own concerns. Cast your eye down the checklist in Extract 1.2 and give yourself time to consider what issues might have been added if the code had been drawn up by a workers' organisation rather than a commercial company. What issues would trade unions, for example, be likely to prioritise, or at least ensure figured prominently, on such a list?

Extract 1.2

'Nike code of conduct'

Nike Inc. was founded on a handshake

Implicit in that act was the determination that we would build our business with all of our partners based on trust, teamwork, honesty and mutual respect. We expect all of our business partners to operate on the same principles.

...

Contractors must recognize the dignity of each employee, and the right to a workplace free of harassment, abuse or corporal punishment. Decisions on hiring, salary, benefits, advancement, termination or retirement must be based solely on the employee's ability to do the job. There shall be no discrimination based on race, creed, gender, marital or maternity status, religious or political beliefs, age or sexual orientation.

Wherever NIKE operates around the globe we are guided by this Code of Conduct and we bind our contractors to these principles. Contractors must post this Code in all major workspaces, translated into the language of the employee, and must train employees on their rights and obligations as defined by this Code and applicable local laws.

While these principles establish the spirit of our partnerships, we also bind our partners to specific standards of conduct. The core standards are set forth below.

Forced labor

The contractor does not use forced labor in any form – prison, indentured, bonded or otherwise.

Child labor

The contractor does not employ any person below the age of 18 to produce footwear. The contractor does not employ any person below the age of 16 to produce apparel, accessories or equipment. If at the time Nike production begins, the contractor employs people of the legal working age who are at least 15, that employment may continue, but the contractor will not hire any person going forward who is younger than the Nike or legal age limit, whichever is higher. To further ensure these age standards are complied with, the contractor does not use any form of homework for Nike production.

Compensation

The contractor provides each employee at least the minimum wage, or the prevailing industry wage, whichever is higher; provides each employee a clear, written accounting for every pay period; and does not deduct from employee pay for disciplinary infractions.

Benefits

The contractor provides each employee all legally mandated benefits.

Hours of work/overtime

The contractor complies with legally mandated work hours; uses overtime only when each employee is fully compensated according to local law; informs each employee at the time of hiring if mandatory overtime is a condition of employment; and on a regularly scheduled basis provides one day off in seven, and requires no more than 60 hours of work per week on a regularly scheduled basis, or complies with local limits if they are lower.

Environment, safety and health (ES&H)

The contractor has written environmental, safety and health policies and standards, and implements a system to minimize negative impacts on the environment, reduce work-related injury and illness, and promote the general health of employees.

Documentation and inspection

The contractor maintains on file all documentation needed to demonstrate compliance with this Code of Conduct and required laws; agrees to make these documents available for Nike or its designated monitor; and agrees to submit to inspections with or without prior notice.

(Nike, http://www.nike.com/nikebiz/)

One issue that might be added by a workers' organisation or trade union, for instance, might be that of freedom of association and the right of workers to organise. Another might be the right to collective bargaining. In fact, the coverage of the codes of conduct vary considerably depending on who instigated the code and the parties involved (Pearson and Seyfang, 2001). Most codes of conduct, it seems, are top-down affairs, drawn up by the companies involved or by trade associations. Some have been negotiated with trade union officials and representatives from NGOs, often with the blessing of government bodies. Others have been drafted with the help of human rights advisers and other ethically minded bodies. Monitoring has also taken a variety of forms, ranging from in-house checks by the companies' own staff or specially commissioned private audits from independent firms such as Price Waterhouse Coopers, to local trade unions and branches of human rights groups, as well as various religious and humanitarian groups (Connor, 2002b; Jenkins et al., 2002). One of the most comprehensive pieces of monitoring to date has been the *2003 Social Responsibility Report* produced by the Gap clothing company (Gap Inc., 2004).

Operating with an in-house team of ninety compliance officers, over a twelve-month period, Gap conducted around 8500 factory visits, the majority of which were in Asia. Figure 1.14 shows the regional breakdown of verified code violations for the Asian region. It makes for interesting reading, if only because the company itself admits that 'few factories, if any, are in full compliance all of the time' (Gap Inc., 2004, p.12). China, the firm's largest sourcing market, is acknowledged as a particular difficulty, especially over outright verbal abuse and coercion, along with the concealment of overtime and the withholding of complete and accurate documentation. In other parts of Asia, in India, Cambodia, Vietnam and beyond, many of the issues highlighted earlier by the antisweatshop movement in recent decades are still to be found: violations over unsafe machinery, environmental hazards, excessive working hours, low wages, and so on.

While 136 plants across the globe had their supply deals terminated by Gap this time around for a variety of violations, in a fragmented industry it would nonetheless seem that total compliance remains an elusive goal. Lern's factory may not have been among those which had their contracts cancelled, but her circumstances are typical of those that corporations such as Gap need to distance themselves from in order to show the consuming public that they are *not* connected to sweatshop abuses. Corporate codes of conduct and monitoring exercises are clearly demonstrations of good intent for many companies. They are

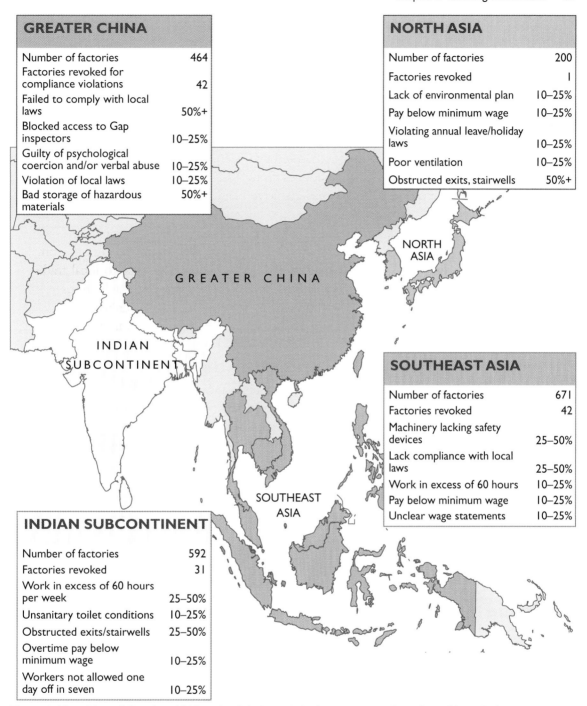

GREATER CHINA

Number of factories	464
Factories revoked for compliance violations	42
Failed to comply with local laws	50%+
Blocked access to Gap inspectors	10–25%
Guilty of psychological coercion and/or verbal abuse	10–25%
Violation of local laws	10–25%
Bad storage of hazardous materials	50%+

NORTH ASIA

Number of factories	200
Factories revoked	1
Lack of environmental plan	10–25%
Pay below minimum wage	10–25%
Violating annual leave/holiday laws	10–25%
Poor ventilation	10–25%
Obstructed exits, stairwells	50%+

SOUTHEAST ASIA

Number of factories	671
Factories revoked	42
Machinery lacking safety devices	25–50%
Lack compliance with local laws	25–50%
Work in excess of 60 hours	10–25%
Pay below minimum wage	10–25%
Unclear wage statements	10–25%

INDIAN SUBCONTINENT

Number of factories	592
Factories revoked	31
Work in excess of 60 hours per week	25–50%
Unsanitary toilet conditions	10–25%
Obstructed exits/stairwells	25–50%
Overtime pay below minimum wage	10–25%
Workers not allowed one day off in seven	10–25%

Figure 1.14   Map of Gap Inc. 2003 code violations, Asia (percentages of number of factories)
Source: adapted from Gap Inc., 2004, pp.14–15

essentially a *counter* to the defamations poured upon them by the antisweatshop movement: sufficient evidence that such companies have at least tried to meet their responsibilities to factory workers on the far side of the globe, even if hardships inevitably persist across the industry.

A rather different conclusion was reached, however, by Oxfam (2004), the Clean Clothes Campaign and various trade union groupings in their reviews of the efforts of the big sportswear firms to fulfil their distant obligations. For them, the 'race to the bottom' continues apace *despite* such companies recognising their responsibilities to the workers who make the trainers, tracksuits and T-shirts for them. At the same time that firms such as Nike, Adidas, Reebok, Puma and Fila adopt corporate codes of conduct leading to more enlightened working practices, they also demand greater flexibility, lower prices and shorter delivery times from their overseas suppliers. Put another way, those companies which have put in place codes and monitoring practices to tackle sweatshop abuses are, on this view, themselves producing the very conditions that encourage their violation. If the global retail firms insist on using the cheapest available source of labour, push for quicker turnaround times and demand flexibility in meeting orders of different sizes, then the factory managers, those such as Mr Chaiyapat in Extract 1.1, have no choice but to pressurise their workers to labour longer and faster, to cut corners on health and safety issues, and to accept illegally low pay levels.

In short, according to the antisweatshop campaigners, it is the instrumental business practices of the big retailers which impose unrealistic expectations on their suppliers if, as is supposed, they really do wish to curb the poor working conditions in their subcontracted factories overseas. The big retail companies, Oxfam and others insist, cannot have it both ways. They cannot have ever-lower production costs with ever-faster delivery times *and* expect factory managers to provide decent jobs at a living wage. It is just not possible to square the circle.

Summary

- During the 1970s and 1980s, countries such as Hong Kong, Singapore and Taiwan benefited from their low-cost advantages in the new global division of labour. Now, however, the gap between rich and poor nations is wider and competition in the world economy greater, prompting campaigning groups to argue that contemporary low-wage economies do not have the options for economic development that their predecessors had.

- In the face of market fragmentation, the antisweatshop movement has sought to *connect* producers and consumers across the globe by linking the big brand retailers directly to sweatshop exploitation abroad. As such, the movement attempted to bring *closer* to Western consumers the distant exploitation and hardships that, it claimed, underpinned their lifestyles.

- Under pressure to *distance* themselves from sweatshop abuses, the big retail corporations adopted corporate codes of conduct which, according to antisweatshop campaigners, have done little to avoid a 'race to the bottom' among the low-wage economies.

So, despite agreement over the fact of sweatshop exploitation in low-wage economies, the two sides to the debate which I have considered in this and the previous section differ markedly as to the economic consequences of that exploitation and who is responsible for it. Their claims and counter-claims over the issues of cheap labour, market forces and economic development are set out in Figure 1.15 to give you a broad idea of their different standpoints.

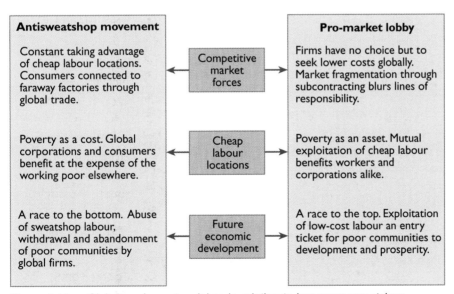

Figure 1.15   Claims and counter-claims in relation to low-wage sweatshop industries

4   Responsibility for elsewhere

Up to now I have focused on the claims of the antisweatshop movement and the counter-claims of those who contest the purely negative conclusions drawn about the exploitation of another country's poor. To that end, I have, at various moments, touched on issues of demands to take responsibility: whether, for instance, responsibility for sweatshops should be divided up in some way between all those connected to the market system which gives rise to them, or placed firmly at the door of the big retailers; whether responsibility for such hardships is greater closer to home than far away; or whether perhaps it would be irresponsible to intervene in market forces in the first place. These are all weighty issues with a much wider relevance than simply in relation to sweatshops. Realistically, in the remainder of this chapter I can only begin to probe them, but we will return to them more fully in later chapters. What I would like to do in this section, therefore, is to stand back from the evidence for the conditions in factory sweatshops – which, as you may recall, are not in dispute – and consider more the issue of what *responsibility for elsewhere* might actually involve.

In one respect, as we have seen, the adoption of codes of conduct by the clothing multinationals, and increasingly in other areas such as toys and footwear, can be taken as a clear indication of the acceptance at the corporate level of demands to take responsibility for working conditions in distant places. However, such actions may also be read in a more cynical manner as a form of damage-limitation exercise to their corporate brands in the wake of negative media publicity and falling sales. Taking responsibility can be good for business in an interdependent global economy where the far off is not as distant as it once seemed. Indeed, many in the pro-market lobby would go further than this and argue that it is a firm's responsibility to participate in the world's markets, in so far as the failure to globalise is tantamount to denying the world's poor a chance to raise their living standards and gain a share in the rising levels of prosperity overall (Moran, 2002; Hartman et al., 2003).

4.1   It's up to the market ...

On this view, market responsibility looks something like this: if left alone, foreign companies will do what they do best, which is to spot an opportunity in the global marketplace, take advantage of it, and then try to keep the spoils of globalisation to themselves until such time that they are forced by market pressures to share them with the local population in the form of higher wages and other such improvements. Or in Krugman's stinging words:

> These improvements have not taken place because well-meaning people in the west have done anything to help – foreign aid, never large, has lately shrunk to virtually nothing. Nor is it the result of the benign policies of national governments, which are as callous and corrupt as ever. It is the indirect and unintended result of the actions of soulless multinationals and rapacious local entrepreneurs, whose only concern was to take advantage of the profit opportunities offered by cheap labour. It is not an edifying spectacle; but no matter how base the motives of those involved, the result has been to move hundreds of millions of people from abject poverty to something still awful but nonetheless significantly better.
>
> (Krugman, 1997, pp.3–4)

The working conditions in the global factories may be awful at times, as indeed many in the pro-market lobby readily admit, but that does not alter their argument that a firm's responsibility lies in exploiting opportunities as they arise across the changing map of global uneven development. A world spatially differentiated by levels of wealth and income provides an opportunity for the poorest areas to exploit their low-cost competitive advantage and raise themselves out of poverty. The poor themselves, on this reckoning, have a responsibility to themselves, along with governments and local administrations, to attract overseas firms and allow market forces the possibility of realising a virtuous circle of growth. One could argue that this was precisely the kind of responsibility exercised by the 'Asian Tigers' in the 1970s and 1980s, when the governing administrations in Hong Kong and Singapore, for instance, actively courted foreign multinationals and the work they brought with them.

This notion of market responsibility implies that it is precisely the kinds of demands espoused by the antisweatshop movement that are *irresponsible*. Because the movement lays the blame for sweatshop exploitation at the door of the big multinationals, particularly those in North America and Europe, and exerts pressure on consumers to take note of the conditions under which their shirts and socks are made so that they, in turn, may put pressure on the multinationals, the whole process can lead to a gross distortion of market forces. At the end of this line of blame is the Indonesian factory manager who, on being informed by a contract multinational that he will have to pay more to the women he employs to stitch trainers, either forces them to work harder and faster or subcontracts production to a less visible workplace, possibly even to home workers. In either case, it is the workforce who lose out as a result of well-intentioned campaigns, even to the extent of losing their jobs.

For the pro-market lobby, it is precisely the feelings of guilt induced among consumers by often well-meaning campaigners which distorts the whole process. By insisting that sweatshop conditions exist elsewhere for their benefit, the antisweatshop movement has somewhat misguidedly made many consumers feel guilty about the clothes that they buy and many other manufactured goods. For those who wear the clothes or play with the latest electronic gadgets, the idea that they are in some way to blame for the harm carried out elsewhere, in their 'name' so to speak, is not only misleading, it could also result in jobs lost, factories closed down, and the only feasible route out of poverty for some countries blocked.

After all, so the pro-market lobby point out, it is only because antisweatshop campaigners have made a connection between the clothes worn 'here' and their distant manufacture over 'there' that we feel anything at all. In one sense the connection is arbitrary and depends upon a sense of shame being successfully invoked. Why, they insist, do we not care in the same way for those we have no connection to, yet who suffer far more than those fortunate enough to hold jobs in garment factories: those scraping a subsistence living in the fields or scavenging for scrap on the garbage heaps, for example? Also, they ask, why should anyone take responsibility for what happens elsewhere, other than the corporate firms directly involved, especially when there are so many pressing economic issues closer to home?

In response, the antisweatshop movement and other transnational NGOs stress the interdependency of all forms of economic activity nowadays, direct or otherwise. But, importantly, they also emphasise that faraway consumers, retailers and government officials may *not be to blame* for what happens elsewhere, on the far side of the globe. But they do bear a responsibility. The political theorist, Iris Marion Young, reflecting on the nature of the antisweatshop movement's claims, believes that the movement deliberately distinguishes blame from responsibility and only asks consumers to exercise *responsibility* in relation to sweatshops overseas. It is to her arguments that I now turn.

4.2 ... or it's all down to connections

For Iris Marion Young, the responsibility of those in North America and Europe towards distant others does indeed rest with their connections to injustices elsewhere, but it would be a mistake to stretch this line of reasoning too far. Although these connections, whether as a consumer, boardroom executive or shop manager, can establish a line of responsibility, as was claimed in Section 3.1, for Young this is only the starting point and not the end point of our involvement. We do not have to worry endlessly about exactly where the shirt on our back comes from or think that we are in some way to blame for the harm done by ruthless factory managers elsewhere, but, she argues, we should be aware that we are connected to an economic *system* which allows sweatshops to persist across the globe. As Young understands it, those in the antisweatshop movement are not demanding that everyone should care about workers on the other side of the world simply because they suffer oppression and injury – as do many people in other kinds of contexts. Rather, it is because we are all part of much bigger processes which enable those conditions that we should do what we can. We may not be to blame for suffering elsewhere, but in this and many other cases, we are connected to it. As she goes on to say:

> The harm the workers suffer comes most immediately at the hands of factory owners and managers who set hunger level wages and inhumane hours and intimidate anyone who tries to change these conditions. These owners and managers themselves operate, however, in a huge global system that both encourages their practices and constrains their ability to modify those practices – because of a realistic fear of being undercut in a highly competitive environment. The antisweatshop movement argues that all the persons and institutions who participate in the structured processes that produce this constraint should take responsibility for the condition of the workers. We are connected to them; we wear clothes they make; we sell them in our stores.
>
> (Young, 2003, p.40)

Our connection to a system which produces these harms and injustices means that we have a political responsibility to do something about them. The intolerable conditions endured in sweatshops, wherever they may be, come about through the actions of many different people operating in ways that, were they aware of the final consequences, they may well choose not to adopt. The same unedifying spectacle, the same soulless multinationals and rapacious local firms figure in Young's account of factory sweatshops as much as they do in Krugman's, but this time the argument is not to leave them well alone; it is to intervene in a global system that encourages the worst practices to ensure economic survival. Left to their own devices, sweatshop economies will not lead their workforces out of poverty, but deeper into it. Accepting political responsibility, on this view, means, first and foremost, understanding how individuals, groups and institutions are tied into the global market system and then acting upon those connections.

Activity 1.5

I would like you to turn to Reading 1A by Iris Marion Young (2003) entitled 'From guilt to solidarity: sweatshops and political responsibility', which you will find at the end of the chapter. As you read through it, consider what makes responsibility 'political' as opposed to 'legal' for Young. You will also see that she identifies four features of political responsibility which distinguish it from blame. I would like you to focus on *two* of those features. The first is the idea that responsibility is political when it is *shared*, by virtue of the fact that together our actions contribute, often in some small way, to sweatshop conditions abroad; and the second is the notion that our responsibility to those in distant sweatshops arises through our everyday behaviour when, as a matter of course, we try on, buy or sell the items – clothes, shoes, electrical appliances, whatever – made in faraway factories.

The reading is fairly compressed, but as I understood the two features of political responsibility, this is what I took Young to have in mind.

Whereas legal responsibility involves assigning direct, traceable blame for outcomes, we have seen that sweatshop production often involves a myriad decisions and actions, responsibility for which is shared by many. Shared responsibility for events elsewhere is political, we can suppose, because little will happen to change sweatshop conditions abroad unless students, workers, consumers, sales assistants, bureaucrats, buyers and the like join in *collective action* with others to persuade the big decision makers to get involved. Everyone has a share of the responsibility, including the exploited workers themselves (so they are not helpless 'victims'), because it is our collective actions – innocuous or otherwise – which gave rise to sweatshops in the first place. Of course, not all responsibilities are of the same order or magnitude; some groups such as factory owners and government institutions are more caught up in the system, some such as the big multinationals are more powerful than others, and some are more capable of bringing about change at arm's length. For this reason, those with only consumer spending power at their disposal should use it to influence those who can effect change – the big corporate retailers, the global regulatory bodies and such.

Young also wants to argue that our responsibility for others elsewhere does not arise through exceptional circumstances, but from the commonplace buying and selling practices which characterise the global marketplace. Most of us when we shop for this or that expect the goods to be available and on sale at an affordable price; the retailers take it upon themselves to stock the goods and expect companies further down the line to procure them from wherever, and so on, until we reach the overseas factory manager and the workers on the assembly line who expect, but rarely get, a living wage. There is nothing unusual about this set of market connections, much of it is conventional business practice, yet those on the factory floor suffer. But if this outcome is puzzling, Young argues that it is our responsibility to bring into question what 'business as usual' means and where it can lead. If our demand for cheap clothing and other consumer items prevents others from earning a living wage, then we should first reflect on what we take for granted when we shop.

To put it another way: if we think that sweatshops are, at root, really the result of a dishonest contractor's dealings or those of a rogue factory manager, then the solution is merely to address these exceptional cases and the problem will go away. Normality is restored by punishing those who are to blame. If, however, contractors and managers alike are both caught up in an economic system which leaves them no margin to improve factory pay and conditions, there is nothing exceptional about such circumstances and, therefore, no one to punish. It is not that we are all to blame, rather it is that our part as consumers in a much larger set of ordinary economic transactions makes us responsible for what price we are willing to pay for goods made elsewhere and the conditions under which they are produced.

What all this seems to boil down to for Young – and it is one of the reasons why staff at the North American clothing company, Gap, find themselves inspecting thousands of remote, scattered workplaces – is that the political responsibility that flows from our connections can exert pressure on others to bring about geographically far-reaching changes. That does not mean to say, however, that those people in the more affluent parts of the world who take responsibility for elsewhere are the only means by which change can come about. Local forms of pressure – the poor themselves, for example, who have a voice through trade unions, social movements, local radio or the internet – can also bring about improvement and change. It is not simply down to what people in wealthier countries can do; rather, it is about the reach and mobilisation of different voices, groups and movements acting together – within the limits of their abilities and resources – to ensure that factory workers producing for Western markets do so under decent working conditions, properly regulated and enforced. In that sense, Gap's compliance officers are but one part of a much larger equation.

Summary

- The question of who is responsible for factory sweatshops in the poorer regions of the globe remains a passionate political issue, in North America and beyond. Views on how responsibility for overseas sweatshops should be exercised differ between those who believe that it should be left to market forces to improve conditions and those who consider that everyone, as a consumer, bears some responsibility for their perpetuation and should intervene to bring about change.

- For the antisweatshop movement, those in wealthier contexts who benefit from overseas sweatshop production are responsible, but *not to blame*, for such conditions. Whereas factory owners and managers are culpable, distant consumers and other agencies are *politically responsible* in that they have a collective responsibility to change our everyday buying and selling practices so that factory conditions elsewhere improve.

5   Conclusion

Throughout this chapter, a major concern has been to show how the *demand* of the antisweatshop movement that we not only respond to, but take responsibility for, economic injustices, no matter how distant, is an intensely controversial one. Claims by campaigning groups such as Oxfam and Christian Aid that consumer demand for cheap branded goods perpetuates poverty wage levels in the sweatshop industries are countered by claims from the pro-market lobby which point in an altogether different economic direction. Whether the issue is one of factory sweatshops in East Asia, or further afield in Mexico and Central America, or indeed worker exploitation more generally in relation to the agricultural foodstuffs that we eat and drink, there are pressures on us to respond to the controversial demands thrown up by life in a globalised world.

As part of understanding the nature of such demands and the claims that back them up, I have also been keen to show how events often thought about as distant from a particular audience, such as shopkeepers, retailers or consumers, can be *drawn closer* by political appeals to evoke an immediate response. Equally, it is possible to find ourselves *distanced* by the sheer complexity of global events so that any response, immediate or otherwise, may often appear futile or pointless. In this way, when it comes to matters of global injustice, the distinction between what is near and what is far may not be best defined by mere physical distances; instead, political demands and global processes are involved in making new kinds of distances and proximities.

In the following chapter, we take this understanding of proximity and distance a step further by exploring new forms of media in a variety of global settings – where physical distance is often no barrier to contact.

References

Broham, J. (1996) 'Postwar development in the Asian NICs: does the neoliberal model fit reality?', *Economic Geography*, vol.72, pp.107–30.

Castree, N., Coe, N.M., Ward, K. and Samers, M. (2004) *Spaces of Work: Global Capitalism and Geographies of Labour*, London, Sage.

Clean Clothes Campaign, 'CCC photo exhibit', http://www.cleanclothes.org/ (accessed 11 March 2005).

Connor, T. (2002a) 'Nike in Thailand: Lern's story', http://www.oxfam.org.au/campaigns/nike/reports/lern.html (accessed 4 March 2005).

Connor, T. (2002b) 'Re-routing the race to the bottom? Transnational corporations, labor practice codes of conduct and workers' right to organise – the case of Nike Inc.' in Hernandez-Truyol, B.E. (ed.) *Moral Imperialism: A Critical Anthology*, New York, New York University Press.

Dicken, P. (2003) *Global Shift: Reshaping the Global Economic Map in the 21st Century* (4th edn), London, Sage.

Donaghu, M.T. and Barff, R. (1990) 'Nike just did it: international subcontracting and flexibility in athletic footwear production', *Regional Studies*, vol.24, no.6, pp.537–52.

Gap Inc. (2004) *2003 Social Responsibility Report*, San Francisco, CA, Gap Inc.

Hartman, L.P., Arnold, D.G. and Wokutch, R.E. (2003) *Rising Above Sweatshops: Innovative Approaches to Global Labor Challenges*, Westport, CT, Praeger.

Hartman, L.P. and Wokutch, R.E. (2003) 'Nike Inc.: corporate social responsibility and workplace standard initiatives in Vietnam' in Hartman, L.P., Arnold, D.G. and Wokutch, R.E. (2003) *Rising Above Sweatshops: Innovative Approaches to Global Labor Challenges*, Westport, CT, Praeger.

Hartwick, E.R. (2000) 'Towards a geographical politics of consumption', *Environment and Planning A*, vol.32, pp.1177–92.

HSBC (2003) 'The future of work migration – an international bank's perspective' in *Financial Times* (in association with Nasscom) (ed.) *Outsourcing to India: The Next Steps*, London, FT.

Indian Chamber of Commerce (2004) 'India Inc. newsletter', http://www.indianchamber.org/al/index.asp (accessed 2 March 2004).

Jenkins, R., Pearson, R. and Seyfang, G. (2002) *Corporate Responsibility and Labour Rights: Codes of Conduct in The Global Economy*, London, Earthscan.

Klein, N. (2000) *No Logo*, London, Flamingo.

Krugman, P. (1997) 'In praise of cheap labour: bad jobs at bad wages are better than no jobs at all', http://web.mit.edu/Krugman/www/smokey.html (accessed 9 July 2004).

Liu, K. (2003) *Research Report on Global Purchasing Practices and Chinese Women Workers*, Shenzhen, Institute of Contemporary Observation.

Moran, T.H. (2002) *Beyond Sweatshops: Foreign Direct Investment and Globalization in Developing Countries*, Washington, DC, Brookings Institution Press.

Nike, http://www.nike.com/nikebiz/nikebiz.jhtml;bsessionid=SIBV3FRDDEN3GCQCGJFCF4YKAIZB2IZB?page=25&cat=code (accessed 30 June 2005).

Oxfam (2004) *Play Fair at the Olympics*, Oxford, Oxfam GB.

Oxfam Hong Kong (2004) *Turning the Garment Industry Inside Out: Purchasing Practices and Workers Lives*, Hong Kong, Oxfam Hong Kong.

Oxfam International (2004) *Trading Away Our Rights: Women Working in Global Supply Chains*, Oxford, Oxfam International.

Pearson, R. and Seyfang, G. (2001) 'New hope or false dawn? Voluntary codes of conduct, labour regulation and social policy in a globalizing world', *Global Social Policy*, vol.1, no.1, pp.49–78.

Wolf, M. (2004) *Why Globalization Works*, New Haven, CT, Yale University Press.

Young, I.M. (2003) 'From guilt to solidarity: sweatshops and political responsibility', *Dissent*, Spring, pp.39–44.

Iris Marion Young, 'From guilt to solidarity: sweatshops and political responsibility'

Liability vs. political responsibility

I think that this claim of responsibility, implicit in the antisweatshop movement, as well as some other contemporary labor and environmental movements, is rather novel. It involves an argument that agents are responsible for injustice by virtue of their structural connection to it, even though they are not to *blame* for it. My main purpose in this essay is to outline the elements of this argument and contrast it with the more familiar concept of responsibility as blame or liability.

The most common model of assigning responsibility derives from legal reasoning about guilt or fault for a harm inflicted. Under the fault model, one assigns responsibility to particular agents whose actions can be shown to be causally connected to the circumstances of the harm. This agent can be a collective entity, such as a corporation, treated as a single agent for the purposes of assigning responsibility. The connected actions must be voluntary. If candidates for responsibility can demonstrate that their causal relation to the harm was not voluntary, that they were coerced or that they were in some other way not free, then their responsibility is usually mitigated if not dissolved. When the agents are causally and freely responsible, however, it is appropriate to blame them for the harmful circumstances. A concept of strict liability departs from this model in that it holds individuals liable for an action even if they did not intend the outcome, or holds them liable for a harm caused by someone under their command. While different in these respects, responsibility as fault and strict liability share two other features important for distinguishing them from political responsibility. The fault or liability model is primarily backward looking; it reviews the history of events in order to assign responsibility, usually for the sake of exacting punishment or compensation. Assigning responsibility to some agents, on this model, also has the function of absolving other agents. To find this person or group guilty of a crime usually implies that others accused of the same crime are not guilty.

Assuming that I am right so far, the antisweatshop movement must understand responsibility differently. The universities and consumers it targets are not themselves to blame for the working conditions. They are connected to those conditions only indirectly and in a highly mediated fashion through market relations and other complex structural processes. Although many people would like to say that such a mediated connection implies that they are not responsible at all, the movement argues that institutions, individual consumers, and faraway decision makers in the clothing industry, are responsible in a different sense, which I want to call political responsibility. There are four features of the idea of political responsibility that distinguish it from blame or liability.

1   **Political responsibility does not mark out and isolate those who are considered to be responsible.** A blame model of responsibility distinguishes those who are responsible from others who, by implication, are not responsible. Such isolation of the one liable or blameworthy person from all the others is an important aspect of legal responsibility, both in criminal and tort law. Because they argue that organizations or collectives, as well as individual persons, can be blamed for harms, most accounts of collective responsibility also aim to distinguish those who have done the harm from those who have not.

    But many harms, wrongs, and injustices have no isolatable perpetrator; they result from the participation of millions of people and institutions. Endemic large-scale homelessness in an otherwise affluent society, for example, is arguably an injustice without an identifiable perpetrator. Some people and institutions perform specific actions or enforce policies that can be shown as contributing to homelessness, but they do not intend to do that, and what they do only has this effect insofar as it is supplemented and mediated by other actions even further removed from that outcome. For other cases of injustice some specific perpetrators can be identified and blamed as immediate causes, but these too are enabled and supported by wider social structures in which millions of people participate. I have suggested already that the injustices of inhumane labor conditions should be analyzed on these two levels. In the conception of political responsibility, then, finding that some people bear responsibility for injustice does not necessarily absolve others.

2   **Political responsibility questions 'normal' conditions.** In a blame or liability conception of responsibility, what counts as a wrong is generally conceived as a deviation from a baseline. Implicitly, we assume a normal background situation that is morally acceptable, if not ideal. A crime or an actionable harm consists in a morally and legally unacceptable deviation from this background structure. The process that brought about the harm is conceived as a discrete, bounded event that breaks away from the normal flow of events. Punishment, redress, or compensation aims to restore normality or to 'make whole' in relation to the baseline condition.

    A concept of political responsibility in relation to structural injustices, on the other hand, doesn't focus on harms that deviate from the normal and acceptable, but rather brings into question the 'normal' background conditions. When we judge that structural injustice exists, we are saying that at least some of the accepted background conditions of action are morally unacceptable. Most of us contribute to a greater or lesser degree to the production and reproduction of structural injustice precisely because we follow the accepted and expected rules and conventions of the communities in which we live. Usually we enact standard practices in a habitual way, without explicit reflection on what we are doing, having in the foreground of our consciousness and intention our immediate goals and the particular people we need to interact with to achieve them.

The antisweatshop movement well illustrates this challenge to normal structural background conditions. It asks consumers, universities, and other institutions that contract with retailers, brand-name clothing companies, and many other agents, to reflect on the hitherto acceptable market relationships in which they act. It challenges all the agents that are part of the economic chain between the workers who make garments and the people who buy and wear them to ask whether 'business as usual' is morally acceptable.

3 **Political responsibility looks forward rather than backward.** Blame and praise are primarily backward looking judgments. They refer to an action or event assumed to have reached its end. The purpose of assigning responsibility as fault or liability is usually to sanction, punish, or exact compensation. Such backward looking condemnation may partly have a forward looking purpose; we may wish to deter others from similar action in the future or to identify weak points in an institutional system that allows such blameworthy actions, in order to reform the institutions. Once we take this step, however, we may begin to move toward a conception of political responsibility. For many people may be bound to undertake those reforms, even though they are not to blame for past problems.

Political responsibility doesn't reckon debts, but aims at results, and thus depends on the actions of everyone who is in a position to contribute to those results. Taking political responsibility in respect to social structures emphasizes the future more than the past. Because the causal connection of particular individuals or even organizations to the harmful structural outcomes is often impossible to trace, there is no point in seeking to exact compensation or redress from some isolatable perpetrators. If we understand that structural processes cause (some) injustices, then those of us who participate in the production and reproduction of the structures should recognize that our actions contribute to the injustice. And then we should take responsibility for changing the processes. To return to the sweatshop case, the main objective of this movement is not to compensate workers for past wrongs but to make social changes that will eliminate future harm. (Such a project cannot be undertaken, of course, without reflection on the past: we need to understand the history of processes that produce specific outcomes, and in this sense must be backward looking.)

4   **Political responsibility is shared responsibility.** If the injustice is a
result of structural processes involving many individuals and
institutions engaging in normal and accepted activities, the necessary
change requires the cooperation of many of those individuals and
institutions. Discharging my responsibility in this situation means
joining in collective actions with others. We share responsibility for
organizing changes in how the processes work. Working through state
institutions is often an effective means to change structural processes,
but states are not the only tools of effective action. The antisweatshop
movement has begun to create information-sharing and monitoring
institutions whose purpose is to connect workers in specific locales to
solidarity organizations far away who try to hold manufacturers to
account for working conditions. Our responsibility is political in the
sense that acting on it involves joining in a public discourse where we
try to persuade one another about courses of collective action that will
contribute to social change.

An important corollary of this feature of political responsibility is that
many of those properly thought to be victims of harm or injustice may
nevertheless have political responsibilities in relation to it. In a fault
model of responsibility, blaming the victims of injustice serves to
absolve others of responsibility for their plight. In a conception of
political responsibility, however, those who can properly be called
victims of structural injustice often share the responsibility to try to
change the structures. In the case of labor exploitation, the workers
themselves ought to resist if they can.

Conceptualizing political responsibility as distinct from blame is important
for motivating political action. When people feel that they are being
blamed, they tend to react defensively. They look for other agents to
blame instead, or they make excuses that mitigate their liability. Such
practices of accusation and defense have an important place in morality
and law. When the issue is how to mobilize collectives for the sake of
social change, however, such rhetorics of blame and finger-pointing lead
more to resentment and refusal to take responsibility than to useful
action. If corporate executives or ordinary people buying shoes believe
that antisweatshop activists are blaming them for the conditions under
which the shoes are produced, they rightly become indignant, or scoff at
what they perceive as the extremism of the movement. Distinguishing
political responsibility from blame or liability allows us to urge one
another to take responsibility together for the fact that our actions
collectively contribute to the complex structural processes that produce
the working conditions we deplore. Most of us have not committed
individual wrongs; rather, we participate by our normal and on the face
of it innocuous actions in processes that produce wrongs.

(Young, 2003, pp.40–2)

Chapter 2

Media and communication in a globalised world

Roger Silverstone

Contents

1   Introduction

Over the centuries, a major strand of human ingenuity has been directed towards the development of technologies that bring what is distant closer to hand. Each of these technologies – that is, until the most recent – has the prefix *tele*, the Greek word for 'far off'. In order of appearance, the telescope, the telegraph, the telegram, the telephone, radio-telegraphy (the radio) and the television each brought some aspect of the world within reach. As seeing, signalling, writing, talking, hearing, broadcasting and communicating across distance became increasingly less constrained by the limits of face-to-face communication, so human beings were progressively freed from the bounds of physical proximity. Bringing the world closer to home has involved both the transcendence of distance and the compression of time. Not only could the otherwise invisible and inaudible world be made part of the everyday experience of larger and larger numbers of people, but today many such connections can be managed in real time.

As these technological developments have gathered pace and begun to reinforce, as well as replace, each other, it is as though the planet has begun to shrink. In the minds and imaginations of those receiving such communications, as well as of those responsible for sending them, a sense of a shareable world has emerged, a world that is, potentially, constantly and immediately available and accessible. There is little doubt that the world that has been brought into being by the increasing presence and use of these communication technologies is one of powerful connection. The possibility of seeing and talking to globally dispersed family or friends; sharing information in real time with business partners or colleagues; and knowing what is happening on the other side of the planet as well as down the street, because it can be seen on a screen or heard on a speaker – these are the components of an intensely mediated world: that is, a world in which many, if not most, interactions take place through media of various kinds.

The possibilities of such a shareable world have intensified with the emergence of the internet. The internet (what might

Defining time–space compression

Central to the speeding up of life, both institutional and personal, are the various new technologies, above all media and communication technologies, which have enabled and sustained high levels of immediate and continuous flows of information. Places and people can be in instant contact with one another, and the speed of communication can allow all kinds of actions to be taken more quickly than before. With particular reference to the late twentieth century, David Harvey (1989) sees what he calls 'time–space compression' as enabling an accelerated version of capitalism: 'the history of capitalism has been characterized by speed-up in the pace of life, while so overcoming spatial barriers that the world sometimes seems to collapse inwards upon us' (Harvey, 1989, p.240).

otherwise have been called the 'telecomputer') has both intensified and speeded up this process of global connectivity. Email, chat rooms and the World Wide Web each offer distinct modes of communication and information retrieval which, for those who have access to the networks, have together added a new and powerful dimension to what geographers have called the compression of time and space in our globalised world. Indeed, the dreams and fantasies of those first confronted with these radical and technologically-led changes, both at the end of the nineteenth century when such changes began to gather pace and at the end of the twentieth century when that pace accelerated, have in many significant respects become realities.

Activity 2.1

Read the following three quotations, noting when they were first written. What aspects of technological change seemed most compelling to the writers?

> The editor rules the world; he receives ministers of other governments and settles international quarrels; he is the patron of all the arts and sciences; he maintains all the great novelists; he has not only a telephone line to Paris but a telephote line as well, whereby he can at any time from his study in New York see a Parisian with whom he converses. Advertisements are flashed on the clouds; reporters describe events orally to millions of subscribers; and if a subscriber becomes weary, or is busy, he attaches a phonograph to his telephone, and hears the news at his leisure.
>
> (from 'How electricity will help out the editor of the future', *Electrical Review*, 2 February 1889, a summary of Jules Verne, *Yesterday and Tomorrow*, quoted in Marvin, 1988, pp.216–17)

> You stay at home and send your eyes and ears abroad for you. Wherever the electric connection is carried – and there need be no human habitation however remote from social centers, be it the mid-air balloon or mid-ocean float of the weather watchman, or the ice-crushed hut of the polar observer, where it may not reach – it is possible in slippers and dressing gown for the dweller to take his choice of the public entertainments given that day in every city of the earth.
>
> (Edward Bellamy, 1897, quoted in Marvin, 1988, p.200)

> Early in the next millennium your right and left cufflinks or earrings may communicate with each other by low orbiting satellites and have more computer power than your present PC. Your telephone won't ring indiscriminately; it will receive, sort, and perhaps respond to your incoming calls like a well-trained English butler. Mass media will be redefined by systems for transmitting and receiving personalised

information and entertainment ... The digital planet will look and feel like the head of a pin. As we interconnect ourselves, many of the values of a nation-state will give way to those of both larger and smaller electronic communities. We will socialise in digital neighbourhoods in which physical space will be irrelevant and time will play a different role. Twenty years from now, when you look out a window, what you see may be five thousand miles and six time zones away. When you watch an hour of television, it may have been delivered to your home in less than a second. Reading about Patagonia can include the sensory experience of going there.

(Negroponte, 1995, pp.6–7)

Putting aside the question as to what my right and left cufflinks or earrings might wish to say to each other, the vision is clear and consistent enough and can, in broad terms, be endorsed. To live in a globalised world is to live in a mediated world, a world that exists for most of us not through direct experience, but through the images, sounds and stories we receive on a daily (in many cases an hourly) basis, on the screens and through the speakers scattered around the home or office and, increasingly, in the form of the Walkman, the iPod or the mobile telephone, attached to the person. To live in a mediated globalised world is to live in a world which has the potential to be constantly accessible, visible and within easy reach, and that idea has excited commentators, including the three quoted above, for more than a century.

Defining mediation

Mediation refers to what media do, and to what we do with media. It is a term that includes both the media of mass communication (radio, television and the World Wide Web, as well as the press) and the media of interpersonal communication (fixed and mobile telephony, and email, as well as the letter). It suggests that these media actively form a space in which meanings can be created and communicated beyond the constraints of the face-to-face, and which is becoming increasingly significant for the conduct of public, institutional and private life. Audiences are part of this process of mediation, because they continue the work of the media in the ways in which they respond to, extend and further communicate what they see and hear via the world's multitude of screens and speakers.

From the very beginning, media technologies have been seen as machines for the interconnection of dispersed populations, compensations perhaps for the decline of community and neighbourhood and the decrease in face-to-face interactions which are often thought to characterise life in the modern world. New technologies of mediation and communication have become our constant companions in, and essential preconditions for, the management of proximity and distance, economically and politically as well as socially and culturally. The connections that we might or should have with those in distant sweatshops, as discussed in Chapter 1, to a significant degree hang on their visibility on the pages and screens of the media.

Yet to live in a shareable world is a not necessarily to live in a shared world. A shareable world is one in which various kinds of media offer the prospect and the possibility, but not the guarantee, of interconnection among otherwise disconnected individuals, groups and nations. Many of us do not have access to these new technologies, or the interests or skills in using them. Many of us find their use unsatisfactory, feeling the weight of the distance that remains rather than the proximity which connects, as we talk to friends or try to come to difficult business decisions, without the benefits of face-to-face interaction. More than this, we might want to question whether these new technologies really are bringing us closer together.

Activity 2.2

Take some time to reflect on your own day's communication. How much of it has depended on the use of technology? How much of it did you instigate and how much were you on the receiving end of? How much of it felt compromised by the absence of face-to-face interaction: the impossibility of cross-examining the newsreader, or judging real warmth or truthfulness in the body language of the person to whom you were speaking?

Your answers will begin to suggest how complex, intense and, indeed, demanding such mediated communications are. As the American social scientist Ithiel de Sola Pool (1977) once noted in writing about the telephone, media technologies have double lives. They connect and separate at the same moment. However intense the mediated communication with a parent or a lover across the telegraph wires or via satellite communication, that intensity is compromised by the absence of physical co-presence and its immediacy, by the absence, perhaps, of smell or touch. In contrast, of course, we often embrace the illusion of connection that such mediation enables. It suits us. There can even be some relief in not being in face-to-face contact. There are things that can be said on the telephone or by email which would be inappropriate, difficult or compromising without the distance that technology brings. Perhaps in part for precisely these reasons, many of us enthusiastically embrace what the technologies enable.

Communication, then, is always flawed; we can never guarantee its effectiveness. It can generate both comfort and discomfort. Moreover, our capacity to reach the other person means that the other person is equally capable of reaching us. While we may value being connected, we may value less being vulnerable to the connections claimed by those others: the cold-calling telephone sales, pop-up Web advertising, spam emails, offensive television programmes and other unwanted communications which puncture our personal electronic space with their demands for our attention. Our participation in a mediated world often brings challenges and responsibilities although we tend to think only of facilities and rights. Such participation can produce dependence but we often think only of the independence it affords. In many significant respects it can keep the world and its demands at bay even when we think of it as being constantly available and continually present, visible on our screens and audible through our speakers, on command, twenty-four hours a day.

In this chapter, I will propose that the extension of our reach, which the media enable, brings the world close to hand, but that this sense of closeness, the sense of being in touch, involves new demands and new responsibilities and also gives rise to new ways of keeping the world at a distance. Demands are made on us to be available to those close to us, to be accessible and responsive to the continuous flow of telephone calls, emails and messages that personal communication technologies have brought in their wake. In a globalised world, however, there is also often a particular demand to recognise that mediated access to the lives and worlds of those who may be less fortunate than ourselves requires our increased engagement with those lives and worlds. Perhaps, though, like me, you find that sometimes you just have to switch off! Literally – switch off the television, turn off your mobile phone, close down your internet access, or switch *on* the answering machine. However, we also 'switch off' just by ignoring or not responding to the messages of a mediated world.

With this in mind, we might well ask whether the media's overcoming of physical distance is, in many significant respects, more apparent than real. In this chapter, I will explore the paradox that, while all kinds of global connections, communications and communities are made and sustained, this does not always result in a meaningful overcoming of distance. On the contrary, we will see that the media can create an illusion of proximity, such that the world stays where it is and we where we are, and that meaningful connection between the two is confined to the exchange of images, sounds and stories; it does not often or easily extend to action, intervention or care.

This chapter will focus, then, on how the globalised media, in their transcendence of physical distance, actually do, or do not, bring those involved into meaningful and sustainable relationships with each other. It will explore how we manage our individual lives and our personal spaces, given the demands that are made on us through conversational and interactive as well as broadcast media; and it will ask what kind of broader responsibilities might be required of us since, through the media, we have access to the demands of a globalised world.

Answering these questions requires us to dig a little deeper into the dynamics of media and to try to understand their distinctiveness. Doing so involves a consideration, in Section 3, of the media as work – that is, as practice – in which technologies and infrastructures, producers and audiences are all involved. Section 4 then presents a number of case studies in order to explore in more detail the processes involved in global mediation, first at an individual, then at a collective and finally at a global level of communication. In all of these we consider how the media can create a sense of proximity to distant people and places, while at the same time it can work to push the world away.

Let us begin, in Section 2, with the media themselves.

Chapter aims

♦ To consider to what extent new media technologies bring distant people and places together, enabling new kinds of relationships and communities to be formed.

♦ To explore how the globalised world which such media and communication technologies have enabled is a shareable, but not necessarily a shared, world, where the ideal of perfect communication is compromised by inequalities of access, by the basic paradoxes of communication at a distance, and by how we, as individuals, manage and respond to the media.

♦ To consider how the new proximities that global media enable bring with them demands and new responsibilities.

2   The dynamics of media and communication

Language – that is, natural language – is the primary means of communication for human beings. Natural language in the face-to-face situation, unmediated by technology, has been the only means of effective communication for the greater part of human history. Writing, then print and then the whole slew of electronic media have fundamentally and irrevocably changed the way in which human communication takes place. But face-to-face interaction, in its immediacy, intimacy and intensity, still survives as the gold standard which, as I suggested in Section 1, electronically mediated communication, notwithstanding its reach and range, can never quite match.

Of course, the face-to-face is never perfect and oral communication even between two equals in a perfect setting of mutual understanding can never be guaranteed as pure. Language requires a set of skills which those who use it will develop in different ways and in different degrees. Interlocutors will vary in their power and their command of these skills and communicative resources. They need to trust each other. In addition, ideas, meanings, even sounds, change or become distorted, however minimally, in their exchange. Most communication has something of the Chinese whisper about it. All communication, even face-to-face, is flawed. There will always be things that are misunderstood, that mislead, remain unsaid or are unsayable. Even in the immediate presence of the other, in the micro-geography of person-to-person interaction in a shared social space, there are distances.

In the literature on electronic mediation, however, it is the face-to-face that provides the starting point for any discussion of mediated communication. The sociologist John Thompson distinguishes between three kinds of interaction which he refers to as 'face-to-face interaction', 'mediated interaction' and 'mediated quasi-interaction'. The distinctions are identified in Table 2.1.

Activity 2.3

Think of one example of each of the three types of interaction outlined in Table 2.1. How do they compare generally in terms of user – that is, your – satisfaction? What problems, if any, do you have with each of them?

Table 2.1   Types of interaction

Interactional characteristics	Face-to-face interaction (e.g. face-to-face conversation)	Mediated interaction (eg. telephone conversation)	Mediated quasi-interaction (e.g. radio)
Space–time constitution	Context of co-presence; shared spatial–temporal reference system	Separation of contexts; extended availability in time and space	Separation of contexts; extended availability in time and space
Range of symbolic cues	Multiplicity of symbolic cues, including visual, sound, smell, body, context	Narrowing of the range of symbolic cues, for example lack of visual information	Narrowing of the range of symbolic cues, especially no opportunity for immediate response
Action orientation	Oriented towards specific others	Oriented towards specific others	Oriented towards an indefinite range of potential recipients
Dialogical/monological	Dialogical	Dialogical	Monological

Source: based on Thompson, 1995, p.85, Table 3.1

Let us discuss this model for a moment. In addition to what has been said so far about the face-to-face, note how Thompson talks about 'co-presence' and the 'multiplicity of symbolic cues': that is, our ability to read meaning from many different aspects of the event, including body language, facial expressions or perhaps even smell. Face-to-face communication is immediate, intense (even when it might merely be a ritual form of 'Hello' with a neighbour you pass in the street) and focused. Above all, it is dialogical: that is, it presumes and involves interaction among people, in this case people who are in close physical proximity.

In many ways what Thompson calls mediated interaction is similar, especially in relation to dialogue and focus, but the intervention of technology – the telephone, the internet – allows for the linking of distant contexts. As a result, the interaction is less intense and narrower in its range of cues, even though it is more powerful in terms of its ability to reach across space.

What Thompson calls mediated quasi-interaction brings a very great change to the processes of mediated interaction, since it is primarily a one-to-many form of communication. Broadcasting is its paradigm. Radio and television, like the printed press before them, provide a top-down environment for communication, one that is defined principally by a communication from the centre – from Fleet Street (the traditional home of the national press in the UK) or Broadcasting House, from where BBC radio was, and to a significant extent still is, broadcast. Because it is one-to-many and, like mediated interaction, allows the separation of contexts while maintaining the immediacy of space–time relations, it is less rich and less focused. Moreover, it is monological rather than dialogical in that it does not generate a response. For the most part, radio and television in their broadcast mode do not invite interaction. The internet, and to an extent interactive television, of course, are changing this.

There are two related points to be made about this model, and particularly its account of mediated quasi-interaction with its stress on the monological nature of the interaction. Although the model is very helpful for understanding different types of mediated *social* interaction, it is in some ways a little too simple in its account of mediated *quasi*-interaction. For, while such forms of one-to-many mediation bring the world home to us, they do not operate only in a one-directional fashion: they also invite different kinds of responses and offer different kinds of challenges. So perhaps we need to suggest that all mediated communication, even that of the broadcaster, has something of the dialogical about it. Its audiences are not merely receivers. They process what they hear, and talk about it, and sometimes write letters of complaint or of enthusiasm. Such interaction, limited though it may always have been, is now being inscribed into the technology itself. Television is indeed becoming modestly dialogical.

When we watch television or listen to the radio, we will each be doing so in different ways, in different contexts and with varying degrees of attention. We are invited to engage with what is being broadcast, although we can refuse to do so. If we do find ourselves giving a soap opera, a sports event or a news item our attention, we are already doing something with it for ourselves (it pleases us, it makes us think); if we go on to discuss it with family or friends, we are then also working with it and our experience of it with others in a wider social context. We might have imaginary conversations with the characters in our favourite sitcom and dream of meeting the actors, but we might also have arguments in the pub with our friends about the invasion of Iraq or an off-side decision in last night's football game. This kind of activity, or work, is a crucial part of the process of mediation. It transforms the monological into the dialogical, by recognising that even one-way communication is not all one way. It suggests that, if we are to think carefully about the media, we need to think about our role as audiences and participants in the process and, indeed, the nature and extent of our possible responsibilities for it.

Activity 2.4

Turn now to Reading 2A by John Thompson (1995) entitled 'The media and modernity', an extract from his book of the same title, which you will find at the end of the chapter. Take a while to read through it. It raises a number of issues in relation to how media are produced and how they are used by audiences. You will have a chance to return to this reading later in the chapter.

For the moment, reflect on the extent to which your own knowledge of the world comes from the media, and the extent to which the media provide resources for social activities, for decision making or for action in your everyday life. How significant is mediated communication to you? How dependent do you think you are on the information and communication you receive through the mass media? These questions are useful to think about now, but you might find your answers change as the discussion in this chapter develops.

The global media, both those that enable immediate dialogue and those that might subsequently encourage it, involve forms of work not just by producers and those who appear on the screen, but also by audiences.

Mediation, then, is the product of human agency. It requires the involvement of a range of actors, and it has consequences for the lives of others. We know who the actors are: they are the owners and producers, performers and subjects, as well as the regulators of the media, local, national and global. But they are also the audiences for, and users of, the media, those – indeed all of us – who listen, read, watch, think and talk about the media's content: the ideas, images, facts and opinions which are constantly available to us.

All this work, by the different agents involved in mediated communication, has effects in and on the world. In their broadcast mode, the media provide many resources for us to manage our place in the world, to come to understand or misunderstand it. Our dependence on mediated imagery and stories of the world of which we otherwise have no or little knowledge is a central feature of media in a globalised world. The media therefore provide us with many, if not most, of the tools we seem to need to make sense of this globalised world in which many of us now find ourselves living.

Summary

- Face-to-face and mediated communication offer different opportunities for making connections between people.
- The media play a powerful role in enabling our understanding of the otherwise unknowable and unreachable world of distant events.
- The media are able to transform the relationship between distance and proximity, but individuals who use the media also shape the relations between events and people nearby or far away by their own choices and responses.

3   The work of global media

This section explores the theme of mediation as work, by focusing on the involvement of institutions – that is, of governments and corporations – in determining how the basic technologies of mass communication (principally radio, television and the internet) have come to be defined historically, sociologically and geographically. It then discusses the role of producers, who can be both individuals and institutions, in their work of determining media content and in making judgements and decisions about what will or will not appear on the screens or pages of the world's media. Finally, the attention shifts to the work of users and audiences, and to the issue of how we manage or do not manage the demands that the media make on us as we go about our everyday lives. Through all these actors, we will explore how the media work to bring otherwise distant contexts and people into relationship with one another, and how the new proximities of a mediated world have their limits, or can even be refused.

3.1   The work of institutions

Even if the resources for mediation are essentially technological, we need to understand the technological as something more than simply itself. It is never naked: never merely the machine. Technologies involve the creation of networks and systems and the application and enhancement of skills, knowledge and creativity. Media technologies require those activities, in both production and consumption, in order to be effective. Turning on the computer and linking to the internet immediately connects the user to a network of electronic connections and switches, hosts and terminals, which have been regulated (albeit to a limited degree) by governments, and which require skill and literacy if we are to make the most of them. The internet does not exist as an effective technological solution to the problems of communication or information retrieval without these social inputs and without our participation in it.

It is when media technologies enter social life, both that governed by public and commercial institutions and that of the individual user, that they become significant to us. It is only then that their identity and function become influential on, and just as crucially become influenced by, the values, beliefs, expectations and judgements of those who engage with them, wherever they happen to be in the social world. Of course, some actors have more power than others to define the ways in which media technologies change and develop. Radio was originally designed as a two-way interactive device for military and commercial purposes, but once it was commandeered by the state, above all in the UK after the First World War, it was turned into a broadcast technology to be embraced by a national population of an increasingly suburban and mobile society (see Figure 2.1).

The internet has a similar history. It too began life as a project of the military and was then appropriated by those most involved in its development – principally scientists and academics and their circles – as a free and freeing network of interactive communication, which promised to provide a clear alternative to commercially dominated,

Figure 2.1   At home with the media: listening to radio in 1923

non-interactive broadcasting. Since these beginnings, internet use has expanded exponentially and risen greatly in popularity in wealthier parts of the world, although its growth has been far less dramatic in poorer countries (see Figure 2.2). Yet it is possible to suggest that the internet too is struggling to maintain its status as a space for free and genuinely interactive communication under pressure both from governments (to regulate content and protect vulnerable users), on the one hand, and from commerce (to ensure it is a money-making undertaking), on the other.

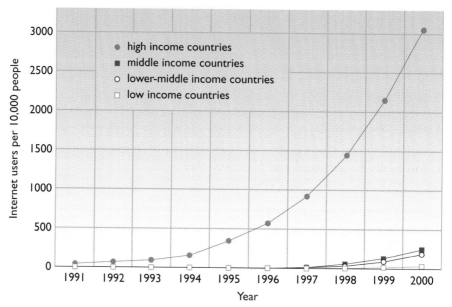

Figure 2.2   The growth of internet use
Source: Wallsten, 2003, Figure 1

Finally, in our everyday engagement with and use of these media, we too mould them to our needs, sometimes quite profoundly and significantly: for example, file sharing on the internet and text messaging on mobile phones were both activities initiated by users; they were substantially unanticipated by those responsible for creating the computer networks and the mobile phone services.

There is inevitably a tension between what a technology can and cannot do, between its potential and its power. A tension also exists between the capacity of users of all kinds – from powerful institutions, such as the transnational media corporations and governments, to individual users – to mould it in their own interests. Indeed, the story of nineteenth- and twentieth-century media culture has, for the most part, been that of the increasing dominance of press and broadcasting: that is, of media that have become the enabling resources for a sequence of projects related to powerful interests and nation-building. Through the appropriation and control of raw technology – moveable type in the first case, wireless speech in the second – governments and commerce created both national markets and national cultures. Taken together, this convergent trajectory could be described as centripetal. At base, it encouraged an inward-looking identification with a national community and with a symbolically, if not a materially, shared national space. Mediated centripetal cultures emerged and came to dominance in a period of society-building following the breakdown of more local or circumscribed communities as industrialisation gathered pace. They underpinned, and also expressed, the strengthening of early twentieth-century nation states, both the liberal democratic and the totalitarian. They were the product of a particular configuration of the work of institutions – in broadcasting, for example, the interests of governments and the early radio manufacturers converged. They have been used, as the BBC, for example, was used, to bring people together, to provide a basis for national citizenship and for a shared, or at least a shareable, national culture (Scannell and Cardiff, 1991).

However, if these national media emerged in the wake of a shift from local to more national communities, we might ask what the effect of globalisation might be on national forms of media. What has been the fate of national media in the wake of globalisation? And what too of that host of new technologies, which one might imagine could render the radio or the television obsolete?

The new media technologies to have emerged since the late twentieth century include the internet and other digitally enhanced or enabled systems of communication such as satellite television or mobile telephony. These have offered new possibilities to societies and cultures that have become less nationally focused and increasingly fragmented and global in perspective and connectivity. In this late modern age, media are becoming centrifugal, enabling people to avoid the constraints of national cultures and connect with one another. Centrifugal cultures are those of ethnicity and migration, lifestyle and taste, fandom and crime, and, of course, the marketplace. Mediated centrifugal cultures emerge through and along the rays of networks; they only occasionally coincide with the frameworks and borders of the nation.

This idea of the digital media, above all the internet, producing a new kind of society – a network society, and arguably a centrifugal society – is one most powerfully advocated by Manuel Castells (2000). His view of this new global space is one that is, in a sense, a mirror of what he takes the new technologies to be – a space of flows and untrammelled movement and one in which, to all intents and purposes, distance, in both space and time, is abolished:

> ... the new communication system radically transforms space and time, the fundamental dimensions of human life. Localities become disembodied from their cultural, historical, geographical meaning, and reintegrated into functional networks, or into image collages, including a space of flows that substitutes for the space of places. Time is erased in the new communication system when past, present and future can be programmed to interact with each other in the same message. The space of flows and timeless time are the material foundations of a new culture that transcends and includes the diversity of historically transmitted systems of representation: the culture of real virtuality where make-believe is belief in the making.
>
> (Castells, 2000, p.406)

Such visions of socio-technical change are valuable in so far as they help focus our attention on the scale and scope of the changes that technologies enable. But it is also very important to acknowledge the uneven spread of these technologies around the world. In a later book entitled *The Internet Galaxy*, Castells (2003) considers this unevenness. He notes, for example, that the geography of the internet is uneven, in terms both of users (see Figures 2.2 and 2.3) and of the control of internet sites. This is often referred to as a 'digital divide' between rich and poor countries. Castells notes that in 2000 North America had about 161 million internet users, to Europe's 105 million, but that the Asia Pacific region, with over two-thirds of the world's population, had only 90 million users: 23.6 per cent of the worldwide total. Africa had only 3.1 million, the majority of whom were recorded as being in South Africa. So while Castells observes that 'Internet use is diffusing fast', he also suggests that 'the diffusion follows a pattern that fragments its geographies according to wealth, technology, and power' (Castells, 2003, p.212). In terms of the production of internet sites, these unequal geographies were even more apparent, with about 50 per cent registered to a US address (Castells, 2003, p.214). The USA and a few other developed countries seem to be producing the majority of internet sites for everyone else.

Table 2.2 shows similar global variations in the presence of some of the key technologies that we have been discussing: radio, television, fixed and mobile telephones and the internet. Note the differences in levels of access, particularly between radio (which is more widely used in poorer countries), television and the internet (which is strongly skewed to wealthier countries), and between the fixed and mobile telephone. As a United Nations report noted in 2000, 'while dominant parts of the world are now being mediated with ICTs [information and communication technologies] at an astonishing pace, 80 per cent of the world's population has never made a phone call. And while it is growing very rapidly, the internet remains the preserve of an elite of between 2 and 5 per cent of the global population' (UNCHS, 2001, p.6).

It should be reasonably clear that any discussion of the role of the media in a globalised world must take into account both its inequalities and its variations, for participation is not uniform and there are many parts of the world – and enclaves even within some of the wealthier countries – which are substantially excluded. As we have seen, it is variations in income levels and the different capacities of governments to supply the required infrastructure that shape the uneven geographies. Not everyone or every place is able to participate in the brave new world of timeless time and flows, or to play a role in shaping how the world is understood through the media, even such relatively open media as the internet.

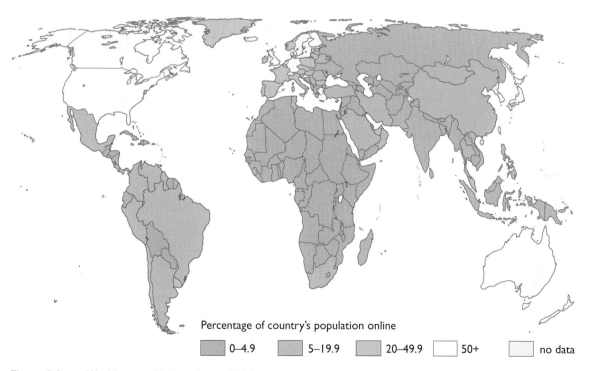

Figure 2.3   World map of internet use, 2005
Source: based on data from Internet World Statistics (2005)

Table 2.2   Uneven global access to communications media

Region	Radios/1000 population (2001)	Television sets/1000 population (2002)	Telephone lines/1000 population (2002)	Mobile phones/1000 population (2002)	Personal computers/1000 population (2002)	Internet users/1000 population (2002)
High income countries For example:	1266	735	585	698	466.9	364
Germany	570	661	651	727	431.3	412
Japan	956	785	558	637	382.2	449
Sweden	2811	965	736	889	621.3	573
UK	1445	950	591	841	405.7	423
USA	2117	938	646	488	658.9	551
Middle income countries	360	326	167	149	45.4	80
Lower-middle income	346	326	164	99	37.7	46
Upper-middle income	466	326	190	241	100.5	149
Low income countries	139	91	28	13	7.5	10
Low and middle income countries combinedby region	257	190	100	62	28.4	50
East Asia and Pacific	287	317	131	24	26.3	44
Europe and Central Asia	447	407	228	196	73.4	87
Latin America and the Caribbean	410	289	168	126	67.4	92
Middle East and North Africa	277	200	107	52	38.2	37
South Asia	112	84	34	8	6.8	14
Sub-Saharan Africa	198	69	15	16	11.9	16
World	419	275	176	110	100.8	131

Source: based on data from World Bank, 2004, and International Telecommunications Union, 2003

The impact of the media – in terms both of availability and content – has been very strongly shaped by the institutions that create and manage them: governments that establish infrastructures and firms that supply and usually charge for services. However, it is the work of the producers of the content of the media that we now turn to consider.

3.2   The work of producers

Media producers are involved in bringing distant images and events to us, at home. The production of radio and television news and current affairs, and the creation of documentary narratives – even, indeed, the performance of soap opera or serial drama, sitcom or chat show – in their various and obviously different ways invite a relationship with a distant other: someone other than ourselves who may be either fictional or non-fictional. The appearance of these figures is an increasing part of our everyday lives. The events or dramas in which they are players are likewise visible and audible components of the world in which we live. Yet, of course, in all these cases, in relation both to the person and to the event, they are otherwise out of reach, beyond immediate experience and distant in space and time.

Producers, both as institutions and individuals, therefore become key figures in the representation of this mediated, distant world, for they make the choices, tell the stories and choose the images that determine how that world will or will not appear on the screens and through the speakers of national broadcasting systems and global websites. The decisions that are made by individual reporters or producers are, of course, constrained by the demands placed on them by both producing institutions and the immediate conditions or circumstances of production. Organisational cultures, political pressures and the dangers of reporting in war zones or in circumstances where there is little time for reflection, conspire to limit – but often limit in consistent and ideological ways – the character of what subsequently appears. Yet what subsequently appears is what stands for the truth, both for those of us who have no other source of information against which to check it, as well as for those who appear as the subjects of the story and who have little or no recourse to challenge how their story is being told.

Defining ideology

Ideology, a term that has its origins, in its current usage, in the work of Karl Marx, refers to 'meaning in the service of power' (Thompson, 1990). In the context of the analysis of the role of media, the study of ideology involves questioning how ideas, values and beliefs are constructed and communicated by and within the media, and often in such a way as to serve and maintain the interests of dominant groups or institutions, and in so doing preserving their power and authority in an otherwise unequal society.

Whichever way one looks at it, towards the subjects and the situations being reported, or towards the listeners and viewers whose understanding of the world increasingly depends on those reports, the responsibilities of production are heavy indeed.

Let us consider the news. News is a significant strand of mass communication. The increasingly rapid demand for, and provision of, information of commercial, military and broadly social significance drove the nineteenth-century press (Chalaby, 1998), as well as providing a staple for broadcasting in the twentieth century, which it still does. The conventions of televised news, almost entirely taken for granted and thoroughly unchallenged, articulate a world view grounded firmly in society and culture, and in the values, for the most part, of national self-interest and parochial preoccupation. On the other hand, the conventional format for news programmes has become increasingly globalised, as newsreaders present on the world's television screens a nightly report of the news of the day in more or less brief fragments of otherwise unrelated narratives. The significance of these fragments for viewers depends on their appearance on a particular night and on their mediated status as news.

News is more than news, however: it is a moral event. As such, its status as a report which is accurate, true or trustworthy is crucial for its persuasiveness. Hence the concern expressed by all those involved – broadcasters, regulators and consumers of news – that news, perhaps above all else in the press and on radio, television and the internet, should present the world objectively and impartially. Indeed, it is news that is increasingly the focus of regulation and self-regulation, as the implicit contract that newsmakers and newscasters have with both their subjects and audiences to report the world honestly and objectively is being made more explicit and therefore more accountable.

However, news brings to the speakers and screens of households around the world a version of that world which, in claiming the audience's attention, is also claiming judgements of significance and meaning. Every inclusion involves an exclusion; every image invites both recognition and identification. The reach of the news is in principle infinite; few corners of the globe are geographically or sociologically off-limits, though many are systematically ignored. Those items that make it into the bulletins are what we, the news audience, are being asked to take notice of and to take seriously.

News, therefore, does not so much reflect the world as construct a particular version of the world and, in common with all other forms of mediation, it is the product of work. News involves gate-keeping (decisions of inclusion and exclusion), framing (the way in which the stories are told, and the choice of those aspects which are deemed to be of significance, and which not) and editorialising (offering opinions and stimulating debate). Given all this, neutrality in any strict sense is impossible and claims to be telling the absolute truth, given the complexities of the world, are difficult to sustain. News is also routinised in its production: its very 'dailiness' imposes all sorts of constraints on the 'what' and the 'how' of selection and report. The recognition that news is the product of many different kinds of work raises wider questions about its significance in contemporary society and its capacity to enable a meaningful relationship with the world beyond our front doors. Given the potential of news to provide us with the knowledge and information we need to make sense of the complexities of the world, both distant and closer to home, its failures will deny us the resources that we need for this and consequently for our participation in the society in which we live.

There is one further element of, and crucial participant in, the media's role in bridging distance to be considered, one that has been only implicit in the discussion so far: the audience. How are we to manage the demands of the world that the media bring: the distant world made close and, just as significantly, the more proximate and immediate, albeit mediated, world of friends, family and neighbours which we may want, from time to time, to keep at bay?

3.3   The work of audiences

There is often a presumption in academic and everyday discourses that audiences are passive receivers of communications from the media. Indeed, this presumption is, to a significant degree, implicit in the discussion of news in Section 3.2 above. Yet both academic and everyday discourses also recognise the capacity of viewers and listeners to respond both critically and creatively – to find ways of distancing themselves from, as well as being able to make use of – what they might see and hear, for their own purposes in making sense of the world and in thinking about their own roles and positions within it. Clearly some of us do more of this than others, and some communications are likely to be more effective, more powerful and more significant than others.

All media provide a set of resources, shaped by institutions and producers, for developing or learning an approach both to the immediate neighbourhood and locality and to the wider world. Our dependence on media in this regard is enormous: there is little escape. Here, though, we encounter a paradox. Our dependence on media for knowledge of the world is total, yet our independence is both possible and necessary. In fact, we use media to manage media. Increasingly, through various forms of interactive media – those that are well-established, such as the telephone, and those that are still quite new, such as email, the mobile telephone, the Walkman and iPod – we find ourselves constructing, through the media themselves, our own responses to the challenges and demands made of us on a daily basis by the media.

The principal challenge with which the media present us is how to respond in our everyday lives – that is, how to position ourselves in relation to the mediated world, the world of constant news and ring-tones. On the one hand, how can we protect ourselves from too much intrusion and information and too much discomfort in the face of troubling images and stories? On the other hand, how can we ensure that we receive the news and the communications that we feel we need in order to go about our everyday lives? In short, how can we construct the proper distance between us and the world around us, so that world is neither too close for comfort nor too far away for understanding?

More generally, there is the question of what to do with the stories and images brought to us by the media, and the extent to which what we see and hear actually touches us and possibly moves us to respond in some way. What happens to such knowledge of the mediated globalised world in the context of our everyday lives? Is it to be shared? Is it to be acted upon? Perhaps we mourn the loss of a great figure, or we contribute financially to a media appeal. We might write letters of complaint to the newspaper or broadcaster when we disapprove of something we have read or watched. Or we might just talk with family and friends, at home or at work, about what we have seen or heard via the media, and in so doing share and compare with those around us our responses, pleasures and frustrations.

This is the dimension of mediation that many have overlooked. It is in the process, too, of making sense of media and communicating that sense to others that audiences can be seen to be responding to the demands that media make on their attention: demands for their participation, and of course, from time to time, demands on their consciences. We can think of this component of mediation as action at a distance, or responsive action in distant contexts (see Reading 2A); that is, action that is either oriented to, or stimulated by, images, ideas or events that are not within our physical reach. The next section explores the work of audiences in managing both the proximities and the distances that communication technologies make possible.

Summary

- Key actors in the process of global mediation include: the institutions of mass communication and their command of media technologies; the producers of media content, particularly news; and the audiences whose participation is so often overlooked.

- The distinction between mediated centripetal and centrifugal cultures brings out some of the different ways in which social relationships are produced at a distance through the media.

- The prominence of global media and the way in which they bring demands and challenges from distant people and places into our everyday lives raises important issues of how audiences might choose to respond to and manage mediated information and interactions.

4   Too close for comfort, too far away to care?

In this section I will be looking at examples of the challenges which emerge from a mediated world and how they might, or might not, be managed. I will start with the individual and the management of personal space and then move on to discuss how the media are enabling new forms of community and raising new questions of responsibility. In doing so, we will be able to explore the mediated relationship between distant events and everyday experience in order to understand the significance of media in a globalised world, and their consequences for our lives in the twenty-first century. Do the media bring the world too close for comfort? Or are distant events still too far away for us to care about?

4.1   Living with mediation

This first section looks at the personal management of technologically mediated demands to be connected, to be part of a globalised world. The section examines the capacity of individuals to construct for themselves a space which offers them a modicum of control, the possibility of accepting the challenges of a mediated world, and of containing those challenges by incorporating them into their individual everyday lives in manageable ways. The focus, then, is on the individual and his or her capacity to mould these media to their own interests.

Activity 2.5

Read Extract 2.1 'Walkman talk' in which young people talk about how they use their Sony Walkmans to manage their journeys to work and their movement through public space as they listen to music. As you read, keep the following questions in mind:

1   Are young people keeping the world at bay with these media technologies? Or do you think they are finding new ways to engage with the world?

2   How do their comments compare with your own experiences?

Extract 2.1

Walkman talk

Most of the music I chose was very evocative of something and I associated it with a particular part of my journey. It became a way of describing that this part of the journey is bearable. You can get through this part. I remember there was a big escalator change at Green Park and I thought 'Right! If I don't have that particular music for that, then I'll fast forward it to get to it and then I can go up.' Like that it made it easier not to let work encroach onto non-work time. It was a way of not allowing thoughts like I've got that deadline and a meeting with so and so. Because the journey to work was so uniform and intrusive.

(Chris)

When you start commuting it's very unsettling not to know where to put your eyes. The Walkman makes you one step removed from the situation. Also the music is quite comforting, or is something familiar superimposed on everything else ... It's a way of passively acknowledging that [you're] not going to talk to anyone, and that what's around them is not relevant to [you]. It blocks out and it certainly alters reality. You're not fully there ... It emphasises the step of removal from where you are.

(Chris)

I'm aware of the fact that I'm different from other people walking down the street because I'm listening to my music. But it doesn't make me feel anxious. It puts me in a good mood actually. You don't feel lonely. It's your own environment. It's like you're making something pleasurable you can do by yourself and enjoy it.

(Sara)

We've walked out of the pub down the local high street and we've both got the headphones. We've got the two headphones in one Walkman. Just for a laugh we go dancing down the high street. People are just looking at us.

'What's going on?' Purely for a laugh in the local village. They're used to us now. I've lived there for ten years. It amuses us you know. We'll sit in the bus stop and our arms are going up ... It's a performance. The High Street on stage.

(Ben)

(quoted in Bull, 2000, pp.63, 73, 80, 112)

These examples of how people choose to manage media illustrate how media technologies – and we can include the mobile phone, the Walkman and the iPod in this category – might empower users by offering the possibility of gaining a measure of control in an often overcrowded mediated world. Such technologies can become tools both for establishing one's own presence in an otherwise anonymous and cacophonous global media space, and for constructing a sense of personal and comfortable distance between oneself and that world. In the examples given above, Chris uses music to keep work from encroaching on non-work time, and to keep other commuters at a distance, so that there is no need to engage in conversation. Ben, on the other hand, uses music to assert his presence through 'performance' – the High Street becomes his 'stage'.

Other media technologies – the answerphone, voicemail, personal digital video recorder (PVR), burnable DVD and MP3 recorder, for instance – provide the means to assume control of sometimes unwelcome mediated intrusions into personal space. For example, the phone call can be kept at bay by voicemail or the answerphone; an endless stream of music and television can be chosen, edited and stored in iPods and PVRs. So, many media technologies allow the user to creatively manage the sometimes overwhelming possibilities for communication that, in many cases, go with the user wherever he or she happens to be.

With yet other forms of media technologies, such as personal home pages, web-cam sites, web-logs ('blogs') and video web-logs ('vlogs'), the openness of the internet offers the opportunity for a reversal of the demands to distance oneself from the world. This can signal a bid to position oneself in a world without obvious boundaries, and to invite a response from an otherwise invisible audience and a potential network of like-minded souls somewhere out there, somewhere else. Rather than creating a distance from others, the internet has encouraged a desire to be connected and involved and to communicate with people anywhere. At little or no cost, and with few additional skills, many people have been enabled to write about themselves, their ideas and their preoccupations, indeed any aspect of their everyday life, and to 'publish' this online. Such publication does not guarantee a readership and, given the overwhelming amount of information and equally overwhelming number of websites available, it would be rash to assume that many such 'publications' are widely read, or even read at all. Yet they are proliferating. Indeed, one estimate suggests that, on an average weekday, over 15,000 new blogs are created (Sifry, 2004), indicating that a new blog appears online somewhere in the world every 5.8 seconds.

Extract 2.2 presents an example of a blog posted on a collective blogging site (www.livejournal.com) from a regular contributor in Malaysia who, in December 2004, reported his experience of the cataclysmic tsunami released by an earthquake west of Sumatra in the Indian Ocean.

Extract 2.2

The blog

Home was hit by tidal wave

practically lost everything ... family is fine ... thank god ... *lost of words to rant* to all out there ... appreciate what you have ... even the smallest things and events that u consider irrelevant ... 'cause after this mishap ... well ... views on life have changed a lot for me.

sigh back to cleaning up and getting home back on its feet ... *hugs back those who are going to give me some hugs and moral support*

ps: if i dun reply fast enough its because i am away from work and away from a com (only @ work place is computer available

Ronnie

(Tan, 2004, 30 December)

Ronnie Tan's posting juxtaposes a report on the experience of a globally significant event with an intensely personal, almost private, reflection on the ordinariness of his everyday life. And it is a posting which invites, but may never receive, a response.

Each of us uses these media and communication technologies in our own distinctive ways: the Walkman, the mobile phone and the iPod in the realm of private communication; the internet blog in the strange space that is both public and private. The personal relationships we construct through a range of different media are unique to each person. We can think of this as producing, through our own particular combination and use of media, our own 'media signature'. Such a signature can be seen as a unique, though never static, manifestation of global media culture, in which individuals are able to grasp, and develop, a distinct, both private and public, personal but globally connected web of communications. Through this they can both manage the demands of globalised media and find a space, a voice, within it for themselves. Such a signature expresses the particular solution that each of us is able to create in the management of the demands of the media in our everyday lives. In so doing, we also create our own relationships to near and far places – perhaps keeping some close-up events at a distance through the music we enjoy on our iPods or Walkmans, while bringing other faraway events close up as we find ourselves drawn to pay attention or to take action of some kind.

However, there is more to the global media than the challenges and opportunities that they offer the individual, for from the very beginning these media have been used in wider projects of building communities within which the individual takes second place to a shared project of collective identity building and action. Here the pressing issue is whether attempts to use media to create communities, which might stretch over vast distances, can successfully create new forms of proximity.

4.2   So close and yet so far: the mediation of community

Communities can seem very real to us in so far as the sense of community – of shared values and beliefs – is grounded in history through inherited tradition or common memory, and in society through living in proximity to each other. But communities are also imagined. They are believed in. Most communities you might think of, apart perhaps from very small villages or neighbourhoods, only ever appear symbolically and emerge through the sharing of activities or the attachment to symbols: the flag, the team, the hero. In this symbolic space such sharing and attachment is less, or barely, dependent on the realities of face-to-face social interaction, or a genuinely shared past. Such attachments emerge, when they do, from participation across distances in a shared culture, a culture enabled by the media since, most significantly, the emergence of the nineteenth-century national press.

The idea that the spatially separate but shared and synchronous activity of reading a newspaper has the power to create a strong sense of national community, perhaps the first real example of the media as centripetal, was developed by Benedict Anderson (1983) as a principle of the historical analysis of the formation of the state. Anderson's idea of the 'imagined community' was a significant component of his analysis of the convergence of capitalism and vernacular language which emerging nation states, above all in Europe, increasingly drew upon in the eighteenth and nineteenth centuries as they sought to build empires and to mobilise populations behind national projects of commercial and political enterprise. The newspaper represented and expressed that convergence: a national medium in a shared language read daily by an increasingly literate population, who in doing so could, and did, he argued, absorb a shared national culture and imagine themselves as belonging to the same community. Here Anderson is indicating how reading a national daily newspaper contributed to making a nation as an imagined community:

> The obsolescence of the newspaper on the morrow of its printing ... creates this extraordinary mass ceremony: the almost precisely simultaneous consumption ('imagining') of the newspaper-as-fiction. We know that particular morning and evening editions will overwhelmingly be consumed between this hour and that, only on this day, not that ... The significance of this mass ceremony – Hegel observed that the newspaper served modern man [*sic*] as a substitute for morning prayer – is paradoxical. It is performed in silent privacy, in the lair of the skull. Yet each communicant is well aware that the ceremony he performs is being replicated simultaneously by thousands (or millions) of others of whose existence he is confident, yet of whose identity he has not the slightest notion.

(Anderson, 1983, pp.39–40)

Defining the nation as an imagined community

'The nation is imagined because the members of even the smallest nation will never know most of their fellow members, meet them, or even hear them, yet in the minds of each live the image of the communion. ... The nation is imagined as limited because even the largest of them ... has finite, if elastic boundaries, beyond which lie other nations. No nation imagines itself coterminous with mankind [*sic*] ... Finally, it is imagined as a community, because, regardless of the actual inequality and exploitation that may prevail in each, the nation is always conceived as a deep, horizontal comradeship.'

(Anderson, 1983, pp.6–7)

This notion of a national medium of communication was one very much at the heart of John Reith's project, as the first Director-General of the BBC, in the early 1920s. The BBC would provide what has since been called 'social glue' for the UK. It would generate a national audio and then, with television, an audio-visual centripetal culture linking together individual households otherwise separated by their own thresholds and their own private lives, as well as by wider regional geographies and cultural identities. Radio would become the hearth, perhaps, as well as the heart of the nation. In its everyday consistencies of voice and programme schedules, and in the reporting of national ceremonial, political and sporting events, radio was instrumental in providing the basis for a national culture, or at least a sufficiently sustainable illusion of national culture, bridging distances and inviting individual and collective participation in a mediated public sphere. This was especially the case during the Second World War, when there was a common enemy against which to unite.

In more modern times, however, as I have noted above, it is possible to suggest that this national project of mediating distance is no longer what it was. The media now encompass a global sphere and there are many more of them. Furthermore, as we have seen, those media have become much more responsive to individual demand, at a time when individuals and groups are less dependent on the nation for their identity and culture and more likely to seek and use the media to find others like themselves, wherever in the world they happen to be. We can perhaps date the beginning of this shift from mediated centripetal to the mediated centrifugal culture quite precisely, with the first satellite television broadcast between the USA and the UK on 11 July 1962, which connected two previously separate national mass media (see Figure 2.4).

Such changes have produced two kinds of consequence in the mediation of distance. The first is what might be called the global event; the second is the virtual community. Both make demands on us, to be participants with others in distant places beyond our immediate sense and experience. However, we can choose either to respond to or decline the 'invitation' to engage.

Global media events, in Daniel Dayan's and Elihu Katz's (1992) discussion of them, have the capacity to transform a global population, albeit momentarily, into a global community. This is possible principally because such events are broadcast live, in real time, to a potentially global audience who are, for that moment, transfixed by the immediacy and by the power of such broadcasting to obliterate distance, perhaps almost literally, in the communication of high emotion.

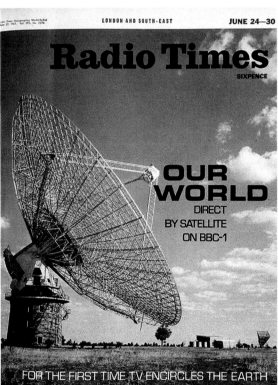

Figure 2.4   The beginning of mediated centrifugal culture: the first satellite television broadcast on 11 July 1962

Global media events invite the viewer, wherever he or she happens to be, to engage with and be part of something taking place somewhere else; in other words, they invite the kind of attention and participation which otherwise would be restricted to the viewer's own world, close at hand (see Figure 2.5). The attack on the World Trade Centre, the assassination of President Kennedy, the moon landing, the funeral of Princess Diana, the tsunami in the Indian Ocean, together with other events such as a final of the football World Cup, the Live Aid concert, the Senate Watergate Hearings and the trial of O.J. Simpson – each of these events, broadcast by television in an interruption of the rhythms of daily life, had the capacity to draw together a global audience. In some ways they were able to stop time and to transform space.

Activity 2.6

Think about, and perhaps make brief notes on, the media events that have been important to your own life, and the mark they may have made on you. How significant were they in connecting you to globally distant events, and in what ways, however distant in time now, do they still have meaning for you? Complete the following sentence: ' I can remember exactly where I was when I first read about or saw ...'.

Then turn again to Reading 2A at the end of the chapter and remind yourself of Thompson's discussion about how different kinds of audience might see the same media event differently. In the case of the events you have just jotted down, can you identify different audiences who might have reacted in different ways?

Global media events, Dayan and Katz (1992) suggest, are transcendent, breaking the mould of mundane reporting and daily broadcasting. They can be celebrations or moments of horror or mourning. They have the capacity to create social networks and to generate gossip, rumour, stories and theories. They change public opinion and our concept of where we are in the world. Indeed, global media events can change our sense of place and location and even shift our centre of personal gravity.

However, the extension of the reach of the media (and through that the extension of our own reach), with its centrifugal consequences, is not confined only to moments of high drama. The convergence of broadcast, satellite and internet-based communication has opened up the media environment to an almost infinite range of connections, many of which build on existing loyalties as well as developing claims for new ones. Two examples will help to illustrate this more routine

Figure 2.5   Global media events: Brazil winning the football World Cup in 2002;
a moon walk in 1969; the attack on the World Trade Centre, New York, 2001; the
assassination of US President John F. Kennedy in 1963; the tsunami of 2004

globalisation of media culture. Both involve the formation of new networks and new communities based on shared and quite specific interests. These examples provide additional evidence of the ways in which global media, as well as creating demands for attention and response, also provide opportunities for creative engagement in a new territory, as it were: the boundless globalised territory of the electronic media, or what is now known as cyberspace. The first example involves football and the second soap opera. Both involve the globalisation of what we might call fan culture.

Football, like the media, has become global. What was once, in the UK at least, the sport of village and town and of the working class, and the subject of intense local commitment and cross-generational male devotion, has now become globalised. From its professionalisation during the late nineteenth and early twentieth centuries – a professionalisation that paralleled the industrialisation and urbanisation of the country – it has become a sport that no longer depends on local players and on supporters who would walk or catch the tram to the stadium on a Saturday afternoon. Instead, international players are bought and sold to replace the home grown, and the stadium, while still literally in place, is nevertheless taken elsewhere, to physically distant places, by television, the internet and the mobilisation of supporters all over the world. The fixtures are no longer simply either home or away, but both at the same time.

Cornell Sandvoss (2003) suggests that football supporters are now a global community. He takes Chelsea as an example. Chelsea supporters are spread all over the world: Chelsea Football Club has some twenty-nine fan clubs in nineteen countries outside the UK. Supporters identify strongly with a team that many of them will never have seen except on television; they will buy the team strip from supporters' shops in Hong Kong or Tokyo, or online, and they will communicate with each other, with more or less intensity, through chat rooms and supporters' home pages on the World Wide Web. As a Chelsea fan living in Norway reports:

> We are on the board of our supporters' club, so we use a lot of time, also for these activities, to organise travels, tickets for home games and we, myself, try to make some activities in Norway, people getting together. We have our football club in Oslo every year. We are playing in Chelsea shirts against other teams from Norway [who] play Manchester United and Arsenal and Liverpool and everybody. So I would say, football is one of the top priorities in life. And Chelsea is one of the top priorities.
>
> (Elspen, Chelsea fan, Norway, quoted in Sandvoss, 2003, p.99)

The World Wide Web has become the site of what many have suggested are virtual communities: networks that draw together those who have both the technology and the skills to manage it, of course, but also the intensity of commitment to a single topic, enthusiasm or, indeed, anxiety. Virtual communities can be considered as centrifugal: that is, as networks that form around the margins and across the borders of nations and communities of propinquity.

Defining virtual communities

'Virtual communities are social aggregations that emerge from the Net [the internet] when enough people carry on ... public discussions long enough, with sufficient human feeling, to form webs of personal relationships in cyberspace.'

(Rheingold, 1993, p.5)

Nancy Baym (2000) expands on the nature of virtual communities in her book on soap opera fans. Her claim is that the interactions that emerge online, despite the absence of any other connection, are sufficient to make them genuinely social: they involve new forms of expressive communication, the exploration of possible public identities, the creation of otherwise unlikely relationships and the development of behavioural norms. Such interactions are sustained for long enough and deeply enough, she suggests, that online becomes a location for the formation of meaningful social groups. She also suggests, however, that such communities still depend on, and must be understood in the context of, the real everyday lives of those who participate: in other words, the communication may be virtual, but for it to survive and have value it needs to be grounded in the physical and bodily space of both person and home.

Football, soap opera and some of the more benevolent global media events (as well as the more tragic ones), are each examples of the ways in which the globalised media provide opportunities for engagement with those otherwise beyond reach. In general, they are there for those who want to respond to them, and they are invisible to those who do not.

However, some other kinds of events and images, usually those which arrive on our screens and speakers uninvited, as it were, can make demands on us that are unwelcome or discomforting, rather than being a source of pleasure or excitement. The global media, in shrinking the planet, also confront us with a range of challenges that are both new and gripping, and that claim directly, and perhaps even require, a response. It is to these that we now turn.

4.3   Mediating demands at a distance

Let us take the example of a controversy that arose during the US occupation of Iraq. On the evening of 28 April 2004 the US television channel, CBS, broadcast an episode of its regular show *60 Minutes II*. It included photographic images of US soldiers posing with their tortured prisoners in what had been, not long before, Saddam Hussein's most notorious prison, Abu Ghraib. The prisoners were portrayed in degrading positions, even naked. The pictures had been taken by the soldiers themselves who had also posted them on the internet. They caused a sensation and for quite some time served as defining images of the invasion and subsequent occupation of Iraq. The storm of controversy they provoked was as complex and as polarised as one might imagine. Commentators savaged the US for its hypocrisy and its willingness to ride roughshod over human rights; others suggested that, in effect, all was fair in love and war, and that these were enemies whose individual and collective threat to US security justified such measures. Yet others took the view that these were images produced of, and by, the very few bad pennies in a US army fully dedicated to peace and humanity in an increasingly troubled world. Yet even others, including the head of the army enquiry Major General Antonio M. Taguba, talked of systemic failings. President George W. Bush declared himself disgusted and described what was represented in the photographs as 'un-American' and 'unacceptable' (Hersh, 2004).

The media event that was generated around these images raises a number of interesting issues in relation to trends in the production of and response to media images in a globalised world. One is the coming together, or convergence, of different media in producing media events. In this case the technologies involved were the privately owned digital cameras which seemed to be ubiquitous among service personnel; the internet through which the images were circulated privately, at least to start with, among fellow servicemen and servicewomen; and television and the press to which the images were subsequently leaked. The movement of images and text between media forms is, technologically, the product of digitalisation, which makes such transfers easy and often quite seamless. It is also, however, the product of a set of institutionalised expectations and practices, on the internet and in the various broadcast media, to seek and find sensational images from wherever possible and turn them into headline stories for global consumption.

A further issue, which I have already touched on in Section 4.1 above, is the intense desire which many people are able to express on the internet to project their own experiences into a wider world. In this case the players were the US servicemen and servicewomen in Iraq who recorded and documented their everyday lives and felt, in many cases, quite content to share those lives with anyone who would be willing to 'stop by' online. New technologies have contributed to a significant shift in the freedom for individuals to express themselves in public space without shame and self-consciousness, and in the difficulty that governments and other regulatory bodies have as a consequence in controlling or, indeed, censoring such communications.

Finally, the Abu Ghraib example brings home to us vividly the way in which mediated communication transforms both proximity and distance. These images were of a hidden, and otherwise distant, part of a faraway war and military occupation. Their dissemination on prime-time television catapulted those distant places into the living rooms of many Americans not only in an extraordinarily vivid but in a shocking way. The images represented a personal and private reality for those who took them, yet the horror of what they showed was met with revulsion and disbelief by many. For many observers, they demanded a response of some kind – from the government, from international agencies responsible for protecting human rights. But they were often described by audiences in the USA as unbearable to look at, as if their transgressions had to be pushed back into distant invisibility once more. Elsewhere, the photographs met with different reactions, not least on the streets of Basra and Baghdad in Iraq where they provided yet more evidence of the misdeeds of what was widely seen as an occupying force.

Given their ubiquity and given our dependence on them, the media are central institutions in representing the distant world. Choices are made about who or what to include and exclude, and about the way in which other people – victims and perpetrators, the exploited and the exploiters, the named and the nameless, the celebrity and the man or woman in the crowd – are represented. These choices frame a way of seeing the world that lies at the heart of life in a globalised world and of our orientation towards those who are otherwise unknown to us. They offer a viewpoint, which is arguably neither one of ignorance nor of knowledge but lies somewhere indeterminate between the two, from which those who receive such representations will make their own judgements. And those judgements will have consequences for the ways in which both individuals and whole societies think and act in response to the demands of a globalised world.

Summary

■ The mediation of social life depends in significant part on the ways in which individuals work with, manage or use their media, whether these are personal technologies, such as the mobile phone or the Walkman, or relatively impersonal ones such as broadcasting.

■ The mediation of community is undergoing a transformation with the globalisation of media technologies and the expansion of their reach and range, as well as their increasing interactivity.

■ The media can transcend distance by making things globally visible, but they can also reinforce it by hiding or disregarding those aspects of the world that are discomforting or threatening. Mediation can thus produce distance and proximity simultaneously.

■ There are significant implications of these media practices for those of us who depend on the media for our understanding of the world, and on our capacity to make the judgements we need to make if we are to orient and conduct ourselves responsibly in the globalised world.

5   Conclusion

I have argued that the demands that media make upon us in this globalised world are substantial but full of paradoxes. Compared with face-to-face interaction, which is often problematic enough, and in which those involved are nominally equal and make efforts to express themselves and understand each other within the constraints of intimacy, immediacy, mutual trust and responsibility, mediated interaction (and mediated quasi-interaction) offers a huge number of challenges.

At the heart of these challenges is the tension between proximity and distance and the question of how to structure, case by case, moment by moment, event by event, a sense of both closeness and a proper distance such that the world is seen and understood in its reality; in other words, in ways that both make sense to us and, when it is appropriate, also enable or encourage a response from us. Without such positioning, and without the fulfilment of the promise of the overcoming of distance which the media have inscribed in their fundamental communicative capacities, we will be victims of what we might think of as the illusion of proximity: a false and misleading sense of closeness which actually preserves distance because it leads to little or nothing by way of engagement with the realities behind the images.

As I have also been arguing, however, there is a further illusion that needs to be identified: the illusion that what appears on the screens and through the speakers of the global media is all that there is. This is an illusion which involves our forgetting that the media often disguise, distort or simply refuse to acknowledge distant realities whose real and effective proximity we need to recognise if we are to participate fairly and responsibly with others on this shrinking planet.

The globalising media offer us a shareable, but not necessarily or inevitably a shared, world. The question, of course, is whether or not we want to participate in such a world, and whether or not we trust the media to represent it fairly and honestly, for to share in something is also, however minimally, to take responsibility for it. In the context of the globalised media, this responsibility is a double one. It concerns the media themselves, the work that they do in generating their version of the world, the content they provide and our critical skills in relation to that provision. It also concerns the realities behind the images and, perhaps above all, the realities of the vulnerability and suffering of fellow human beings who appear, if and when they do, on our screens. There are, of course, limits: our own limits. The press of electronic communications, both those addressed to us personally and those circulating more generally, has to be managed, and there are technologies which allow us to do that. In shutting out these communications, though, are we not also shutting out the world? And if we shut out the world, how can we meaningfully and ethically go on living in it?

We have seen that one way in which the media might be enabling us to engage responsibly in a globalised world is expressed in the difference between the centripetal media of the nineteenth and twentieth centuries (the press and broadcasting), and the increasingly centrifugal ones of the late twentieth and early twenty-first centuries. Centrifugal media do seem to offer more, and possibly more real and effective, opportunities to create our own media cultures and our own routes to participation in a globalised world, though not unequivocally and neither uniformly nor equally. For, as we have also seen, not all of the world's population has meaningful access to such technologies, never mind the skills and motivation to use them in these ways.

Furthermore, the globalising media also undermine the mutuality of what we might think of as genuine communication. Participation in major media events is limited for the most part to that of being a bystander, a witness at best. Participation in online communication is limited by our capacity easily to close down the connection. In both of these cases our actions are likely to have little or no consequence for anyone other than ourselves. Instant disengagement, as well as instant engagement, comes with a press on the remote control or a click on the mouse. In the world of global media, things out of sight really are things out of mind.

The globalised media increase, in their claims for our attention, the scale and range of our responsibilities in the world, but at the same time, and indeed in the same communications, they effectively provide us with the means to downplay or ignore them. Distance can be both transcended and reinforced; proximity can be both real and imagined. While such a contradiction requires that the media themselves should take on a greater and a more self-aware responsibility for what they are doing and how they communicate the world to their audiences, it also requires those audiences to engage more critically and reflectively with the media and with what the media transmit. This is a tall order, certainly, on both counts. But we might think that our global future depends on it.

References

Anderson, B. (1983) *Imagined Communities: Reflections on the Origin and Spread of Nationalism,* London, Verso.

Baym, N. (2000) *Tune In, Log On: Soaps, Fandom, and Online Community,* London, Sage.

Bull, M. (2000) *Sounding Out the City,* Oxford, Berg.

Castells, M. (2000) *The Rise of the Network Society. The Information Age: Economy, Society and Culture,* vol.1 (2nd edn), Oxford, Blackwell. (First published in 1996.)

Castells, M. (2003) *The Internet Galaxy,* Oxford, Oxford University Press.

Chalaby, J.K. (1998) *The Invention of Journalism,* Basingstoke, Macmillan.

Dayan, D. and Katz, E. (1992) *Media Events: The Live Broadcasting of History,* Cambridge, MA, Harvard University Press.

De Sola Pool, I. (ed.) (1977) *The Social Impact of the Telephone,* Cambridge, MA, MIT Press.

Harvey, D. (1989) *The Condition of Postmodernity,* Oxford, Blackwell.

Hersh, S. (2004) 'Chain of command: how the Department of Defence mishandled the disaster at Abu Ghraib', *The New Yorker,* 17 May.

International Telecommunications Union (2003) *World Telecommunication Development Report,* Geneva, ITU.

Internet World Statistics (2005) www.internetworldstats.com (accessed 31 May 2005).

Marvin, C. (1988) *When Old Technologies Were New,* Oxford, Oxford University Press.

Negroponte, N. (1995) *Being Digital,* London, Hodder & Stoughton.

Rheingold, H. (1993) *The Virtual Community: Homesteading on the Electronic Frontier,* Reading, MA, Addison Wesley.

Sandvoss, C. (2003) *A Game of Two Halves: Football, Television and Globalization,* London, Routledge.

Scannell, P. and Cardiff, D. (1991) *A Social History of British Broadcasting, Part 1 1922–1939,* Oxford, Blackwell.

Sifry, D. (2004) 'Technorati tracks 3 million blogs', *Technorati,* 7 July, http://www.sifry.com/alerts/archives/000356.html (accessed 19 February 2005).

Tan, R. (2004) www.livejournal.com/users/ronnietan (accessed 21 January 2005).

Thompson, J.B. (1990) *Ideology and Modern Culture*, Cambridge, Polity.

Thompson, J.B. (1995) *The Media and Modernity: A Social Theory of the Media*, Cambridge, Polity.

UNCHS (2001) *Cities in a Globalising World*, Global Report on Human Settlements, London, Earthscan and UNCHS.

Wallsten, S. (2003) *Regulation and Internet Use in Developing Countries,* AEI-Brookings Joint Center for Regulatory Studies, http://www.aei-brookings.org/admin/authorpdfs/page.php?id=262 (accessed 21 April 2005).

World Bank (2004) *World Development Indicators*, Washington, The World Bank.

Reading 2A

John Thompson 'The media and modernity'

Just as the development of communication media creates new forms of acting for distant others, so too it gives rise to new kinds of 'responsive action' which take place in contexts far removed from the contexts of production. Thanks to ... the media, individuals can receive and respond to actions and events which take place in distant locales. At the same time, responsive action is severed from the dialogical character of face-to-face interaction and can unfold in ways that are difficult to monitor and control, giving rise to a new kind of mediated indeterminacy which can have large-scale consequences. In order to pursue these issues further, we must examine in more detail the social organization of receptive activities.

Like all kinds of action, the reception of media products takes place in particular spatial–temporal contexts. What is unique about receptive activity is that (a) the spatial–temporal context of reception does not overlap with that of production, and (b) there are multiple reception contexts which do not overlap with one another. While reception contexts do not overlap in space (and may not coincide in time), nevertheless they may share certain characteristics, depending on the nature of the technical medium deployed. In the case of television, for instance, the primary reception region is often (though by no means always) a particular room in a private domestic residence. This primary region is often separated from peripheral regions in the same residence by means of physical barriers such as walls and doors. The relation between primary and peripheral regions in a context of reception is not the same, however, as the relation between front and back regions in the production sphere or in a face-to-face interaction. For recipients do not participate in the televisual quasi-interaction in the same way as producers ... If certain areas and forms of behaviour are excluded from the quasi-interaction of recipients, this is done for other reasons – for example, to minimize interruption or interference, or to manage the presentation of self in the face-to-face interaction that takes place among recipients within the primary reception region.

Since recipients cannot generally respond directly to producers, their forms of responsive action are not part of the quasi-interaction as such. In responding to the actions or utterances of producers, they generally do so as a contribution to *other* interactions of which they are part, such as the interaction among recipients who have gathered together in front of a television. In this way media messages acquire what I shall describe as 'discursive elaboration': they are elaborated, refined, criticized, praised and commented on by recipients who take the messages received as the subject matter of discussions with one another and with others. The process of discursive elaboration may involve individuals who were not party to the mediated quasi-interaction – in the way, for instance, that individuals may describe what they saw on television to friends who did not watch the programme. Hence media messages may acquire an additional audience of secondary recipients who did not themselves participate in the mediated quasi-interaction, but who assimilate some version of the message through face-to-face interaction with the primary recipients.

In a world characterized by multiple forms of media transmission, it is also common for media messages to be taken up by media organizations and incorporated into new media messages, a process that can be described as 'extended mediazation'. There is a relatively high degree of self-referentiality within the media, in the sense that media messages commonly refer to other media messages or to events reported therein. For example, a morning newspaper may report what a government minister said in a television interview the day before, an interview during which the minister was commenting on a reported incident, and so on. An individual who did not see the interview or hear the earlier report of the incident will have other opportunities to learn about them, either through other mediated quasi-interactions or through face-to-face interactions with individuals who did. Moreover, those individuals who did see the interview or hear the earlier report will have the opportunity to review their understanding of the incident or of the minister's comments by reading the newspaper report, or by discussing the various events and messages with others.

... the process of receiving media messages may extend beyond the initial activity of reception within the primary reception region. I use the term 'appropriation' to refer to the extended process of receiving messages. ... 'to appropriate' is 'to make one's own' something which is alien or strange; it is to find a way of relating to it and incorporating it into one's life. In so doing individuals draw on their background knowledge, their acquired skills and dispositions and the resources available to them. These social attributes are key elements in a process of appropriation that begins with the initial reception of media messages but extends well beyond it, involving other contexts, other individuals, other messages interwoven with those initially received.

While the diverse contexts of reception may have certain common characteristics, it is important to emphasize that the social attributes which individuals bring to these contexts are not everywhere the same. Since mediated quasi-interaction makes messages available to an indefinite range of recipients who are far-flung in space (and perhaps also in time), the diversity of social attributes which individuals bring to bear on the reception process is likely to be much greater than that found in face-to-face interaction. Moreover, in the case of face-to-face interaction, differences in the social attributes of the interlocutors will be reflected in the interaction – in the way, for instance, that some individuals participate actively and effortlessly in a conversation while others hesitate or remain silent. In the case of mediated quasi-interaction, by contrast, differences in the social attributes of recipients are not reflected in the quasi-interaction as such (except in so far as producers seek to take these differences into account – for example, by using language which will be intelligible and acceptable to a wide range of recipients). Social differences among recipients affect primarily the ways in which they relate to the messages they receive, how they understand them, appreciate them, discuss them and integrate them into their lives. Hence the appropriation of media messages must be seen as an ongoing and socially differentiated process that depends on the content of the messages received, the discursive elaboration of the messages among recipients and others and the social attributes of the individuals who receive them.

The reception and appropriation of media messages are ways of acting in response to others who are spatially and temporally remote. It involves individuals in a set of activities (watching, listening, reading, discussing, etc.) which are stimulated by the actions of others who are situated in distant locales. In many cases, these responsive activities will unfold in ways that are varied and unrelated to one another, reflecting the diversity of the contexts in which the messages are received. But it is also clear that in some cases the actions of distant others, relayed via media such as television, can give rise to what I shall call *concerted forms of responsive action*. That is, recipients may respond in ways that are similar and that may even be explicitly coordinated, either by some aspect of the media message or by a relatively independent agency operating within the contexts of reception. Let us examine some of the ways in which this can occur.

One type of concerted responsive action arises when individuals react in similar ways to mediated actions, utterances or events, although the individuals are situated in diverse contexts and there is no communication or coordination between them. We can regard this as concerted but uncoordinated responsive action. An example would be the actions of individuals who hear through the media that the sales tax will be increased on a certain date and respond by purchasing consumer goods before that date, resulting in a surge in retail sales. This outcome is the result of the discrete and largely uncoordinated actions of individuals who respond in similar ways to an item of reported news. In practice, however, most concerted actions of this kind generally involve some degree of coordination which stems from a combination of discursive elaboration and extended mediazation. The recipients of media messages commonly discuss these messages with others in their immediate social milieu, and the views and actions of others may influence their own behaviour. Moreover, some degree of coordination may be provided by the media, which may, for instance, encourage individuals to purchase goods by predicting or speculating about a surge in retail sales, or by reporting a surge in sales that is already under way (a mediated version of the bandwagon effect). In such cases, concerted responsive action is to some extent the unintended outcome of a media message or of the ongoing commentary on the responses to a media message.

We can distinguish this type of concerted action from another type which occurs when individuals respond in similar ways to symbolic devices that are explicitly intended to coordinate recipient response. The importance of these devices stems in part from the peculiar nature of mediated quasi-interaction. Unlike the interlocutors in a face-to-face situation, the producers of media messages are not in a position to monitor directly the responses of recipients and to modify their action in the light of this feedback. Moreover, since recipients do not share a common locale, they are not in a position to monitor the responses of other recipients (except those with whom they directly interact) and to modify their behaviour accordingly. In these circumstances, producers may employ a range of symbolic devices whose aim is to elicit similar responses among absent recipients – what I shall call 'intended mechanisms for the coordination of recipient response'. A well-known example of such mechanisms is the use of prerecorded laughter sequences in TV sitcoms. By simulating audience responses at key points in the narrative flow, the prerecorded laughter sequences serve as audio cues intended to initiate similar responsive action among absent recipients. A live studio audience can also be used as a mechanism for coordinating recipient response ... If a live audience is included in the front region of the production sphere, recipients can see how others (albeit carefully selected others) respond to the principal communicators and may even feel that they are part of a collective audience whose responses they broadly share.

Of course, the use of mechanisms intended to coordinate recipient response may not always give rise to concerted responsive action. The very structure of mediated quasi-interaction is such that producers cannot monitor directly the ways in which their messages are received, and cannot take remedial action to secure the desired response. The responsive action of recipients may be guided by the message but it is not controlled or determined by it, precisely because the responsive action of recipients is not part of the reciprocal interaction with producers but is a new set of actions belonging to a diverse set of contexts in which a great variety of abilities, expectations and priorities are brought to bear on the messages received.

Let us now consider a third form of concerted responsive action, that which acquires some degree of organization and coordination within the contexts of reception. Here we are dealing with forms of collective action which are stimulated and nourished by mediated images, actions and utterances.

These forms of collective action can vary from relatively diffuse clusters of individuals acting in similar or partly convergent ways, on the one hand, to well-organized social movements with clearly articulated goals, on the other. In most cases these forms of collective action draw support from a variety of sources; the role of the media is one among a set of elements which give rise to and sustain the concerted actions of individuals. But there can be little doubt that in some cases the media have played (and continue to play) a very important role and that, if mediated images and information had not been available to recipients, the forms of collective action would not have developed in the way, to the extent and with the speed that they did.

It seems likely, for example, that the extensive and vivid coverage of the Vietnam War was at least partially responsible for the strength and concerted character of the anti-war movement. The Vietnam War was the first major American military involvement overseas which was covered in detail by television. The vivid images of napalm attacks, wounded soldiers and civilians, screaming children and frightened refugees, as well as reports of US military setbacks and rising death tolls, fuelled the controversy in the United States concerning the legitimacy of the intervention and provided individuals with readily available grounds for protest. In the light of the Vietnam experience, it is not surprising that military establishments in the United States and elsewhere have sought to exercise much tighter control over the media coverage of armed conflicts and skirmishes. During the Gulf War, the military authorities imposed tough guidelines on journalists, and access to the front was strictly controlled. Reports compiled and transmitted by one of the few Western correspondents remaining in Baghdad – Peter Arnett of CNN – were denounced by the Bush Administration. The considerable effort invested in seeking to control the media representation of the war is testimony to the fact that, in the age of the media and especially television, wars must be fought on two fronts: on the battlefield and in the home, where images of the battlefield and its costs are made available to the individuals on whose support the war effort ultimately depends. While political and military authorities may justify their attempts to control the media on the grounds of battlefield logic (such as the need to prevent disclosures which would put the lives of soldiers at risk), they are well aware that much more is at stake. They know that mediated images and information have the potential to stimulate forms of responsive action, criticism and dissent which may weaken the war effort.

The revolutionary upheavals in Eastern Europe in 1989 provide another example of the ways in which media messages can stimulate and nourish collective action by individuals located in distant contexts. There were, of course, many factors that contributed to the extraordinary events which occurred during the last three months of 1989. These events were the cumulative outcome of many years of economic impoverishment and oppressive political control, and they were precipitated by, among other things, the new political thinking introduced by Gorbachev. But it seems unlikely that the revolutionary upheavals of 1989 would have occurred as they did – with breathtaking speed and with similar results in different countries – in the absence of extensive and continuous media coverage. Not only did television provide individuals in Eastern Europe with a flow of images of the West, portraying life conditions which contrasted sharply with their own, but it also provided Eastern Europeans with a virtually instantaneous account of what was happening in neighbouring countries, as well as in neighbouring cities or locales in their own countries. East Germans had long been able to receive West German television, and the images of refugees crowding into embassies in Prague and Budapest, and eventually being escorted to the West and greeted as heroes, could hardly fail to have an explosive impact in East Germany. When the Berlin Wall fell on the night of 9 November, the images of young people celebrating beneath the Brandenburg Gates and hacking at the wall with pickaxes were transmitted live around the world.

In Czechoslovakia the pressure for political change mounted throughout October and November. When the mass demonstration in Prague on 17 November was brutally suppressed by police, foreign television crews were on hand to film the events and the footage was subsequently screened, amid much controversy, within Czechoslovakia itself. Even in Romania, where the national media were strictly controlled by the state, individuals were able to learn about the dramatic changes taking place elsewhere in Eastern Europe, and elsewhere in their own country, by tuning in to radio and TV broadcasts from the Soviet Union, Hungary and Yugoslavia. As conflict intensified within Romania, control of the means of television broadcasting became a crucial stake in the battle. When the Ceauescus were finally arrested, tried by military tribunal and executed by firing squad, their crumpled bodies were filmed beneath a bullet-ridden wall and transmitted via television to an astonished audience in Romania and throughout the world.

These examples illustrate some of the ways in which the development of communication media, and especially television, has introduced a new and fundamentally important element into social and political life. By providing individuals with images of, and information about, events that take place in locales beyond their immediate social milieux, the media may stimulate or intensify forms of collective action which may be difficult to control with the established mechanisms of power. It seems likely that the concerted action displayed in the streets of Leipzig, Berlin, Prague, Timioara, Bucharest and elsewhere in Eastern Europe was, to some extent, action stimulated by the activities of distant others whose aims and aspirations, successes and failures, had been relayed via the media. Moreover, given the nature of modern electronic media and the availability of satellite relays, images and information can be transmitted across vast distances with very little time delay. Individuals in Bucharest can know something about what is happening in Timioara as quickly – even more quickly – than individuals in

Timioara, and the events unfolding in Romania can be watched more or less as they unfold by millions of viewers around the world. Hence the actions and reactions which are stimulated by the media can be linked together closely in time while separated in space, thus comprising a chain of events which can transcend the boundaries of particular nation-states and rapidly slip out of control.

The phenomenon of concerted responsive action highlights the fact that the media are not simply involved in reporting on a social world which would, as it were, continue quite the same without them. Rather, the media are actively involved in constituting the social world. By making images and information available to individuals located in distant locales, the media shape and influence the course of events and, indeed, create events that would not have existed in their absence. Moreover, the individuals involved in these events may be well aware of the constitutive role of the media. They know that what they say on radio or television will be heard by thousands or millions of others who may respond in concerted ways to what is said. They know that, by watching television or listening to the radio, they can learn something – however partial – about what is happening beyond their immediate social milieux, and they can use this information to guide their own action. They know that, by controlling the flow of images and information, the media can play a crucial role in controlling the flow of events.

These examples of concerted responsive action also highlight the fact that, while any particular instance of mediated quasi-interaction generally involves a   one-way flow of information or communication, in the actual circumstances of social life the patterns of information flow are often much more complicated. For in actual circumstances there is often a plurality of sources and channels of communication, so that individuals may find themselves in the position of being both producers and recipients. So, for instance, a political leader who appears on television from time to time may also routinely watch television, read newspapers, etc. Similarly, individuals who are normally recipients of media products may act in ways which become televisable events, and which in turn elicit televisable responses from others. In this way the media come to form part of the very field of interaction within which different individuals and groups pursue their aims and objectives. This media-constituted field of interaction is not like a face-to-face situation in which the interlocutors confront one another directly and engage in dialogical conversation. Rather it is a new kind of field in which face-to-face interaction, mediated interaction and mediated quasi-interaction intersect with one another in complex ways. It is a field in which the participants use the technical means at their disposal to communicate to distant others who may or may not watch or listen to them, and in which individuals plan their courses of action partly on the basis of the images and information they receive through the media. Of course, within this mediated field of interaction there are some individuals who have much more opportunity to use the media to their advantage than others, much more opportunity to appear within the front regions of the production spheres and to communicate to distant others. But, as the upheavals in Eastern Europe attest, this advantage does not always give individuals the ability to control the course of events. Given the fact that there are multiple channels of transnational communication which particular governments may find difficult to restrict, and given the fact that the reception of media messages is in any case a relatively independent process that producers cannot completely control, the mediated field of interaction is a field in which relations of power can shift quickly, dramatically and in unpredictable ways. The development of the media has helped to create a world in which fields of interaction can become global in scale and the pace of social change can be accelerated by the speed of information flows.

The growth of multiple channels of communication and information flow has thus contributed significantly to the complexity and unpredictability of an already exceedingly complex world. By creating a variety of forms of action at a distance, enabling individuals to act for distant others and enabling others to respond in uncontrollable ways to actions and events taking place in distant locales, the development of the media has given rise to new kinds of interconnectedness and indeterminacy in the modern world.

(Thompson, 1995, pp.109–18)

Chapter 3

Reaching out: the demands of citizenship in a globalised world

Clive Barnett

Contents

1   Introduction

In Chapters 1 and 2, we saw that people are increasingly called upon to respond to processes and events that take place beyond the boundaries of their own countries. Chapter 1 discussed demands that wealthy consumers should take responsibility for 'sweatshop' labour conditions on the grounds that their actions as consumers have consequences for the lives of people living far away. Chapter 2 showed how global media bring all sorts of events much closer to us so that they demand our attention in new ways. In this chapter, we will look at another set of demands that involves both the stretching out of processes over distance and the drawing of things close together: the demands that states make of citizens and, in turn, that citizens make of states.

Globalisation is reconfiguring the relationship between states and their citizens. In many countries, people have come to expect more and more from the state, in terms of being able to provide services, deal with environmental problems or provide stable economic growth. We often talk of these expectations as 'rights'. Having rights means that one can demand certain things from the state. At the same time, states increasingly expect their populations to act as good citizens. It is often said that being a citizen comes with various 'responsibilities'. In return for conferring rights, states demand that their citizens act in 'responsible' ways. Yet just what does this mean: what is a 'good' citizen?

Activity 3.1

Before we go any further, it might be helpful to ask what being a citizen means to you.

1   Make a list of the activities that you have undertaken in the last year that, in your opinion, count as 'being a citizen'.
2   Take a look at your list, and think about which of the activities you have listed involve demands being made of you by the state, and which of them involve you exercising rights or making demands of the state.

Some of the activities on my own list included voting in an election and signing a petition; these are actions I have undertaken voluntarily. I have also regularly paid my taxes, and I have had to pay a speeding ticket as well; these are duties or obligations imposed upon me by the state, and they are quite difficult to avoid!

Broadly speaking, it seems that being a citizen is a combination of two sorts of activities:

1   Making demands of the state, or exercising rights.

2   Meeting certain obligations imposed by the state.

However, what about the other side of this definition – what is this thing we call the 'state'? The state actually refers to a wide range of institutions, actors and organisational forms that undertake a number of different activities:

- States raise taxes and regulate financial markets.

- States are sometimes involved in the direct management of economic production.

- States might invest in infrastructure provision (for example, transport networks).

- States provide different sorts of welfare provision (for example, health care, housing and pensions).

- States mobilise resources and people for national defence, protection and warfare, and usually they are the only legitimate source of the use of violence in their territories.

- States provide educational services (for example, schools and universities).

- States provide an infrastructure of law, criminal justice and policing.

- States confer rights of citizenship upon people (for example, they issue passports, process immigration applications and administer asylum claims).

- States engage in all sorts of cultural activities, ranging from radio and television services to rituals of national celebration that help to mobilise a sense of national belonging and legitimacy.

The key question that this chapter addresses is: how are the *demands* made by states of citizens, and by citizens of states, changing in a globalised world? In answering this question, we will explore how the changing pattern of demands between states and citizens is shaped by the changing *reach* of both state capacities and citizenly action, as globalisation has exposed both states and citizens to new kinds of influences and new opportunities for interaction beyond national borders.

Section 2 discusses what citizenship rights and practices have entailed at different times and in different places. Section 3 examines some of the basic practices that shape the relationship between states and citizens.

It looks at how the state can extend its reach over *distance* in order to influence the activities across its territory. This extension of reach across territory enables the state to come into close *proximity* with citizens. Section 4 then assesses the changes to state and citizen relations that are characteristic of a globalised world. First, it investigates the ways in which the state's reach has become more finely tuned to making detailed interventions within territories, so that the demands made of citizens are more differentiated than before. Second, it considers the ways in which the reach of citizenly action can now extend far beyond the confines of national territories to make demands upon distant actors.

Chapter aims

- To examine the ways in which the demands made by states of citizens, and by citizens of states, are being transformed in a globalised world.

- To understand how the relations between states and citizens are determined by their respective capacities to bring each other into reach in order to influence their decisions and activities.

- To explore how the reach of the state and the reach of citizens involves the extension of influence over distance by forging new relations of proximity.

2   Formations of citizenship

In this section, we will look at how states and citizens come into contact with each other, and consider how this varies over time and between places. We will see that this variation depends on the kinds of relationships of proximity and distance that are established between states and their populations. The section will illustrate the variable formation of citizenship by investigating the way in which the process of state formation in modern Europe went hand in hand with the development of a distinctive style of citizenship, and then by comparing this to the pattern of state formation in post-colonial Africa.

Section 1 introduced the idea that being a citizen involves various activities of making and responding to demands, and furthermore that the state engages in all sorts of activities in which it makes demands of people or responds to their demands as citizens. Putting these two together suggests that citizenship can be understood as an ongoing relationship between people and the agents of the state in which each side has certain enforceable rights and obligations.

What is meant by rights and obligations here? An important point to note is that citizenship develops through ongoing conflicts over just what these rights and obligations should be. These conflicts are fought over the demands by the state for resources such as taxes, food, land and military personnel, and over the demands by citizens for such things as security, the provision of material entitlements and political participation. Rights are the demands that can be made of other actors, while obligations are the demands that must be met in response to demands from other actors. The example of citizenship in modern Europe illustrates what is meant by thinking of citizenship as a relationship of demands, rights and obligations.

2.1 State formation in Europe

The development of citizenship in Europe was built around the idea that citizens were members of unified national communities. This involved defining citizens as sharing the same cultural, ethnic or religious identity: as members of nation states.

You will recall that one set of state activities mentioned in Section 1 was the mobilisation of people and resources for military purposes. In Europe, it was through warfare and conquest that states were consolidated into large territorial units with clear boundaries (Tilly, 1990). This process also involved the state extending its activities into the routines of people's lives. As modern wars became more expensive and complex, so nation states were faced with an imperative to mobilise more and more resources from their own populations. One solution was the increasingly widespread collection of taxes levied directly on members of the population as a means of establishing a stable stream of revenue for the state. This represented a new demand made by the state of its population. Over time, paying taxes became a basic obligation of all citizens.

If one part of the development of citizenship in Europe involved the state imposing new obligations on its citizenry,

Defining the nation state

The concept of the nation state refers to a type of political community in which two forms of social solidarity coincide. First, a 'nation' refers to a community in which there is a strong sense of shared identity based on claims to common culture, language, history and attachment to land. Second, the 'state' is an independent political unit with recognised boundaries and a population of citizens. The nation state is the product of the ideology of nationalism, according to which each nation should be able to exist autonomously within a clearly bounded territory governed by its own state apparatus.

how did this process actually work? In order to collect taxes from all citizens, states had to develop efficient, nationwide systems of revenue collection and administration. An infrastructure had to be put in place that could measure and monitor the economic activity of individuals, households, towns, cities and regions. The state also had to collect taxation and keep track of government expenditure. One of the earliest expressions of this sort of administrative infrastructure was the development of modern postal systems. These first emerged as a means of enabling officials of the state to maintain contact with each other across long distances. They enabled information and revenue to be quickly and efficiently circulated around a country. In time, postal systems developed into systems for communication between states and citizens, as well between citizens themselves. In this way, the state was able to keep track of distant events and keep in touch with officials scattered in various corners of their territory. Once the state was able to do this, it became possible to keep track of and in touch with its citizens as well. The ways a state becomes involved in the everyday activities of all its citizens, no matter where they are in the state's territory, is what can be termed the 'reach' of the state.

Did the extension of the reach of European states over distance simply involve an increase in the capacity to coerce people into doing what rulers wanted? In reality, demands for increased taxation often met with stiff resistance from citizens. One example is the attempt by the British state to impose heavier taxes on the citizens of its colonies in America in the 1760s and 1770s. The British government found it very difficult to impose these taxes on its faraway territories, and the attempt to do so provoked serious, even violent, conflict (see Figure 3.1). Colonists in America demanded that they should only pay taxation in return for rights of political participation. The slogan 'No Taxation without Representation' became the rallying cry of the American Revolution, which eventually led to Britain ceding control of these distant colonies, and to the foundation of the United States of America.

The Bostonian's Paying the Excise-Man, or Tarring & Feathering
Plate I.

Figure 3.1   Conflict over demands for taxation: Bostonians tarring and feathering a tax collector, 1774

This example shows that successfully raising revenue through direct taxation depended on states being able to develop forms of cooperative rule based on mutual relations of give and take with their population. People only cooperated with demands for taxes, or for military service, in return for concessions by the state. States and their populations struck a series of bargains whereby the state was allowed to tax more by making concessions to those being taxed. At times, these bargains took the form of granting rights of political participation and representation, whereby citizens gained a degree of influence over state decision making as well as rights to scrutinise those decisions and hold rulers accountable. Sometimes, these bargains have involved states providing an array of material benefits to their populations, such as free education or health care.

What does this historical overview of the pathway to citizenship in Europe and North America tell us? First, it demonstrates that the development of citizenship involves a conflict over the demands that states can impose upon citizens. Second, it shows that in order to make these demands stick, states have to respond to the demands made by citizens in return. Consequently, this relationship is one of mutual demands and concessions. Third, it indicates that, in this case, the ongoing relationship of conflict and cooperation involved a steady intensification of interaction between states and citizens. The state's ability to reach over distance involved the development of various practices that drew states and citizens into close proximity, whether this involved paying taxes, doing military service, communicating with officials or going to school.

There is a strong temptation to think of this story of European state formation as the normal pathway to citizenship, but we should be wary of making hasty generalisations from this one case. The reason for looking at this example is not because it is the benchmark against which to judge other examples of state–citizen relationships. However, there are two important lessons to learn from this case, and which we can apply to other contexts:

1   The precise meaning of citizenship is shaped by the conflicts fought over the demands that states and citizens can successfully make of each other.

2   These conflicts are shaped by the degree to which states are able to reach into the routines of everyday life to create new forms of proximity between the state and its population.

If citizenship is shaped by the conflict between the demands made by states of citizens and the concessions made by states to citizens in

Defining colonialism

Colonialism refers to rule by one sovereign entity over another group of people, nation or state, which is subordinated by the colonial power. Colonialism is often associated with the physical occupation by colonisers of the colonial territory in a more or less permanent process of settlement. From the late fifteenth century through to the mid twentieth century, various European powers established colonial possessions around the world. For instance, the Spanish colonised large parts of the Americas until a wave of independence movements established autonomous nation states at the beginning of the nineteenth century. British colonialism reached its high point from the second half of the nineteenth century with the colonisation of India and large parts of Africa, before anti-colonial movements led the way to independence in the two decades after the Second World War.

return, and if the outcome of these conflicts is in part shaped by the capacity of states to extend their reach, we can see that citizenship rights and obligations will change over time and will vary from place to place.

We can examine these variations by considering an example that seems, at first, to contrast sharply with the European example we have just explored. This is the example of state formation in Africa in the twentieth century, both before and after the end of colonialism.

2.2 State formation in Africa

The African experience provides an interesting contrast to the model of state formation derived from European experience. In the European case, states gradually insinuated themselves into the routines of everyday life throughout their territories, but only by ceding rights to citizens in return. The incentive for the state to raise revenue through direct taxation led to the roll-out of an extensive administrative infrastructure across territories, as well as the conceding of various rights of participation, representation and entitlement to citizens by the state.

In contrast, many African societies today are characterised by a relative scarcity of the state, due to the limited ability of states to extend their reach uniformly over territory. The ability to collect taxation is a good indicator of the reach of any state. In this respect, many African states extract relatively few resources from their societies. Since the wave of independence in the 1960s, most African states have depended for their revenue on indirect taxation, especially taxes on foreign trade, and on revenue from non-tax sources, in particular from mineral concessions (for example, oil in Nigeria or copper in Zambia). This pattern of revenue collection is partly due to the ways in which post-colonial states in Africa are inserted into global networks of trade and investment, which leads them to orient their economies to external export markets.

What does this pattern of revenue collection have to do with citizenship? The taxing of international transactions only requires a state to exercise tight control over the access points at its borders; it does not really require reach across a territory or close proximity to citizens. Thus, ruling elites in many African states have had less incentive to strike the kinds of cooperative bargains with their populations required to establish and maintain steady revenue streams from personal direct taxation. The reliance on indirect taxation and non-tax revenue therefore weakens the link between the need for government revenue and the need to maintain routine contact and cooperation with ordinary people.

As a result of the lack of a strong motivation to develop administrative systems to mobilise tax revenues from populations, the reach of the state over territory tends to be highly uneven in many African countries. The state is often only a real presence in people's lives primarily in and around large urban areas where it is relatively easier to tax populations: 'Instead of African states gradually consolidating control over their territories as time progresses, even the most basic agents of the state – agricultural extension workers, tax collectors, census takers – are no longer found in many rural areas' (Herbst, 2000, p.19).

The absence of these sorts of agents of the state in many places in Africa indicates the relatively low levels of integration of many areas into consolidated national territorial systems of administration and rule. Under both colonialism and independence, many African states have had difficulty exercising effective authority over large, consolidated territories. The reach of states is either not very extensive, or where it does extend over distance, does so only in shallow and sporadic ways. This means that the state is much less of a presence in people's lives in many parts of Africa than in other parts of the world, so that there is less close interaction between the state and citizens. This is because many African states do not make extensive demands upon their populations, and it means that people have fewer opportunities for making demands upon the state as citizens.

This pattern is slowly changing as more and more African states, such as Kenya, Nigeria and Zambia, try to introduce effective systems of tax collection, often under pressure from international loan agencies and aid donors. However, these efforts are hindered by a suspicion among many citizens within these countries that they will not see many benefits from increased taxation. Attempts to levy taxes on basic goods like petrol, diesel and kerosene are often met with strikes and protests from people who can hardly afford these items already (see Figure 3.2). Once again, we can appreciate that the demands of the state for taxation can lead to conflict with citizens unless the state can persuade ordinary people that they will benefit in some way from improved amenities and services.

Figure 3.2   Attempts to increase taxation often provoke conflict with citizens: Zambian workers protest against tax increases

As noted earlier, we should not presume that one case study can provide a benchmark against which to judge other examples. Therefore, what can we learn by the contrast between state formation in Africa and Europe?

First, insofar as African states are characterised by a less extensive reach over their territories than other states, this is not because they are 'less developed' than states elsewhere. It is because state-making and citizenship formation has followed a different trajectory in Africa than in Europe, not least because of the legacy of European colonialism itself. The boundaries of today's African states are the product of European colonialism but, during the period of colonialism, European powers often exercised what was known as 'indirect rule'. The system of indirect rule involved the use of local chiefs or tribal leaders to implement colonial policies. These local intermediaries were empowered to collect tax revenue within their jurisdictions on behalf of the colonial state. This meant that the colonial state was able to exercise rule over territory without really extending its reach very deeply into all aspects of colonial societies. As a result, the end of colonialism has meant that many post-colonial African states inherited poorly consolidated state infrastructures with only limited reach across territory (Mamdani, 1996).

Second, in many African countries the state is a relatively scarce presence in people's lives, and, as a result, people's encounters with the state are likely to be much more sporadic than routine.

Consequently, the African example illustrates the same two lessons that we took from the case of European state formation, that citizenship is determined by conflicts between states and citizens as they are brought within reach of one another through their respective demands. For historical as well as contemporary reasons, the reach of the state in many post-colonial African countries is quite limited. This is because African states have had less capacity and less incentive to reach out uniformly across their territories. Accordingly, these states have had less cause to reach into the routines of people's ordinary lives and draw them into close proximity with the agents and representatives of the state and, in turn, relationships of conflict and cooperation with citizens are that much more irregular.

Summary

- Citizenship is shaped by the conflicts and bargains made between citizens and states over the rights, obligations and demands that each can enforce against the other.

- A crucial factor in determining the outcome of the conflicts and bargains made between citizens and states is the capacity of the state to reach out over distance into the contexts of people's ordinary lives.

- Where states reach out to citizens over distance, this can provide an opportunity for citizens to make demands of the state in return for meeting the obligations imposed upon them.

- The rights and obligations that tie citizens and states together change over time and space, and vary from country to country.

- A lack of close proximity between the state and its citizens means that the state is likely to impose fewer demands upon its population, but also that people will have fewer opportunities and occasions for levying their own demands as citizens upon the state.

3 Making states, making citizens

So far, we have seen that relationships between states and citizens are formed through conflicts and bargains over the demands that each can make of the other. Moreover, these conflicts are shaped by the degree to which states are able to reach into people's everyday lives and establish a close and routine relationship with them. Yet how is this process of reaching out over distance to create a relationship of close and constant proximity actually achieved by states?

One of the most striking things about globalisation is that it has coincided with a proliferation of independent states. There are many more independent states in the world now than there used to be. Therefore, living in a globalised world involves living in a world with lots of states, and this means that there are lots of different ways in which citizenship is organised and practised around the world.

In 1945, when the United Nations (UN) was founded, it consisted of only 51 member-states, mostly from Western Europe, North America, Central America and South America. Most of Africa and Asia consisted of colonial territories controlled by European states like the United Kingdom, France, Holland and Belgium. From the late 1950s onwards, these colonial territories gained independence, and so the number of UN member-states steadily grew: to 99 in 1960, including a number of newly independent West African states; to 127 in 1970, including new states in the Caribbean, East Africa and the Middle East. This number continued to grow slowly throughout the 1970s and 1980s as the last European colonies became independent states. In the early 1990s, another wave of new independent states was formed with the break-up of the Soviet Union and Yugoslavia, and the UN grew from 159 member-states to 189 between 1990 and 2000.

We saw from Section 2 that states have to be made, and this growth in the number of nation states suggests that there has been a lot of state-making going on. What is involved in making a new state? One thing it entails is building relationships with populations and making these populations into good, responsible citizens. State-making goes hand in hand with citizen-making. This can be done by creating new symbols of national identity – flags and national anthems, for example. Saluting a flag or singing a national anthem can provide opportunities for people to identify with one another as members of the same community, even without knowing one another or without being in the same place as their fellow citizens. Chapter 2 showed that radio and television can play an important role in drawing people together around shared images of national belonging by broadcasting sports events, national celebrations or, more mundanely, by drawing together disparate places into the same daily national news programmes.

However, another important dimension of state-making and its relationship to the formation of citizenship is the ability of states to keep track of and to monitor their populations, as we saw in Section 2. So, how exactly do states get to 'see' their populations?

3.1   Seeing like a state

To examine the question of how states 'see' their citizens, we can look at the example of South Africa. South Africa is not a completely new state, but it did only become a unified, democratic state in the 1990s. An important demand that has been placed on the newly democratic South African state is the expectation that it will improve the living standards of the majority of poor, black citizens. Since 1994, when the first inclusive democratic elections were held in South Africa, the population census has been given a crucial role to play in pursuing development programmes designed to meet this obligation. Census information is collected to assist in developing policies that aim to redistribute resources to the urban and rural poor, as well as to monitor the success of these policies in achieving socio-economic equity. Thus, a census is one means by which a state can keep track of, or 'see', who lives where and what is going on in its territory.

Activity 3.2

Turn now to Reading 3A entitled 'Second democratic population count vital to effective development', which you will find at the end of the chapter. The reading is taken from a publication of the ruling African National Congress (ANC), part of a wider publicity campaign for Census 2001 in South Africa, and it explains why a national population census has been considered such an important part of the process of development and democratisation since the end of apartheid in 1994.

1   Try to identify the different uses to which census information is going to be put.

2   How is the information going to be collected – what sorts of interactions between people and the state are involved in carrying out the census?

You may have noticed various ways in which the census information is going to be used. For one thing, the detailed information about education, employment, income, housing, and so on is important for government planning and policy making, particularly plans and policies that aim to deliver services and infrastructure to all South Africans. For example, one of the most pressing issues in South Africa is access to clean, potable water, and so having information about the numbers of households that still do not have piped water is important for planning future policy on delivery of water services (see Table 3.1). Furthermore, keeping track of this sort of information over time is important for monitoring the progress of these policies once they have been planned and implemented.

Table 3.1   Households in South Africa with access to piped and other sources of water, Census 2001

Source of water	Number of households
Piped water to dwelling	3,617,603
Piped water inside yard	3,253,861
Piped water to community stand < 200 m from dwelling	1,202,276
Piped water to community stand >200 m from dwelling	1,392,628
Borehole	270,882
Spring	210,444
Rainwater tank	67,680
Dam/pool/stagnant water	113,892
River/stream	725,719
Water vendor	83,634
Other	267,086

Source: Statistics South Africa, 2003a

The capacity to 'see' population and territory is a distinctive feature of many modern states. Much of what states do is dependent on the capacity to survey, count and monitor all sorts of activities and phenomena within their territories in order to intervene and change them (Scott, 1998). Various statistical and visual technologies for 'seeing' population and resources (for example, censuses, surveys, maps and plans) have become an important means by which states find out about their citizens. These technologies are, if you like, ways in which a state is able to objectify aspects of social and economic life. Nonetheless, from looking at the uses to which the South African census is put, we find that this capacity to objectify society is driven by the aim of intervening in and changing the patterns of people's lives as well. In South Africa, measures are put in place to improve people's lives by providing housing, water or electricity in part as a response to the demands placed upon the state by citizens.

More generally, the South African state's ability to 'see' its population and territory from a distance, objectively, depends on its ability to reach out into every corner of the country. The census is just one example of an administrative system through which the state reaches out over distance by scattering its representatives to the four corners of its territories. The example of the census helps us to appreciate how the ordinary business of managing a modern state is possible because all sorts of agents of the state are present in everyday lives of citizens. These agents include everyone from police officers, judges, doctors and nurses and schoolteachers to census takers, traffic wardens and social workers. These agents of the state engage directly with people when they administer justice, investigate crime, monitor births, marriages and deaths, or deliver various services like health care or education.

Clearly, the capacity of the state to 'see' all sorts of mundane activities – who lives where, who earns what, how many qualifications people have – depends on a decentralisation of all sorts of agents dispersed across a large number of locations. At the same time, all those dispersed, anonymous officials and bureaucrats are linked together through the constant transfer to and from the central organs of the state of information, rules, regulations, targets and results.

The reach of centralised state authority over distance depends on making the state a real, felt presence across the whole extent of its territory. This can take the form of regular systems of taxation; the establishment of extensive postal systems; the establishment of systems for the registration of births and deaths; or less frequent but still regular events like censuses or national elections. All of these activities involve collecting lots of information about distant contexts and bringing all this information together to be analysed, assessed and made the basis of further decision making. Thus, the process of state-making involves the construction of extensive networks and flows of information, materials and people (Allen, 2003).

Let us look again at the South African census to illustrate this process of decentralisation and centralisation. This example shows us that censuses are very difficult exercises to organise, carry out and then make use of. Census forms need to be delivered, either by post or by hand, to every household in the country. Once completed, these forms need to be collected together by the agency responsible for the census – Statistics South Africa – either being returned by post or collected in person. This agency then undertakes the task of analysing the data and, by using all the information collected, produces a vast array of different representations of life in South Africa in the form of tables, maps and diagrams (see Figure 3.3). This information is then disseminated to

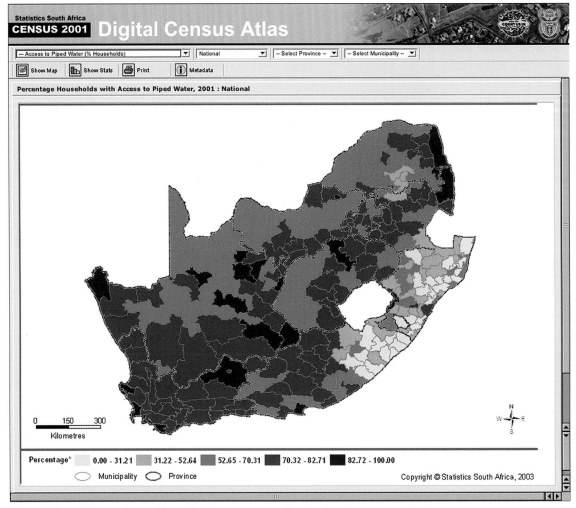

Figure 3.3   Percentage of households with access to piped water, Census 2001
Source: Statistics South Africa, 2003b

government departments, to businesses and also to citizens through public information initiatives, schools and universities, and through newspapers, radio and television. The extension of the reach of the state therefore involves a constant relay of people, material and information around territories. We will return to consider this process further in Section 3.2.

The South African census is an example of a newly democratic state endeavouring to extend its authority over a wider range of activities than before by extending its ability to monitor or 'see' the conduct of people in the places where they live and work. It helps us to understand that extending reach over distance in fact involves two processes:

1   First, many agents of the state have to interact directly with people and places in order to monitor, survey and regulate various activities.

Part of what we mean by reach is to do with making the state proximate to its citizens, bringing them up close and into contact.

2   Second, all of the information collected by dispersed agents of the state has to be transported and translated to central authorities. Therefore, the other part of reach involves a circulation over distance of people, information and materials, and their collection at some central point of decision making.

It is important to emphasise that a state's capacity to reach across distance in order to survey the whole country depends on quite mundane activities, such as sending out lots of census enumerators to knock on people's doors, or posting census forms. These sorts of mundane practices do the work of linking up dispersed activities.

Consequently, we can think of a census as one mechanism for bringing distant activities or phenomena close together by inscribing information onto a simple form, which is then collected with millions of other forms at centres of analysis, calculation and planning. Through this process of relocation, what is distant and dispersed can be brought together and represented in new ways as proximate. This is, in some measure, what it means to 'see' like a state. Examining how a census is physically undertaken also helps us to understand how census information, once collected and analysed, can in turn become part of the relationship between states and citizens, and can be used to support the demands of citizens as much as it can be used to impose the expectations of the state.

We have also ascertained that implementing all the measures that are planned by using census information involves further, direct engagements with citizens. This close engagement between states and citizens is another aspect of 'seeing' like a state, and it is through these engagements that people also get to 'see' the state. We can now consider this aspect of the relationship between states and citizens – how citizens 'see' the state – in more depth.

3.2   Seeing the state

The example of the South African census in Section 3.1 shows us how states 'see' citizens. A census is an occasion when the state engages directly with people. In turn, the information collected provides the basis for further direct engagements by the state with citizens by helping to shape policies for delivering water, employment, housing or health care. This means that a census also creates opportunities for people to 'see' the state. In this section, we will explore how states are experienced by people in direct and indirect ways.

We have seen how state-making and citizenship depend on the development of a broad range of widely dispersed practices of management, regulation and administration. The extension of the reach of the state over distance involves bringing the state into close, routine proximity with ordinary people. However, this process of extending reach by creating new proximities with citizens is not simply a one-way, top-down imposition by states. The state is a presence in people's lives, and because many of the activities of the state depend on the cooperation of ordinary people, extending the reach of the state makes it possible for people to exercise various sorts of influence of their own when interacting with the state and its agents – to make their own demands of the state, as was noted in Section 2.

The South African census involves thousands of state officials going around the country trying to count people who live in all kinds of places. Yet it seems that the success of the South African census depends on people being willing to cooperate with census enumerators when they turn up to distribute census forms and ask questions.

The South African government went to great lengths to try to persuade people to take part in the census, running an expensive media campaign to raise awareness of Census 2001. This included radio programmes explaining the census in various African languages, television adverts in which soap stars encouraged people to take part, as well as storylines dealing with the census in the most popular soap operas. The sorts of media technologies discussed in Chapter 2 were used to reach into people's everyday routines in order to explain and justify the whole exercise. This awareness campaign was deliberately aimed at overcoming the suspicion that many black South Africans, in particular, have towards the state, a suspicion derived from a long history of oppression during colonialism and apartheid.

It transpires that the South African census depends not only on the capacity of the central government to reach out into every corner of South African society by sending out many census enumerators to count people; its success also depends on people having a degree of trust and confidence in the purposes and value of the exercise itself. Convincing people that the information they provide will be confidential and anonymous is very important to the success of the South African census. The efforts that the South African state goes to in order to ensure that people do take part in the census – and the fact that these efforts take the form not of coercive threats but attempts to inform and persuade – tell us that the capacity of the state to extend its authority over large numbers of people living in a large territory depends not so much on its ability to impose itself on those people but more on its capacity to secure their cooperation.

Thus, the census is an occasion when the state makes a certain sort of demand of its citizens. In this case, what is at stake is mainly a demand for cooperation in providing information, and it depends on the state being able to come into direct contact with people, on the doorstep, in their homes.

However, this also means that being counted in a census is one occasion when people get to 'see' the state. If making demands of citizens depends on the state coming into close contact with people and requires at least a minimal degree of cooperation, then might it not also be the case that the extension of reach over distance also generates occasions where people are able to levy their own demands upon the state? In the South African case the census opens up the opportunity for citizens to demand that the state deliver the services it is recording, such as piped water, more effectively across the country.

Let us look at another example, this time from India. How the Indian state 'sees' its population is driven by the imperative to make poverty, inequality and other social problems visible so that the state can intervene to alleviate them. In India, poverty is made manifest by the same sorts of techniques we have already discussed – through censuses, surveys and other statistical and mapping technologies. These become the basis of policy initiatives and administrative procedures that seek to intervene directly in the routines of ordinary people in order to change the characteristics of whole segments of the population – through public health programmes, poverty relief, employment schemes, education provision, and so on. All of these measures involve the direct engagement between agents of the state and citizens, for example in hospitals, clinics and schools. These engagements are all occasions when citizens 'see' the state (see Figure 3.4).

The ways in which the state is made present in people's lives depends on how the various engagements, where people come into close proximity with the state, are structured and performed. There are two aspects to making the state proximate in people's everyday lives.

First, there is the material presence of the state in people's lives. This includes the location of government buildings (for example, police stations, hospitals and schools) which serve as the physical spaces in which encounters with the agents of the state take place. It also involves various mediated interactions – listening to the radio, watching television, or receiving a tax form or a speeding fine in the post.

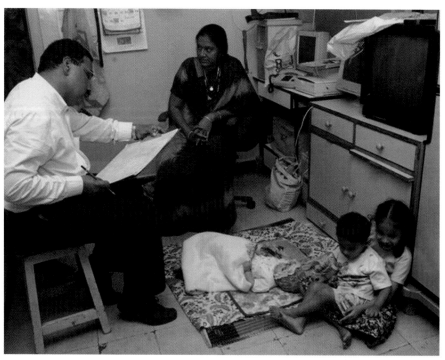

Figure 3.4   India's population census: one occasion when citizens 'catch sight' of the state

Second, there are encounters with agents of the state who mediate between the state and ordinary citizens. How these encounters are performed – how people are treated by a police officer, a tax official or a doctor or nurse – is an important aspect of how people learn to 'see' the state. Both of these aspects of 'seeing' the state are illustrated in this description of how a poor, rural Indian woman might encounter the state:

> When a widow goes to the Block Development Office to collect her pension she makes contact with 'the state' in the form of a lower-level official and by entering a designated building. For example, she might be required to sign a particular piece of paper on an official's desk. But these encounters are rarely conducted as the rulebook says they should be. The widow will often be kept waiting for hours in the sun or the rain, and she might have to call on a relative or fixer to get her business moving. Small payments might also have to be made to the accountant and/or his peon, and sometimes the payment she receives will be several rupees short. The widow might expect this, although her expectations will vary from place to place according to the conventions of political society. The point is that she will have learned to see the state not just through her 'own eyes', but with regard to wider understandings of government.

(Corbridge et al., 2005)

In rural India, people learn to 'see' the state through these sorts of formal and informal encounters. Consequently, their direct and indirect experiences of the state are likely to determine the extent to which they are willing to cooperate when faced with some claim made by the state. These experiences are also likely to shape people's inclinations to make demands of their own back to the state and its officials.

It is easy to think of these sorts of demands in terms of large-scale, collectively organised campaigns – for the right to vote, for example, or to change some specific area of policy to do with access to education, water or provision of health services, or reducing pollution. We will look at this sort of demand by citizens in more detail in Section 4. Yet people can also make claims of the state in more mundane ways, on those occasions when they encounter officials as individuals in daily life. Even poor women in rural India are able to engage positively with the state as citizens. The widow referred to above, for instance, might challenge the informal rules that account for her long wait in the sun or the rain by demanding that officials respect the rules that are supposed to structure their interaction: 'She is able to demand her pension, and occasionally to stand her ground, precisely because the state has defined her as a citizen with rights, and because it has given her scraps of paper to prove her entitlement to welfare benefits' (Corbridge et al., 2005).

This example from rural India shows us how even the poorest citizens are, in certain circumstances, able to levy their own demands upon the state. This might take the form of claiming entitlements or it might simply involve demanding to be treated fairly and with respect by a government official. In both cases, by establishing a relation of close proximity with their populations, states open themselves up to being made subject to demands by people acting as citizens – that is, as members of a political community with legally enforceable rights.

In this section we have seen that the capacity of states to 'see' their populations and territories depends on their ability to reach out over distance to come into close contact with people. At the same time, this extension of the reach of the state provides opportunities for people to 'see' the state. In Section 2 the extension of the reach of the state was related to the demand that citizens pay taxation in order to support the revenue base of the state. In this section, we have seen that the extension of the state can be related to a different sort of demand, as the state endeavours to extract information from people, which depends on the cooperation of citizens. So if the extension of the reach of the state into everyday life means that the state is, in certain respects, much closer to people than it was before, this also means that people are able to interact more directly and proactively with the state to exercise their rights as citizens.

In summary, the interactions between states and citizens are shaped both by the efforts of the state to reach out and influence aspects of economic or social life, as well as by efforts of ordinary people to pull in the state to ensure the delivery of certain services or material entitlements. In the next section, we will look in more detail at how both of these efforts are being reconfigured in a globalised world.

Summary

- States are able to 'see' their populations and territories by reaching out over distance to come into contact with citizens and, at the same time, this enables citizens to 'see' the state.

- The reach of the state over distance involves the development of material infrastructures and organisational procedures through which the state is made proximate to people's lives.

- 'Seeing like a state' is not only a matter of an omnipotent authority imposing its will on a subordinate population; it provides opportunities for people in turn to make demands of their own.

4   Reconfiguring states and citizens

In Section 3, we looked at how the state 'sees' its population and territory, and how citizens 'see' the state. In both cases of 'seeing like a state' and 'seeing the state', the capacity of the state to reach out is a crucial factor, not only in imposing obligations upon people, but also in providing opportunities for people to engage the state more directly by claiming entitlements or exercising rights.

Now, what difference does living in a globalised world make to how states 'see' their citizens, and how they make demands of them? And what difference does living in a globalised world make to how citizens 'see' the state, and to how they make demands of it?

We have emphasised that the precise ways in which these processes of reach and making demands work will vary from place to place. This means that citizenship will also be geographically and historically variable. In this section, we will explore examples of the different types of relationships that can develop between states and citizens under conditions of globalisation. Globalisation alters the ways in which states exercise their capacity to reach into people's lives, and this has important consequences for how states and citizens engage one another to make and respond to demands.

4.1   Fragmented citizenship

A striking example of how relationships between states and societies
are changing in a globalised world is found in a number of rapidly
globalising newly industrialised countries (NICs) in Southeast Asia,
including Malaysia, Indonesia, Thailand and Singapore, as well as South
Korea and China.

These countries are among the so-called 'Asian Tigers' discussed in
Chapter 1. Their experience of rapid economic growth, capitalist
industrialisation and urbanisation is often attributed to the highly
interventionist policies of their governments. They have been
considered models of 'developmental states'. In this type of state, the
government was actively involved in economic management to foster
the transformation of industrial production and rapid economic
growth. This entailed the state establishing companies, providing
subsidised loans to companies and investing heavily in fixed
infrastructure to sustain economic growth.

As models of developmental states, these Asian states were also
characterised by particular relationships with their own populations.
They are often referred to as 'strong states', which means that the
bargain struck between state and citizens in this formation of citizenship
puts more emphasis on the state's ability to promote and sustain high
levels of economic growth in order to deliver steady improvements in
standards of living, rather than on the extension of widespread civil
liberties and rights of effective political participation and representation
that characterised the European example discussed in Section 2.

In the 1990s, this trajectory of national economic development
underwent significant revision in response to the increasing
internationalisation of production systems and the ever more intense
globalisation of finance markets. States found themselves less able
directly to control economic activity. However, rather than being
powerless in the face of these forces, these states have been able to
reconfigure and refashion their capacities to respond to changed
circumstances. A crucial factor in determining the ways in which these
states have responded to global forces has been that, while the global
economy is largely beyond their control, they still have considerable
capacity to manage their own populations. NICs in Asia have adopted
strategies that aim to bring people and resources within the reach of
the state in order to connect them in new ways to global markets. This
has led to them being characterised as 'post-developmental states'. The
basic goal of this form of post-developmental state is to produce a

Defining developmental and post-developmental states

The concept of the developmental state refers to the commitment of an autonomous bureaucratic leadership to deploy the capacities of the state in the pursuit of national economic development, where this is usually understood to involve industrialisation and steady economic growth. The legitimacy of a developmental state depends primarily on its ability to continue to ensure that the benefits of steady economic growth are distributed to all of its citizens. Models of this type of state include post-Second World War Japan and South Korea. The concept of the post-developmental state refers to the recent emergence of an approach to developmental goals that shifts from promoting the growth of domestic industries and enterprises towards using the authority and capacity of the state to attract foreign investment and to shape citizens as skilled employees and entrepreneurs, while also distributing the benefits of economic growth more differentially among social groups.

skilled, entrepreneurial middle class that can actively form links with global markets by virtue of its educational qualifications, business acumen or access to domestic capital.

Post-developmental states therefore trade off a reduction of control over direct economic production for heightened management of their populations, and this is expressed in states making greater demands of their citizens to be more flexible and entrepreneurial.

How exactly is this demand that citizens be more flexible and entrepreneurial actually managed? There are two strategies that characterise the ways in which post-developmental states engage with their populations, and both of them aim to *fragment* citizenship in certain ways.

The first strategy consists of states treating particular segments of society in different ways; people are accorded different rights and entitlements depending on their class, gender, and ethnic or racial identity. For example, in Malaysia and Singapore this differential treatment builds upon prior categorisations of the population into distinct ethnic groups that date back to the colonial period. Both of these states differentiate citizens by ethnicity, gender, class and nationality, so that different ethno-racial categories become the basis for entitlements and rights. Since independence, certain groups have been given special, privileged status in Singapore (ethnic Chinese) and Malaysia (Malay bumiputera). The identity of these groups is maintained in part by classification schemes such as censuses and surveys. These schemes of ethnic and racial categorisation are now being used as the basis for calculating the potential market value of different population groups.

In this way, different segments of the population are given different privileges, entitlements and protections depending on how the state wants them to participate in globalised market activities (Ong, 2000). This involves the further enhancement of the privileged status of some groups compared with others. With this shift, values of expertise, risk-taking and entrepreneurship are replacing ethnicity and political loyalty as the key to how different groups engage with the state. This amounts to an attempt to create policies that produce some segments of the citizenry as attractive to capital because they are experts or entrepreneurs, and other segments as attractive to capital because they are flexible, low-paid labour. Consequently, the first way in which citizenship is becoming fragmented in post-developmental states is through the differential treatment of particular population groups as potential segments of labour markets. This strategy is closely related to the second strategy through which citizenship is fragmented.

The second strategy involves dividing the national territory into distinct zones of economic and administrative activity (Ong, 2004). A good example of this strategy is the development of Special Economic Zones (SEZs) and Special Administrative Regions (SARs) by China since the 1970s (see Figure 3.5). SEZs are zones that are economically and administratively autonomous from the rest of China's centrally

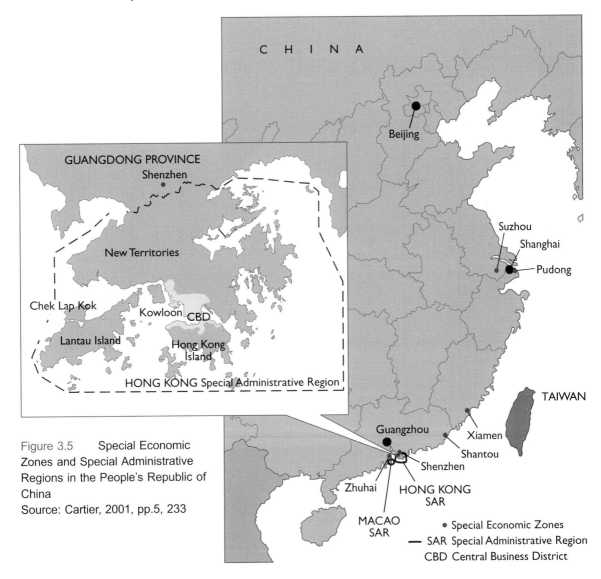

Figure 3.5 Special Economic Zones and Special Administrative Regions in the People's Republic of China
Source: Cartier, 2001, pp.5, 233

planned economy. They are designed to attract capital investment through relaxed regulations and incentives for foreign investors. Therefore, people in these zones live and work in different conditions from people in other parts of China. They may be paid more, but they are also likely to be expected to be more flexible in their work and employment practices than workers elsewhere in the country. Chinese citizens have been able to establish their own businesses in these zones, and so are plugged into the global markets discussed in Chapter 1 that reach all the way to high streets in the West.

SARs were developed as a way of China managing the incorporation of Hong Kong in 1997 and Macao in 1999 following the end of British and Portuguese colonial rule respectively. These are zones of relative political autonomy as well as economic and administrative autonomy, in so far as people living in these zones enjoy a greater degree of civil liberties and political rights than citizens in the rest of China. People living in these zones enjoy a relatively higher degree of personal and political freedom, and have more opportunity to influence the policies of state actors than in other parts of China.

The differential treatment of population groups and the differential zoning of territory are the two strategies through which post-developmental states have pursued policies that effectively fragment citizenship within nation states. Rather than extending reach uniformly over territory, these strategies involve reaching out to manage different groups of people or different zones of territory in starkly different ways. This means that depending on where people live, work, or the identity they are ascribed, the state extends varying types of citizenship rights as part of a calculated strategy to connect with broader global flows of capital and finance. In both cases, the aim of these differentiating strategies is to draw the national economies into closer proximity with global flows of investment and trade.

From the perspective of how states reach out to citizens, globalisation seems to be associated with the development of a range of new mechanisms that no longer treat the national population as a uniform whole, nor treat the economy as a single, integrated, bounded national system. In both respects, post-developmental states are now exercising their capacities to reach into society in order to differentiate more finely groups of people and different locations.

In an era of fragmented citizenship, states are being reconfigured to be more responsive to the interests of some people than others, depending on their potential value to international labour markets. However, recalling what we have learned so far about the relationships between states and citizens, if in a globalised world there is a shift in the sorts of demands made by states of citizens, should we not also expect the kinds of demands made by citizens of states to be changing?

4.2   Flexible citizenship and transnational activism

In this section, we will look at how the restructuring of states and economies under globalisation also provides opportunities for people to act in new ways as citizens. The fragmentation of citizenship discussed in Section 4.1 means that some citizens are likely to be able to express their demands and exercise their rights more effectively than others. This will depend on where these citizens live and on their positions within social and economic hierarchies.

For example, one finds an increasing willingness and capacity among the managerial, expert and professional workers to circumvent and benefit from differential citizenship regimes in different countries (Ong, 1999). This is contributing to an increase in transnational migration (which will be discussed further in Chapter 4). One feature of transnational migration is the development of dual citizenship arrangements. Dual citizenship confers on some people the status of 'citizen' of a particular national community without requiring that they permanently live or work there, or that they relinquish citizenship status in another country. This is one example of *flexible* citizenship (Ong, 1999), in which people are able to make demands of more than one state to gain the benefits, entitlements and rights that result from being a citizen.

Thus, being able to act as a flexible citizen is related to the capacity to act transnationally. This means being able to engage not only with a state of which one is a resident, but also with states that are far away. Flexible citizenship is a phenomenon that depends upon people being able to extend the reach of the demands which they make as citizens to encompass more than one state, and indeed to encompass non-state actors such as firms or NGOs as well, with which they might only have a remote or temporary relationship.

The capacity to act transnationally in order to make demands as a citizen is not only available to a relatively privileged global

Defining transnational

The term transnational is most fully developed in studies of migration, where it refers to a pattern of migration that is distinct either from the permanent relocation from one country to another or from merely temporary residence in a foreign country. Transnational migration, in contrast, involves a process of ongoing movements and interactions between more than one country. It refers to the process whereby migrants, rather than relocating completely from one place to another, effectively live in more than one place, having homes and work in more than a single nation state.

The term 'transnational' is also used to describe other phenomena. For example, transnational activism refers to the sustained interaction between activist networks organised across national boundaries, engaging with opponents who may or may not continue to be embedded at national levels.

class of professionals, business people and entrepreneurs. As globalisation increasingly shapes many aspects of people's social and economic life chances, political mobilisation often has to go beyond the borders of the nation state (Miller, 2004). Transnational political activism is another example of people adopting flexible strategies in order to enforce and secure the rights that people are meant in principle to have as members of nation states. By saying that transnational activism is an example of flexible citizenship, we mean that it can involve people addressing their demands to more than one single state. Moreover, they may address their demands to a number of different actors beyond their own state, and not just states but multinational corporations and international governmental organisations as well. To examine this process in more detail, let us return to South Africa, where we will look at an example of transnational citizen action on behalf of poor and marginalised groups of people.

Section 3 showed that all South Africans now enjoy equal citizenship rights by virtue of living in a democracy. These rights include basic civil liberties as well as rights to democratic participation and representation. The South African Constitution also recognises various rights of social and economic citizenship, and these include a right to a clean and healthy environment:

> Everyone has the right
>
> (a) to an environment that is not harmful to their health or well-being; and
>
> (b) to have the environment protected, for the benefit of present and future generations, through reasonable legislative and other measures that
>
> (i) prevent pollution and ecological degradation;
>
> (ii) promote conservation; and
>
> (iii) secure ecologically sustainable development and use of natural resources while promoting justifiable economic and social development.
>
> (South Africa, 1996)

The nominal right to a clean and healthy environment raises a number of questions about the meaning of citizenship in a globalised world:

- Who is obliged by this constitutional clause to ensure this right? We might think that it is primarily the responsibility of the South African government to ensure that this objective is achieved.

However, can the South African government be expected to guarantee this right in the face of powerful domestic imperatives and global forces that encourage further industrial development?

- Should multinational companies and foreign investors be bound by the South African constitution? After all, they might be responsible for some of the environmental problems that this clause is meant to address.

- If you think that multinational companies and foreign investors should be bound by the South African constitution, how can this obligation be enforced? If we cannot necessarily expect the South African government to demand that such bodies clean up their operations, can anybody else be expected to make this demand, and make it effectively?

One place in South Africa where these issues have become a source of explicit political contention is in the city of Durban. The south Durban industrial basin is the country's second largest concentration of industrial activity. It is also one of the country's worst pollution 'hot spots'. Pollution has been a pressing concern for local communities in south Durban for decades. Local residents, who are predominantly poor black people, live in very close proximity to a host of 'dirty industries' (see Figures 3.6 and 3.7). As a result, these residents reside in a highly polluted urban environment. The residential areas of south Durban suffer very high levels of air, ground and water pollution, not least because of their contiguity to two oil refineries, a paper and pulp factory, and a number of petrochemical plants.

Figure 3.6   The proximity of residential areas to industry in south Durban

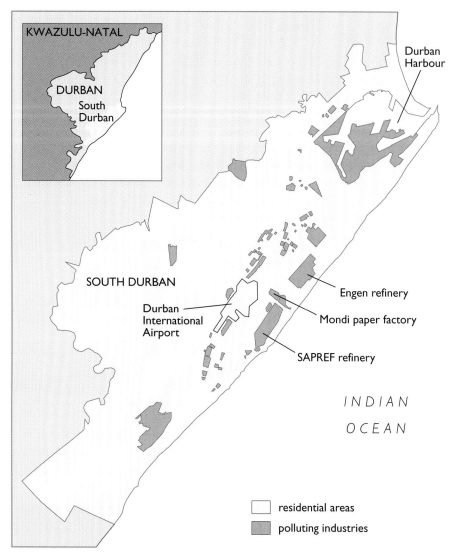

Figure 3.7   Industrial development and residential areas in south Durban
Source: Danmarks Naturfredningsforening and South Durban Community Environmental
Alliance (SDCEA), 2004

Among the worst polluters in the area are the two oil refineries. One
of these, the SAPREF (Shell and BP South African Refineries) refinery,
is jointly owned by two multinational oil companies, Shell and BP
(British Petroleum). The other refinery, the Engen refinery, is owned
by Petronas. Petronas is Malaysia's state-owned oil and gas company,
which has expanded its operations beyond Malaysia's borders in recent
years. As a result, people living very close to polluting industries – and
experiencing high levels of asthma, cancer and other health problems
as a consequence – are faced with the problem of engaging with
corporations whose headquarters are far away.

Activity 3.3

Turn now to Reading 3B by Tony Carnie (2000a; 2000b) entitled 'The poison in our air' and Reading 3C by Myrthe Verweij (2003) entitled 'Leaking pipelines: Shell in South Africa', which you will find at the end of the chapter. The two readings are about pollution in south Durban. Reading 3B is from a local newspaper, *The Mercury*, and reports on the apparently high incidence of cancers in south Durban, and on whether these are related to air pollution levels in the area. Reading 3C is from a pamphlet produced by a Dutch environmental NGO, Milieudefensie, which works closely with Durban-based environmental activists. This extract discusses pollution from oil pipelines under the ground.

As you read, note down your thoughts on the following questions:

1   What sorts of demands are being made by local communities regarding air and ground pollution?

2   To whom are they making their demands?

Among other things, the demands made by local communities include the need for further scientific research into the causes of health problems in the Durban area, as well as better monitoring of pollution from industry. Their demands also include that industries do more to conform to international standards of pollution emission.

You might also have noticed that responsibility for meeting these demands is divided between a number of different actors. One set of demands is that corporations who own the worst polluting industries should do more to clean up these operations. Yet there is also the demand that the South African government should do more to enforce existing pollution standards. So, just how do local communities try to enforce these demands in order to make them into binding obligations for the state and for both domestic and foreign corporations? What strategies of reach do they employ to make their own government and these powerful actors, especially foreign firms, respond to their demands?

Since South Africa's first democratic elections in 1994, local activists in Durban have made creative use of their new rights of citizenship. Whereas under apartheid, black people in South Africa were denied the status of full citizenship rights, now government departments are bound by law to be more accountable, transparent and participatory in their relationships with all South Africans. Nonetheless, this still requires people to engage in various citizenly practices to try to influence state agencies. Accordingly, activists in south Durban have mobilised local people in support of their campaign to reduce pollution in the area. Their primary aim has been to draw attention to the health problems that local communities face by virtue of living so close to polluting industries. The activists have organised demonstrations, protests and public meetings which are all forms of collective activism aimed at publicising pollution issues, demonstrating the extent of public concern around them, and establishing the degree of support for the activists organising around these issues.

Chapter 2 showed that media can be one important mechanism through which events and causes are brought close to people, and these forms of activism have been designed to do just that. Activists have been successful in attracting a great deal of sustained news coverage about pollution issues in the south Durban area, in local and national media. In this way, activists have been able to bring pollution issues to the attention of powerful national politicians and policy makers. They have made it possible, indeed imperative, for powerful actors to 'see' the pollution problem in their area. Since the South African government is publicly committed to improving the living standards of poor South Africans, this form of activism has been successful in using media coverage to reach out to the state and oblige it – to shame it almost – into paying more attention to the problem. Furthermore, this sort of activism seems to have had tangible results. The national government has responded to the demands of the community by implementing a programme of pollution monitoring and scientific research into health problems in the south Durban area.

This is an example of citizens engaging in collective action by mobilising support locally and nationally in order to reach out to the state and impose certain obligations upon it (Low, 2001). So far, we have only talked about citizens reaching out to the government of their own state, to which they belong as citizens. On the face of it, there does not seem to be anything 'transnational' about the process described above. What about the demands that are being made by environmental activists of transnational companies? What about enforcing the obligations of foreign corporations? How do citizens go about trying to reach out to them?

In fact, activists from Durban have not limited their campaigning to the channels of citizen–state engagement in their own country. They have also engaged in various sorts of transnational activism, reaching out to cooperate with activists in other countries.

One thing the activists have done is to *reach out to pull in* certain sorts of resources that help them to make demands upon the South African government. For example, much of their transnational activity has involved the mobilisation of scientific expertise to support the local communities' claims about the unacceptably high levels of air and ground pollution in the Durban area. An instance of this is called the 'Bucket Brigade'. This is an idea borrowed from environmental justice campaigners in the USA. The Bucket Brigade is a procedure enabling local residents to take their own air samples by using a simple bucket device, as the name suggests, that they can use in and around their homes and neighbourhoods. These samples are then sent to university research centres in the USA to be analysed. The results enable activists back in South Africa to confront both government and businesses with hard facts about levels of toxins in the air. As in Section 3.1, where we saw that the state extends its reach by circulating information and materials over distance, in this case activists are doing much the same thing, sharing information and sending materials back and forth across national boundaries.

You will also recall that in Section 3.1 extending reach involved both the extension of influence over distance and the ability to bring things close together and into contact. The science-based campaigning by environmental activists involves this second aspect of reach as well. For example, South African activists have established a collaborative relationship with the largest citizen-based environmental organisation in Denmark, Danmarks Naturfredningsforening (The Society for the Protection of Nature in Denmark). This collaboration has included a scientific comparison between the levels of air pollution produced by the two oil refineries in south Durban with the levels produced by refineries in Denmark. The research showed that the emission of sulphur dioxide (SO_2) from the two South African refineries in Durban was far higher than the levels from Danish refineries (see Figure 3.8). SO_2 is a major cause of asthma and other chronic respiratory illnesses as well as a cancerous pollutant. Emissions of particulate matter – liquid and solid aerosols like soot – were also higher in Durban than in Denmark (see Figure 3.9).

This comparison of the data on refinery pollution in Denmark and South Africa illustrates the process of making two distant places proximate to each other very well. The relationship across national boundaries between two sets of campaigners enabled the two places to be brought close together, not least in the form of tables, graphs and charts that literally put Danish and South African refineries alongside one another. This comparison emphasised the different pollution standards applied in these two countries. In turn, bringing these two different contexts into contact in this way enabled activists in South Africa to argue that their own government should enforce the stronger standards of environmental protection that are used elsewhere in the world.

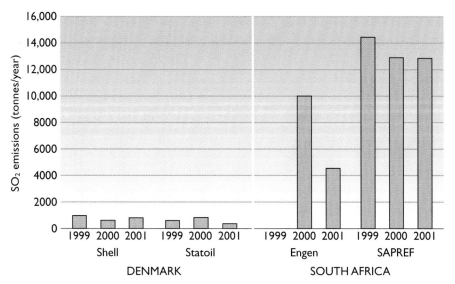

Figure 3.8   Annual sulphur dioxide emissions from Danish and South African oil refineries
Source: Danmarks Naturfredningsforening and South Durban Community Environmental Alliance (SDCEA), 2004

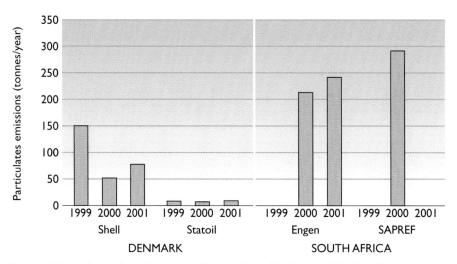

Figure 3.9   Annual particulates emissions from Danish and South African oil refineries
Source: Danmarks Naturfredningsforening and South Durban Community Environmental Alliance (SDCEA), 2002

The collaboration is an example of reaching out across distance in order to pull in expertise that is not necessarily easy to access in South Africa. This sort of collaboration is not only aimed at the South African government, to try and make it enforce existing pollution legislation; the activists from south Durban have also *reached out to influence* the global corporations that own the refineries located in south Durban.

This process of reaching out to influence global corporations is illustrated by another dimension of the transnational activism developed by activists from the area. The multinational oil company Shell is one of the owners of the SAPREF refinery in Durban, and activists from Durban have linked up with an international campaign coordinated by Friends of the Earth that aims to force Shell to be more accountable to the local communities impacted upon by its activities. This campaign brings together citizens from countries as far afield as the Philippines, Nigeria, Brazil, the USA and South Africa. The campaign produces an annual report, *The Other Shell Report*, to coincide with Shell's annual shareholders' meetings. On these occasions, the campaign brings together activists from all of these locations to lobby and protest in person at the annual general meetings (AGMs) in London and The Hague (see Figure 3.10). Some of these activists own one single share in Shell, which enables them to attend the shareholders' meetings and raise sometimes embarrassing questions about the company's operations around the world.

Both aspects of the process of reaching out (to pull in, to influence) are illustrated in this example: the establishment of connections over distance between similar campaigns located in different places around the world; and bringing together representatives from these campaigns

Figure 3.10   Transnational activism: campaigners at the Shell AGM

to lobby directly, up close and in person, the companies that are responsible for the industries polluting in those different places.

This type of activism works by generating new forms of proximity between actors located in different parts of the world. It does so by establishing all sorts of linkages, relays and interactions over distance. The same process of reaching out as was shown in the process of state formation in Section 2 is at work here. However, in this case it is citizens who are the main agents of the process, and extending reach is a means of making demands of the state, as well as of other actors, and a means of enforcing them. In the same way that Section 3 demonstrated that an important aspect of the state's ability to extend its reach involves finding ways to 'see' distant phenomena, the example of transnational activism shows that an important part of this sort of campaigning involves various efforts at making pollution 'visible' to distant actors – by publicising pollution problems in the media, or by producing statistical and diagrammatic representations of pollution emissions.

It seems that the ability of citizens to draw states *and* corporations into their reach – to engage them in dialogue, to lobby them or to protest about their actions – depends on some of the same capacities that enable states to draw citizens into relationships of enforceable rights and obligations. In this section, we have seen three ways in which the reach of citizen action can be extended transnationally:

1   Through the circulation of various forms of communication or media output such as scientific reports, books, newspaper coverage, emails and websites.

2   Through the movement of materials, for example sending air samples overseas to get them analysed.

3   Through the movement of people such as activists travelling to corporate AGMs or visiting other communities with similar concerns.

The example of transnational activism shows that these sorts of activities can be used to make demands either by reaching out to pull in resources that enable citizens to enforce demands close to home, or by reaching out to influence other actors or events that are located far away.

There is one final point to take from this example. It seems, on the face of it, a very good example of how globalisation might produce 'global' forms of political activism. Yet this example shows us that this does not mean that national rights of citizenship have ceased to be important. Just as the capacities of states are being reconfigured rather than eroded by globalisation, so the sort of flexible citizenship we have looked at in this section combines both national and transnational activities. The strategies used to reach out beyond national boundaries by South African activists have been adopted in order to try to enforce nationally prescribed rights to a clean and healthy environment. The example of transnational environmental activism discussed here certainly spills over the borders of contained nation states, but it does so to try to enforce the obligations of non-state actors such as multinational corporations to deliver rights guaranteed in principle by a national constitution. This has involved South African activists drawing on the support of actors in other places; it has involved Dutch and Danish citizens, for example, lending their support to South African activists; and it has involved these and other actors 'pooling' their citizenship resources to lend their support to broader transnational campaigns for globally enforceable policies on environmental issues.

Summary

- In a globalised world, states are actively reconfiguring their capacities. One feature of this process is the differential treatment of populations within national territories. This is leading to the fragmentation of citizenship, where different segments of society are given different combinations of enforceable rights and obligations.

- Forms of flexible citizenship are also being developed in response to the demands of living in a globalised world. These often involve types of transnational activity in which people conduct their activities in more than one state, or reach out beyond their own countries to draw on the support of citizens of other countries, to lend them their support, or to address demands to powerful actors located far away from the countries in which they live.

5   Conclusion

This chapter started by asking the question: how are the demands made by states of citizens, and by citizens of states, changing in a globalised world? In Section 2, we saw that this question could only be answered if we understood how the changing relationship between states and citizens is shaped by the changing reach of both state capacities and citizenly action. Thus, as a first step in answering the chapter's key question, we explored the practical ways in which states have been able to extend the effective reach of their authority over large distances in order to consolidate control of their territories. Sections 2 and 3 discussed how this process of extending the reach of the state over distance actually involves bringing the state into close proximity with citizens. Moreover, this process of linking up dispersed locations leads to the development of reciprocal, cooperative forms of relations between states and populations in which citizens are able to levy demands of their own upon states.

In the process of reaching out to citizens, states have used all sorts of techniques and strategies. In Section 3 we considered a few of the ways of extending the reach of the state, using examples such as censuses, taxation schemes and poverty alleviation programmes. These have helped us to see how variable state–citizen relationships can be, and we looked at examples from Europe, Africa and NICs in Asia to investigate the different intensity of engagements between states and citizens.

In turn, there is a diversity of ways in which citizens can bring the state within their reach in order to influence and engage powerful actors. This may involve voting, being counted in a census or survey, protesting or claiming an entitlement. These and other forms of citizen activity aim to exercise rights, whether these are rights to material entitlements, civil liberties or political participation.

In both cases – of states engaging with citizens or citizens engaging the state – reaching out over distance is a means of drawing people, things or events closer together. We have seen that this can enable states to collect information or to deliver services; people to interact with state officials; or citizens in one country to cooperate and communicate with citizens in other countries.

In Section 4, by examining the changing relationship between states and citizens through the prism of their respective capacities for reaching out, we have been able to see that far from dwindling away in the face of globalisation, the state retains considerable capacity in a number of areas. This is especially true in the area of attributing citizenship status and regulating citizenship practices, which is discussed further in Chapter 4. We identified a trend towards the increasing fragmentation of citizenship rights within nation states; this involves the development of a more differentiated form of reach, with the state using various strategies of segmentation and zoning to fragment the roles and rights of different groups of people. However, we also looked at the emergence of flexible strategies from citizens themselves; they have developed new ways of both cooperating with other actors across national boundaries, and contesting against distant actors.

To conclude, we can offer an answer to this chapter's key question: how are the mutual demands of states and citizens changing in a globalised world? The demands made by states of citizens have become more finely attuned to the need for ensuring global economic competitiveness. At the same time, the demands made by citizens of states have also expanded to include demands for political participation in more than one state, and for protection from the consequences of globalisation, including environmental hazards. In both cases, this changing pattern of interaction between states and citizens in a globalised world, structured around demands and counter-demands, is shaped by the variable capacity of both states and citizens to reach out beyond the confines of national boundaries in order to establish new forms of proximity with flows of foreign investment or networks of transnational activism.

References

Allen, J. (2003) *Lost Geographies of Power*, Oxford, Blackwell.

ANC Today (2001) 'Second democratic population count vital to effective development', vol.1, no.37, 5–11 October, http://www.anc.org.za/ancdocs/anctoday/2001/at37.htm (accessed 7 August 2005).

Carnie, T. (2000a) 'The poison in our air: how bad is the pollution and who controls the polluters?', *The Mercury*, South Africa, 13 September.

Carnie, T. (2000b) 'The poison in our air: now what needs to be done', *The Mercury*, South Africa, 15 September.

Cartier, C. (2001) *Globalising South China*, Oxford, Blackwell.

Corbridge, S., Williams, G., Srivastava, M. and Véron, R. (2005) *Seeing the State: Governance and Governmentality in India*, Cambridge, Cambridge University Press.

Danmarks Naturfredningsforening and South Durban Community Environmental Alliance (SDCEA) (2002) *Comparison of Refineries in Denmark and South Durban in an Environmental and Societal Context*, Copenhagen and Durban.

Danmarks Naturfredningsforening and South Durban Community Environmental Alliance (SDCEA) (2004) *Applied Meteorology and Climatology in South Durban*, Copenhagen and Durban.

Herbst, J. (2000) *States and Power in Africa: Comparative Lessons in Authority and Control*, Princeton, NJ, Princeton University Press.

Low, M. (2001) 'States, citizenship and collective action' in Daniels, P., Bradshaw, M., Shaw, D. and Sidaway, J. (eds) *Human Geography: Issues for the 21st Century*, London, Longman.

Mamdani, M. (1996) *Citizen and Subject: Contemporary Africa and the Legacy of Late Colonialism*, Princeton, NJ, Princeton University Press.

Miller, B. (2004) 'Spaces of mobilization: transnational social movements' in Barnett, C. and Low, M. (eds) *Spaces of Democracy: Geographical Perspectives on Citizenship, Participation and Representation*, London, Sage, pp.223–46.

Ong, A. (1999) *Flexible Citizenship*, Durham, Duke University Press.

Ong, A. (2000) 'Graduated sovereignty in South-East Asia', *Theory, Culture and Society*, vol.17, no.4, pp.55–75.

Ong, A. (2004) 'The Chinese axis: zoning technologies and variegated sovereignty', *Journal of East Asian Studies*, vol.4, pp.69–96.

Scott, J. (1998) *Seeing Like a State: How Certain Schemes to Improve the Human Condition Have Failed*, New Haven, Conn., Yale University Press.

South Africa (1996) *Constitution of the Republic of South Africa*, ch.2, no.24, Pretoria, South African Government Press.

Statistics South Africa (2003a), 'Households in South Africa with access to piped water, Census 2001', http://www.statssa.gov.za/census2001/digiAtlas/index.html (accessed 7 August 2005).

Statistics South Africa (2003b), 'Percentage households with access to piped water, Census 2001', http://www.statssa.gov.za/census2001/digiAtlas/index.html (accessed 7 August 2005).

Tilly, C. (1990) *Coercion, Capital and European States*, Oxford, Blackwell.

Verweij, M. (2003) *Leaking Pipelines: Shell in South Africa*, (trans. B. Plantenga), Amsterdam, Milieudefensie.

Reading 3A

'Second democratic population count vital to effective development'

Census 2001

The proper direction and application of government development policy will benefit greatly from the results of South Africa's second democratic population census, which takes place from 10–31 October. The census will provide detailed statistical information vital to the effective development of the country and its people.

Its success depends however on the cooperation of all South Africans, and the ability of the census officials to reach every corner of the country within the three week period. About 80,000 representatives of Statistics South Africa will count and record the details of the people living in South Africa's 10 million households, hospitals, hostels, hotels, prisons, other institutions, as well as the homeless.

The results of the census provide statistics for planning not only by government, but also by business, foreign investors and individuals. Census 2001 will help measure the changes and improvements in South Africa since the last census in 1996. It will track progress in delivering services and infrastructure in each community, and will also be used for calculating budget allocations to provincial and local governments.

The Census 2001 questionnaire covers demographic, social and economic areas. Questions relate to education, housing, migration, economic activity, employment status, mode of travel and income.

The confidentiality of information gathered on individuals is protected by the Statistics Act. Census 2001 officials adopt an oath of secrecy and all information is published in a way that ensures individuals aren't identified.

(ANC Today, 2001)

The poison in our air

How bad is the pollution and who controls the polluters?

Tony Carnie

There is no doubt that some of the chemicals and pollutants wafting around south Durban can kill you – if they are present in large enough doses, or after prolonged exposure at harmful levels.

But little is known about the present dosage levels in the air. Most of the current information is based on guesswork, estimates and speculation rather than physical measurements of the air which people take into their lungs.

This is what the Council for Scientific and Industrial Research (CSIR) scientific research body concluded three years ago when it tried to assess the problem during a South African Rand (R) 2 million Strategic Environmental Assessment (SEA) study funded by Durban metro council:

'Information on air quality in south Durban is generally scanty and inadequate. There is no comprehensive list of air pollutants in the area, let alone an indication of the ambient (ground level) concentrations of these pollutants, or an indication of probable effects.'

Which, in short, means: 'We are groping in the dark.'

Nevertheless, the researchers suggested that planning for industrial expansion would have to proceed on the basis of a 'limited knowledge base', combined with tighter controls.

It was not possible, they said, to work out how much pollution there was in the air, nor how much more pollution could be absorbed safely in the future.

But they do know for certain that sulphur dioxide levels are frequently above South Africa's outdated limits – and at times they are two to four times higher than the World Health Organisation's more stringent standards.

But sulphur dioxide (which has been linked to increased lung cancer cases in a study of non-smoking Californian residents) is just one of the pollutants. What about the nastier stuff which is put into the air by south Durban's myriad big and small industries?

What about benzene, for example, which is a proven carcinogen? What about xylene, chromium VI, cadmium and hexavalent chromium, which can also cause cancer or major health problems?

Other possible sources of pollution, according to the CSIR, are phenols, aldehydes, hydrocarbons, mercury, acetone and dioxins, to name just a few. And when you mix these together and combine them with pollution from motor vehicles and other sources, you get a very nasty little cocktail of pollutants. No tests have been done on this cocktail effect in Durban.

There are laws which are intended to control air pollution, but the Atmospheric Pollution Prevention Act dates back to 1965 and there are no legally enforceable ambient air quality standards. Most of the air pollution estimates also come from the major polluters themselves, because the system of control is based on 'cost-effective' British legislation.

On the ground, the principle of cost-effectiveness has translated into a single air pollution officer keeping a check on polluters through KwaZulu-Natal (KZN) for more than a decade. Recently, however, the ranks of the inspectorate swelled to two full-time government inspectors, supplemented by a small band of municipal inspectors.

But perhaps the biggest weakness of the system, said the CSIR, was that there was no management of the 'total' air pollution load. In other words, individual polluters might be controlled to some limited extent – but there was no limit on the overall pollution from a multiplicity of sources.

Yet despite these glaring shortfalls in air pollution monitoring, a three-year strategic environmental assessment study commissioned by the metro council recommended recently that the city should promote massive petro-chemical expansion and industrial development in south Durban.

Community spokesmen tore their hair out in frustration. Durban had spent R2 million on the SEA study to establish the environmental impact of future industrial development in this area – but a human health study apparently fell 'outside the scope of the study'.

For people like Mr Bobby Peek and Mr Rory O'Connor, of the South Durban Community Environmental Alliance, this is an unacceptable situation.

The alliance says it supports job-creation and economic growth, but insists that further development cannot be at the cost of neighbouring residents.

Mr Peek, director of the environmental justice body groundWork, says south Durban is currently bearing the brunt of air pollution from industry, but Durban city centre will not be spared as pollution knows no boundaries.

'If sulphur dioxide, benzene and other chemicals are found in high concentrations in south Durban, then it is a short distance for them to be blown over the bay. A city centre that becomes known for its high levels of toxins with associated health impacts is not going to be a top tourist destination,' he said.

(Carnie, 2000a)

The poison in our air

Now what needs to be done

A special investigation by
Tony Carnie, Chief Reporter

Perhaps it's irrelevant at this late stage to recall some of the lies told to the people of Durban nearly 50 years ago by the former owners of the Engen fuel refinery in Durban.

Because everyone trusts that the world has moved on today, and that the new Malaysian owners of the refinery – and other role players – will not repeat the mistakes of the past when they plan for the future.

Yet in looking towards this future, it is worth taking a brief journey back into history to a bitter showdown in Durban in 1954.

That was when the first refinery was build at Wentworth.

At the time the refinery was a much smaller affair. It had not sprawled out yet to the front doors of Merebank residents.

Ten years later, when Mr N P Govender moved into his house in Badulla Road, there was still a big forest across the road from him, filled with monkeys. He also remembers a motor car race track not far away.

But that's all gone now. One day he opened his front door and found that the refinery had expanded all the way to his front gate. He also has to keep his windows closed when the wind blows towards him to keep out the stench of the refinery.

He is also a widower. His wife 'Baby' died nine years ago at the age of 47 from lung cancer. Mr Govender says she never smoked.

Directly opposite him, on the very far side of the refinery, long-standing Bluff resident Margaret Sharp also has fond memories of the old days.

Her husband, who was a smoker, has cancer of the throat. Her son (who also had an operation for cancer) has moved to Cape Town with his two daughters, who both suffer from asthma.

Mrs Sharp's fondest memories include swimming near Anstey's Beach on moonlit nights.

'Mrs Anstey had a little round restaurant where we used to go for a fruit salad, brown bread and glass of milk. It used to be so lovely here.

'We can still watch dolphins and whales swimming past our house, but now I have to wipe the grime off our door every day and wash the curtains frequently because they turn black so quickly.

'It wasn't like this 50 years ago and then one day they built a refinery. We didn't know it was being built until it was up.'

That was the year more than 1000 Bluff residents gathered at the old Harcourt Hotel because a number of people had started waking up with headaches and nausea in the middle of the night from the foul smells emanating from the Standard Vacuum oil refinery.

Feelings were running so high that Durban mayor Percy Osborn cancelled his holiday in the Drakensberg to attend the public meeting and to issue an ultimatum to the refinery: 'Stop the pollution or shut down!

'We are not prepared to sacrifice the Bluff to the interests of industrial development,' he told cheering residents.

Councillor Sidney Smith also drew loud applause when he challenged the assumption that the refinery 'cannot be touched' just because it costs £6 million to build.

'I ask you: Where lies the country's national interests: the making of profits by an oil company, or the health and homes of its citizens?'

A few days later Stanvac Refinery's board of directors issued a 'Statement to the people of Durban'.

'We assure the Durban public that scientific tests show that there has been no measurable pollution of the atmosphere as a result of the refinery.

'The Durban refinery is among the most modern in the world. And – most important of all – Standard Vacuum has proved itself a responsible organisation. It would shut down its facilities, without regard to cost, if they were endangering the health of the community.'

Mayor Osborn, not surprisingly, said he was 'a little amazed' by these statements, considering the refinery had previously acknowledged its role in polluting the air.

'We are not blind to the importance of this industry to Durban', said Mr Osborn, 'but when the company decided to establish a refinery here, an undertaking was given that there would be no nuisance.'

Almost five decades later, very little seems to have changed. If anything, the level of air pollution in south Durban (from a wide variety of sources) is worse than ever.

And the precise impact on the health of neighbouring communities has still not been investigated by officials.

So what should be done?

The city's health department says R1,5 million is available to conduct a health study, but the money has not been spent

because of a stalemate with residents on how it should be spent.

The South Durban Community Environmental Alliance wants some of the money spent on epidemiological studies, which would compare health information from south Durban with other areas which are not polluted.

But Mr Neil Larratt, the city's principal environmental health officer, believes the money would be better spent analysing what chemicals are present in south Durban and where they come from so that immediate action could be taken to reduce the risks.

'You can do studies which might prove that there are cancer clusters or that the asthma rate is higher than normal. But where does that leave you? It won't tell you who is to blame, or where the carcinogens are coming from, or provide any pollution reduction strategy. We believe that epidemiological studies will consume the whole budget and that it would be better to rapidly target the various sources responsible for pollution and then set clear targets for reductions.'

The community alliance, on the other hand, insists that any risk assessment study should be combined with a health study to establish the true level of the problem. And if there isn't enough money for both, the authorities need to find more from somewhere else.

'And until the government has a clear programme of environmental governance accepted by all stakeholders, the problems in south Durban will increase and have a more negative impact on a city dependent on tourism and clean air,' says community spokesman Bobby Peek.

SAPREF believes there should be an overall attack on all emissions, including tighter control on vehicle maintenance and by developing cleaner motor fuels with less sulphur and lead.

It says the government has asked the oil industry to prepare new 'clean' fuel specifications before March 2001, for implementation in 2006.

Engen says the height of chimney stacks in parts of south Durban is limited because of proximity to the airport, and believes that relocating the airport to La Mercy would allow south Durban industries to build taller chimney stacks to disperse their pollution.

It also believes all new cars should be fitted with catalytic converters to reduce benzene and other dangerous exhaust gases.

Mr Narend Singh, the KwaZulu-Natal environment minister, says he is alarmed by the results of The Mercury's cancer survey in Merebank and wants an urgent investigation in collaboration with the Department of Health and Durban metro.

'It is intolerable that entire communities should be put at risk. We need wide and rigorous research to establish beyond doubt the effects of exposure to industrial gases and effluents. After that, some hard decisions might need to be taken as to residential location against continued industrial activity.'

Mr Valli Moosa, the national minister of environment affairs, says he is also concerned about the health of communities, and that polluters 'will be put on clear terms soon'.

It was unfortunate that no comprehensive health study had been done yet, mainly because of the complexity, cost and duration of such a study, but he said a 'task team on health assessment' in south Durban had been formed recently to oversee the project.

The Cancer Registry believes the government should increase its budget or set up a new dedicated registry for KwaZulu-Natal and Durban to assess scientifically the number of cancer cases.

Bluff resident Norman Barrett (who has cancer of the ear and who watched his granddaughter, Lynsey, die from leukaemia), says the health problems he knows about in the neighbourhood cannot all be dismissed as coincidence.

'I've always believed the Bluff was a deathtrap. My grandchildren were sick here so often we had to move them to Pinetown eventually. Even now we get vile, terrible smells coming up from the Island View and King's Rest area.

'I'm sorry, but this is not just "one of those things". Someone has to take some action now. How much longer can we wait? How many more people have to die?'

The constitution says: 'Every person has the right to an environment which is not harmful to his or her health and wellbeing.'

But right now, the constitution does not seem to apply in Durban south.

We need to start looking for better answers and better solutions. It's the least we owe our children ...

(Carnie, 2000b)

Reading 3C

Myrthe Verweij, 'Leaking pipelines: Shell in South Africa'

In Durban, South Africa, Shell shares an oil refinery with BP or British Petroleum (Shell and BP South African Refineries, hereafter: SAPREF) that has been the source of many problems involving damage to the environment, as well as safety and health issues. The underground pipelines that deliver the refinery's finished products run through residential areas and have over the past few years been the cause of many, and sometimes, enormous spills. SAPREF was the cause of the largest petrol spill in South African history. (In July 2001, more than one million litres of petrol leaked into local soil.)

Other areas have also been affected by incidents. The SAPREF storage terminal has been the site of a large spill involving the highly toxic tetra-ethyl lead. Even before this incident, Shell Global Solutions had recommended that SAPREF modernize its rust-detection techniques.

There has been an explosion at the refinery itself which resulted in a giant poisonous cloud of hydrogen fluoride. In addition, thousands of litres of crude oil, benzene, and fuel oil have been – and continue to be – 'spilled' during everyday operations in places like Durban's harbour.

SAPREF has a history of corporate irresponsibility and SAPREF's behaviour in these cases would be unacceptable in the Netherlands. The local community and environmental organisations have tried for years to force SAPREF to be more mindful of the environment they operate in. These organisations have also demanded that the refinery be more forthcoming with vital data. How many spills along the pipelines and storage terminals can be accounted to the refinery? And precisely what sorts of substances were released into the environment? What has been, and what continues to be, spilled and leaked into the environment on a daily basis? And what kind of guarantee can SAPREF offer when it comes to the safety of the surrounding residential areas and the health of the local population?

Local environment organisations and citizens have demanded that the refinery replace all of its pipelines as a precautionary measure. Most of the pipelines are, like the refinery, some forty years old. SAPREF's own inspections revealed that in many places the pipelines showed a deterioration of over 50% of the wall thickness.

Over the past few years there have been so many leaks that repairing them does not seem to make much sense any more. After all, the pipelines run under and through residential areas. But even if, as SAPREF claims, all of the pipelines have been tested and repairs have been made or pipe sections have been replaced, independent investigations of the test results and repair records have not been able to get off the ground. Existing information has not been made publicly available and thus SAPREF's claims cannot be adequately verified. Furthermore, some of the leaks actually occurred along pipelines that had recently been tested or repaired.

At the request of numerous South African organisations including the South Durban Community Environmental Alliance (SDCEA) and groundWork (Friends of the Earth South Africa, a sister organisation of Milieudefensie), Milieudefensie investigated SAPREF and specific incidents involving SAPREF. In correspondence, Milieudefensie urged SAPREF and Shell to find solutions to specific problems.

Not only the refinery, but both the Shell headquarters in London and The Hague, have refused to answer our detailed questions and provide specific information regarding pollution, leaks, the current condition of the pipelines, and the demand to have these pipelines replaced. Shell refers back to SAPREF. But after some seven years of discussions on environmental issues, the dialogue between SAPREF and the local community remains in deadlock. In fact, the conversations have only further exacerbated a situation of mutual distrust.

That is why Milieudefensie, along with its partner organisations, has decided that the time has come for Shell's main offices to intervene. The Shell Group must take its responsibility, especially if it wants to live up to the reputation it is trying to portray as a responsible, open, and concerned enterprise. Having advertised this promise, Shell cannot now renounce it. Milieudefensie, along with the local community, is convinced that Shell should replace the pipelines as a precaution. Because of the lack of independent investigations into the condition of the pipelines, and considering the levels of pollution that SAPREF has been responsible for thus far, only a total replacement of the entire pipeline network can provide a reasonable guarantee that future leaks, spills, and accidents will be averted.

The number of spills and incidents caused by carelessness has to be drastically reduced. In the event of an incident, SAPREF must be more careful when it comes to those living in the immediate vicinity of its facilities. This means they should inform people in a timely fashion, and, if necessary, evacuate the area. SAPREF must develop a better information dissemination policy.

The history of this refinery reveals the urgent need for international binding regulations for companies, including on environmental issues. South African legislation (and the understaffing of local authorities who must enforce the regulations), in combination with voluntary guidelines such as those produced by the Organisation for Economic Cooperation and Development (OECD), do not appear to be enough to motivate SAPREF to become a more responsible enterprise.

(Verweij, 2003, pp.4–5)

Chapter 4

A place in the world: geographies of belonging

Karim Murji

Contents

1   Introduction

A few years ago, I attended a family reunion in Toronto, Canada. Around 120 of my relatives came to this event from across Canada, the USA and the UK. The reunion was organised around the production of a booklet tracing the family trees of the seven children of my great grandfather, who migrated from western India to Zanzibar in East Africa towards the end of the nineteenth century. Most of his children (and most of those gathered in Toronto) were born into what was for a while part of German East Africa, then Tanganyika as part of the British Empire, and then Tanzania following independence (see Figure 4.1). The occurrence of this event, far from where most of us were born, and the places from which we travelled to it, indicate the journeys and distances covered in four generations of a family, our migrations across three continents, and the different places with which we could feel a sense of belonging.

One reason for introducing this story is that it makes me think about origins and identities, as well as different ideas of what 'home' was and is. 'East African Asian' is a category and identity that many of my family would recognise and sign up to in terms of our origins, though it

Figure 4.1   The author's family, photographed in Tanzania in the early 1960s

must feel remote to those born in Europe and North America. Yet, 'East African Asian' is itself an anomalous term, indicating a connection to two continents, but describing different countries, religions and communities. 'Asian' or a little more precisely, 'South Asian', is closer to our external appearance, and although we have grown accustomed to thinking of ourselves as Asian, many of my relatives have never even been to Asia. Our citizenship and nationality is mainly British or Canadian, even though very few of us seem to think of ourselves as having a 'British Asian' or 'Asian–Canadian' identity. We would also identify ourselves as Muslims, despite the fact that we do not have close connections to what is considered to be the 'Muslim world', nor – by virtue of belonging to a distinct sect – any significant association with the majority of Muslims. This relates the story of one family, although it reflects the wider history of a whole community in which pinning down precise identities and clear origins and belongings is not straightforward. As I hope this story suggests, there are different locations that people can feel pulled towards – or be proximate to – and made distant from in physical and emotional terms; and there are several answers, rather than a single answer, to the question of where migrants belong.

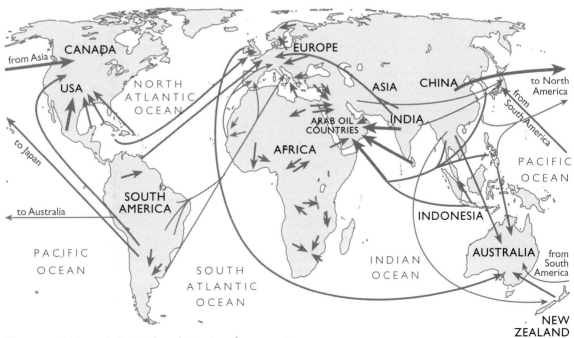

The arrow thickness indicates the relative size of movement

Figure 4.2   Global migratory movements from 1973 to 2002
Source: Castles and Miller, 2003, p.6

A second reason for opening with this story is that the four areas it touches upon are the sources of the examples used throughout this chapter. These areas – South Asia, East Africa, North America and Britain – are parts of the world which have historically been closely 'connected up', not least as components of the British Empire and through a common claim to the English language, as well as culturally and institutionally.

This chapter uses the example of migration and migrant lives to explore questions about demands associated with geographies of belonging. Figure 4.2 indicates the main movements of people around the world between 1973 and 2002. It is widely accepted that international migration has become a more significant and pressing political issue in recent years. It often seems to be regularly in the news, and a focus for policy discussions about how to control, regulate or manage it. As Table 4.1 shows, the number of international migrants has been increasing steadily over decades, and this trend shows no sign of reversing (Table 4.1 and Figure 4.2 also show that migration is not evenly spread across the world). The physical movement of people and of cultures is often seen as emblematic of a globalised world in which connections and mobilities across the world are intensified and enhanced. It is, in part, as a result of all this movement that national boundaries are thought to be of declining significance (although you will remember that Chapter 3 questioned this assertion). Indeed, migration is sometimes seen not just as characteristic of a globalised world, but as a key factor producing global change (Castles and Miller, 2003).

In this context, migrants are very often represented as the outsiders or strangers coming from 'far away' into 'our' space. Nevertheless, the story of my own family history has already suggested that the geographies of migration are more complicated than that. Connections of various kinds between two distant places can exist well before someone makes a decision to migrate from one to the other (both may be part of the same empire, for example), and migration may make links between more than two places. Given the significance of migration to contemporary globalisation, it becomes important to understand the complex geographies of belonging that migrations often produce. Looking at migration offers a particular insight into attachment to more than one place.

The apparent porosity of borders can conjure up an image of migrants who are capable of just picking up their belongings and travelling at will. This, however, neglects the ways in which there are barriers to migration, both physical and symbolic. As Chapter 3 discussed, states

Table 4.1   International migrants living in various world regions, 1960–2000

Major area	Number of international migrants (millions)					Average annual rate of growth of the number of international migrants (%)				International migrants as a share of the population (%)		Distribution of international migrants by region (%)	
	1960	1970	1980	1990	2000	1960–1970	1970–1980	1980–1990	1990–2000	1960	2000	1960	2000
World	75.9	81.5	99.8	154.0	174.9	0.7	2.0	4.3	1.3	2.5	2.9	100.0	100.0
Developed countries	32.1	38.3	47.7	89.7	110.3	1.8	2.2	6.3	2.1	3.4	8.7	42.3	63.1
Developed countries excluding USSR	29.1	35.2	44.5	59.3	80.8	1.9	2.3	2.9	3.0	4.0	8.3	38.4	46.2
Developing countries	43.8	43.2	52.1	64.3	64.6	−0.1	1.8	2.1	0.0	2.1	1.3	57.7	36.9
Africa	9.0	9.9	14.1	16.2	16.3	0.9	3.6	1.4	0.0	3.2	2.0	11.8	9.3
Asia[1]	29.3	28.1	32.3	41.8	43.8	−0.4	1.4	2.6	0.5	1.8	1.2	38.6	25.0
Latin American and the Caribbean	6.0	5.8	6.1	7.0	5.9	−0.5	0.7	1.3	−1.7	2.8	1.1	8.0	3.4
Northern America	12.5	13.0	18.1	27.6	40.8	0.4	3.3	4.2	3.9	6.1	12.9	16.5	23.3
Oceania	2.1	3.0	3.8	4.8	5.8	3.5	2.1	2.3	2.1	13.4	18.8	2.8	3.3
Europe[2]	14.0	18.7	22.2	26.3	32.8	2.9	1.7	1.7	2.2	3.3	6.4	18.5	18.7
USSR (former)	2.9	3.1	3.3	30.3	29.5	0.5	0.5	22.3	−0.3	1.4	10.2	3.9	16.8

[1]Excluding Armenia, Azerbaijan, Georgia, Kazakhstan, Kyrgyzstan, Tajikistan, Turkmenistan and Uzbekistan.

[2]Excluding Belarus, Estonia, Latvia, Lithuania, the Republic of Moldova, the Russian Federation and Ukraine.

Source: World Economic and Social Survey 2004 (United Nations, 2004, p.25)

make considerable efforts to control migration – to select who can or should come in. In recent years, the United Nations (UN) has noted that many governments are becoming less hospitable to migrants, and that about 40 per cent of the world's nations have adopted policies that aim to lower immigration. States can also impose, in a more or less friendly fashion, various demands about the nature of belonging in terms of citizenship, culture and customs. Very few people travel or migrate to wherever they wish; there are ties and connections that can enable migration and make it a matter of choice, but migration is also constrained. Constraints may be financial or economic, though they can also be emotional (for example, family ties) and cultural (for example, language and community networks).

Therefore, despite the existence of connections and networks across the globe, migrants do not just circulate freely; they are sometimes made to settle, and frequently make demands to settle, to find a place in the world. So migrants make demands both to belong and to settle. But they also find themselves subject to a range of demands. Some of these come from people and institutions in the place where the migrants have arrived; other demands come from the place they have left. It is to this issue of the demand to belong and the various forms it takes that this chapter is directed. To introduce this, we can begin by asking what 'belonging' means.

Activity 4.1

Briefly, think about your own ideas of what 'belonging' means and jot down a few thoughts. What are the places and people that you feel you belong to?

Your answer to Activity 4.1 might have included families and friends that you feel connected to; it might also have covered a number of places or associations where you feel you belong – a neighbourhood or community, a region or country, a club or some other grouping. Belonging can therefore contain multiple attachments that sometimes overlap, or which may be discrete. Some of these settings are situations or associations that we can choose to be part of, indeed to some extent we express our identities by selecting the places or groups where we think we belong. Others, though, are not the product of our own choices – hardly anyone chooses their family, or their name; we do not control where we were born or, most of the time, the countries of which we can be citizens. In between these two options, there might be groups or communities that we wish to belong to, but cannot for some reason. We may live in a place to which we do not feel we belong (whether that is a domestic or a national space), or we do not see ourselves as members of a local or national community.

Belonging, this exercise suggests, is both a matter of choice and feeling, as well as a condition given to us and imposed upon us. To belong entails feelings of being at ease although, paradoxically, it can also contain a sense of unease at the same time, and with various possibilities in between those two. Consider, for example, the ways in which people may see their families and relatives as both a blessing and a curse (Chapter 2 examined the way that communication technologies can be used to manage these mixed feelings). Belonging contains a sense of being at home, even though home may not always be where we feel we belong. For instance, is home 'where I was born' or 'where I am now'? (Westwood and Phizacklea, 2000). Ambivalent feelings about home are sometimes seen as a key to migrant sensibilities, of belonging not in one place or another, but in some sort of 'third space' that is more than just a combination of the other two. Belonging, in this chapter, refers to a sometimes uncertain and unfixed sensibility that is produced out of people's awareness of the people and places they feel close to, whether these are 'far away' or 'nearby', and the interrelationship between the two.

The three main sections of this chapter look at geographies of belonging – the demand to belong – in different and overlapping ways. Section 2 gives a historical overview of the migration of one group, East African Asians, touching on both the political context of their movements and their experiences of migrating. The next two sections then focus in more detail on each of these, with Section 3 looking at migrant experiences in contemporary London, and Section 4 examining a particular example of a state – India – and its relations with some of its migrant people. I will consider how the sense of something being 'close by' or 'far away' is a social relationship, not one of physical distance per se: distance and proximity can be both created and imposed. People, states, the media and markets use various 'distancing' techniques to hold migrants at arm's length, through either denial or refusal of their connections to and stake in a nation or a place. The denial that migrants can belong somewhere is expressed legally or socially (as in the case of East African Asians in Section 2), or through culturally 'placing' migrants elsewhere (discussed in Section 3), or by asserting their difference (as with Non Resident Indians in Section 4). At the same time, all of these people can be brought nearer, or they can employ methods to make themselves seem closer, by stressing their roots and historical connections to a particular place, adopting a local rather than national or transnational sense of identity and belonging (Sections 2 and 3) or through 'long distance nationalism' that reaches into faraway places (Section 4).

The materials in this chapter draw on qualitative sources – personal accounts, a novel and anthropological studies – that emphasise what a migrant sensibility may entail. In other words, they are often concerned with the emotional and cultural dimensions of proximity and distance. Conforming to legal or social demands, such as citizenship or culture, can make being

Defining culture

Culture is a word with many uses and meanings. Generally, it refers to what is distinctive about a group, a community, a nation or a people – their 'way of life'. It embodies their ways of making sense of the world, the meanings that they attach to things and practices, and how these are expressed. We can feel that we belong to a culture to the extent that we identify, or feel at home, with it; conversely, people sometimes feel unease with cultures that they do not share or understand.

close or being far away seem like a binary choice – you're either in or out. But this binary is often hard to map onto real lives. It is the more fluid and sometimes ambivalent senses of belonging that this chapter seeks to draw out. Consequently, this chapter treats most of the binary divides that permeate discussions of migration (for example, hosts/outsiders, sending/receiving countries, and push/pull factors) as redundant, and suggests that 'proximity' and 'distance' are tangled together in migrant sensibilities. Although generalising about the migrant experience is difficult because the causes, types and effects of migrations are very diverse, this chapter tries to develop a perspective that emphasises how belonging is created through connections, shared histories and the diverse spaces and networks that are created to link 'us' and 'them', and 'near' and 'far'.

Chapter aims

- To understand the demands that migrants make, and that are made of them, to belong to particular places.

- To examine the changing relations of proximity and distance that cut through and across migrant lives, as they build connections across different national boundaries and often maintain close ties to more than one place.

- To explore the senses of belonging that migrants can create through their links and attachments to different places.

2 Transnational migrants

This section explores the migration of East African Asians in the nineteenth and twentieth centuries. It looks at some of the political factors shaping that migration and some aspects of migrants' cultural experiences. This discussion will show how different migrants have different capacities to move and to settle, and how many continue to identify with distant places even as they find ways to make a home in a new context.

2.1 Twice migrants

The opening story in the Introduction to this chapter indicates that migration is not necessarily a one-off journey. Families and communities can have experience of multiple migrations, perhaps extending over several generations. As a result of this, the anthropologist Parminder Bhachu described East African Asians in Britain as 'twice migrants' (Bhachu, 1985). Her work focuses on the Sikh community who migrated from the Punjab to East Africa in the early years of the twentieth century and then on to Britain, mainly in the 1960s and 1970s. In East Africa near the end of the nineteenth century, around 32,000 indentured labourers were recruited to work on building the railway, of whom around 6500 stayed on in East Africa because of the new economic opportunities they found there (Lall, 2001). The tied migration of indentured labour and the 'free' migration of Indians who went to East Africa to take up commercial and administrative openings in the colonial order points to the occurrence of different forms of migration at the same time, making migration more than a singular process such as 'labour migration'.

Table 4.2   Indians in Africa, 1920

	Kenya	Tanganyika[1]	Uganda	Zanzibar[1]
Total population	3,300,000	5,000,000	3,600,000	138,000
Indian population	42,000	23,500	20,000	15,000
European population	19,000	9000	2000	

[1]Tanganyika and Zanzibar now make up Tanzania.

Source: Chaliand and Rageau, 1995, p.153

Bhachu's account of the East African Sikhs who emigrated to Britain is significant for three reasons. First, she argues that they did not have a marked orientation to a 'home country' – either in South Asia or in East Africa. Being removed from India gave them a qualitatively different experience from the 'direct migrants' from South Asia for whom emigration to Britain was a first move. The latter had, for the first generation at least, a stronger identity and association with India that included a 'myth of return', a belief that they would one day be returning to their home countries. It was because such journeys rarely occurred that the idea of returning came to be seen as a myth.

Second, having become a settled community in East Africa, the Sikhs – like other East African Asians – already had their own networks and resources. The Sikhs were a technically skilled workforce in East Africa. The education system shaped by the British Empire meant that they arrived in Britain with cultural skills, such as familiarity with the language and with British institutions, making them relatively prosperous migrants possessing both cultural and social skills and resources. For Bhachu, these two factors meant that Sikh communities from East Africa made progress more quickly than direct migrants from India, because they were 'closer' to Britain and more 'distant' from India. Even though direct migrants from India arrived in Britain before the East African Sikhs, they did not possess the same expertise, linguistic facility and communications networks to develop community structures at the same pace. Thus, different places of origin (although both were part of the British Empire), as well as different orientations to migration, underline the different make-up of these Asian communities in Britain. An absence of or a lack of identification with a fixed place of origin – either South Asia or East Africa – led some Sikhs to see themselves as settlers, making new homes in the countries they had arrived in. This was less the case with direct migrants, who may, in the early years at least, have seen themselves as likely to return home.

The third point made by Bhachu in her discussion of differences between 'twice' and 'direct' migrants indicates that changes in the nature of these differences occur over time. 'Distant' events can rework social relations and bring Sikhs with different migration histories closer together. A major event, for example, was the burning of the Golden Temple in Amritsar in 1984 by the Indian Army. This served to mobilise a common 'Sikh' identity politics that cut across boundaries of origin, and helped to draw the different migrant communities closer. Indeed, calls for an independent Sikh homeland can connect and unite Sikhs across the world. Overall, however, Bhachu's analysis points to the diversity of migrant experiences and expectations along class and caste lines, as well as countries of origin, and the ability to prosper in a 'new' society. She challenges the common assumption that such Asian migrants are oriented towards a homeland culture that provides a sense of common cultural identity. 'South Asian' migrant experiences are varied and diverse, as are the patterns of belonging and identity.

By the mid 1990s, Bhachu (1995) refers to thrice and even quadruple migrants who have moved on from Britain to the USA, Canada and Australia. They are able to do so, she argues, because they are skilled in the 'game of migration' – of particular note is their command of English and familiarity with bureaucratic institutions in the West. Along with this is an expertise at reproducing cultural institutions and community infrastructures in which, Bhachu says, the role of Asian women has been particularly important and generally overlooked because women are often seen as docile, subordinate to men, and mainly home-makers. Migrants do not just move to 'make a home', they carry 'a home' with them and this can be vital in linking a sense of self with a sense of place, as the geographer Alison Blunt (2003) points out.

From this discussion, we can see that the capacity to respond to demands – in this case to settle, to fit in – varies among migrant groups. Community expertise in migration, involving several events or movements across generations, enables some people to be more mobile across national boundaries and to settle more easily in different contexts. It is also important to note that migrations have a gendered dimension that requires an understanding of mobility and connections at household and family levels, in addition to national and global levels.

2.2 Journey to the West

To look further at the connections between East African Asians and Britain, we now turn to an article about the play *Journey to the West*, directed by Jatinder Verma.

Activity 4.2

Please read the article from the Guardian Unlimited website in 2002, reproduced as Reading 4A. As you do so, consider the following questions:

1 Would you regard Jatinder Verma as being 'proximate' to or 'distant' from Britishness? In what way(s)?

2 Why does Verma think *routes* are more important than *roots*?

3 What you think he means by referring to East African Asians as 'world citizens'?

Verma, like Bhachu, stresses that East African Asians are multiple migrants. The article observes that the schooling Verma received in Kenya – designed by the Cambridge University Board and including the work of Romantic poets such as Keats and Wordsworth – made him familiar with the English language, though not in a way that was of use on his first encounter with a cockney London bus conductor. Verma recalls a feeling of Britain being a hostile place for migrants in the 1960s and early 1970s – a period when being called an 'immigrant' was intended as an insult (just as 'refugee' and 'asylum seeker' have been in recent years). That hostility displaced or dislocated migrants from a sense of belonging in the nation. Racism and

Figure 4.3   Jatinder Verma, listening to actors in rehearsal, 2003

discrimination sought to exclude Asians from claiming a stake, or making a home, in a new land, denying them a place symbolically and, sometimes, violently. The demand to settle may encounter a response that denies that demand. Thus, there are some ways in which Verma seems 'proximate' to Britishness. However, there are other ways in which he feels himself distant from Britishness, such as the moments when he felt he was being pushed away by people already here, who refused to allow him to belong.

Verma's comment about routes raises an important theme because it questions the view that there is a fixed relationship between place, identity and culture. The idea of routes – rather than roots – emphasises that identity and belonging are formed from the experience of real and imagined journeys and connections. These link people, places and histories in ways that resist the easy categorisation of Britain with whites, or Africa with blacks, for example. Identity and belonging, Verma argues, are more about the routes that connect Britain with East Africa, rather than the often constructed claims about who is really British (Section 3 discusses this further). Routes are counterposed to roots because routes are regarded as dynamic and forward-looking, while roots are thought to be static and historical (Woodward, 2003). Roots are often proclaimed by far right nationalist groups and seem to be more about origins and 'where you're from', whereas routes bring out the movements and flows – cultural, geographical and emotional – that make up 'where you're at'. Indeed it is a criticism made of Alex Haley's well-known book and 1970s TV series, *Roots*, that it fed 'Afrocentric' ideologies that seem more concerned with slavery and with finding a 'true' identity in Africa, than with living in the here and now.

The stress on routes is contained in the idea of East African Asians as 'world citizens', of people seemingly regularly on the move and able to make a home in different places in the world. As we have seen, the very term, East African Asian, links a group of people to two continents, while they also identify with a third separate part of the world – Europe. The geographies of belonging that this reveals do not operate on a national

Defining diaspora

Diaspora refers to the scattering or dispersal of a people across the world. Examples include the Jewish, African and Irish diasporas. The people of a diaspora are thought of as, or feel themselves to be, sharing some common ancestry or origin, although that may be geographic (originating from the same place, whether a country or a continent) or ethnic. In the former case, diasporic identities link migrants to a particular territory or homeland that they identify with or feel a sense of belonging to. However, as well as identities rooted to a place, diasporas can transcend and go beyond place-based identities, particularly national identities, in demonstrating attachment to more than one place. Diasporic identities exemplify mixed forms of culture that are part of both 'here' and 'there'; diasporic cultures emerge in new forms in different places.

level, which limits and ties the idea of belonging to nation states. Instead there is a transnational and diasporic belonging and identity that contains elements of Indian, East African and British cultures, formed out of the historical, political and cultural connections between these parts of the world. East African Asians possess a transnational sense of belonging, something that extends across and beyond nation state boundaries As we saw in Chapter 3, transnationalism is a useful description because it implies that the globalised world is one in which the state has been traversed but not necessarily bypassed altogether (Westwood and Phizacklea, 2000). Indeed, the state can still be important when it comes to some forms of belonging, particularly rights to citizenship, through which governments regulate the entry of non-nationals, or aliens. In this light, the fluid relationship that, according to Bhachu and Verma, East African Asians have towards their 'Indian roots' and their 'British routes' becomes a little more complicated.

In the early part of the twentieth century, people in India protested about discrimination against Asians in East Africa; in doing so, they demonstrated a sense of responsibility for, and connection with, them. Equally, from afar, East African Asians expressed solidarity with the struggles for Indian independence. However, after independence in 1947, the attention of the Indian government turned inwards towards nation-building and national integration. This required a political identity that could not include the distant 'satellites of expatriate Indians living all around the world', who were largely 'ignored and held at arm's length' (Lall, 2001, pp.5–6). East African Asians were encouraged to settle in the countries in which they lived. For both economic and political reasons, though, they chose not to opt to take the citizenship of the newly independent countries of East Africa (which was open to them for a limited time after independence). Thus they were, as Lall (2001) points out, technically aliens in their 'own' countries. The citizenship choices the East African Asians made actively signalled a 'distance' from their homeland, and a potentially mobile belonging to or identification with a place 'far away', to which many of them had never been. In spite of taking on the identity of being 'East African Asians', settling, learning the local language and, in some cases, intermarrying, their connections and roots to this place were, if not shallow, at least transplantable.

Following independence in East Africa in the early 1960s, East African Asians with links to Britain found themselves in an odd situation where they could not be citizens of India, nor could they fully belong to Britain. After 1947, they had been classed as British subjects who were citizens of the United Kingdom and Colonies. The issue of citizenship did not really begin to matter until the British Immigration Acts from 1962 onwards started to make it more difficult for such groups to migrate to and settle in Britain. At this time, East African Asians could still technically have 'returned' to India, though many had never been there. Lall (2001) argues that the only ties they felt to India were of language and culture, whereas British nationality offered economic benefits. There were, however, other forms of proximity and belonging to Britain in terms of schooling, language and institutions, as was shown in both Bhachu's and Verma's accounts. This situation came to a head twice. First, in 1968 the British government announced it was planning immigration quotas for British subjects. This prompted a number of Kenyan Asians to enter Britain before the restrictions came in. India said it would deny entry to any British passport-holding East African Asians because they were no longer its responsibility (although it did permit the entry of some Kenyans, they became legal aliens and were restricted in their ability to own property and invest in businesses).

Second, in 1972 the Ugandan government led by Idi Amin decided to expel all Asians from the country. India's arm's-length relationship with its diaspora made it willing to accept only limited responsibility for them. At this time, the media and some politicians in Britain warned of an 'invasion' by East African Asians, and the city of Leicester famously issued advice to Ugandan Asians not to settle there. Thus, the underlying message was that East African Asians did not belong, legally or symbolically, to either India or Britain.

This brief account of changing relations between East African Asians and India and Britain indicates a number of things. It suggests that migrant senses of belonging can be about feeling both close to somewhere and distant from it at the same time: recall Jatinder Verma's love of words, his formal English education, and his reaction to the racism he encountered on his arrival in England.

The discussion in this section also suggests that relations of proximity and distance can change over time. The connections and networks established by the British Empire link people across space and time, through a shared language, schooling and culture. Both these historical and cultural roots, and the routes travelled by migrants and their ancestors, may be used to express a sense of proximity to a land far away. Even without a shift in their physical location, East African Asians have in the course of the last century identified and not identified with both Britain and India. As twice and thrice migrants, they have roots in more than one place. Yet despite the significance of their multiple routes and transnational migrations, East African Asians found that stressing their legal connection to Britain was necessary in seeking to belong to it in the 1960s and 1970s.

Citizenship of a nation state (being part of it legally, though not necessarily identifying with it or feeling a complete sense of belonging) therefore still matters to migrants today, and contradicts the image of migrations occurring across a supposedly borderless, globalised world.

Summary

- Some migrations entail complex chains of connections and networks across generations that militate against a sense of fully belonging to one place or one nation.

- Belonging can be formed through a sense of cultural and emotional proximity across distance, as well as through the way homes are made and communities built by migrants on their arrival in a new place.

- The state still has a key role to play in responding to migrants' demands to belong, and in determining their right to settle in a place.

3   Mixed belongings

Section 2 took a broad, historical overview of one group of migrants, East African Asians, examining some of the cultural, economic and political contexts shaping their experiences. This section focuses on the experiences of migrants directly, and explores how some migrants feel about belonging in and to Britain. It draws upon the best-selling novel *White Teeth* by Zadie Smith, which considers the different ways people have of belonging to the places they live in and to the places they have links with.

White Teeth is a multi-layered novel, and its themes include history, memory, fate and identity. It portrays three families in contemporary London: the Joneses are a British-Jamaican family; the Chalfens are white, of European origins; and the

Figure 4.4   Zadie Smith accepting a prize for her novel *White Teeth*, January 2001

Iqbals – who are the main example used here – are from Bangladesh. The Iqbals consist of Samad, a Bengali immigrant, Alsana, his much younger wife, and their twin sons, Magid and Millat. All the families are migrants in some sense, and *White Teeth* can be read as a depiction of intersecting migrant lives and of Britain as a nation of immigrants, albeit ones who have arrived and settled at different times. In the novel, belonging and geographies of proximity and distance mean rather different things for first and second generation migrants; these meanings are also gendered and generationally varied.

The location or setting for these tales of multiple connections and misunderstandings between and within families is unfashionable Willesden in north-west London. Here collide the histories and people who all come from 'somewhere else', but whose past and present criss-cross and overlap in a distinctive place where the globalised world comes 'home'. Local, national and more diasporic senses of place help to shape the characters' identities as well as the multicultural environment that they inhabit and help to make up. A sense of place and of self is created out of both roots and routes. The mixed-up world the novel depicts is not an accident but an illustration of one of its themes: there are no pure origins or distinct geographies of 'here' and 'there' that demarcate 'them' and 'us'; migrant lives are not only deeply enmeshed with the history and character of a nation, they help to make it what it is. An illustration of this is O'Connell's Pool House, a venue where two of the older men in the novel meet regularly. Despite its name, it is neither Irish nor a pool house '[but] run by Arabs ... [who] will cook you chips, egg and beans, or egg, chips and beans, or beans, chips, eggs and mushrooms but not, under any circumstances, chips, beans, eggs and bacon' (Smith, 2000, p.159). In spite of this Muslim ban on pork, however, the Pool House doubles up as a gambling den.

Activity 4.3

To get a flavour of the serio-comic style of the novel, which often uses humour to make telling points, and to introduce some of its themes, please turn to Readings 4B and 4C that are from the novel *White Teeth* (Smith, 2000).

As you read the extracts, consider these questions:

1   What different kinds of belonging can you see in the first extract?
2   In the second extract how are events 'far away' understood by Alsana and Samad? What does this suggest about what home, belonging and identity mean to them?

The novel signals to me that a sense of belonging can be tied to different places, and that there are different levels of identification. For the parents, belonging seems to refer to the more or less distant countries of Bangladesh or Jamaica, or Britain. For the children, however, belonging is local and tied to Willesden or London. The latter embody a kind of 'post-immigrant' sensibility, in which their identities and belonging are influenced at least as much (or probably more) by being of and from 'here' than a sense of their origins from somewhere else. Their 'roots' are local and proximate, and not necessarily fashioned by the 'routes' travelled by their parents. While all migrants are weighed down by their histories – 'they cannot escape their history any more than you yourself can lose your shadow' (Smith, 2000, p.399) – they do not all feel or experience it in the same way.

Despite the generational and gender differences between Samad and Alsana, though, they share enough of an immigrant cultural sensibility to worry that their roots and identity will disappear in the mixture of the world around them. The Jamaican side of the Jones family also shares this concern. Mixture, the physical and symbolical pile-up of the past and the present, the near and the far, is feared by some white nationalists too, as we can also see in the first extract. The fact that the children – Irie and Millat in this case – do not seem to share this concern marks out a second generation perspective.

This theme of the differences between generations is manifest in other ways in *White Teeth*. Irie is drawn towards the Chalfen family, and away from her own family, because they 'dealt in the present... [and] didn't drag ancient history around like a chain and ball' (Smith, 2000, p.281), which reinforces the image of roots as backward looking. Nonetheless, the difference between generations is evident in the Chalfen family too. For example, at one point Joyce Chalfen asks:

'You look very exotic. Where are you from, if you don't mind me asking?'

'Willesden,' said Irie and Millat simultaneously.

'Yes, yes, of course, but where *originally*?'

'*Oh*,' said Millat, putting on what he called a *bud-bud-ding-ding* accent. 'You are meaning where from am I *originally*'.

Joyce looked confused. 'Yes, *originally*.'

'Whitechapel,' said Millat, pulling out a fag. 'Via the Royal London Hospital and the 207 bus.'

(Smith, 2000, p.275)

This response emphasises that home and origin is a locality – east London – not the somewhere 'distant' that the question invites. Millat's resistance to and mocking of the question illustrates his denial of the 'placing' implied in the question 'where are you from?' Although it may indicate simple curiosity, it can contain the insinuation that wherever you are from, it is not 'here' but 'there', which is somewhere much further away than the East End. Even if you were born 'here', the question signals an obsession with origins. Since we all came from somewhere else originally, 'how far back do you want? How far will *do*?' (Smith, 2000, p.72), the novel asks. A stress on origins, like some versions of roots, maintains that identity is based on a long and perhaps distant sense of the past, whereas – subjectively – some migrants, like Millat, insist that felt identity is made rather than given. Both his roots (Whitechapel) and his routes (the 207 bus) are determinedly local and near, not distant and far.

Despite the inter-mixture that *White Teeth* highlights, it also draws attention to those who contest and deny the rights of migrants to settle and make a home. Demands to find a place may be rejected by others. The common slogan voiced by the far right in Britain over more than five decades is 'send them back home', or 'they should all go back home', which *White Teeth* calls 'the oldest sentence in the world' (Smith, 2000, p.142). The 'they' or 'them' referred to here usually means black and Asian migrants and their descendants, yet sometimes other white people (the Irish, for example) have also been the targets of exclusion. This refusal of proximity suggests that hostility is as likely as hospitality when we come 'near' to people. The nation, in this case, is constructed or defined as an exclusive space where only some can belong – you can only be in or out according to this logic. The more fluid relationship that migrants have towards Britain as a 'home' is not easy to pin down, as *White Teeth* suggests, but while its meaning may be more open-ended it still constitutes a place of belonging. Home and belonging may not just be about being in the nation. Rather, migrants 'place' themselves by identifying with localities 'near by' as well as 'distant' places far away.

Within a family, the generational split is notable in Samad's feeling that both his boys are losing their way and their identity. When Samad learns that Magid has taken to calling himself Mark, he sends his son 'home' to Chittagong for a proper education because 'tradition was culture and culture led to roots... [they] were ... the ropes one throws out to rescue drowning men' (Smith, 2000, p.168). The appeal to roots here reflects fears about a growing distance between parents and their offspring, even when they share the same domestic space. In the meantime, Millat becomes a playboy and joins a militant Muslim organisation, the Keepers of the Eternal and Victorious Islamic Nation – KEVIN – though they are aware that they 'have an acronym problem' (Smith, 2000, p.255). Magid eventually returns to England, speaking precise English and sporting the demeanour of someone educated at a private school. Not surprisingly, Samad is bewildered at how things work out: 'The one I send home comes out a pukka Englishman, white suited, silly wig lawyer. The one I keep here is fully paid-up green bow-tie-wearing fundamentalist terrorist. I sometimes wonder why I bother' (Smith, 2000, p.349).

The joke here is that 'home' and 'away', 'here' and 'there' are, inevitably, hard to 'place' or to pin down and, wherever they are, they are no guarantors of identity or belonging. In other words, if 'Englishness' can be created just as much 'there' as it can 'here', there are no privileged identities and belongings rooted in a place. Magid, the product of a private education in Bangladesh is 'far away' but turns out a 'pukka Englishman' (or rather, he represents one kind of patrician Englishness), while his twin, Millat, stays 'close' at home, but adopts the values of a group which rejects 'the West'. This, however, is also a home-made identity as the jokey acronym of Millat's group – KEVIN – implies just how British they are. The younger people in the novel fashion a syncretic cultural belonging that is not reducible to 'parent' or 'host' cultures. Their responses to the demands to belong deny this either/or choice that they are apparently presented with; instead new and different senses of place and belonging emerge.

Furthermore, tradition and roots are no guarantors of identity and belonging either. While Millat does after all 'return to the fold' and embrace Islam, his form of religious practice is something that Samad finds hard to comprehend. So even when Samad and Millat are 'close' in religious and cultural terms, there is little understanding between them. Time, in terms of age and generation, is a source of distance between people who are spatially close. The novel makes this a wider theme: 'A distance was establishing itself, not simply between *fathersons*, *oldyoung*, *borntherebornhere*, but between those who stayed indoors and those who ran riot outside' (Smith, 2000, p.190).

Samad's character captures a first generation migrant's sensibility – an ambivalent sense of belonging in Britain, at the heart of which is a sense of loss. Towards the end of the novel he concludes that, 'the *very idea* of belonging ... seems like some long, dirty lie' (Smith, 2000, p.349). Seemingly caught between 'East' and 'West', Samad embodies, 'the unhappy contradiction of the migrant sensibility [in] the chilling fear of having lost a certain sense of time and place ... Parallel to this loss is the anxious realization that having gained entrance to another space does not amount to a feeling of full acceptance' (Papastergiadis, 2000, p.74). This feeling explains why Samad holds on to an idealised sense of home 'far away', while decrying the immediate space that he and his family occupy. For his family, however, belonging has varying meanings and senses for different generations and genders.

In spite of her other differences with Samad, Alsana also worries that 'here' is a corrupting place where 'roots' and identity are lost through 'Westernisation' and 'Anglicisation' among young second and third generation migrants – 'you're becoming more and more English' as Miri Song (1997) heard Chinese parents express it. Alsana's concern is about the Chalfens' influence on Millat: 'They're Englishifying him completely! They're deliberately leading him away from his culture and his family and his religion' (Smith, 2000, p.297). Thus, the threat of the 'near' and 'here' is embodied in another family to Alsana. The way in which physical proximity can be full of cultural distances is brought out in the same exchange. When her niece suggests that Millat is 'looking for something as far away from the Iqbals as possible', Alsana replies, 'But they [the Chalfens] live two roads away', to which the niece responds, 'No, Auntie. *Conceptually* far away from you' (Smith, 2000, p.298).

'Near' and 'far' mean different things to Alsana and Samad in other ways too and we can see this in the second extract from *White Teeth*. On hearing about the assassination of the Indian prime minister in 1984, Samad both misinterprets and reworks Alsana's concerns to his own purposes. For her the event means something personal – death and retribution on the streets, perhaps including people she knows and feels involved with. For Samad, however, the same event means something quite abstract – the state of both the Indian and British nations. While she is relieved to be 'far away' from something she feels emotionally close to, he is 'distant' from the event itself but unhappy at the state of the world around him. They display different kinds of attachments to the 'far away', Alsana's attachment being much more personal than Samad's. His idealisation of the 'far away' (or at least, those parts he regards as home) goes hand in hand with the denigration of the 'near by'. Proximity and distance are interwoven and, in this example, help to define one another.

In this section I have argued that there is a variety of different kinds of routes and roots, and of belonging. These vary among different generations and produce a range of senses of belonging to place(s), that may be local, national or transnational. The cultural and emotional proximity that some migrants feel for their places of origin is seemingly remote for their offspring, and *White Teeth* makes clear the differences between first and second generation sensibilities and the different forms of belonging that these entail. In the shape of the children, and their refusal to see the world through their parents' eyes, the novel gestures towards a 'post-immigrant' sensibility. Here again, though, among the second generation, there are different ways of belonging. Gender differences may also contribute to different kinds of belonging and responses to conditions of proximity and distance. There is no one way of being or belonging. The demands to settle and to make a home take many different forms throughout the novel, from the almost total assimilation of the seemingly most English family, the Chalfens, to the varying responses of the Iqbals and the Joneses. The novel does not proclaim that only the former are truly British, but that all of the families help to refashion what it means to be British by staking out different responses to, or kinds of, belonging. The differences within families, and some of the similarities across them, signal that there is not a single migrant outlook, but a number of mixed ones.

Summary

- Migrants display local, national and transnational senses of belonging and identification; these are varied and complicated by gender and generational factors.

- Some migrants may have ambivalent feelings about where they belong.

- Different kinds of proximity and distance – physical, cultural, emotional – cross-cut each other in migrants' family relations, and in the relationships they have with friends, neighbours and others.

4   Home and away

This final section of the chapter turns to South Asia, the region to which most of the migrants we have been looking at are linked. It explores some of the diverse and changing relations between India and its diasporas in order to examine more carefully the role of the state in relation to international migration. Both this chapter and Chapter 3 have suggested that the state continues to exert significant influence on who it will allow to settle in its territory, and to whom it will give what kind of citizenship. This section, in contrast, looks at the role of the state, not in relation to people who wish to enter a country, but in relation to people who have already left a country. The example of the category of 'Non Resident Indian' (NRI) (and the associated one, Person of Indian Origin or PIO) illustrates how some Indians and Indian-descended people living abroad are pulled 'closer' to India sometimes, but held at a 'distance' in other ways. NRIs experience senses of 'closeness' and 'distance' from a homeland, though often without any physical or actual movement, in part because of the Indian state's policies towards them. This section therefore explores the construction of migrant senses of proximity and distance through institutional and political processes, but as we shall see, even these processes often also depend on and evoke emotional experiences of belonging.

As we saw briefly in Section 2 and Activity 4.2, Indian migrants are made up of very different kinds of groups who have moved for a range of reasons. In the nineteenth century under British colonialism, around 1.5 million Indian indentured workers were recruited as relatively cheap labour after the abolition of slavery, and migrated to East and South Africa, the Caribbean and Southeast Asia (see Figure 4.5).

In the twentieth century, before and after Indian independence in 1947, many migrants left India for commercial reasons and moved to Britain, North America and Australia, as well as parts of Africa (see Figure 4.6). In the second half of the twentieth century, Indian migrants became identified with the 'brain drain' from India as they left to seek more lucrative jobs in 'the West'. For example, Indian emigration to the USA quadrupled between 1970 and 1996 (Singh, 2003) as India became a leading exporter of professionals. These 'sponsored' migrations have a selective bias towards professions required in the West, although they entail both a 'pull' (from receiving states) and a 'push' from families and individuals who choose career paths that will enable migration to the West. As well as these permanent migrations, since the 1970s there has been marked Indian migration to the Gulf States, much of it short term. Temporary migration also characterises the frequent seasonal migrations of Indian workers to neighbouring countries such as Sri Lanka and Nepal.

There are an estimated 11 to 20 million Indians living abroad in between 70 and 130 countries in the world today (Lall, 2001; Dubey, 2003; Parekh et al., 2003). What it means to call all these people 'Indian' or part of an 'Indian diaspora' is open to question because, as we have seen, the ways in which connections and origins to India operate take different and inconsistent forms. The groups who are

Figure 4.5   The movement of Indian workers in the nineteenth century
Source: Chaliand and Rageau, 1995, p.146

Figure 4.6   Indian migrations in the nineteenth and twentieth centuries
Source: Chaliand and Rageau, 1995, p.155

included in these figures have diverse patterns of migration and settlement. Not all of them claim or feel any link with India itself. Some have never been there, nor have any idea of returning to a 'homeland'. Added to that 'extreme heterogeneity' (Singh, 2003, p.4) are differences of religion, caste and class, which suggest that there is much work involved in imagining connections between such diverse groups and individuals in a way that enables them to be called an 'Indian diaspora'. While it is common to acknowledge that diversities exist, claims are still made that there are essences that link all emigrant Indians. Dubey (2003), for example, recognises considerable variations among Indians abroad who have adapted in various ways to the situations and countries in which they live. Nonetheless, he claims this has 'never subsumed their identity [which] ... springs from their deep faith in their civilization and their spiritual heritage'. According to him, they believe strongly in heritage and common values and, while they wish to see their children prosper, they also want them to 'adopt Indian family values. The global identity of Indian Diasporas is distinct because of these preferences, practices and aspirations' (Dubey, 2003, p.iii). Lall (2001) also argues that members of the diaspora retain an Indian consciousness that links them to the 'motherland'.

However, differences are easier to spot than commonalities. For instance, a recent survey (Parekh et al., 2003) found that in Trinidad and South Africa there is some resurgence of cultural pride in 'Indian-ness'. Yet that does not signal a wish for a permanent or fixed link with the 'homeland'. Some level of association with 'Indian culture' (which is in any case very diverse) is common among Indian diasporas across the world, but that is a quite different matter from an actual identification with the nation of India. Alternatively, in Sri Lanka, Sinhalese nationalism leads to a denial among many that they have any connection to the Indian diaspora, even though the whole population could claim to be descended from India in some way. The people of what are now the countries of Pakistan and Bangladesh are infrequently mentioned in accounts of the Indian diaspora, despite the fact that all of them can also claim to be of Indian descent. So who is and who is not counted in and claimed for the Indian diaspora is a selective process, and some definitions involve a particular imaginative exercise in tracing connections across time and space to work out who is 'in'. Even in its imagined form it is hard to identify an essence that binds all 'Indians' to a 'motherland' in South Asia.

The terms 'Non Resident Indian' (NRI) and 'Person of Indian Origin' (PIO) are of relatively recent origin. They date from some time in the 1970s and were first mentioned in the Indian parliament in 1984 (Lall, 2001). Their invention reflects the process in which geographies of connections (and disconnections) between Indians 'here' and 'there' came to be articulated. In the narrowest legal sense, an NRI means a citizen of India who lives abroad, a definition first developed to enable such people to invest in Indian property and businesses. The category of NRI was thus created in order to attract economic investment in India. Since 1999, the purchase of a PIO card confers certain advantages such as not having to apply for a visa, and parity of treatment with NRIs. The economic benefits of NRI/PIO status have been to the fore in both the creation and take-up of this category. The Indian state seeks to attract investment, and some investors in the Indian diaspora want the privileges of NRI/PIO status when investing in India. The economic motivation surrounding NRI/PIO status explains why the NRI/PIO policy has been targeted very selectively. As Lessinger observes, 'In theory any member of the Indian diaspora could qualify for these privileges. In practice, the new policy has been aimed at the wealthiest and best-connected immigrants in the US and Europe' (Lessinger, 2003, p.176).

Nevertheless, the process of drawing in or binding Indians 'far away' takes more than an economic form. For example, the media in India have hailed and celebrated the success of Indian fashion, cuisine, literature, theatre and films as part of an NRI phenomenon that reflects India's cultural glory in the West (Chattarji, 2005). This indicates the role of the media in bringing the far off closer, a point made in Chapter 2. The appeals by the Indian government to NRIs also signal the attempts of states to reach across borders, to try and exercise power at a distance beyond their own territories.

However, Indians abroad have been the subject of changing and contradictory attitudes that have made them both 'closer' to and more 'distant' from India over time. Several episodes reveal how Indian governments have sought to attract but also at times to repel Indians living elsewhere. In the 1970s, India did consider how to attract NRIs to 'return' to or invest in the country, principally due to concerns about the 'brain drain' caused by scientists leaving India. Following attempts at economic liberalisation first in the 1980s and then from 1991, NRIs have been encouraged to buy Indian property, business and government securities. High interest rates have been available to NRIs for depositing foreign exchange in Indian bank accounts, along with tax breaks for business investment and government bonds at favourable prices. As well as the economic incentives, NRIs have been wooed by governmental appeals to a range of emotions: their nationalism, their sense of being part of a greater India, 'to ideals of national development ... to primordial sentiments of Indianness and belonging, and to immigrants' residual guilt at having left poverty and underdevelopment behind them when they migrated' (Lessinger, 2003, p.176). As Chattarji (2005) suggests, the appeal to NRIs combines resurgent nationalism with economic pragmatism where the 'pull' or demand on NRIs relies as much on cultural and emotional ties as on economic ones. Nonetheless, the significance or quality of such connections between a nation and some of its diaspora is subject to different opinions. Some see these monetary flows as significant in helping to avert a balance of payments crisis in India (Jain, 2003), although others think it has had a more limited impact because opening the door to multinational corporations has been more important economically (Lall, 2001).

Whatever the scale of their involvement in and identification with India, the response of the NRIs has not been passive. They have sought to use their influence at a distance in calling for reform of India's economy and education system, and pressed for the appointment of a minister for NRI affairs. Such proposals have pitted migrants against their 'homeland' and resuscitated moves within India to create greater 'distance' from NRIs by resisting these proposals, in part due to fears that the proposals will give NRIs undue influence on Indian politics as well as its economy. This reveals the ambivalent attitude towards NRIs in India. Hence, the government has resisted the desire among some NRIs for dual citizenship. Moreover, when 'they' come 'here', NRI can come to mean 'Not Really Indian'. Lessinger (2003) notes that ordinary citizens in India 'often refer to all overseas Indians as NRIs, talk about the summer months, when immigrants return for visits and holidays, as "the NRI season", and identify a certain kind of Westernized consumption as "NRI style"' (Lessinger, 2003, p.175). Those who fear that 'Westernisation' is corrupting and undermining Indian culture accuse NRIs of being 'crassly materialistic' (Lessinger, 2003, p.167) and deride their impact on Indian culture.

Yet at the same time, other NRI activities that reach into India across distance are not seen in the same way. The 'long distance nationalism' of some NRIs who fund Hindu nationalist movements undoubtedly has an effect 'here' in India, which is welcomed by some though disparaged by others. Demands to belong, or at least to express a material and cultural identification at a distance, lead to responses that may not always be seen as desirable or welcome.

It is clear, then, that the 'distance' of Indians living outside India, and particularly those in 'the West', operates in more than the economic and political spheres. It has been common to view Indians abroad as cut off from their roots, as people who have been corrupted by licentiousness and lost their moral values. In other words, Indians 'there' are seen as morally and socially distant; they are not like 'real Indians', and the distance between 'here' and 'there' is itself seen as a cause of the gulf or separation between 'real Indians' and NRIs. In the same critical vein, the 'far away' location of NRIs paints them as unpatriotic people who have abandoned their country and their parents (Lall, 2001). This overlooks the possibility that NRI investment in India can be seen as a way of being in touch, of expressing a sense of belonging to, and identification with, the 'motherland'. It might be an attachment through which those who are far from India physically express their sense of closeness to and involvement in it. In other words, NRI investment could be read as an expression of responsibility in answer to a demand to remember those who remain at home, although this generous reading of NRI activity and involvement does not seem to get much of a look in during popular debates about NRIs.

Distance, like proximity, can work in more than one way, though, since, at more or less the same time as NRIs are popularly disparaged, the Indian diaspora across the world can be used to proclaim India's glory and influence in the world in cultural fields such as the arts (Chattarji, 2005). Thus, while the attitude that NRIs are corrupt and materialistic pushes them away or makes them distant from a national culture, the celebration of NRI successes brings them closer, even 'home'. Yet in both situations their actual physical location remains the same. NRIs are apparently welcomed as 'economic migrants', but they are repelled as migrants who seek political influence, albeit from a distance. Culturally, too, they are both celebrated and derided. Consequently, in this example, the state – together with the mass media – is making NRIs distant and bringing them closer at one and the same time.

The example of the NRIs living away from their 'home' but selectively 'pulled' and 'pushed' by it illustrates once again that identity and belonging can be linked to and rooted in more than one place, and that physical 'closeness' or 'distance' is not what produces or reduces a sense of belonging. Also revealed are the different ways in which the Indian state puts into practice its relation with some of its migrant citizens. Migrants who have left India – and their descendants – find themselves the subject of appeals to stay connected with India. These appeals are about money as well as about emotions, and demonstrate that the demands of the state upon its citizens can be made at a distance, and can depend upon evoking feelings such as love of country and guilt. Such appeals also show that the reach of the state can pull its distant citizens closer in some ways, while keeping them distant in others. Distance and proximity are here inseparably entangled.

Summary

■ Migrants are 'pushed' and 'pulled' in their ties to a country by the policies and practices of states even after they have left the country.

■ The emotional qualities of belonging are found not only in the experiences of migrants, but also in the appeals made by the state to its emigrants.

■ Proximity and distance may be inseparable in some senses of belonging, and may be at work simultaneously.

5 Conclusion

This chapter has identified some of the senses of belonging that migrants can experience. In particular, it has suggested that in a globalised world several different kinds of proximity and distance are entangled in migrant lives. Matters of identity, belonging and home are bound up in changing relations of proximity and distance. These relations are made rather than given. On the one hand, migrants sometimes express a sense of belonging to more than one place when they maintain loyalties to, or connections with, where they live, as well as where they came from. They can and do assert sustained connections to places and people in other parts of the world that make them part of both 'here' and 'somewhere else'; in this way they actively make 'distant' places closer. On the other hand, sometimes migrants are positioned in ways that connect them to places with which their links are considerably looser.

Migrants are part of networks that stretch across the world, and these connections may involve demands for extended familial and community involvements and responsibilities and relations of care. Such connections across borders mean that demands from migrants to belong and to find a place in the world also entail connections to places of origin. Migrants are mobile in a literal sense, but also imaginatively as people who connect with more than one place, or can be claimed by more than one place. What seems to be far off can be brought 'closer', while what seems near by can be made 'distant'.

Given all this, belonging, as we saw in the Introduction, can be ambivalent and complex, and this has been illustrated by all of the examples in this chapter. East African Asians, discussed in Section 2, seem to have a mobile sense of belonging that is not located in, or tied to, any one place. At one level, they exemplify the idea of transnational migrants who are seemingly flexible and 'un-rooted'. We might say that their sense of belonging is in part about travelling between places, across distances; as Jatinder Verma says, 'My identity is located on the road' (Guardian Unlimited website, 13 March 2002). In this sense, the experience of the East African Asians seems to be characteristic of a globalised world defined by mobility and interconnections. However, we also saw that their migrations are enabled by the way they carry their home-making and community-building skills with them as they travel, and that women in particular have an important role in enabling East African Asians to settle.

There are times, though, when one kind of belonging – the right to settle in a country conferred by its citizenship – can matter more than any other. The relationship between state and transnational forms of belonging and identification is thus often in tension. Different kinds of belonging were also evident in Section 3, through the example of the Iqbals from *White Teeth* (Smith, 2000). The extracts from the novel reinforce the point that belonging has a gendered dimension. The novel also explores the ways that belonging can vary generationally, and how it can mean a sense of identification with the local as much as with the national or transnational. The novel explores the tension between travelling and settling, but the various characters in the novel also draw on different senses of what is near and far, and attach very different meanings, emotions and values to those geographies. *White Teeth* not only suggests that distance and proximity may be in tension, it tangles them up in a variety of ways. Furthermore, the novel explores some of the emotional dynamics that senses of belonging can create.

The case of NRIs in Section 4 suggests that state policies towards emigrants can also be emotionally loaded, as well as, for example, driven by economic imperatives. Section 4 also showed how migrants and their descendants are subject to demands from afar to belong – economically, culturally – to a 'homeland'. Their responses to such demands mean that they, in turn, make demands on the state, demanding dual citizenship, for example. Belonging in this situation is a two-way street between migrants and states, where demands and responses (and non-responses) circulate across distance in ways that both 'push' migrants away and 'draw' them in. This example of the transnational reach of the state demonstrates that other aspects of migration mobilise both proximity and distance at the same time, as when the Indian government appears to want the investment and cultural status of NRIs but not what it perceives as their lax, Westernised moralities.

One final point about responses to the demands of living in a globalised world helps me to draw this chapter to a close. In each of the main sections the proposition is advanced that there are different kinds of routes and roots. Although there is a view that routes are more 'progressive' than roots because they are more open-ended, and less limited to a place, or to myths of origin, in this chapter we have seen that both roots and routes operate in various ways. Roots may be local, national or transnational. They may be about the importance of family connections, whether these are wished for and maintained or not, as well as about networks of care and involvement at a distance. And routes need not always be progressive; certain visions of diaspora populations insist on a myth of origin, for instance. Whether rooted or routed, migrants make demands to belong and settle where they are, and find themselves the subject of demands from the places and people they have left.

Thus, the key proposition of this chapter is that either/or binaries do not help us to understand migrant lives. Both home and away, routes and roots, and proximity and distance combine to shape senses of place and of belonging in the world – they are interlinked rather than separate. However, the ways in which these elements combine and interrelate are contingent and not fixed. What produces proximity is a variety of cultural, economic and emotional ties and appeals such as the historical connections between East African Asians and Britain, the co-presence of migrants in a locality, or the pull on migrant Indians by their 'homeland'. At the same time, we can see the reverse occurring through a similar variety of distancing strategies. Belonging is fashioned out of both proximity and distance, which means that what is near and what is far are not separate but interlinked in a range of different ways.

References

Arnot, C. (2002) 'Staging a survival', http://society.guardian.co.uk/societyguardian/story/0,,666048,00.html, 13 March (accessed 19 April 2005).

Bhachu, P. (1985) *Twice Migrants*, London, Tavistock.

Bhachu, P. (1995) 'New cultural forms and transnational South Asian women' in van der Veer, P. (ed.) *Nation and Migration*, Philadelphia, Pa., University of Pennsylvania Press.

Blunt, A. (2003) 'Home and identity' in Blunt, A., Ogborn, M., Gruffudd, P., May, J. and Pinder, D. (eds) *Cultural Geography in Practice*, London, Hodder Arnold.

Castles, S. and Miller, M. (2003) *The Age of Migration* (3rd edn), New York, Guilford Press.

Chaliand, G. and Rageau, J-P. (1995) *The Penguin Atlas of Diasporas*, London, Viking.

Chattarji, S. (2005) 'Reportage on the Indian diaspora in the UK and US in Indian media' in Gupta, S. and Omoniyi, T. (eds) *The New Orders of Difference*, Ontario, de Stiller.

Dubey, A. (ed.) (2003) *Indian Diaspora: Global Identity*, Delhi, Kalinga Publications.

Haley, A. (1976) *Roots: The Saga of an American Family*, New York, Doubleday Books.

Jain, P. (2003) 'Culture and economy in an "incipient" diaspora' in Parekh, B., Singh, G. and Vertovec, S. (eds) *Culture and Economy in the Indian Diaspora*, London, Routledge.

Lall, M.C. (2001) *India's Missed Opportunity*, Aldershot, Ashgate.

Lessinger, J. (2003) 'Indian immigration in the United States' in Parekh, B., Singh, G. and Vertovec, S. (eds) *Culture and Economy in the Indian Diaspora*, London, Routledge.

Papastergiadis, N. (2000) *The Turbulence of Migration*, Cambridge, Polity Press.

Parekh, B., Singh, G. and Vertovec, S. (eds) (2003) *Culture and Economy in the Indian Diaspora*, London, Routledge.

Singh, G. (2003) 'Introduction' in Parekh, B., Singh, G. and Vertovec, S. (eds) *Culture and Economy in the Indian Diaspora*, London, Routledge.

Smith, Z. (2000) *White Teeth*, London, Hamish Hamilton.

Song, M. (1997) '"You're becoming more and more English": investigating Chinese "siblings'" cultural identities', *New Community*, vol.23, pp.343–62.

United Nations (2004) *World Economic and Social Survey 2004: Part II International Migrations*, New York, United Nations.

Westwood, S. and Phizacklea, A. (2000) *Transnationalism and the Politics of Belonging*, London, Routledge.

Woodward, K. (2003) *Social Sciences – The Big Issues*, London, Routledge.

Staging a survival

Chris Arnot on a new play that maps out the ongoing odyssey of east African Asians

It's lunchtime in the Maharini restaurant on Clapham High Street, south London. Jatinder Verma sits under a picture of smiling women picking tea on a plantation and orders the meat curry. The man on the Clapham omnibus, which pulls up outside at regular intervals, could well be looking enviously through the window. Curry has, after all, displaced the roast beef of olde England as the favoured dish of the average British citizen – a measure of how much Britain has changed since Verma first boarded a London bus in 1968.

Verma is now artistic director of Tara Arts, Britain's oldest Asian theatre company, which is currently celebrating its 25th anniversary with an epic production called Journey to the West, opening tonight.

His own journey to the west began at the age of 14. He arrived from Kenya with his mother, younger brother, three sisters and a planeload of fellow Asians. President Jomo Kenyatta had made it clear they were no longer wanted in his increasingly 'Africanised' country. Prime minister Harold Wilson had made it equally clear they were not wanted here either. His government's commonwealth immigration bill was being rushed through parliament in an attempt to stop Gujeratis and Punjabis from east Africa exercising their right to British citizenship.

The Verma family arrived on the evening of Valentine's Day, but there was little love in the air for these desperate immigrants being herded through Heathrow to face blank stares, frank glares and hostile headlines on every news stand. 'Relatives took us as far as Victoria, where we had to catch a bus to Holloway Road, in north London,' Verma recalls. 'One thing that's stayed with me is the smell of detergent from so many launderettes. I also remember being shocked when I looked out of the window and saw a white man emptying dustbins. I was even more shocked when the bus conductor spoke to me and I couldn't understand a word he said.'

Verma's formal education in English – Keats, Wordsworth, exams sent to Nairobi by the Cambridge University board – had not prepared him for Cockney. But he was nothing if not adaptable. East African Asians of his generation were expected to know Punjabi, Hindi and Swahili, as well as English. He has since forged a career from his love of language.

Journey to the West is written as a trilogy, set in 1901, 1968 and 2001. But in each of the eight British cities and towns where it tours, there will be an opportunity to see all three parts together over seven hours. Four years ago, the company explored the 1968 episode through the play Exodus. No sooner have we walked from the rehearsal room to the restaurant than Verma begins to explain why he felt the need to broaden his scope.

'Exodus raised two questions,' he says. 'Why did so many Asians find their way to countries like Kenya and Tanzania in the first place? And what happened to the children of those who migrated to Britain in 1968?' Part of the answer to the first question is that Gujeratis had traded along the east African coast for centuries. At the end of the 19th century, famine in the Punjab coincided with a demand for skilled workers to extend the railway to the cotton-growing area around Lake Victoria.

'Gujeratis provided the materials,' says Verma, 'migrating Punjabis provided the labour.' And British imperialists creamed off the profits. Once the railway reached the lush highlands, white farmers carved themselves huge plots. A law was passed in 1913, preventing Africans and Asians from doing likewise. Its provision lasted 50 years, until Kenya gained independence at the end of 1963.

In Nairobi, the three communities were strictly segregated. Different living quarters, different schools, different hospitals. 'You could move around a bit more after independence,' says Verma, 'but I didn't mix socially with any white people until I came to Britain.' As a Hindu, though, he did mix freely with Muslims. 'It was a frontier society,' he explains, 'and Asians had to get on with each other. We used to go to each other's festivals, and that carried on for a long time when we came to this country.' That it is no longer the case, partly because of the rise of militant Islam and partly, he feels, because of globalisation and the need to be distinctive. 'It's no longer enough to be lumped together as Asians. We're living at a time when your ethnicity is becoming more and more important.'

So is this epic play an attempt to identify his roots? 'It depends how you're spelling the word,' he muses. 'I prefer to think of it as r-o-u-t-e-s. Roots lead backwards. Routes are more progressive, leading you to make connections with others. I'm not interested in the particular village in India where my grandfather came from. My identity is located on the road. East Africans are a real conundrum for modern anthropologists because, in some ways, we represent the future, beyond ethnicity. In a truer sense, we are world citizens. I know people who are moving on again, to America. It's as if, having taken the first step out of India, our people are perpetually on the move.'

Those arriving here in 1968 could have been forgiven for wanting to move on again as soon as possible. It was a turbulent year, to put it mildly. 'The assassination of Martin Luther-King made us feel like we were losing one of our own,' says Verma. 'Then Enoch Powell made his "rivers of blood" speech, which made us feel we could be booted out at any time.'

Verma was shouted and spat at on his way to school in south London. 'Enoch's right,' he was told, time and time again. Inevitably, he was called a 'Paki bastard', although he had no experience of Pakistan.

Former Asian residents of Nairobi and Dar-es-Salaam were used to a standard of living much higher than the conditions they found here in the so-called 'mother country'. Verma and his team have recorded many interviews while researching his plays, and a common theme running through them is disgust at having to share rooms and outside toilets. Members of the Kukadia family from Leicester, for instance, vividly remember the 10-minute walk to the public baths, where they would wait 45 minutes for their turn.

They soon became familiar with another queue – outside the only Asian shop in the area. Today, it would be difficult to name an exotic spice or vegetable which is not available in Leicester. 'When we first came here,' says Verma, 'we could only rent rooms from Asian people because whites apparently hated the smell of our cooking. Now curry is the national dish.' Not that he would give credit for that entirely to his own people. What he does say is that east Africans have often been the 'engines' of Asian commerce. 'They have endured and added their story to the story of the nation,' he adds, as another Clapham omnibus pulls up outside the Maharini.

(Arnot, 2002)

Reading 4B

Zadie Smith, 'White Teeth'

This has been the century of strangers, brown, yellow and white. This has been the century of the great immigrant experiment. It is only this late in the day that you can walk into a playground and find Issac Leung by the fish pond, Danny Rahman in the football cage, Quang O'Rourke bouncing a basketball, and Irie Jones humming a tune. Children with first and last names on a direct collision course. Names that secrete within them mass exodus, cramped boats and planes, cold arrivals, medical checks. It is only this late in the day, and possibly only in Willesden, that you can find best friends Sita and Sharon, constantly mistaken for each other because Sita is white (her mother liked the name) and Sharon is Pakistani (her mother thought it best – less trouble). Yet, despite all the mixing up, despite the fact that we have finally slipped into each other's lives with reasonable comfort (like a man returning to his lover's bed after a midnight walk), despite all this, it is still hard to admit that there is no one more English than the Indian, no one more Indian than the English. There are still young white men who are *angry* about that; who will roll out at closing time into the poorly lit streets with a kitchen knife wrapped in a tight fist.

But it makes an immigrant laugh to hear the fears of the nationalist, scared of infection, penetration, miscegenation, when this is small fry, *peanuts*, compared to what the immigrant fears – dissolution, *disappearance.* Even the unflappable Alsana Iqbal would regularly wake up in a puddle of her own sweat after a night visit by visions of Millat (generically *B B*; where *B* stands for Bengali-ness) marrying someone called Sarah (aa where 'a' stands for Aryan), resulting in a child called Michael (*Ba*), who in turn marries somebody called Lucy (aa), leaving Alsana with a legacy of unrecognizable great-grandchildren (Aaaaaaa!), their Bengali-ness thoroughly diluted, genotype hidden by phenotype. It is both the most irrational and natural feeling in the world. In Jamaica it is even in the grammar: there is no choice of personal pronoun, no splits between *me* or *you* or *they*, there is only the pure, homogenous *I*. When Hortense Bowden, half white herself, got to hearing about Clara's marriage, she came round to the house, stood on the doorstep, said, 'Understand: I and I don't speak from this moment forth,' turned on her heel and was true to her word. Hortense hadn't put all that effort into marrying black, into dragging her genes back from the brink, just so her daughter could bring yet more high-coloured children into the world.

Likewise, in the Iqbal house the lines of battle were clearly drawn. When Millat brought an Emily or a Lucy back home, Alsana quietly wept in the kitchen, Samad went into the garden to attack the coriander. The next morning was a waiting game, a furious biting of tongues until the Emily or Lucy left the house and the war of words could begin. But with Irie and Clara the issue was mostly unspoken, for Clara knew she was not in a position to preach. Still, she made no attempt to disguise her disappointment or the aching sadness. From Irie's bedroom shrine of green-eyed Hollywood idols to the gaggle of white friends who regularly trooped in and out of her bedroom, Clara saw an ocean of pink skins surrounding her daughter and she feared the tide that would take her away.

It was partly for this reason that Irie didn't mention the Chalfens to her parents. It wasn't that she intended to *mate* with the Chalfens ... but the instinct was the same. She had a nebulous fifteen-year-old's passion for them, overwhelming, yet with no real direction or object. She just wanted to, well, kind of *merge* with them. She wanted their Englishness. Their Chalfishness. The *purity* of it. It didn't occur to her that the Chalfens were, after a fashion, immigrants too (third generation, by way of Germany and Poland, née Chalfenovsky), or that they might be as needy of her as she was of them. To Irie, the Chalfens were more English than the English. When Irie stepped over the threshold of the Chalfen house, she felt an illicit thrill, like a Jew munching a sausage or a Hindu grabbing a Big Mac. She was crossing borders, sneaking into England; it felt like some terribly mutinous act, wearing somebody else's uniform or somebody else's skin.

(Smith, 2000, pp.281–3)

Reading 4C

Zadie Smith, 'White Teeth'

So it was with surprise that Samad greeted the vision of a violently weeping Alsana, at 2 a.m. on 31 October, hunched over the kitchen table. He did not think, *Ah, she has discovered what I am to do with Magid* (it was finally and for ever Magid), because he was not a moustachioed villain in a Victorian crime novel and besides which he was not conscious of plotting any crime. Rather his first thought was, *So she knows about Poppy*, and in response to this situation he did what every adulterous man does out of instinct: attack first.

'So I must come home to this, must I?' – slam down bag for effect – 'I spend all night in that infernal restaurant and then I am having to come back to your melodramatics?'

Alsana convulsed with tears. Samad noticed too that a gurgle sound was emanating from her pleasant fat which vibrated in the gap between her sari; she waved her hands at him and then put them over her ears.

'Is this really necessary?' asked Samad, trying to disguise his fear (he had expected anger, he didn't know how to deal with tears). 'Please, Alsana: surely this is an overreaction.'

She waved her hand at him once more as if to dismiss him and then lifted her body a little and Samad saw that the gurgling had not been organic, that she had been hunched *over* something. A radio.

'What on earth —'

Alsana pushed the radio from her body into the middle of the table and motioned for Samad to turn it up. Four familiar beeps, the beeps that follow the English into whatever land they conquer, rang round the kitchen, and then in Received Pronunciation Samad heard the following:

> This is the BBC World Service at 03.00 hours. Mrs Indira Gandhi, Prime Minister of India, was assassinated today, shot down by her Sikh bodyguards in an act of open mutiny as she walked in the garden of her New Delhi home. There is no doubt that her murder was an act of revenge for 'Operation Blue Star', the storming of the Sikhs' holiest shrine at Amritsar last June. The Sikh community, who feel their culture is being attacked by —

'Enough,' said Samad, switching it off. 'She was no bloody good anyway. None of them is any bloody good. And who cares what happens in that cesspit, India. Dear me ...' And even before he said it, he wondered why he had to, why he felt so *malevolent* this evening. 'You really are genuinely *pathetic*. I wonder: where would those tears be if *I* died? Nowhere – you care more about some corrupt politician you never met. Do you know you are the perfect example of the ignorance of the masses, Alsi? Do you know that?' he said, talking as if to a child and holding her chin up. 'Crying for the rich and mighty who would disdain to piss upon you. Doubtless next week you will be bawling because Princess Diana broke a fingernail.'

Alsana gathered all the spit her mouth could accommodate and launched it at him.

'*Bhainchute!* I am not crying for her, you *idiot*, I am crying for my *friends*. There will be blood on the streets back home because of this, India and Bangladesh. There will be riots – knives, guns. Public death, I have seen it. It will be like Mahshar, Judgement Day – people will die in the street, Samad. You know and I know. And Delhi will be the worst of it, is always the worst of it. I have some family in Delhi, I have friends, *old lovers* –'

And here Samad slapped her, partly for the old lovers and partly because it was many years since he had been referred to as a *bhainchute* (translation: someone who, to put it simply, fucks their sisters).

Alsana held her face, and spoke quietly. 'I am crying with misery for those poor families and out of *relief* for my own children! Their father ignores them and bullies them, yes, but at least they will not die on the streets like rats.'

So this was going to be one of those rows: the same positions, the same lines, same recriminations, same right hooks. Bare fists. The bell rings. Samad comes out of his corner.

'No, they will suffer something worse, much worse: sitting in a morally bankrupt country with a mother who is going mad. Utterly cuckoo. Many raisins short of a fruitcake. Look at you, look at the state of you! Look how *fat* you are!' He grabbed a piece of her, and then released it as if it would infect him. 'Look how you dress. Running shoes and a sari? And what is that?'

It was one of Clara's African headscarfs, a long, beautiful piece of orange Kenti cloth in which Alsana had taken to wrapping her substantial mane. Samad pulled it off and threw it across the room, leaving Alsana's hair to crash down her back.

'You do not even know what you are, where you come from. We never see family any more – I am ashamed to show you to them. *Why did you go all the way to Bengal for a wife*, that's what they ask. *Why didn't you just go to Putney?*'

Alsana smiled ruefully, shook her head, while Samad made a pretence of calm, filling their metal kettle with water and slamming it down on the stove.

'And that is a beautiful lungi you have on, Samad Miah,' she said bitterly, nodding in the direction of his blue-towelling jogging suit topped off with Poppy's LA Raiders baseball cap.

Samad said, 'The difference is what is in here,' not looking at her, thumping just below his left breast bone. 'You say you are thankful we are in England, that's because you have swallowed it whole. I can tell you those boys would have a better life back home than they ever – '

'Samad Miah! Don't even begin! It will be over my dead body that this family moves back to a place where our lives are in danger! Clara tells me about you, she tells me. How you have asked her strange things. What are you plotting, Samad? I hear from Zinat all this about life insurance ... who is dying? What can I smell? I tell you, it will be over my dead body – '

'But if you are already dead, Alsi –'

'Shut up! Shut up! I am not mad. You are trying to drive me mad! I phoned Ardashir, Samad. He is telling me you have been leaving work at eleven thirty. *It is two in the morning.* I am not mad!'

'No, it is worse. Your mind is diseased. You call yourself a Muslim – '

Alsana whipped round to face Samad, who was trying to concentrate his attention on the whistling steam emerging from the kettle.

'No, Samad. Oh no. Oh no. I don't call myself anything. I don't make claims. *You* call yourself a Muslim. *You* make the deals with Allah. *You* are the one he will be talking to, come Mahshar. *You*, Samad Miah. You, you, *you*.'

(Smith, 2000, pp.170–3)

Chapter 5

Envisioning demands: photographs, families and strangers

Gillian Rose

Contents

1   Introduction

So far this book has argued that to live in a globalised world is also to live in a demanding world. The antisweatshop campaign explored in Chapter 1 demands that affluent consumers should take responsibility for the working conditions under which their trainers and T-shirts and televisions were made. Chapter 2 examined how many forms of communication – from email to telephones – make insistent demands for a reply of some kind. Chapter 3 focused on some of the demands made by democratic states on their citizens, and by citizens on their states and beyond: demands to pay taxes, to be counted by censuses, to shift the location of responsibility for environmental change. And Chapter 4 explored the demands made by migrants to belong to a place.

These four chapters also explored a range of responses to those various demands. After all, if something is demanded, it is a request to someone or some organisation to do something. Yet, as we also saw, not all demands are acted upon. There are strong counter-arguments made against the antisweatshop campaign, for example, which suggest that sweatshops are inevitable, or that they are not a bad thing anyway, or that consumers in the developed world are not responsible for them. Many people resist the invitations to intimacy extended by various kinds of communication technologies. Many people also resist the efforts made by governments to integrate them into a nation state. And migrants may refuse to belong to a place on any terms; they may make their own sense of place, sometimes with quite distant countries or contexts.

This book has claimed that these demands and responses are part of the making of various geographies of proximity and distance, and that it is these geographies that produce the complex patterns of globalisation today. To explore these further, this chapter considers one important element of many different kinds of demands: photographs.

Photographs are central to the way that many of the demands of campaigning organisations and groups are made. If you think for a moment about some recent demands that you have encountered – perhaps in newspaper advertisements, something arriving in the post or a demonstration you have seen or taken part in – photographs are likely to have been prominent in most, if not all, of them. Indeed, nowadays, especially in affluent countries, photographs are found just about everywhere: in books, papers, leaflets and magazines; in houses, art galleries, hospitals, libraries, archives; on billboards, advertising hoardings, buses and trains. All these sorts of photographs make at least one kind of demand: a demand for our attention. This chapter looks at how photographs have become part of more or less organised campaigns to make certain demands more visible, and considers their particular effects on those demands. It also explores more generally how photographs are involved in making the proximities and distances that shape the globalised world in which we live.

Ever since its invention in Britain and France in the 1850s, photography has been one means by which the world has become globalised; it has been used to show different parts of the world to each other. Many kinds of travellers in the second half of the nineteenth century took cameras with them to record the people and places they saw as they journeyed; they also showed their photographs to various audiences on their return home. In the twentieth century, popular publications like the magazine *National Geographic* continued this tradition, producing heavily illustrated essays about places far away from most of their readership. Photographs have been carried by migrants since the beginning of photography too; the photograph in Figure 4.1 in Chapter 4 of this book, for example, has travelled with members of Karim Murji's family from Tanzania, where it was taken in the early 1960s, to Britain later that decade, and was scanned and sent digitally to Canada and East Africa in 2002. With the development of mass tourism (and affordable cameras), many of us now take pictures ourselves when we travel, and look at them once we have returned home. Television news programmes and documentaries, as well as photographs in newspapers, also bring distant places close to their viewers. Photography, then, is another aspect of the globalising mediation discussed in Chapter 2 of this book.

Photographs seem to bring distant places close to us because they enable us to see places vividly and in detail. They offer a sense of visual proximity, even presence. Many charities and campaigning groups that are concerned with distant places use photographs in their appeals for action or for money as a means of getting people in one place to see what the problem is in another part of the world, or what can be done about it. Photographs are central to demanding what Chapter 2 calls 'responsive action in distant contexts'. An obvious example is the use of photographs of hungry children to solicit donations for famine relief.

Yet once a photograph has become part of a specific demand, in a newspaper report or on a website, for example, what happens then? What sorts of responses might it elicit, and how does that contribute to understanding further the contemporary geographies of globalisation?

This chapter tries to answer those questions. It focuses on the responses photographs get when they are put to work on behalf of a specific, explicit demand. Section 2 looks at two typical examples of non-governmental organisations (NGOs) using photographs within campaigns, and explores how the photographs bring distant places close as part of a demand for action on the part of the photographs' viewers. Section 3 explores a more unexpected way in which photographs can be put to work in relation to a demand, when a photograph refers to something that is in some way missing or absent. The idea that something might be absent in relation to a photograph helps us to understand better how important emotional responses are in making connections that span the globe. The chapter then explores why some photographs get no response at all, emotional or otherwise, by looking in Section 4 at the familiar family snap, and in Section 5 at ways in which photographs – and the demands they represent – can be ignored.

Finally, at the end of the chapter, there is a photo-essay produced in collaboration with the photographer Owen Logan. While most of this chapter concentrates on responses to photographs that are part of campaigns, the photo-essay explores some aspects of the production of a set of photographs that make a series of demands. These demands centre on the need to see the global oil industry differently from the way it is usually presented. At the end of the chapter you'll have your own chance to reflect on and respond to these campaigning photographs that are a little different from other photographs that this chapter discusses, and from campaign photographs you are most likely to encounter every day.

Chapter aims

- To explore how photographs of people or places far away and in need of help can move us to respond to a demand.

- To examine how campaign photographs work to produce senses of proximity, distance and absence.

- To explore how part of the effect of photographs has to do with the unpredictable emotional responses they provoke.

- To examine why some photographs, particularly those showing disasters in less affluent parts of the world, can elicit little or no response from their viewers in more affluent regions.

2   How photographs bring distant places close

To start thinking about how a photograph works as part of a demand, we can look at two typical examples of photographs used by campaigning organisations. Figures 5.1 and 5.2 show part of two leaflets produced in 2004 by a couple of NGOs working for global change. In its leaflet, Oxfam describes itself as 'working with others to find lasting solutions to poverty and suffering', while Friends of the Earth (FoE) says its aim is to 'inspire solutions to environmental problems'. Both organisations are active within the UK, where these leaflets were distributed, but both chose to use photographs from elsewhere in the world in these particular appeals. Both leaflets are making a number of demands.

Girls collecting clean water from taps set up by Oxfam.

Day by day

Oxfam has been working with the people of Kenya since 1963. Prolonged droughts have driven many parts of the country, such as the Turkana District, into crisis. In 2000 alone, 2.2 million people across the country were in need of emergency aid. As one drought followed another, the people living in Turkana never recovered. Today, pastures remain dry, and water sources remain empty.

In human terms, the cost of this drought is enormous. People are living in fear that they will not be able to feed their livestock, and so lose their main source of income. Anna Nangolol, who lives in the affected Turkana region is clearly worried:

"This drought has been very bad. Past droughts have been shorter and rains have come. This one seems never to finish."

Boy collecting water for his family.

Thanks to the support of regular givers, like yourself, we are able to help the people of Turkana. We are distributing food, supporting the repair and maintenance of handpumps, and building reservoirs to sustain livestock during dry periods. Cash-for-Work programmes are also being set up to help people earn a dignified living, whilst delivering the long-term development they so desperately need.

But with millions of people facing severe food shortages, **every extra pound** you can afford could make a huge difference.

A little bit more

Figure 5.1   A double-page spread from a leaflet mailed out to Oxfam supporters in the UK, 2004

Climate change will change ...
your health, your money, your world, your life

Did you know?
85 per cent of Britons would be prepared to change the way they live in order to lessen the impact of climate change.
BBC National Poll, July 04

An alarming increase in greenhouse gases like carbon dioxide from burning coal, oil and gas is warming up our planet.

35 per cent of our electricity is produced by burning coal in power stations.

The frequency of extreme weather events is rising. Insurance claims for storm and flood damages in the UK have doubled to over £6 billion in the last five years and could triple by 2050, according to the Association of British Insurers.

The World Health Organisation estimates 160,000 people a year die from climate change. Water shortages, agricultural failure, flooding and heatwaves are some of the real threats climate change poses.

The polar bear is just one of over a million species facing possible extinction within decades. Other animals affected include walruses, sea lions and penguins or closer to home, the UK's beech woodlands.

Government action to tackle climate change is essential, but the choices we make in our lives can also make a significant difference.

Be part of this change

Figure 5.2   A double-page spread from a flyer distributed in the UK by Friends of the Earth, 2004

Activity 5.1

Look at the photographs and read the text reproduced in Figures 5.1 and 5.2. What demands do the photographs and text make on you? How do the photographs contribute to the demands? Think about what they show you and how they are showing it.

For me, the most obvious demands are, first, a demand that we read the leaflets and, second, demands for money and for action. The Oxfam leaflet, which was sent in the post to people who already make regular donations to Oxfam, is asking for 'a little bit more' – a little bit more money to enable Oxfam to distribute more food and water and build more infrastructure in Kenya (the other countries featured in the leaflet are Brazil and Nicaragua). The FoE leaflet is demanding that its readers 'be part of this change' by making small alterations to their lifestyles in order to tackle climate change. But what are the photographs doing?

Both leaflets are trying to convince their readers to take some sort of responsibility in relation to people and environments. Nevertheless, both organisations seem to think that just writing about this is not enough to make the point – they have included photographs too. Furthermore, the kinds of photographs they have chosen to use are rather different. FoE uses pictures of the consequences of the problem of climate change: floods, parched soil and endangered animals.

Oxfam, on the other hand, has used positive images of its work in Kenya: children happily using the water supply it has provided for them. The inclusion of the children in the photographs suggests that they want what Oxfam does too; they too want change. Whatever they show, though, it seems that photographs are a necessary part of these campaigns. And in this, as I have already noted, FoE and Oxfam are hardly alone. It is quite unusual to encounter a campaign or an organisation that does not use photographs in some way or another.

Perhaps groups such as FoE and Oxfam feel that, precisely because there are so many photographs around these days (not to mention TV, computer and mobile phone screens), their messages will seem boring if they just use written text. However, these photographs are also letting their UK audience see something of the need to act to ameliorate climate change and of the effects of Oxfam's work in distant places. They are being used to bring those distant places close to UK viewers. Therefore, the photographs are making a faraway place proximate. In the FoE leaflet, the aim of this is to show what is at risk; the thrust of the Oxfam photographs, in contrast, is to show what has been achieved. In both cases, the photographs are being used as evidence to support the demand from each organisation that we do something. Not only are we being told what needs to be done, through the photographs we can see the need for it with our own eyes. We become witnesses to it.

In these examples this 'witnessing' effect depends on photographs of people and places as they appeared in real life when the photo was taken. But there are other ways of using photographs as evidence of how the world is. For example, completely new images can be created by pasting different photographs together. The photo-essay at the end of this chapter in part uses this technique, of creating new photographs from existing ones, in order to visualise aspects of a globalised world that are otherwise difficult to see.

The straightforward immediacy of the images in Figures 5.1 and 5.2 is harnessed in rather different ways by FoE and Oxfam, though. FoE uses the photographs in Figure 5.2 to evoke a notion of responsibility very similar to that outlined by Iris Marion Young (2003) and discussed in Chapter 1 of this book. The photographs do not show the actual connections between the readers of the leaflet and the effects of climate change – it is the text of the leaflet that makes them clear – but they do claim to show the results of those connections. Oxfam, on the other hand, is using the photographs to incite action on somewhat different grounds. Its leaflet is not claiming any direct connection between its reader and young people in Kenya (although in fact Oxfam frequently argues that there are structural connections between poor countries like Kenya and rich ones like the UK). In this particular example, Oxfam is inviting our sympathy with a situation by allowing us to see and read about it directly. The immediacy of the Oxfam leaflet is intended, I think, to cut through the complexities involved in tracking global connections, whether direct or indirect (complexities which we explored in Chapter 1), in order to establish a sense of involvement in what the photographs in the leaflets show.

Activity 5.2

Some of the photographs you have already seen in this book are part of campaigns; for example, Figures 1.3 and 1.5 in Chapter 1 are used by the Clean Clothes Campaign. Do they also bring distant places close? And do they also ask you to act as a witness? Do they make connections between you and what they show, or do they ask you to feel compassionate about someone or something that you have no connection with?

It seems that there are two different ways of envisioning the geography of responsibility in the photographs we have looked at so far. One depends on tracing the actual connections between an action and its result, and the other depends on establishing a feeling of sympathy with those whose lot should be improved. Whichever kind of responsibility is invoked, however, the assumption of both FoE and Oxfam is that once some sense of responsibility is indeed established, often through the proximity brought about by photographs, action will follow. We will change from witnesses to activists, and do something: dig into our pockets and donate money, or make lifestyle changes to ameliorate climate change.

Many discussions of photography pay a great deal of attention to how powerful the immediacy of some photographic images can be. Elizabeth Edwards (2001) has called this the 'rawness' of some photographs; the information they carry can be so direct, so powerful that it makes what is pictured feel not only proximate to a viewer, but actually present. A photograph that carries a presence, as well as making something proximate, shows something so intensely that it grabs its viewer and will not let go. An example of a photograph used in a campaign that has this effect on me is one used by the International Campaign for Justice in Bhopal. Bhopal is a city in India, and also the site of a pesticide factory owned by Union Carbide. An explosion on the night of 3 December 1984 has killed 20,000 people to date and left many others with long-term illnesses. In its appeals for money to help the victims of the disaster, the Campaign uses a photograph of the face of a child blinded by the explosion being buried. The child has sightless, staring eyes, and I find it hard to describe how intensely they affect me. Photographs that have such presence (and by no means all do) can carry immense emotional power.

Activity 5.3

Take a moment to consider whether there are any photographs used as part of campaigning demands that have affected you in some intense way. If there are, did you respond to the demand they were helping to make?

Photographs with such raw presence are not common, and moreover they often do not affect everyone in the same way. If you can, ask someone else to do this same activity and compare your answers. Did you choose the same photograph? Did their photograph have the same effect on you as on them?

It is sometimes claimed that the presence carried by some photographs has the power to shift social or economic or political or environmental processes. Typical of this claim is a book called *Photographs that Changed the World* (Monk, 1989), which includes several photographs that have been reproduced hundreds, if not thousands, of times: a photograph of survivors of the Buchenwald concentration camp in 1945; a 1968 photograph of a naked child running terrified down a road in Vietnam, burning with napalm; the *Challenger* space shuttle exploding in 1986, for example. The editor of that book, Lorraine Monk, says about these photographs that, 'every one of them has been undeniably influential. Because of them and the information they revealed, the world was ever after a different place ... perceptions of reality were forever altered' (Monk, 1989, p.1). I think this argument rather exaggerates the power of photographs to act on their own, however. Although it is clear that photographs are used in all sorts of campaigns and are an important part of many demands, they are just that: *used by* campaigning groups and organisations, as *part of* their demands. As the examples from FoE and Oxfam show, photographs are often used alongside written arguments and explanations (just as newspaper photographs are always accompanied by written text that explains them), and their precise effect depends as much on those explanations as it does on the proximity or presence in the photograph. Furthermore, as we have noted, not all photographs affect everyone the same way.

Nonetheless, although we make sense of photographs by reading the written materials that invariably accompany them, it remains the case that the proximity of photographs – the way they bring what they show close to their viewer – and, more unpredictably, their presence – the raw intensity of their impact – are very important elements of the demands made in many campaigns. Photographs bring something happening elsewhere close and present to viewers who could not otherwise witness what the photographs show, and demands are made more imperative by the proximity and presence carried by photographs.

Summary

- Photographs can make distant places and people proximate to their viewers by showing them sights they could not otherwise see.

- Some photographs have such an intensity that they seem to make present what they show. This presence feels not only close up but also raw and compelling.

- Campaigning groups often use the qualities of proximity and presence in photographs to show the need for change, to mobilise support for change or to present evidence of change.

- Campaigning groups assume that looking at such photographs as part of a demand will help to inspire action in the viewer.

3   How photographs show what is absent

The previous section argued that some photographs which are used as part of demands are effective because they make an issue unavoidably close to someone who can do something about it. Thus, Oxfam brings photographs of Kenyan young people collecting and carrying water in their village to UK residents in the expectation that, faced with such evidence, the UK residents will act to ensure that such collection continues to be possible. Not all photographs make demands through proximity or presence, however. Many photographs depend for their impact on some notion that something or someone is missing in relation to the photograph. That is, some photographs not only bring a place or a person close to their viewers; they can also work as a reminder of things or people who are not there. This section explores examples of this. It looks at the way that photographs can be mobilised to make some kind of demand not by making something proximate or present, but by evoking some kind of absence.

In campaigns, photographs are often used as part of demonstrations and protests, and this section looks at three rather different examples of this. It argues that the photographs' impact comes, not only from the proximities and presence they produce, but also from their particular uses of absence. In all these examples, there are photographs which show people who are in some way missing from the actual protest action. The photographs are there as *substitutes* for these missing people. The differences between the three examples are to be found in the various effects that these three kinds of substitutions have. It is these effects that can tell us something about how the impact of photographs often has much to do with people who are absent and, more generally, about how absence plays a part in shaping demands.

3.1 'A new form of social protest': the visual petition

The first example of photographs being used in demonstrations and protests is a protest organised between 2003 and 2006 by three campaigning organisations: the human rights organisation Amnesty International, Oxfam and the International Action Network on Small Arms. Their joint campaign was called 'Control Arms'. It was a campaign against the global arms trade and the violence, crime and human rights violations that they argued follow in its wake. The campaigners wanted a legally-binding, international arms trade treaty to help stop weapons being sent to destinations where they might undermine human rights, fuel conflict or exacerbate poverty. The way they chose to involve people and force governments to agree to an arms trade treaty was to make what they called a 'visual petition'. Now, a petition is usually made up of signatures which indicate that the people who signed their names agree with what the petition is about. This visual petition, however, was not interested in signatures. It wanted photographs.

The petition was called the 'Million Faces petition'. The Control Arms campaign invited individuals to send it, via email, a digital photograph of themselves which had to show their names (or a slogan) and locations written either on their hands or on a piece of paper they were holding. Each photograph had to come from an individual email address; like signatures on petitions, each photograph had to represent an actual individual. The campaign workers then checked the photographs to see they were appropriate, and put them on the Control Arms website. People who did not want their pictures on the web, or who were under 16, could use a prepared image provided by the campaign. The point of collecting one million faces by 2006 was that in the summer of that year, the United Nations (UN) was holding a conference on the arms trade to which the petition would be presented. Figure 5.3 shows the location of petitioners as at November 2004.

According to the campaigners, the fact that this was a *visual* petition served two purposes. The first was to create 'a powerful visual symbol of solidarity linking people from all over the planet in their call to

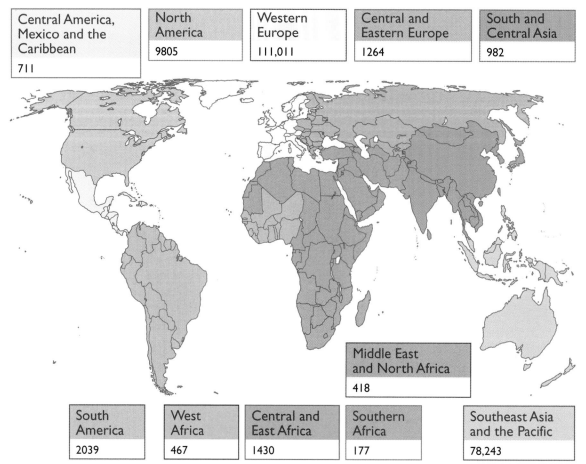

| Central America, Mexico and the Caribbean 711 | North America 9805 | Western Europe 111,011 | Central and Eastern Europe 1264 | South and Central Asia 982 |

| Middle East and North Africa 418 |

| South America 2039 | West Africa 467 | Central and East Africa 1430 | Southern Africa 177 | Southeast Asia and the Pacific 78,243 |

Figure 5.3   A map of the number of people who had signed the 'Million Faces petition' by November 2004
Source: http://www.controlarms.org

demand an end to the arms crisis' (Control Arms, 2004). On the website, you could see the many, many other people who, perhaps like you, were calling for the regulation of the arms trade. Here we can see again the way in which photographs bring distant people and places close. The web pages showed thousands and thousands of faces, from many parts of the world. However, the sheer number of photographs, on screen after screen after screen, was also evidence of the scale of support for the campaign. Section 2 highlighted the assumption in campaigning leaflets that if a photograph showed something clearly, it would help to prompt action from its viewer, and the Control Arms campaign also seemed to suggest something similar. In this case though, it was not evidence of the problem or its solution that was shown, but evidence of the will to make a solution. The proximity and the size of the photo gallery were being used to inspire solidarity with a particular campaign.

The second use of the Control Arms visual petition, according to its organisers, was that it allowed a new kind of protest to take place. Control Arms was planning to bring the petition – the photographs – to the 2006 UN conference on the arms trade 'as a powerful visual message of support for the Control Arms campaign', to support its call for an end to irresponsible arms trade (Control Arms, 2004). Although the million people pictured would not be there in person, their photographs would. Through their photographs, they would become part of a protest event.

The conviction that a visual petition will have some kind of political effect therefore depends on two things. First, it depends on the belief that the size of a protest matters for its impact, and, second, it depends on the way photographs are seen to make something close. Whether it is a photograph of parched earth in an FoE leaflet that drops through your letterbox, or a photograph of a protest movement member on a website or at a conference, the impact of these photographs depends on the way the photograph brings the earth or the movement member proximate to you or, for example, to the delegates at a UN conference. However, these are only photographs! They are substitutes for people, not the people themselves. The actual people are missing from the planned protest. Their absence is in fact crucial to the success of this sort of campaign, which depends on the impact of big numbers. It would be quite difficult to get a million people protesting outside a UN conference venue; it is much easier to get a million photographs there. The substitution of people with their photographs enables the protest to happen on a much larger scale than would otherwise be possible.

Obviously, when any petition, visual or otherwise, is handed over to its intended recipient, not all its signatories are present. Other kinds of photographic absence can have a much more resonant effect, however.

3.2 'Not in my name': how absence might matter

To demonstrate a more resonant effect of photographic absence, let's look at a second example of a protest that used photographs of people. The years 2002 and 2003 saw many demonstrations in the major cities of the world against the US-led invasion of Iraq. One of the groups who organised the demonstrations in the UK was the Stop the War Coalition. A slogan it used frequently in its publicity for the anti-war protests was the phrase 'Not in my name'. Noticing that the governments of the UK and the USA were justifying their aggression by saying they were doing it for the sake of the safety of all their citizens, the Coalition wanted to point out that not all citizens were

Figure 5.4   A demonstration in Edinburgh in November 2004 organised by the Stop the War Coalition

convinced by their reasoning. Drawing on the two-way relation between citizen and government explored in Chapter 3 of this book, the Coalition pointed out that many citizens in fact felt their safety (and that of many others) would be threatened more by going to war in Iraq than not. Hence the slogan 'Not in my name'. Directed at the government, it insisted that not everyone wanted the war, and that the government was therefore ignoring the wishes of a significant number of its citizens. (The same slogan, or variations of it, has also been used by a number of other protest groups around the world.)

People took to the streets in large numbers in anti-war protests, often chanting 'Not in my name' or holding posters saying that. However, it was not only the people in these demonstrations who were explicitly articulating that position. The words 'Not in my name' were also given to those in the marches too young to talk, and to those not actually present at the protest at all. As Figure 5.4 shows, some protesters were carrying photographs of people not on the march, and those photographs were shown as if the people they pictured were also saying 'Not in my name'.

In part, these photographs were working in the same way as the visual petition organised by Control Arms. They were being used as substitutes for people who couldn't get to the actual demonstration, as a means of boosting the number of protestors and therefore the impact of the protest. The placards were also giving voice to those too young to talk or to understand, or too young to be taken on long, cold marches. Moreover, I think something else was also taking place, particularly when protestors were using photographs of young children. To me, the use of these photographs in demonstrations demanding peace suggests that war threatens the future of the children pictured. This was certainly the case in an earlier moment of the peace movement in the UK during the 1980s, when the Campaign for Nuclear Disarmament was demanding an end to nuclear weapons. In protests then, photographs of children were used to show the future lives that nuclear weapons were seen as threatening, lives that needed protecting and not obliterating. In the Stop the War Coalition demonstrations, the fact that the children pictured were often missing from such demonstrations might be about more than the practical difficulties of bringing young children on marches. It might imply something more important: if the protest at which their photographs are present fails, then the children's futures may disappear too. These children may not have a future if peace does not prevail. Their literal absence from the protest thus might also symbolise the possibility of them being made 'absent' in the future: their future deaths.

As the 'Million Faces petition' example demonstrated, photographs that show people supporting a campaign are useful because they boost its numbers, whether on a website or at a conference or on a march. In the case of the 'Not in my name' marchers, the photographs also indicated that something that might potentially *not* exist (in the future) was an important part of the campaign. The threat of violence and the risks that war posed to children were also implied by the use of photographs as substitutes for people.

Shadowing the photographs of children carried in demonstrations against the invasion of Iraq in 2002 and 2003 in places like Edinburgh, however, were the photographs of Iraqi children killed by invading troops – and indeed by Sadam Hussein's brutal regime. The next example looks at the effects of using photographs of people who have actually gone missing in the most brutal of circumstances. It allows us to explore further the power of absence in relation to photographs and demands.

3.3   Photographs demanding justice for the dead

Every Thursday afternoon, since 1977, in the Plaza de Mayo in Buenos Aires, Argentina, a group of women known as the 'Mothers of the Disappeared' meet. They often carry a family photograph, yet another example of photographs being used in demonstrations. These photographs show their children, who as adults were some of the women and men who disappeared while Argentina was ruled by a right-wing military dictatorship between 1976 and 1983. In this period, the Argentine military abducted anyone it suspected of 'subversive' activity; somewhere between 10,000 and 30,000 people were taken from their homes, never to be seen again by their families. Many mothers of these 'disappeared' started to search for their children, meeting each other again and again at police stations, detention centres, mortuaries and prisons; eventually, in April 1977, a few decided to meet weekly at the Plaza. Initially, fourteen women came. Soon about 150 women were regular participants, and in 1979 they constituted themselves formally into the organisation Asociación Madres de Plaza de Mayo. Their initial demand was straightforward: they wanted to know what had happened to their children.

As time passed and neither their children nor any information about them appeared – indeed, the bodies of thousands of the disappeared have never been found – the women of the Asociación divided into two groups, although they still work together. One group – Madres de

Figure 5.5   Members of the Asociación Madres de Plaza de Mayo demanding an investigation into the fate of children born in captivity to disappeared mothers, Plaza de Mayo, Buenos Aires, July 2000

Plaza de Mayo-Linea Fundadora – works to establish the cause of death of each of the individuals abducted. The other group – which still calls itself the Asociación Madres de Plaza de Mayo – works to ensure that the collective fate of the disappeared is remembered and never recurs. Both groups also work with others; for example, they work with an organisation that tries to unite the children of those disappeared with their original families. Both groups are active in relation to the authorities in Argentina and to organisations outside Argentina, particularly human rights organisations.

In the many photographs that exist of both these groups, the women are very often pictured with photographs of their disappeared children. In this case, though, the photographs obviously do not carry the implication that these children might disappear in the future, as was the case with the 'Not in my name' protestors. Here, the children have really disappeared already. They are absent in relation to these photographs because they have most likely been murdered by the military regime.

The Madres are not the only protest group to use photographs as part of their actions. Demonstrations about many other kinds of brutalities also often mobilise photographs of lost loved ones (see Activity 5.4 below). However, let's consider the case of the Madres in Buenos Aires a little further in order to explore the effects of using photographs in this way in some detail.

Clearly, one way in which the Madres are using their photographs is to mark the fact that their children are missing, murdered. Yet when they are part of demonstrations the photographs also strengthen the demands the Madres are making. All the accounts of the Madres' action are agreed on this: the photographs deepen the intensity of their protest. The Madres are using the photographs to give an emotional depth to their demands. They can do this because they feel that the connection between the mother and the photograph of her son or daughter is particularly emotionally charged. Drawing on their Catholic faith, the Madres believe that there is a profound connection between a mother and child; indeed, they feel it is an unbreakable bond which continues even after death. And so, when they gather at the Plaza de Mayo, a photograph certainly substitutes for the child, but with an intensity that resonates with both this faith in the closeness between a mother and her child, and with its loss.

This emotional attachment between a mother and the photograph of her dead child means that, although the child is absent, it feels as if he or she can be made present again through the mother's feelings.

The Madres have organised marches during which they carry their children's photographs, this time enlarged to the size of posters, with their names, ages and dates of disappearance. One mother described these marches as being 'the first time that our kids had come out in the streets with us to march since their disappearance' (Mellibovsky, 1997, p.133); it is as if the children are actually with their mothers once more.

Witnesses to these marches have also talked about the startling effect of these posters on them. As a result of the rawness of photographs, the way photographs show us things so directly, and because of the emotional charge these photographs held for the Madres, the photographs seemed especially vivid. Yet, of course, these onlookers knew that all the people in the photographs were dead. Indeed, the photographs resonated so strongly precisely because their subjects had gone. Although some bystanders – and indeed some Madres – felt that the photographs somehow brought the disappeared back on to the streets of Buenos Aires and made them present again, it could also be said that the absence of the disappeared was there too.

These marches ended with the Madres lined up in front of the president's residence holding their posters, the faces on the posters confronting the soldiers guarding the building. (The decision to march to the president's residence reflected the Madres' view of where responsibility for the disappearance of their children lay: not with the president personally, perhaps, but certainly with the state's army and police force of which the president was the head.) People who saw these confrontations talk about the mix of presence and absence that these photographs produced. The faces staring from the posters at the impassive faces of the soldiers became so intense, so raw, so loaded with loss, with the possibilities of what might have been but could not now be, that witnesses spoke of the photographs outfacing the soldiers who were guarding the residence (Mellibovsky, 1997).

In this case, then, the substitution of an absent person by his or her photograph is not intended to boost the numbers taking part in a protest on the assumption that the more people present, the more powerful the protest will be. Instead, the photographs are making the protests more powerful because of the emotions they evoke. The photographs are of the *absent* – the missing – and their impact is in making them *present* again, with an intensity that could force change.

The precise demands being made by the Madres carrying their photographs onto the streets of Buenos Aires are diverse. One is that those who tortured and murdered the disappeared should be brought to justice, a demand made all the more valid after the democratic government that succeeded the dictatorship in 1983 made prosecuting

Figure 5.6   Asunción, Paraguay, 2004

these individuals extremely difficult, and those few that were prosecuted were pardoned in 1990. Other demands are that the individual fates of all the disappeared should be known, and that the social justice to which so many of the disappeared were committed should be realised. To reinforce these demands, the photographed faces of the disappeared are used. Their presence is a reminder about what was possible and what should have been possible: the future lives that should have been lived. Their absence is a reminder of the wrongs that have been committed and the ongoing need, as the Madres see it, for justice of various kinds.

Figure 5.7   Independence Square, Luanda, Angola, 2003

Photographs of people missing or dead are used as part of many demands. In Figures 5.6 and 5.7 we can see two further examples of photographs being used in this way.

The protestors in Asunción photographed in Figure 5.6 are at a temporary shrine erected opposite a supermarket which burned down in August 2004; the building flouted safety regulations about fire escapes and at least 374 people died in the blaze, including the boy pictured. The women queuing in Luanda (Figure 5.7) are waiting to show their photographs on a prime-time television show, 'Nação Coragem' – 'Courageous Nation'. The photographs are of relatives who disappeared during the course of Angola's civil war, which finally ended in 2002. The women are hoping that their relatives will watch the show and get in touch to be reunited with their families; in many cases, though, they do not know if they are alive or dead.

Activity 5.4

In terms of the effects of the photographs, there are several differences between Figures 5.6 and 5.7, and also between them and the case study from Buenos Aires. Thinking about the discussion of the Madres, compare the three examples in terms of:

1   The absences evoked by the photographs. Who is absent and why? Does it matter why they are absent in terms of the effect their photograph has on you?

2   The demands made with the photographs. Apart from the photographs, what do you need to see or know in order to understand what demands are being made in each example? Do the photographs make much sense on their own?

3   The location of the protests. The Madres took their photographs to the site of those they deemed responsible for the disappearances of their children. What notions of responsibility, if any, are suggested by the locations of the other two protests?

Photographs do not always have the same effects, even when similar sorts of photographs are used in broadly similar ways. This is both because different people react differently to the rawness or presence of photographs, and because photographs are put to work differently in different situations. Therefore, the use of photographs in the sorts of protests illustrated in this section does not necessarily lead to one specific kind of demand. In fact, photographs can be put to work to make very different sorts of demands; even the Madres have two organisations pursuing two somewhat different aims.

It is now possible to suggest that the role of photographs in a globalised world is not only about making viewers in one part of the world witnesses to the need for change in other parts of the world – although that is one task to which photographs can be set, as Section 2 showed. Nor is the role of photographs only to mobilise ever larger numbers of people in campaigns for global change – even though, as Sections 3.1 and 3.2 showed, they can be used like that. What all the examples in this section have shown is that what is missing in relation to photographs can also be central to their effects. Paradoxically, perhaps, given that photographs are in some ways all about showing things, photographs can also show us what has gone, what is absent, what is no longer there. Photographs make people and things proximate and present, they bring them 'here' from somewhere else, sometimes in very intense ways, but they can also work as powerful reminders of things that are not, or may no longer be, 'here' at all.

Summary

- Photographs can evoke absence as well as presence. They can show what is not there, either because it is somewhere else or because it has, or may have, disappeared.

- The absences in photographs can have various effects and can be highly emotive.

- Some campaigns assume that the intense sense of presence evoked by the absences in photographs will help to inspire action in the viewer.

4   Family snaps: potent or bland?

You might have noticed that nearly all the photographs used in the examples in Sections 3.2 and 3.3 were family photos. By 'family photos', I mean photographs that show one or more members of a family, and which are taken for viewing by members of that same family. Sometimes that means that the photograph was snapped by a family member, often a mother or a father – taking photographs seems to be especially important in families with children. Yet many family photo collections also contain photographs taken by professional photographers, either in their studios, or at somewhere like a graduation ceremony, a school or football club, or a wedding.

Family photos are very common in many parts of the world. And they travel the world too. Photographs are often sent to family members living far away; indeed, family snaps are one way in which global connections are made and remade. Photography as a technology became popular in precisely the same period that larger and larger numbers of people from Europe began to migrate long distances. The second half of the nineteenth century saw huge flows of people from the countryside to the newly industrialising cities in Europe; a great number of individuals and families migrated further, across continents and oceans. Many, many of these migrants carried photographs to remind themselves of the families they had left behind and might never see again, as do many migrants today. Indeed, family photos are one way in which the complex senses of belonging explored in Chapter 4 are articulated.

However, while this kind of photograph is taken in order to be seen by family members, wherever they are, these photographs do seem to move out of the private family sphere for which they were intended and into more public sorts of spaces quite frequently. (This may be another example of the involvement of individuals in centrifugal mediated cultures, as Chapter 2 suggests.) The family photo in Figure 5.8, for example, travelled from an album in its family home in the USA, to the mailbox outside, to the front page of the UK newspaper *The Independent* in 2004 when the man it pictures, Nick Berg, was executed in Iraq. When a family photo moves from its intended audience of a family and out into wider circulation, it is useful to think a little more about exactly what kind of impact it might have by virtue of its status as a 'family snap'.

4.1 The intensity of family photos

Family photos can be very powerful objects. The raw impact of photographs is often heightened in the context of family viewing. People often feel strongly about family photos, because they feel strongly about family. Some deeply resent the way their parents' photograph albums are full of pictures of their older siblings but contain so few snaps of themselves. Some cherish family photos, spending hours making albums, ensuring that especially precious ones are kept in a fire-proof box. Some people can be moved to silence or tears by a photograph of a person or place, others to anger and bitterness.

Figure 5.8   Photo of Nick Berg attached to a mailbox in West Whiteland, Pennsylvania, USA, 2004

In just a few minutes soldiers will break down your door. They've already killed your father and raped your daughter. Now they are coming for you. What should you take? Quick. Think. Money? Your passport? A family photo? **You have two minutes left to decide...**

Figure 5.9   The cover of a leaflet appealing for funds, distributed by the Refugee Council in the UK, 2001. The leaflet suggests that family photos might be as important as money or a passport to someone fleeing for their life

The intensity of feeling with which family photos can be seen is a major reason for their mobilisation as part of protests and demonstrations. Indeed, Section 3.3 of this chapter has already discussed how the strong emotions provoked by family photos motivated the Asociación Madres de Plaza de Mayo to use them as part of their demands for justice.

4.2   The recognisability of family photos

Family photos can provoke strong emotions, but this is not the only reason for their impact. Also relevant is the fact that the photographs tend to be very recognisable sorts of images.

Family photos taken in homes and on holiday are very conventional in what they picture. The mundane realities of family life are invisible in most family photo collections; instead, photographs show families together, at leisure, and (apparently) happy. While the odd snap of a screaming baby might make its way into an album, on the whole family photos do not picture domestic labour or family fights or teenage tantrums. Nor do they usually have the often striking visual qualities of the photographs used by NGOs in their campaigns. Focusing might be erratic; people are pictured with their eyes shut or their feet cut off.

Photographs taken in professional photographers' studios for family use tend to be predictable too. Children's classes and football teams all over the world, for example, are lined up in the same conventional way for their group photographs to be taken. Many migrants send studio portraits that show them at their best to family elsewhere. Stuart Hall (1991) has written about the studio portraits that Afro-Caribbean immigrants to the UK in the 1950s had taken of themselves, for instance. These studio photographs showed their subjects in their best clothes or in the uniform of a profession. They were sent back to Jamaica or Trinidad 'as "evidence" that you had arrived safely, landed on your feet, were getting somewhere, surviving, doing all right' (Hall, 1991, p.156). Many migrants today continue to do the same thing, for much the same reasons; the outward signs of success might have changed, but a studio portrait still captures people looking happy and successful.

Their conventional qualities mean that family photos are recognisable kinds of photographs. Many people take them, all over the world. As a result, when the photographs travel out of the family and into other sorts of situations, their recognisability as family photos comes with them. A consequence of this is that people in quite different places are invited to identify with that recognisability. In some ways, the photograph on the placard carried by the person demanding justice for her murdered child is just like the one of my son on my mantelpiece. Even though I know I can never look at the placard photograph and feel the same as that mother does when she looks at it, I do imagine that I have looked at photographs of my own son with similar kinds of feelings (this might be a mistaken assumption, of course). As well as the absent presence that pictures of murdered people evoke, the use of family photos encourages a *sense of identification* with the people using those photographs. Those people are like us, in some way, with their ordinary photographs, so we should empathise with their plight.

Thus, the use of family photos in campaigns for justice works for several reasons. As Section 3 argued, it works in part because photographs substitute for real people. It can work too because of the haunting absence that emanates from photographs of the dead. Furthermore, it works because of the predictability of family photos.

The apparent similarity between the viewer and the campaigner in the way they share family photography might produce a direct sympathetic bond between them. That sympathy can then be a basis for action on the part of the viewer.

4.3   Family photos: quickly forgotten?

The recognisability of family photos, then, has certain useful effects for campaigns demanding justice. This recognisability also points to another quality of family photos, though: their banality. Family photos are not the most aesthetically exciting of visual images. They are in fact often blurred and wonky, and their content is conventional and fairly predictable. Moreover, when the family photo album is taken out, or the holiday snaps or photographs of the new baby or wedding photographs are passed around, there are often so many of them that some viewers get bored. And that is if they get passed around at all: many photographs get a quick flick through once they return from the developers or a brief slideshow when they are downloaded on to a computer, and that is it. They are rarely looked at again.

Although the recognisability and familiarity of family photos are important in evoking support for demands, it is also possible to see that family photos have rather ambivalent qualities. On the one hand, they can be extraordinarily powerful emotionally; they can render the loved ones of viewers present in ways that seem expressive beyond words. Something of the character of protests using family photos would be lost without an appreciation of the emotional intensity of the photographs. Nonetheless, presence is an unpredictable quality in photographs and so, on the other hand, many family snaps – probably most family snaps – sit unobtrusively, in a frame on a mantelpiece or stuck under a fridge magnet or in a box, gradually fading into invisibility.

This raises a pressing question, I think, in relation to the work of photographs in a globalised world. The fact that family snaps get ignored questions the assumption that photographs showing evidence of the need for change always help to prompt their viewers into some kind of action. You will recall that Sections 2 and 3 of this chapter suggested that the proximity, presences and absences of photographs were often assumed to provide evidence of the need for change, and that the sight of such evidence was a crucial part of achieving a response to a demand. Family photos, however, despite their often intense emotionality, often get ignored. They linger in cardboard boxes and albums and on computer hard drives or CDs, unseen; they become part of the taken-for-granted décor of a home, or lie forgotten in pockets of purses and wallets. The next section explores the challenge that this neglect poses to the use of photographs by campaigns and protest movements. Is the assumption that photographs prompt people into action – even the very basic action of looking at them – mistaken?

Summary

■   Family photos can be highly emotionally charged objects.

■   Family photos are also conventional images, and often it is their recognisability that is used to win support for demands by encouraging viewers to identify with the people using them.

■   Family photos can also be ignored because they are often not very good pictures, and because they frequently show the same things again and again.

5   Seen but not seen: denying photographic evidence

In his book, *States of Denial: Knowing About Atrocities and Suffering*, sociologist Stanley Cohen (2001) discusses the way that many demands to act to prevent or ameliorate suffering use photographs as evidence, in leaflets and newspaper adverts and websites, and so on. Cohen is particularly interested in exploring how many of these images are seen but are not acted upon. His term for this state of knowing and not-knowing – or, more accurately in the context of this discussion, seeing and not-doing – is 'denial'. Given the widespread circulation of images of suffering, damage, devastation and horror, why, he asks, with this kind of evidence of the need for action, are most such photographs ignored?

We might ask the same question of much less disturbing photographs. As the previous section noted, many photographs are not exactly ignored, but do not provoke much reaction either; family photos were the example there, but the same applies to many other kinds of photographs, including, very often, ones like those in Figures 5.1 and 5.2. Judging the impact of photographs like those in Figures 5.1 and 5.2 is actually very difficult. Appeals by charities and campaigning organisations that use such photographs usually elicit generous responses from the public. The UK charity Comic Relief, for example, which gets wide television coverage, has given over £210 million to projects in Africa and in the UK since it was set up in 1985; its biennial fundraising event, Red Nose Day, raised £59 million in 2003. However, some appeals meet with very little reaction. In his discussion of Amnesty International's appeals for new members during the 1990s, for instance, Cohen (2001) notes that to pay for the cost of a mailshot of leaflets asking people to join the organisation, about 2 per cent of recipients had to become members. He suggests that a strong response to such a recruitment mailshot will be a response rate of 4 or 5 per cent; a poor response, experienced by the US branch of Amnesty International in 1993, can be a mere 0.5 per cent. Even a good response means that a large number of photographs of tortured and abused prisoners are thrown in the bin: a large amount of denial. There is no reason to think that these figures are unusual. Photographs, as part of demands, are often seen but not acted upon.

The previous section suggested some reasons why family photos are ignored: they can be boring because their quality is often poor and their subject matter is repetitive. Yet those reasons cannot explain why Amnesty, Oxfam or FoE photographs often provoke no action on the part of those who see them, because their materials use a variety of striking photographs. Cohen's discussion of denial suggests some other reasons for not acting on the demands photographs carry. Many of these reasons depend not on the way photographs produce presence or use absence as a means of demanding that responsibility be taken, but on the way a photograph can be seen as part of the distances that also structure a globalised world.

5.1   There are too many images to pay attention to them all

One common response to understanding the denial of photographic evidence is to say that there are simply too many photographs around now to pay attention to them all. Chapter 2 of this book explored a range of ways in which the insistent demands of living in a mediated world are managed using various technologies. The claim is that in affluent countries in particular, photographs are so ubiquitous that, in order to prevent some sort of visual overload, people learn to see things without being deeply affected by them. We thus become hardened to any emotional appeal photographs may have, we ignore terrible evidence when it is shown to us. In a major study of the viewers of television news undertaken at Glasgow University in 1999, one woman was reported as feeling that 'every time you turn on the TV or pick up a paper there's another war starting or there is more poverty or destruction. It is all too much' (Philo, 2002, 177). Consequently, the page is turned or the channel switched, or indifference is cultivated.

No doubt there is some truth to this claim. However, it is also the case that images that make demands on their viewers to get involved in distant places are working in a broader context that shapes what is seen and how it is seen. As this chapter has already shown, photographs work their effects in relation to other forms of knowledge and understanding. We have already explored the importance of Catholicism, for example, to the use of photographs by the Asociación Madres de Plaza de Mayo in Buenos Aires, and the predictability of what gets pictured in family albums. Therefore, to understand the denial of photographic evidence, we need to consider the relevant broader context. In fact, we need to consider the history of how people from more affluent countries see the poorer parts of the world, and to think about how some of that history is still at work today.

5.2   A brief history of colonial ways of seeing

The second half of the nineteenth century was the period in which photography became a widespread technology. It was also the period of extensive expansion by various European states into other parts of the world. Explorers, adventurers, missionaries, soldiers, geographers and anthropologists, among many others, were involved in this colonial expansion. Many of these Europeans carried cameras with them. The Royal Geographical Society (RGS) in London, for instance, supported many expeditions and explorations to lands previously little known to Europeans, and many geographers took cameras to record their discoveries, as geographer James Ryan has shown (Ryan, 1997). The RGS had collected over 75,000 photographs by 1930 in an ambitious attempt to bring together images of as many parts of the world as possible. The audiences for these sorts of photographs were not only the members of the RGS, however. Once back in Europe, explorers would show their photographs as lantern slides at public meetings to large audiences fascinated by what they saw; some sold their photographs commercially as prints or in books; many photographs were also used in school textbooks. These photographs were used to bring distant places close to an audience.

Given the popularity of illustrated public lectures by famous explorers such as David Livingstone, it seems that these photographs were very interesting to a lot of people. In part, they were surely fascinating simply because this was a new technology, and its trick – of seeming to bring distant places very near, and accurately so – was a novel one. In addition, what it brought so near was also new. Genuine curiosity must surely have been part of the attraction of these photographs.

Nonetheless, like so many photographs, these were not working in a vacuum. They were made by photographers educated only in the traditions of Western art, and they often replicated its styles. Landscape photographs taken in China in the 1870s, for example, were influenced by European traditions of landscape painting; the people and animals in photographs of tiger hunts in India in the late nineteenth and early twentieth centuries were arranged according to the conventions of fashionable sporting paintings in contemporary London (Ryan, 1997). The photographers making these pictures were doing so through an already existing set of conventions about the subjects they were seeing, and that knowledge influenced how they chose to picture these places.

Defining Western

'Western' is a term used to describe a set of attitudes, values and beliefs that originated in Europe in the seventeenth, eighteenth and nineteenth centuries. In very broad terms, a faith in science and reason was central to Western attitudes, combined with a conviction that Europe was superior to other places and peoples. These attitudes were then carried to different parts of the world as Europeans conquered and colonised many other places. 'The West' therefore refers more to a set of cultural values than to a physical location. It is important to note that there were many different ways of being Western even in the West, and that many Western values and beliefs were changed by encounters with other cultures.

Moreover, the photographs were received by their audiences in the context of much discussion and debate about these new places and their inhabitants, which would presumably have made many of their viewers interpret the photographs in quite particular ways. Long before cameras were taken to these places, there had been writers – novelists, journalists, travellers – who had described them or artists who had depicted them. Thus, what these photographs showed was pictured and interpreted in the light of these existing interpretations. For instance, photographs of the jungle encountered during an expedition in 1859 in central Africa mirrored existing descriptions written well before the invention of photography (Ryan, 1997). The audiences for these pictures were looking at them through already existing knowledge about the places they were seeing.

Clearly these places looked different from places previously familiar to Europeans, but they were also seen in various ways as inferior. Europeans thought of themselves as civilised, and of other peoples and places as less so. During this period of history they tended to view other peoples as less cultured, more barbaric, less moral and less technologically advanced. Although some colonial explorers and administrators found aspects of other people and places admirable, many felt that their role was to bring Western civilisation to these places as an improvement over – sometimes even as a replacement for – what already existed.

In making sense of what was seen as this profound difference between the colonisers and the colonised, many observers in the later nineteenth century believed that there were distinct, biological differences between different races of people. Photography was frequently used to establish these differences by acting as a record of them, and photographs claiming to represent different 'types' of people living in different places were made more and more frequently. Anthropologists aiming to study such differences sometimes photographed individuals in front of a grid of squares in order to measure their body shapes accurately, and individuals were often measured as well as photographed. In the process, these individuals lost their individuality and came to stand for their racial group instead. Many of these photographs of 'types' were also made for more popular circulation; they were made into *cartes-de-visite* – photographs sold individually that many people collected in albums – and into postcards, as well as being published in popular books describing explorations and adventures.

These sorts of anthropological photographs are complex, and so are their effects. They were important contributors to wider processes of racialisation during colonial times, although it is certainly possible to see in many photographs evidence of colonised people resisting being photographed, being held in place, or looking sullen, or indeed apparently enjoying the experience. Some colonial photographs were utilised for other ends too, for instance in anti-slavery campaigns; Ryan (1997) discusses the photographs used at the turn of the twentieth century to demand an end to the brutal Belgian regime in the Congo. Furthermore, photographs can be reused in different circumstances. We have already seen various family photos leave the family and take to the streets; there are also examples of anthropological photographs being taken back into the family, as it were. Jo-Anne Driessens, for example, is an Australian Aboriginal woman who was adopted by a white Dutch-Australian family when she was two weeks old in 1970 (Driessens, 2003). In her adult life, Driessens has worked with various collections of photographs taken of Aboriginal men and women. In one archive she managed to identify a photograph of her great-grandfather, Charlie Chambers, taken by an anthropological expedition in the 1930s (see Figure 5.10). This photograph was very much in the tradition of the racialised 'type'. As Driessens says, 'it's very controlled and impersonal' (Driessens, 2003, p.20). She admits to having 'mixed feelings about the photo of my great-grandfather', but she also says that 'it plays a very important role in my life' (Driessens, 2003, p.22). As one curator of Aboriginal photographs says, 'Aboriginal people are grateful for the opportunity to find images of their relatives, regardless of who took the photographs or where these photographs are held today' because they enable Aboriginal people to document their own histories which were often lost through processes of forced adoption or family dispersal (Aird, 2003, p.39).

As Section 2 suggested, some photographs may have a rawness, which is not entirely determined by the conditions in which they were made. In some photographs, no matter how demeaning or degrading the conditions in which a person was placed to be photographed, something about that person overcomes those conditions. That person seems to stare straight back at us, across the years; they become a haunting presence.

Nevertheless, NGOs and others who work in less affluent parts of the world are very aware of the history of how certain parts of the world have been seen in the West. They are therefore very careful about how they photograph people for their campaigns. In 1991, the Save the Children Fund published influential guidelines on the use of photographs for fundraising which recognised the continuing legacy of colonial ways of seeing places, and asked instead for images that do not damage the dignity of the children and adults pictured. This demand is still being heeded over a decade later, as the Oxfam leaflet reproduced in Figure 5.1 shows; in the

Defining racialisation

'Racialisation' is the term used to describe the process of assigning humans to separate groups called 'races'. This process can work in a number of ways. Races are most often distinguished on the basis of physical features, for example skin colour or, as in the case of the anthropologists using photographs discussed here, a whole range of anatomical measurements. However, 'racialisation' emphasises the work that has to be done in order to differentiate racialised groups – work which includes, historically, the use of photographs – and use of the term therefore implies that there is little that is natural or inevitable about the specific groups that have been described as 'races'.

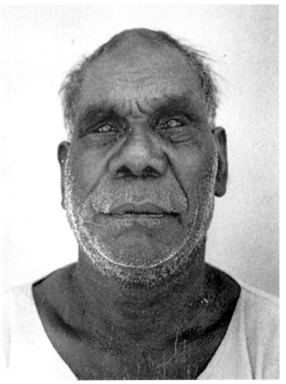

Figure 5.10 Charlie Chambers, photographed by anthropologist Norman Tindale in the 1930s in central Australia

leaflet the Kenyan young people are obviously poor but they are shown as active participants in their own betterment, and they are also given a voice in the accompanying text.

The people whose places and faces were seen so clearly for the first time in the second half of the nineteenth century were brought close to audiences in the colonising nations in ways that they had never been before; sometimes they also became movingly present, for example, to people concerned with colonial injustices. Yet those people were also rendered distant by the whole surrounding discussion of racialised differences. They were visible, close up, but according to prevalent notions of differences between different races of people, they were portrayed as very different from the audiences of these photographs. The proximity which such photographs suggested was thus supplemented with a powerful sense of distancing.

5.3   'It's just like that over there': media representations of developing countries

Although few colonies remain in existence today, there is much evidence that contemporary ways of picturing developing countries remain deeply influenced by colonial imagery. Of course, as Chapter 2 pointed out, any form of mass media always has to select what it represents; the full truth is too vast to show, quite apart from all the debates about what the truth of any particular matter might be. However, the way in which the people and places of less affluent countries are shown by the Western mass media is produced in more or less consistent ways. The mass media of today, by and large, still see developing countries as distant from, and inferior to, the affluent nations of the world. It is this distancing that can appear to absolve viewers in affluent countries from feeling as if they should have any involvement in what they see.

Studies of factual television coverage of developing countries suggest there are four aspects to this distancing process. First, audiences in the rich regions of the world actually see very little of other parts of the world, and this is another feature of the mediated globalisation discussed in Chapter 2. Between 1989 and 2004, the number of factual programmes about developing countries on terrestrial TV channels in the UK halved. While news coverage of developing countries reached very high levels in 2003, this was almost entirely due to coverage of the war in Iraq (3WE, 2004).

Second, the coverage that viewers in the developed world do see of the less affluent parts of the world is highly selective. A high proportion of the images of poorer countries shows war, conflict, terrorism, famine, disease and other disasters. Most of the rest of the coverage concerns sport or the visits of important Westerners to poorer countries. The Glasgow University study of BBC and ITN news in 1999 in the UK, for example, showed that a third of all their news coverage focused on disasters of various kinds (Philo, 2002). Moreover, people local to these events are often shown as victims of them; they are made to look as if they passively suffer the disaster.

The third point made by such studies is that the concentration on disasters and victims encourages the audiences of such images to think that places like Africa are fundamentally different from, and inferior to, 'us'. The Glasgow University study in 1999 also discussed the TV news with groups of TV viewers and found that there was widespread agreement with the claim that, as one group member put it, 'they [Africans] can't look after themselves' (Philo, 2002, p.180). Just as 100 years ago, it seems that in the UK today TV viewers are often encouraged to think that Africans are too backward to cope with their circumstances. Not only does it look as if disasters only happen 'over there', it also looks as if 'they' cannot cope with them. The distance between 'them' and 'us' is still seen, as it was in the colonial period, as a sign of the inferiority of less developed countries.

Finally, the visual images of developing countries that are seen most often in more affluent countries very rarely concentrate in detail on the *connections* between many of these disasters and affluent countries. The idea that 'they can't look after themselves' is legitimated in part because disasters are portrayed as being confined entirely to places or regions separate from the affluent world. Again, disasters in certain parts of the world are distanced from their viewers in affluent countries by a sense that 'they' have nothing to do with 'us'.

Photography is little different from television in this regard. Much contemporary photography distances its affluent viewers from poorer parts of the world by suggesting that those places are disaster-prone, that local people cannot manage those disasters adequately, and that they have nothing to do with the affluent nations of the world. Such places are made to feel far away because they have disasters (while affluent countries rarely do), because they cannot manage (and Western help is necessary), and because there are no apparent connections between people 'here', looking at photographs or watching TV, and 'them' far away over there. In the case of African countries, for example, it appears that:

> postcolonial Africa exists in the consciousness of the general public in the rich world – besides through its sexy music – mainly as a succession of unforgettable photographs of large-eyed victims, starting with figures in the famine lands of Biafra in the late 1960s to the survivors of the genocide of nearly a million Rwandan Tutsis in 1994 ... More recently, the photographs are of whole families of indigent villagers dying of AIDS.
>
> (Sontag, 2003, p.71)

This distancing means that images of disaster are very often met by a sense of hopelessness and despair in their affluent viewers. They see what the photographs show but may have a sense that they have seen this before and they'll be seeing it again, and in any case it is nothing to do with them and it will not change anyway. They may register pictures of famine or flood – they may even be moved by them – but they do not always respond by taking some kind of responsibility for what they see, by making a donation to a relief effort. Even if the affluent viewer donates money when something really terrible happens, he or she often does so with the sense that this is just one more disaster and that nothing can really be done to stop disasters happening again and again. Thus, it is not simply the sheer number of images that makes a lot of people ignore so many of them. In the case of some photographs, the ways in which their audience makes sense of them draw on longstanding ideas about the people and places they show, and those ideas can also make viewers feel helpless and distant in front of such photographs. They are seen but not acted upon: their demand is denied.

Activity 5.5

This section has discussed why many organisations working to end poverty in less developed countries refuse to use photographs showing people as passive victims of disasters far away, but emphasise instead their dignity and their own voices and actions. However, in his discussion of the denial of photographic evidence, Stanley Cohen provocatively questions this position. He says:

> Objections do matter if the starving child and the corpses floating down the river come to represent 'Africa'. But surely these images cannot be repressed. Needless misery, sickness and violence, millions of human beings losing their lives...: this is the problem, the whole problem and nothing but the problem.
>
> (Cohen, 2001, p.184)

Cohen also points out that, although there is rather little evidence about what kinds of demands get most donations, the few studies that have explored this question suggest that, in fact, it is the appeals that use photographs of people as victims, in desperate situations, that receive most money.

Given these two positions, which do you agree with? Why?

Summary

- ■ Many photographs that are part of demands to act are seen but no action follows. The demands they carry provoke no action.

- ■ The denial of photographic evidence happens in part because there are so many images demanding attention that responding to all of them is impossible.

- ■ Photographs are always interpreted by their viewers in relation to other kinds of knowledge and understanding. To understand the denial of photographs used in support of demands for global change, both the history of colonialism and the contemporary practices of the mass media must be considered.

- ■ Much denial of photographic evidence takes the form of distancing viewers from what they see. People and places in need are seen as distant, different and disconnected from viewers in affluent countries. Although those viewers may be moved by what they see they take no action, because they think that they are not responsible or that their action will have no effect.

6   Conclusion

We are now in a better position to understand how photographs of people or places far away and in need of help can move their viewers to respond to a demand. Responses to demanding photographs depend in large part on how presences and absences weave through photographs.

Photographs carry what they show over long distances, and so they are often used as part of demands to get involved in, or to feel responsible for, areas of the world that are thousands of kilometres away from the viewers of the photographs. Many campaigning organisations use photographs as part of their demands because they bring places close to those who have the resources to do something about what the photographs show. Sometimes, for some people, a photograph can also make a place or some people immediately present. Such proximity and presence are understood to offer an opportunity for making some kind of connection between viewers and what they see. Sympathy and engagement might be provoked, even though there are no other apparent connections between the person looking at the photograph and what he or she is looking at. This kind of feeling of involvement with people photographed can be one way in which campaigning photographs have an effect.

Photographs can work with absence too, as we have seen. They can substitute for actual people, living or dead. Photographs often work as a reminder not of what is there, but of what is missing. Such absences can also work to demand the involvement of a viewer by evoking actual or potential loss and grief or horror. Indeed, both the absences and presences that photographs can carry are often used as part of demands because they can be emotionally powerful.

However, the impact of a photograph's rawness is affected by broader ways of making sense of the world. The legacy of colonial ways of seeing is still evident in the way the mass media in the affluent world produce images of the less affluent world. Poorer countries are shown as different, inferior and separate from affluent nations. 'They' are distanced from 'us' and, because of this distancing, more often than not wealthy viewers can remain untouched by the demands made of them to act to change the world. They can be said to be in a state of denial about what photographs supporting demands for change show them.

Yet this distancing effect can be punctured, and what is kept far away can rush back to entangle viewers in what they see. Sometimes this is a matter of reworking the geographies of an image so that distance turns into proximity and separation into responsibility. The Glasgow University study of BBC and ITN news in 1999, for example, made some quite practical suggestions about how to challenge affluent viewers' passivity and hopelessness when confronted with images of war, disaster and famine. In particular, it suggested that if news reports made clearer the connections between the disaster photographed and the people looking at it, then audiences would become very concerned and would want to help. The example given in that study was the civil war in Angola. Initially, the photographs of that war produced horror but also despair and distancing. Once the news audiences were told that the war was funded mostly by the sale of diamonds in Europe and oil in the USA – and they were asked who was wearing a diamond and who drove a car – then they were immediately more engaged by the humanitarian disaster that accompanied the war. In this example, the viewers of a photograph were moved to feel responsible for what they were seeing because they were connected with it: a sense of responsibility akin to that described by Iris Marion Young (2003) and discussed in Chapter 1.

At other times, a photograph just grabs a viewer and will not let go, and it is very hard to say exactly why or how. Although unpredictable, the emotional power of photographs can be very intense, and this is one reason why campaigning organisations will no doubt continue to use photographs to try and involve people in changing the globalised world.

References

3WE (2004) *The World on the Box*, London, 3WE.

Aird, M. (2003) 'Growing up with Aborigines' in Pinney, C. and Peterson, N. (eds) *Photography's Other Histories*, Durham NC and London, Duke University Press.

Cohen, S. (2001) *States of Denial: Knowing About Atrocities and Suffering*, Cambridge, Polity Press.

Control Arms (2004) http://www.controlarms.org (accessed 19 November 2004).

Driessens, J.-A. (2003) 'Relating to photographs' in Pinney, C. and Peterson, N. (eds) *Photography's Other Histories*, Durham NC and London, Duke University Press.

Edwards, E. (2001) *Raw Histories: Photographs, Anthropology and Museums*, Oxford, Berg.

Hall, S. (1991) 'Reconstruction work: images of post-war black settlement' in Spence, J. and Holland, P. (eds) *Family Snaps*, London, Virago.

Mellibovsky, M. (1997) *Circle of Love over Death: Testimonies of the Mothers of the Plaza de Mayo* (trans. M. Proser and M. Proser), Willimantic, Conn, Curbstone.

Monk, L. (1989) *Photographs that Changed the World: The Camera as Witness, The Photograph as Evidence*, New York, Doubleday.

Philo, G. (2002) 'Television news and audience understanding of war, conflict and disaster', *Journalism Studies*, vol.3 no.2, pp.173–86.

Ryan, J. (1997) *Picturing Empire: Photography and the Visualization of the British Empire*, London, Reaktion Books.

Sontag, S. (2003) *Regarding the Pain of Others*, New York, Farrar, Strauss & Giroux.

Young, I.M. (2003) 'From guilt to solidarity: sweatshops and political responsibility', *Dissent*, spring, pp.39–44.

Drilling boom...

"The Standard Oil Company, controlled by the
Rockefellers, with 275 international affiliated companies is the world's largest trust (turnover in
1964: 12 billion dollars). Because of their political
connections and military contacts the Rockefellers procure huge arms contracts for these subsidiary firms; they then sell a part of the shares with
fantastic profits. For example, the shares of the
Itek Corporation founded by them rose within one
year from 2 to 346 dollars!"
(Victor Perlo and Carl Marzani, Dollars and
Disarmament, New York 1960)

Josep Renau, 'The Fascinating Oil King', 1957

Making photographs that make demands: a photo-essay from the Oil Lives images project

Photographs can solicit powerful emotional responses, and are often used to draw people's attention to issues, or to raise awareness of demands. This photo-essay takes a look at how one set of photographs, used as part of a particular demand, was created. It looks at the process of producing images by exploring a series of photographs made with the intention of affecting the way a globalised industry is seen and understood. The industry in question is the oil industry based in Aberdeen, on Scotland's north-east coast, an industry with global ramifications. The photo-essay reproduces several pictures researched and made by Owen Logan in collaboration with the history project, Lives in the Oil Industry, based at the University of Aberdeen.

The oil industry is perhaps the archetypal globalised industry. Dominated by a few multi-national companies, it is highly centralised at the level of corporate power but, like the corporations explored in the first chapter of this book, investment and trade in the oil industry are also highly mobile. The long reach of the global oil economy is a consequence of the distance between the location of significant oil reserves and the location of the major markets for oil. The reserves of oil currently expected to last more than fifty years are all in the Middle East; most of the nations needing large amounts of oil to fuel their economies are not. The global market in oil straddles this distance.

Many countries with either small or no oil supplies of their own – notably the USA, China and several countries in Europe – need steady and guaranteed supplies of imported oil. Since so much of the stability of these economies and countries depends on this fuel, they also have political reasons for trying to ensure the reliability of those supplies. The most obvious demonstration of this, many would contend, was the invasion of Iraq in 2002 by a coalition of countries led by the USA. Some commentators at the time argued that this war was an attempt to control the price, conditions and distribution of the most important economic resource on which the USA depended: oil.

The significance of the oil industry in Scotland is due in some measure to the way it is part of the political and economic relations that span the globe. This makes a place like Aberdeen very dependent on distant events. In terms of making photographs that draw attention to this dependency, it is the global extent of the oil industry that poses challenges for a photographer. How can the full dimensions of the oil industry be adequately represented in a photograph? Like many other global phenomena, the oil economy cannot be made visible to a single camera's eye. Moreover, as this chapter pointed out, what is shown in the mass media is patterned in particular ways. The example there was the representation of poorer countries, but images of global industries are also mediated (to use Chapter 2's term). The life of an oil platform is mostly invisible to the general public buying petrol at their local garage, and the complex role of the oil industry in so much of global economics and politics is rarely shown. As the news photographer Susan Meiselas has remarked, 'the larger sense of the image has been defined elsewhere, in Washington, in the press, by the powers that be, and I can't, we can't, somehow reframe it' (cited in Ritchin, 1989, p.438).

These two problems – the challenge of visually portraying an activity of global extent, and a desire to address relationships and activities which are largely invisible in the global media – have encouraged several photographers to use the technique of montage in order to portray the oil industry. Montage combines two or more images into one; cutting and splicing in this way can bring things that are usually kept apart into close and often startling proximity. The image at the start of this essay is an example of a montage, and so too is the 'War Scrapbook' by Logan. In this way, montage can make the relationships among distant places and people visible in new ways. Logan's aim in using montage in his Oil Lives photographs is precisely to try and reframe how we see the global oil industry.

Activity

Oil Lives consists of a series of photographs of an individual and some written text based on interviews with them. Two are reproduced here with Logan's 'War Scrapbook' in between them. Take some time to look at the photographs and to read the words accompanying them. Try to work out first what parts of the photographs have been brought together from different originals. What do Owen Logan's decisions about how to picture the industry and some of its workers suggest about how he sees the industry?

Bob Ballantyne

electrician – Piper survivor – community education worker

The late Bob Ballantyne survived the 'Piper Alpha' disaster that took the lives of 167 oil workers in 1988. Always a strong trade unionist, Bob never liked the nickname 'Tigers' that is used for off-shore workers. Union supporters often refused the nickname and would call themselves 'pussycats'. Bob was critical of the 'macho' culture within oil companies and spoke of the way it reflects powerful anti-social values at work in the industry.

Unlike the Norwegian oil industry, the development of the UK's North Sea sector was given over to private enterprise. Bob compared the UK and Norwegian approaches to the North Sea industry as being 'the difference between exploitation and exploration'. Bob became a prominent activist against the Occidental oil company following the explosion on Piper Alpha and testified at the Cullen enquiry, which found the company to be 'negligent'. However, the company was never prosecuted and many of the people affected by the Piper disaster still feel that real justice was never done.

Bob went on to work in community education. He died shortly after these photographs were completed.

'The inverted coal
mine' Bob Ballantyne,
UK sector oil
production platform

'Tigers' Bob Ballantyne in the zoo

Owen Logan, 'War Scrapbook', 2004

Flora Macdonald

temp – ground stewardess – office manager – accountant

Flora Macdonald has worked in several jobs that reflected the breadth of the oil economy. Early on in her career she was a ground stewardess at Aberdeen and Stansted airports. In Aberdeen, she saw the increased traffic and new business opportunities accompanying the oil industry.

In a diverse career, Flora enjoyed participating in an exciting new entrepreneurial arena, which appealed to an 'impetuous' side of her character. As a young temp she once threw a typewriter off a desk and walked out of her job. However, Flora's experience of the ups and downs in support companies also points to an equally impetuous process of economic development. She speaks candidly about opportunism in politics, the economy, and in business.

As attention centred on the potential of oil, other industries became disinvested of their importance. Flora now works as an accountant for a fishing company in Aberdeen at a time when the survival of this traditional industry is increasingly precarious.

Flora Macdonald at
Aberdeen airport, circa
1970

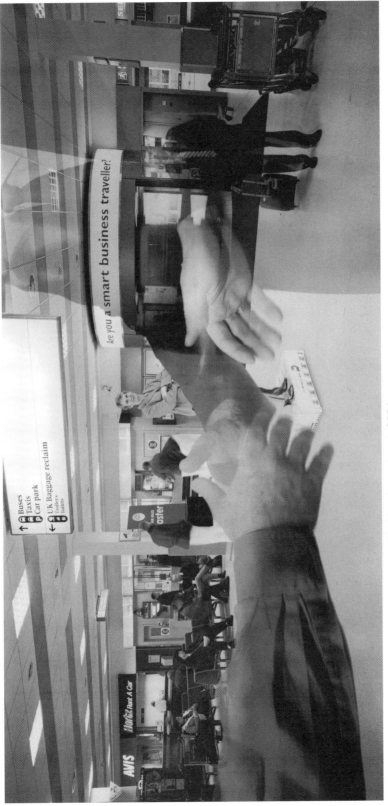

'Where has all the money gone?' Flora Macdonald, Aberdeen airport, 2004

Responding to the way in which the content and style of photographs are so often limited by the production and distribution processes of the mass media, Owen Logan uses digital technology to produce a new way of seeing the oil industry. As you can see, many of his pictures are made by digitally splicing separate photographs together. The effects of these montages are in part about the relationship between what is put together. For example, to me Logan's use of a photograph of an oil platform bathed in light implies a rather glamorous industry, bravely enabling the modern world to function. Yet the colliery winding gear that Owen has inserted into the image as the platform's shadow suggests that the reality might be rather different. What these photographs show and how they show it is intended to challenge conventional ways of picturing the oil industry, making it visible and displaying something of its true, if complex, nature.

These composite images also draw on Owen Logan's close collaboration with people who have contributed their life stories to the Oil Lives history project in Aberdeen. Effectively, the pictures are intended as a visual interpretation of key aspects of the informants' life stories, and the captions of these composite images are quotations from interviews with them. (Here we can see the importance of written text for shaping our understanding of the photographs.) Visualising people's individual stories in this way helps to bring a wider range of experiences of the oil industry into the public sphere. Even if, according to Logan, many people are in denial (to use Cohen's term (2001)) about the critical questions raised by the impacts of the global oil industry and by the dependency on oil which affects producers and consumers alike, these voices from Aberdeen can help to support others who want to confront the full scope of the global oil economy.

Who are those people in denial? One group of people who have misunderstood or misrepresented the role of oil, Logan argues, is the political elite of Scotland. Hence, when offered a commission to produce photographic work for the Scottish Parliament building in 2004, Logan took the opportunity to develop several photographs, and accompanying text, similar to that reproduced here. The demand he was making in that project, as in this photo-essay, was that the true nature of the global oil industry be recognised.

References

Cohen, S. (2001) *States of Denial: Knowing About Atrocities and Suffering*, Cambridge, Polity Press.

Ritchin, F. (1989) 'What is Magnum?' in Manchester, W. (ed.) *In Our Time*, London, Andre Deutsch.

Chapter 6

A haunted world: the unsettling demands of a globalised past

Steve Pile

Contents

1 Introduction: the return of the past, the demands of the past

In Chapter 5, we saw how photographs have been used by UK campaigning organisations, such as Oxfam and Friends of the Earth (FoE), to solicit people's responses to world disasters, such as famines and climate change. Through such images, it was argued, campaigning organisations seek to make us witness events at a distance, even though people might have no direct connection to the events. The intention is to make people respond to those events and to feel that they could do something about them. Images, such as these, are consciously and self-reflectively deployed. They make visible demands upon people to respond. However, there is something else about such photographs. They are often haunting: they catch people emotionally, and they don't let go.

In this chapter, I will explore the idea that, as a consequence of living in a globalised world, we live in a haunted one too. For example, as the campaigns of organisations such as Oxfam and FoE have often shown, the world is haunted by the histories of human destructive power (whether by accident or design) and, moreover, by the earth's own devastating abilities. Let me briefly list some noteworthy, yet disturbing, events that continue to be remembered long after they have happened:

- environmental disasters, such as famines (for example, in Ireland, 1845–50 and Ethiopia, 1984–85), volcanic eruptions (such as Krakatoa, 27 August 1883), earthquakes (such as those in San Francisco, 18 April 1906 and Kobe, 24 January 1995), floods (including Bangladesh, July 1974), tsunamis (Indian Ocean, 26 December 2004) and so on;
- industrial disasters, such as those at Three Mile Island (28 March 1979), Bhopal (3 December 1984) and Chernobyl (26 April 1986);
- maritime tragedies, such as the discovery of the Mary Celeste (4 December 1872), and the sinking of the Titanic (15 April 1912) and Exxon Valdez (24 March 1989);
- political assassinations, such as those of Archduke Franz Ferdinand (28 June 1914), Mahatma Gandhi (30 January 1948), President John F. Kennedy (22 November 1963) and Martin Luther King (4 April 1968);
- politically motivated attacks, such as the release of sarin gas on Tokyo's underground (20 March 1995), the destruction of New York's World Trade Center (11 September 2001) and the Beslan school hostage-taking (1–3 September 2004);

- major battles or the killing of civilians in wartime, such as the Battle of the Somme (1 July to 18 November 1916), the Blitz on London (7 September 1940 to 10 May 1941), the attack on Pearl Harbor (7 December 1941), and the nuclear bombings of Hiroshima (6 August 1945) and Nagasaki (9 August 1945);
- genocide, including the Jewish Holocaust in Europe under Nazi control (1938–45), of Armenians in Turkey (1915–18), of political opponents by the Khmer Rouge in Cambodia (1975–79), and in Rwanda (April–July 1994) and Kosovo (January 1998 to April 1999).

You may or may not have heard of these events. And, you may wish to change this list in a variety of ways, perhaps to include events you feel have been significant. In doing so, you might reflect that while some events are remembered, others fade in the memory, and many are simply forgotten. My point is not simply that there is an ever-lengthening list of disasters, nor even that these disasters are in some sense 'global'. Instead, I am suggesting that these events, though past, continue to influence events today: we still live with these events – not all the time, and not everywhere, but they nonetheless sometimes cast shadows over the globalised world. They do not do so solely through acts of remembrance, or through being evoked in political demands, or through the writing of history, whether enacted by individuals, campaign groups or by states. Events such as these also touch people emotionally. Though separated by many years and by thousands of kilometres, the events can sometimes feel up close and personal: that is, emotionally proximate and present.

There is something else: these events refuse to go away. For whatever reason, these events seem to keep coming back, like ghosts, to haunt the world. For example, the aftermath of the nuclear bombs on Hiroshima and Nagasaki presented a terrifying glimpse of what nuclear war might have in store for the world, while the volcanic eruption of Krakatoa afforded scientists a model of what might happen once nuclear bombs had thrown millions of tons of dust into the atmosphere, and the nuclear disasters at Three Mile Island and Chernobyl reminded everyone that it did not require a war to cause a nuclear holocaust.

Living in a haunted world does not just mean that we are touched by dreadful events, however far away. These events remind us that there is something unfinished about the past. Even though it can sometimes feel as if we live in a world haunted more by the threat of global climate change or environmental disasters than by nuclear wars or accidents, the haunting images of Hiroshima and Nagasaki have not gone away. They occasionally make their presence felt, reminding people that the so-called nuclear age has not ended. In many ways, the bombs that fell on Japan over half a century ago remain unfinished business. The peril of nuclear warfare is an unresolved problem that continues to haunt the world.

This chapter is about a haunted world, then, in two interrelated senses:

1   Haunting indicates that something from the past has caught hold of the present. The past can return in a variety of ways, such as in deliberate acts of remembrance (whether collective or personal), or it can make its presence felt in unexpected, and sometimes alarming, forms. In particular, the idea of haunting suggests that the past has returned because it has not been properly buried. Furthermore, by returning, the past can make demands upon people to resolve its unfinished business.

2   In haunting, the past returns in ways that are highly charged emotionally, and sometimes also politically. Here, we are less concerned with senses of the past that invoke fond memories or detached remembrance, than with those that involve a feeling that something disturbing is refusing to go away. Thus, haunting foregrounds the troubling emotional qualities associated with the return of the past, such as feelings of sorrow, grief or guilt, of torment, terror or horror.

In a globalised world, the past can become unexpectedly proximate and present, even if it happened to someone else, long ago, in another place. We can even talk of a 'globalised past':

1   As a way of acknowledging the historical legacies of previous globalisations, such as those of the British Empire.

2   As a way to talk about how the histories of specific places or peoples become entangled in the formation of the contemporary globalised world. For example, as cultural forms, political struggles or feelings of community reach out from one place to another (see Chapter 4).

The globalised past, then, is part and parcel of the globalised world, and these globalised historical legacies often generate demands upon people. For example, by asking people – sometimes across large distances, over long periods of time – to take responsibility for events in the distant past, or perhaps to maintain traditional customs of a faraway place, or to join long-standing political struggles (whether violent or not), to give aid to long-suffering people far away, or simply to honour the dead.

In previous chapters, we have seen how people – as individuals, campaigning groups and nation states – work to create different kinds of proximities and distances in a globalised world, for example by pushing the world away or, alternatively, by making events far away seem much closer to home. We can think of the globalised past as being handled in a similar way. On the one hand, the past can be placed at a physical distance (far away), or it can be kept proximate (close by). On the other hand, the globalised past can be made to feel either present (here) or absent (not here). It is important, then, to think both about how people make the past either proximate or distant, and also about the effects that the presence of a globalised past can have. In this chapter we also want to explore how pasts that are seemingly absent can suddenly make their presence felt and demand people's attention, whether they like it or not.

To begin exploring how people have dealt with the unsettling demands of a globalised past, I will look first at statues, monuments and memorials. Ironically, the presence of statues, monuments and memorials often implies that the past demands very little of people because the monuments are usually ignored, except by pigeons and other birds. Yet, sometimes, the past can suddenly become a contentious issue and monuments can become an awkward presence in the landscape, demanding that the past is taken into account. To exemplify this, in Section 2, I will examine the experience of Budapest after the fall of the communist regime in 1989: what became of the monuments to Lenin? Section 3 then explores how the traumas of the history of slavery in the American South resonate in deeply emotional ways, bringing these past injustices into the present. Section 4 considers how seemingly distant pasts can return unexpectedly to shape events here and now. The globalised past – distant in both time and space – is often involved in shaping very present demands.

Chapter aims

- ◆ To explore the ways that the globalised past returns to haunt the present.

- ◆ To examine how demands are made by histories that refuse to go away.

- ◆ To consider people's responses to the demands of a globalised past, especially strategies that involve making the past either proximate or distant, either present or absent.

- ◆ To show that the past remains a vital – yet sometimes disturbing – presence in the world, emotionally and politically, even when it seems entirely absent.

- ◆ To consider the emotional and political aspects of haunting.

2   Memorial sites and the unsettling legacies of the past

In this section, I will look at the way the past is ordinarily present in the world: not stunningly, not remarkably, not spookily, but prosaically. Before I go on, however, a quick word of caution. Although statues, monuments and memorials (of various kinds) can be found in many cultures, in many historical periods and in many places, this does not indicate that they all mean the same thing, or have the same kind of significance or importance. Although I will be talking broadly about the demands – sometimes silent, sometimes contested, sometimes ignored, sometimes surprisingly present – that these material objects make upon the world, we should not assume that this is everywhere the case, nor that this has always been (or always will be) the case. With that in mind, let's see just how present the past is in the form of public sculptures, such as statues, monuments and memorials.

2.1   So, the past hangs around, does it?

A walk around the central part of almost any city will quickly reveal the presence of many commemorative public sculptures. Thus, for example, in Liverpool in the UK there are statues celebrating royalty, aristocrats and other famous people; memorials to the dead of various wars; commemorative plaques showing where famous people once lived; and shops selling Beatles memorabilia. At Anfield football ground, an eternal flame burns in memory of the 96 Liverpool fans who died in the 1989 Hillsborough Stadium disaster, and there is the statue of Bill Shankly. On the banks of the River Mersey, there are many memorials to those who were lost at sea, mainly during the Second World War (see Figure 6.1).

Activity 6.1

Take a little time to think about commemorative statues, monuments or memorials in your local area (or in an area with which you are familiar). Ask yourself these questions:

1   What people or events do the statues, monuments or memorials commemorate?

2   Are you aware of any controversies surrounding the statues, monuments or memorials?

3   Are any of these statues, monuments or memorials particularly important to you? (There could be many different kinds of answer to this question, but don't worry if your answer is 'no'.)

Figure 6.1   A selection of statues, monuments and memorials in Liverpool:
Queen Victoria and the Duke of Wellington; a statue celebrating Liverpool Football
Club's legendary manager Bill Shankly; a Beatles memorabilia shop in Mathew
Street; a memorial plaque honouring the merchant marine and Royal Navy sailors
who died during the Second World War; the Hillsborough memorial at Anfield
football ground; and the memorial to those who died while in the King's Liverpool
Regiment

In many ways, statues, monuments and memorials can seem like a durable, immutable presence in the landscape. They may have been built in the past and commemorate people or events in the past, but they seem as if they will survive long into the future, unchanged. Sometimes they are ill-treated, sometimes they are neglected, sometimes they seem just to be convenient perches for pigeons, but less often are they the subject of intense political debate. Arguably, the very durability and immutability of statues, monuments and memorials may be one of the reasons they do not spark fierce political debate. Through their apparent permanence, they let you know their place – and consequently your place – in history. However, in Hungary from 1989 onwards, the statues, monuments and memorials of the past suddenly became a very big issue, for 'history' was subject to revision. Through its monuments and symbols, the communist era continued to haunt the post-communist Hungarian state – maintaining a disturbing presence in the political debates of the day.

2.2   Hungary and the fall of communism: the contested significance of communist-era symbols

Communism in Hungary effectively ended in Spring 1990 with the election of a new national government. Unlike in Berlin and elsewhere in formerly communist East European states, there had been only a little destruction of communist-era symbols in Hungary. In Budapest, there were far fewer headless and toppled Lenins than there had been in Berlin (see Figure 6.2). Nevertheless, communist-era public sculptures came to be an increasingly difficult political problem for the new regime.

Figure 6.2   A statue of Lenin being dismantled, Berlin, November 1991

For sociologist Maya Nadkarni (2003), the existence of statues, monuments and memorials in post-communist Hungary had the effect of casting up Hungary's communist past for scrutiny and debate. In communist-era Hungary, Nadkarni argues, Soviet-style monuments had been built to reinforce the idea that communism was durable and immutable; they embodied the bid for eternity of communism itself. Yet now these same monuments had suddenly become dislocated: they were no longer the permanent markers of a communist state, but awkward remnants of a communist past haunting a yet-to-be-born Western-style democratic state. Their everyday presence in Budapest, and the rest of Hungary, posed a problem: how should this lingering past be dealt with, and what did its continued presence mean? Nadkarni puts it this way:

> After Hungary's failed 1956 revolution against Soviet rule [...] life was characterised by a sense of inertia and eventlessness, of being left out of international trends and outside 'the global course of history'. In the words of historians András Gerő and Iván Pető, 'time seemed to have stopped: socialism was being built, but the construction process appeared to be uncompletable, never ending' [1999, p.7]. By the end of the era, even the promise of a beautiful future had fallen silent, to be replaced by the everyday concerns of 'existing socialism'. Public monuments, rituals, and political symbols continued to buttress the faltering regime's ideological self-justification, however, until almost the last days of its rule. While invisible in their iconicity, the monuments' function as indexes of the unchangingness of everyday life allowed them to take on prosaic (and often ironic) meanings in the urban environment they helped to organise.
>
> (Nadkarni, 2003, pp.195–6)

Nadkarni is alluding to several important factors underlying the haunting significance of communist-era symbols in post-communist Hungary. To begin with, there is the suggestion that Hungary was removed from global history in the wake of the Soviet suppression of the 1956 Hungarian revolution. As a result, Nadkarni argues, Hungarians withdrew from public and political life. Even so, they understood that communist monuments, rituals and symbolism were attempts to create, for the regime, the appearance of permanence and progress. However, instead of the monuments taking on the glorious iconic status that the communist regime hoped for, ordinary Hungarians ascribed to them quite different meanings.

An example is the statue of Captain Ostapenkó. For many in Budapest, the statue represented the beginning of holiday, as it stood at the main exit out of the city leading to a popular vacation destination, Lake Balaton. The popular significance of the statue stood in contrast to the reason for erecting the monument. Captain Ostapenkó, a Soviet military envoy, had been killed crossing between Russian and Hungarian–German lines in 1944, even though he was carrying a white flag of truce. The Russians alleged that the Germans had shot him in the back, although he seems in fact to have been caught in an exchange of artillery fire between both sides. Because of Ostapenkó's association with Russian oppression, during the 1956 Hungarian uprising the statue was badly mutilated and later had to be partially remodelled. Nonetheless, Ostapenkó fared better during the uprising than a statue of Stalin in one of Budapest's main squares; this was cut off at the feet and dragged ignominiously through the streets. However, the situation was different in 1989. By then, how best to deal with these monumental hangers-on from the past had become a question with more than one answer in Hungary.

2.3   What is to be done about communist symbols in post-communist Hungary?

As Nadkarni (2003) suggests, by the 1980s communist symbols had become an ordinary part of the Budapest cityscape, with meanings quite different from those that led to their construction. The question in 1989, though, was political: in a newly forming democratic state, how could communist symbols be dealt with *democratically*? Communist monuments could not be treated in the same way as communists had treated statues and monuments of previous eras, by undemocratic diktat. Thus, the statues, monuments and memorials of the communist era were to be treated almost as if they were the dead bodies – the fallen – of a previous era, now gone forever, but nevertheless to be regarded with dignity, justly.

Figure 6.3   A statue of Lenin in Felvonulasi Ter (Parade Ground Square), Budapest in 1985. The statue was erected in 1965 but was intended to echo the statue of Stalin that had been toppled in 1956

Activity 6.2

Imagine yourself in the immediate aftermath of communism in a former East European state (such as Hungary).

1   What would you have liked to see happen to communist-era public statuary? Write down the reasons for your answer.

2   Do you think your solution to dealing with communist symbols treats them democratically, with justice, and with dignity? Why or why not? And do you care?

The literary historian László Szörényi argued that a Statue Park should be created for communist-era public sculptures (see Baros, 2002). The park would be home, as he envisaged it, to all the Lenin statues: a Statue Park located in a former forced-labour camp. However, the proposal was not met with enthusiasm. Was it fair to treat Lenin in the same way as a political prisoner? Was this the right way to remember Lenin? Indeed, was this the right way to forget the past, by placing it in a prison camp? For many, it did not seem very democratic, or very liberal.

A new site for the public sculptures was subsequently identified: a bare piece of land in the Tétény area, about half an hour's drive from Budapest. Following practices in many Western municipalities, tenders were invited for plans to build the park, including both architectural layouts and business forecasts. The competition was eventually won by an architect called Ákos Eleőd. His tender probably succeeded because he understood that dealing with communist public sculptures was not as easy as creating either a capitalist-style theme park for them or a communist-style prison camp. Instead, the park would act more like a zoo: a place where the best specimens could be cared for, safely quarantined from post-communist public life, but easy enough to visit. The statues were to be kept at a distance, yet not pushed so far away that they could not be visited occasionally. They were to become absent from the city, but not so absent that they were effectively purged from history.

Figure 6.4   A statue of Lenin in Budapest's Statue Park, 2004

For Ákos Eleőd, Statue Park was a way to memorialise the communist past, so that Hungarians need no longer be silent about the suffering they underwent. On the other hand, it was also about the future of a new liberal democratic state, requiring that the communist era be forgotten as new political traditions were created. Yet, among Hungarians, the meanings associated with the statues were contested, variable and indeterminate. Recognising this, at a meeting on 5 December 1991, the General Assembly (Hungary's new parliament) opted to vote on which statues were to be included in the Statue Park, and on which were not. In their voting, the democratically elected representatives tried to take great care to recognise which statues irritated people, and which did not, as well as considering the historical and artistic value of the sculptures. Ultimately, this was meant to be an exercise in democracy itself – a refusal to treat the statues in the same way that the communist regime had treated people. The ghosts of the communist past were being demonstrably, democratically, laid to rest or, for some at least, openly buried in a Statue Park.

For Nadkarni (2003), however, the destruction or relocation of the statues did not just expel the communist past from the everyday landscape; it also repressed many of the personal and collective sentiments associated with the monuments. It smacked of a Soviet-style political cleansing of the physical environment. Nadkarni argues that, by ignoring calls for some statues to be left where they were, the General Assembly had used the statues' removal to create the illusion

Figure 6.5   These two statues used to be situated on one of Budapest's major highways. They were popular landmarks, but they are now preserved in Statue Park. Waving a white flag, Captain Ostapenkó is on the left; in the foreground, the flowers bloom into a red star

that there was a democratically achieved consensus about how to treat them. Nonetheless, there was no such consensus. For example, most argued that the statue of Captain Ostapenkó should be left where it was, at the main exit out of Budapest. Even so, it was one of only forty-one sculptures eventually relocated to Statue Park (see Figure 6.5). By claiming consensus when there was none, the General Assembly's actions bore disturbing similarities to the one-party system in communist Hungary; the Assembly erased dissent. Although the statues have lost the seriousness and significance they were meant to have under the communist regime, the remaining monuments bear witness to a past that has not really gone away. Despite being displaced, the statues continue to haunt Budapest, and Hungarian politics more generally.

You may feel this judgement on the General Assembly to be harsh, especially since it did openly debate the issues. However, the fate of these monuments continues to be politically contested. There was no consensus in the early days of the democratic regime, nor is there one now. The attempt to make the past distant – politically and spatially – by removing the monuments to, and quarantining them in, Statue Park has had the paradoxical effect of keeping the past close by, such that it can still bear witness. Furthermore, the statues left gaps after their removal. In some places, these empty spaces remain. The empty spaces become sites of absence: the location of something that is no longer there, yet which had been all too present. Now, it is these absences that are present, visible in the ordinary landscape. These empty spaces themselves are constant reminders of how an awkward communist past was handled by post-communist Hungary. Absences also haunt Hungary (and elsewhere too).

In some places, pre-communist-era statues have been restored to their original positions, from where once they had been removed to be replaced by communist statues. There is an irony here: one erased past takes the place of another past, which is itself thereby erased. Each past vies for its proper place in the Hungarian landscape. Unlike the public sculptures in Liverpool, those in Hungary – whether present or absent, whether distant or proximate – remain an unsettling presence in the landscape. Comparing Liverpool and Budapest, we might be drawn to conclude that the major difference is that the public sculptures in Hungary became contentious as a result of a regime change from a Soviet-style communism to a more Western-style liberal democracy. However, we should not conclude that Liverpool's statues, monuments and memorials are not contentious in some way or that they are unlikely to become so in the future.

Figure 6.6   The offices of the Hillsborough Justice Campaign, close to Liverpool
Football Club's stadium

Thus, for example, there is an ongoing campaign for justice over the
death of 96 Liverpool fans in the 1989 Hillsborough Stadium disaster,
with the memorial at Anfield acting as a painful reminder that people's
suffering and loss continues (see Figures 6.1 and 6.6). In many ways,
memorials such as this allow the past to be present, to provide a focus
for public acts of memory and mourning. The situation in Budapest
tells us more about how such public memorials function, and it is
worth spelling this out.

2.4   The unsettling legacies of the past

We have seen that public sculptures can act to make present the intentions and ideologies of those who built them. In Budapest, for example, sculptures were the public face of both a faltering communist regime and also a new democratic state; they were used by each regime to appear both durable and also close to the people. Consequently, sculptures projected communist ideologies backwards into the past as well as forwards into the future. They provided a set of reference points for the communist regime, showing where it was, where it was coming from and where it was going to. Perhaps paradoxically, the removal, relocation and replacement of communist icons performed exactly the same function for the new democratic state. Through the destruction of some icons, the relocation of others to Statue Park and the return of pre-communist-era statues, the new Hungarian government projected itself both backwards into the past and forwards into the future.

Therefore, the lack of consensus in the new Hungary about how to dispose of the public sculptures properly was less to do with the statues' association with a terrifying and terrible past than with how communist statues (whether in Statue Park or in their absence from the everyday landscape) acted as reminders that this past continued to shape present-day Hungary: in many ways it had not yet been properly dealt with. We can also see this problem in other places. For example, geographer Karen Till (2005) has noted very similar issues in contemporary Berlin, with its dilemmas over handling the unsettling legacies of its Nazi past. In these situations, terrible histories that cannot ever be quite left behind also suggest the possibility that the same terrors may return to haunt the world. Sometimes, this haunting can be imagined to take the shape of ghosts: ghosts who make demands on the living to resolve, or make restitution for, the injustices and horrors of the past. It is to this issue that we now turn. We will explore this through Toni Morrison's novel, *Beloved* (1987a). Through this novel, we will learn more about the emotional qualities of haunting, but also about how the presence of ghosts can call up the injustices and horrors of the past. Ghosts, like statues, make demands upon the living, although it is not always clear what they want, nor even if it is possible to do as they ask.

Summary

- The presence and, as importantly, absence of statues, monuments and memorials can reveal how the past becomes present within contemporary landscapes.

- Seemingly innocuous aspects of the landscape can suddenly become political, emotional flashpoints for public debate (and, here, you might think of all the other ways this might happen, for example, in debates about the fate of derelict buildings or of proposals for new buildings, especially those alongside historic sites, and so on).

- The past can haunt the physical landscape, even where it has been displaced or erased.

- The past can be spatially very close, but remain distant politically, emotionally and historically – as if waiting for its moment to come again, waiting for an opportunity to return to make its point.

3   The past cannot (always) speak its mind: ghostly appearances, unfinished business and the perplexing demands of the past

In Section 2, we saw that public sculptures can become an unsettling, haunting presence within the landscape. The statues in Hungary took on a disturbing quality – reminding people that the past had not yet gone away, that the injuries and injustices of the past had not yet been properly dealt with, despite all best efforts. Thus, it is unsurprising that communist-era symbols were likened by some to ghosts: ghosts that are a disturbing presence, which refuse to go away and keep coming back. Ghosts themselves are often used, figuratively, to evoke the feeling that the business of the past is somehow unfinished. Frequently, the figure of the ghost is associated with demands for justice, for retribution, for revenge or for reparation. By looking at ghosts, we can learn more about the injustices of the past, and also about what demands these may still place upon the living. This is very much the view taken by sociologist Avery Gordon (1997). She argues that:

> The ghost is not simply a dead or a missing person, but a social figure, and investigating it can lead to that dense site where history and subjectivity make social life. The ghost or the apparition is one

form by which something lost, or barely visible, or seemingly not there to our supposedly well-trained eyes, makes itself known or apparent to us, in its own way, of course.

(Gordon, 1997, p.8).

So far in this book, the demands that are placed upon the globalised world have been consciously articulated, for example by campaigning organisations or state institutions. Commonly, these demands are made effective by making a direct connection between 'the problem' and those who are meant to do something about it. Also, demands often require structural responses, involving wider changes in social organisation – as in Hungary's transition to democracy and the demand to deal with its communist past appropriately. Yet, as Chapter 5 noted, demands also work emotionally: asking people to respond on the basis of empathy or sympathy, even if they have no direct connection with 'the problem'. Ghosts, significantly, tend to make demands on individuals, individuals who often respond on the basis of intensely and personally felt emotions. Indeed, the haunted may have had no direct relationship with, nor even a structural connection to, the events represented by the ghost. This is partly because ghosts themselves are usually disconnected by the passage of time from the horror that created them, from the unfinished business they demand we attend to.

Ghosts, in Gordon's (1997) view, enable us to envisage something that has been otherwise lost or is only barely present in the world. Nonetheless, ghosts often find it difficult to communicate to the living exactly what is going on. Their demands are expressed in moans and groans rather than in words and pictures. You may have a sense of this yourself from ghost stories that you are aware of, whether these are from films, books, personal experiences or word of mouth.

Activity 6.3

For a ghost story that you are familiar with – perhaps even a ghost story that you were told by someone you know – think about the following:

1   Where was the ghost story set? Where was the ghost?

2   Who (do you think) the ghost was? Was it from the recent past, or from long ago?

3   What did the ghost do? Did the ghost seem to want something?

4   How do ghost stories make you feel?

Take a little time to write your answers down; we will return to these at the end of this section.

Often enough, the appearance of a ghost signals an injustice associated with a death. In this section, we will look at a story about a very particular ghost, Beloved. We will gain a strong sense of the emotional qualities of haunting when we read a passage from Toni Morrison's novel, *Beloved* (1987a). Morrison's novel, set in pre-civil war USA, was based on the infamous story of a slave woman, Margaret Garner, who escaped from Kentucky into Ohio across the great Ohio River that marked the boundary between slavery and freedom. However, sometime in late January 1856, Margaret Garner tried to kill all her children rather than allowing them to be re-enslaved. One died. How could she kill her own flesh and blood? Exploring this question is the implicit motivation for Morrison's novel.

Beloved is chilling in many ways, but there are two important features that are worth drawing your attention to. The first is that the circumstances of the girl's, Beloved's, death – namely, slavery – remain unresolved (the unsettled legacies of slavery will be explored further in Chapter 7). The second is that Beloved's story is highly emotive. An important aspect of this concerns the demands that Beloved makes; these are often emotional, inarticulate and formed with a child-like incomprehension of what is going on. In fact, Beloved's demands can never be properly articulated, for no one can really say what it is that she feels she has lost.

Activity 6.4

Turn now to Reading 6A by sociologist Avery Gordon (1997) entitled 'Ghostly matters: haunting and the sociological imagination', which you will find at the end of the chapter. Gordon provides us with background to Toni Morrison's novel, *Beloved* (1987a). As you read, ask yourself the following questions:

1   Why do you think Morrison uses a ghost story to explore the injustices of slavery?

2   How does the character Beloved – who is both a ghost and a child – reveal the horror of slavery?

For Gordon, Morrison conveys the story of Margaret Garner 'quietly and extravagantly' (Gordon, 1997, p.139) through an account of the fictional character Sethe. Gordon says 'quietly', I think, because we are not really told exactly what is going on. Instead, in the novel the reader has to look at the world from Sethe's limited perspective, which is sometimes joyous, sometimes bewildered, sometimes terrified. Sethe is *doubly haunted*: she is haunted by slavery itself, its horrors and inhumanity; yet she is also haunted by her own actions, the killing of her beloved daughter. But by using the figure of a ghost, Beloved, Morrison (1987a) can 'extravagantly' evoke not only the terror of slavery but also the irredeemable losses that slavery caused – its murderous quality – and the extraordinary emotions and actions that it entailed. By telling a ghost story, therefore, Morrison can evoke the haunting qualities of an unresolved past.

The ghost returns both because slavery itself continues to haunt history and also because of the tragic events surrounding Beloved's death. Nevertheless, because she is a child, Beloved is unable to understand what has befallen her. In this way, Morrison implies that it is almost impossible to comprehend what slavery in the American South was actually like, nor to fully appreciate Margaret Garner's actions. Instead, Morrison tries to evoke what it feels like to be bewildered and frightened, haunted.

Activity 6.5

Next, turn to Reading 6B by Toni Morrison (1987a) entitled 'Beloved', at the end of the chapter. You will see that Sethe is haunted by her actions as the ghost of her youngest, Beloved, returns. But Beloved is only a child: what is she to make of her murder by her mother? As you read, consider the following questions:

1   How does Beloved behave?

2   What demands does Beloved make?

3   What do other people (in the novel) think about Sethe's situation?

4   How would Ella deal with Beloved? And why?

Morrison (1987a) passes over various 'true' aspects of Margaret Garner's story in silence. By doing this, she asks the reader to imagine what is going on, and what it is like to be Sethe – without providing a definite answer. The most silent geography of terror, here, is slavery in the American South, from which Sethe was escaping. Slavery: so terrible that Sethe would not let her children fall back into the hands of the white men from Kentucky. Slavery: the ghosts of its past injustices continue to haunt the imagination.

In Morrison's story, the outright injustice of slavery is embodied in the ghostly presence of Beloved. Morrison tells us that the word 'Beloved' was often put on the gravestones of the dead children of slaves as they would often die before becoming old enough to be given a proper name. Sethe's own Beloved returns to haunt her murderous mother.

Still a child, Beloved is petulant, capricious, demanding. She is not in a position to articulate her demands, to make clear what kind of justice she is after, nor even to properly name the person who murdered her. How could she believe such a thing of her mother? How could she even appreciate the conditions of slavery from which her mother was attempting to spare her? How, in truth, could she comprehend the concept of slavery? The injustice that has befallen Beloved cannot be easily appeased. In part, this is because her mother murdered her out of sheer, pure love – not out of baser motivations such as greed or malice; and in part, it is because it was not her mother's fault. Sethe did not invent slavery: she was as much its victim as Beloved.

So, the point Morrison is making is this: Sethe was not a passive victim of slavery – not only did she escape, she also refused to return to it. How you feel about her actions is one thing, but she did act and she never gave up. Furthermore, she also refused to give up her children to slavery. Beloved, however, understands none of this. Instead, she makes ever greater demands upon her mother: demands her mother has to give in to, to the extent that eventually her life and health rapidly deteriorate. Yet how are the living supposed to respond to these demands from the past? In the novel, Ella worries that the past has taken possession of the present:

> Whatever Sethe had done, Ella didn't like the idea of past errors taking possession of the present. Sethe's crime was staggering and her pride outstripped even that; but she could not countenance the possibility of sin moving on in the house, unleashed and sassy. Daily life took as much as [Sethe] had. The future was sunset; the past something to leave behind.
>
> (Morrison, 1987a, p.256)

You may feel that Sethe deserves to suffer for her staggering crime, for her pride. Still, Ella doesn't like the idea that past crimes should take control over the present. The past should not prevent people moving on. For Ella, Beloved had to be exorcised, both because she had moved in and become all 'unleashed and sassy', and also because what was done was done. Ella felt that ghosts should know their place:

> As long as the ghost showed out from its ghostly place – shaking stuff, crying, smashing and such – Ella respected it. But if it took flesh and came in her world, well, the shoe was on the other foot. She didn't mind a little communication between the two worlds, but this was an invasion.
>
> (Morrison, 1987a, p.257)

Ella doesn't mind a little communication between the worlds of the living and the dead, in fact she respects ghosts. Even so, she does not want to be conquered by their presence. The implication is that ghosts have a proper place, where they can legitimately exist. This proper place lies between the worlds of the living and the dead, between the past and the present. Nonetheless, Beloved has something to communicate, even if she herself cannot understand what it is, let alone express it. With increasing frustration, and making ever greater demands, Beloved continues to haunt Sethe.

Beloved's inability to say clearly what she wants has the effect of prompting the reader of Morrison's novel to wonder about what Beloved would say if she could. In particular, who would she blame for her situation? Who should take responsibility for the injustices of slavery that made her into a ghost? Her mother? The white men of Kentucky? History? Us as readers, living in a world still shaped by slavery? The ghost is central to these questions: Beloved demands attention, demands that someone takes responsibility (compare this to Chapter 1, Reading 1A). Sethe, for her part, doesn't know what to do about Beloved: she is trapped in her melancholia, her despair. There seems no way out of this situation for either of them.

Now, remind yourself of your answers to Activity 6.3, especially the first question about where the ghost was.

The novel *Beloved* (Morrison, 1987a) is a reminder that society in the USA is still haunted by the unresolved legacy of slavery. The appearance of the ghost is evocative of traumatic events in the history of that society. Haunting, in this case, is as much about the emotional and personal consequences of slavery as it is about the evils of slavery, a globalised system of exploitation. Ghosts, such as Beloved, can help reveal how places are haunted by the past. However, they do not simply tell us about a lost, or half-forgotten, past. Ghosts also let us know *where* the past comes from. Indeed, in a globalised world, the past can return to remind people of connections between places long forgotten. The return of these globalised pasts creates the nagging problem of not just *how* to deal with the demands of the past, but also *where* to deal with them. In Section 4, the disputes and dilemmas created by some old bones discovered in a north Devon cove will help us to explore some questions about where the past returns from.

Summary

- Ghosts can bring the past into uncomfortably close proximity, often unexpectedly.

- Ghosts evoke intense feelings such as fear, shame, guilt, indignation, incomprehension and inconsolable sorrow.

- Ghosts can help us to recognise that an injustice has taken place and that this wrong remains unresolved.

- Ghosts do not always make clear and concise demands, nor offer straightforward solutions. They can signify the enormity and complexity of past injustices.

- Ghosts ask people to take responsibility for past events, even if they have no direct connection to, or even knowledge of, them.

4   'From hell, bound for damnation': from where does a globalised past return?

On 17 February 1997, Jeanne Hardwick of the Ilfracombe Museum in England telephoned local historian Pat Barrow to tell him that someone had found some bones at Rapparee Cove near Ilfracombe Harbour. Barrow was already well known for his research on the wreck of *The London*, which had foundered at Rapparee Cove on 9 October 1796. Bones had been discovered previously, but never in such quantity. It seemed that a storm had uncovered part of the history of *The London* that had lain hidden for two centuries (see Figure 6.7).

In this section, we will be less concerned with how this history came unexpectedly to haunt the present, but with *where* this history came from. Where had these bones come from, and what did it mean now that they were lying in a small coastal port in north Devon, England? The idea that we live in a haunted world reminds us that we are not always aware of all the threads of history that comprise places, and that these threads sometimes need to be carefully traced out not only across time, but between different places too. In this regard, it is helpful to think of places as being knots of history and geography, as Chakrabarty argues (2000).

The idea behind the expression 'knots of history and geography' is that specific threads of history and geography come together at certain points. So far in this book we have seen that the globalised world is characterised by various connections between different places. These

Figure 6.7   The dig conducted by Bristol University archaeologists at Rapparee Cove in February 1997

become entangled in specific ways at particular sites. This chapter has shown how past globalisations also shape places today. So, the way the threads of history and geography become entangled gives particular places their peculiar characteristics. Thus, for example, we can explore the knot of history and geography associated with the dispute over the Lenin statue in Budapest's Statue Park (see Figure 6.4) by following the threads of communism stretching to the former Soviet Union; of democratic protest linked to the West; of popular or nationalist sentiment drawing on the pre-communist past; of capitalism reaching across the globe; of artistic sensibilities; and so forth. Embedded in Budapest's treatment of Lenin is a particular knot of history and geography. And much the same can be said of many other sites and situations.

Let us begin to unravel the knot tied at Rapparee Cove by following the threads associated with the sinking of *The London* in 1796.

4.1 'From hell ...': the bones that haunt Devon

After the discovery of human bones in Rapparee Cove, Pat Barrow uncovered an account of the wreck of *The London* (see Figure 6.8) in a book titled *Old Times in the Westcountry: Stories and Legends*, published around 1873, which contained a series of cuttings from the Ilfracombe Parish Magazine (Barrow, 1998, pp.34–5). Here is the anonymously written tale, which seems at first glance to be an eye-witness account of the terrible fate of *The London*.

It was late in the evening when a gun was heard faintly booming in the distance. A fine vessel was seen in distress. Who fired the gun is a question I cannot answer, but it was thought most probably it was one of the crew, for the master of the vessel wanted no assistance as it turned out. Finding that he was in a position from which he could not extricate himself, it was supposed that he had determined to die rather than let it be known that he was trading with human freight; that his vessel was loaded with fellow human beings as slaves. An Ilfracombe pilot bravely ventured out in response to the signal, but was not allowed to board her. 'Where are you from?' demanded the pilot. 'From hell, bound for damnation,' was the awful answer given by the ruffian captain, who had on board such invaluable treasure – a cargo of human life with gold and specie, the worth of which none shall ever answer. 'Pilot away,' exclaimed the captain, 'We want no assistance, we're bound to perish,' and soon the assertion was realised, and the noble vessel sank beneath the gurgling waters, amidst the agonising cries and shrieks of those on board, thus ruthlessly and desperately deprived of precious life. In the morning the beach was covered with the bodies of the unfortunate Negroes, washed up by the tide; and amongst them, a strange and pitiful exception, like a pearl amongst Rubies, was a lovely creature, a youthful lady. A naked lily fair,

The Bark 'London' who came from St. Lucia with 150 black Prisioners and was wrecked in Raparree Cove - October 9th 1796 in attempting to save lives 46 was unfortunately drowned

Figure 6.8   The wreck of *The London* painted by John Walter some time between 1834 and 1839. Walter's painting depicts the sinking of *The London* on that fateful night in 1796

Figure 6.9   Rapparee Cove, 2004. Note the close proximity of the cove (in the foreground) to Ilfracombe and its harbour (in the background): *The London* was not far from safety

lying dead, and cold. Whether it was the body of a captive, or the captain's wife, none could ever tell, but the sea had made no distinction between the white and black victims.

As the waves moved the sand on the beach, heaps of shining coins in gold met the sight of the astonished inhabitants, who were busily removing the dead bodies to the out-houses of the Britannia Hotel. The sight was a wondrous and not unwelcome one. Eagerly they rushed to the treasure. The cry was raised by someone, 'Stop, first bury the dead.' They hesitated, but the inward voice of conscience re-echoed the mandate, and they returned to their work, and the bodies were hastily buried in the hillside, this being the most convenient spot near at hand, thereto rest until the resurrection morn. Whether the gold was got afterwards I don't recollect; but I dare-say a good deal was secured.

(Anonymous, *c.*1873, quoted in Barrow, 1998, pp.34–5)

It is worth observing that this account contains some familiar ghost story tropes: a storm, mysterious alarming sounds (often bells or clanking chains, in this case ominous gunfire), a doomed vessel, a ruffian sea captain, riches untold and the dead – including a pearl among the rubies: white and cold. And not all of the gold had been 'secured'; a gold coin was found in Rapparee Cove on 14 January 1978. This find sparked frenzied digging at the site, which revealed more coins, mostly dating from the period 1675 to 1725. These finds, and subsequent investigations, seemed to confirm the legend of *The London*. Nevertheless, Barrow recalls that there were other, conflicting, stories about the wreck: 'about bodies being drowned with iron fetters still on their legs, and skulls washed up in the cove' (Barrow, 1998, p.27).

Stories about the bones of Rapparee Cove had circulated for over two centuries: whose bones they were had also incurred much speculation. Could they be the bones of Irish rebels, or Spanish sailors from the Armada? It was in 1997 that many bones were eventually discovered, almost inevitably after a dark and stormy night. Exactly as legend had it, the bones appeared to have been placed in a shallow grave, close to the beach. It seemed that the victims of *The London* had indeed been hastily buried, without a second thought or proper ceremony, suffering indignity in death much as they had in life. Now the bones of the dead had returned, but what stories did they have to tell? Barrow's archival investigations turned up this account from 1796:

> This evening a very melancholy accident occurred at Ilfracombe. A ship, called 'The London', from S. Kitts, having on board a considerable number of blacks (French Prisoners) was driven on the rocks near the entrance of the pier during a violent gale of wind, by which about 50 prisoners were drowned.
>
> (Annual Register, 1796, quoted in Barrow, 1998, p.33)

Therefore, it would appear that the bodies belonged to black French prisoners of war, originating somewhere in the Caribbean. Suddenly, the bones reached out across geography as well as history. If ghosts were present in the cove, haunting a small part of the Devon coastline, then, as geographer Vron Ware (2002) argues, they now also haunted the Caribbean, as histories of slavery combined with histories of resistance to the expansion of British colonial interests (James, 1938). In fact, it seemed that the bodies belonged to ex-slaves from the former French colony of St Lucia.

Having gained freedom from slavery under the French in 1794, yet fearing re-enslavement, St Lucian free slaves, known as the Brigands, fiercely resisted both French and British attempts to take control of the island (Devaux, 1997). By 1796, St Lucia was in a state of chaos. This prompted the British to land a large force of an estimated 12,000 soldiers on the island. Although the Brigands initially managed to hold off the British forces in a series of hard-fought battles, they were outnumbered and outgunned. By the end of 1797, the British had succeeded, despite a series of dispiriting reversals, in cornering the

Brigands at Pigeon Island. With their numbers and supplies dwindling, the ex-slaves eventually surrendered in 1798. The surviving Brigands were immediately re-enslaved, exactly as they had feared. Throughout the two-year campaign, captured Brigands were deported to England, along with treasures looted from French estates.

This raises the following question: did the bones of Rapparee Cove belong to prisoners of war or to slaves? In other words, were captured Brigands being treated as French soldiers, as St Lucian prisoners of war, or as (re-enslaved) slaves? Furthermore, was Captain Robertson, master of *The London*, intending to sell the captives on arrival at his destination, Bristol? Though selling slaves had been illegal in England since 1772, the law was widely flouted. It was possible that Captain Robertson intended to make a quick profit by selling the captives (Barrow, 1998). It has been argued that he must have felt guilty about something to refuse help and to go down with his ship. Maybe. Maybe not. It is worth remembering that British cities such as Bristol and Liverpool grew rich on the Atlantic slave trade, to which memorials in both cities now testify: there are memorials to those such as Bristol's Edward Colston (1636–1721) who became rich from slavery, and memorial plaques to the unnamed, untold millions of slaves who suffered.

To confuse matters further, analysis of the bones by archaeologists at Bristol University casts doubt on whether the dead were from the Caribbean at all. The bone chemistry suggested the remains might instead belong to north Devon folk: Devon fish-catchers, perhaps (who also travelled far and wide). This uncertain history and geography produced a problem; if you want to remember the tragedy, how can you erect a memorial to mark the events when you don't know who or what you are memorialising?

Moreover, as events unfolded, simply remembering became only one possible response to the discovery of the bones. After the bones were unearthed, Rapparee Cove was visited by a number of politicians and dignitaries. These included Member of Parliament Bernie Grant, who demanded an apology from the UK government for its role

Defining the Atlantic slave trade

The Atlantic slave trade began in the mid fifteenth century and continued until the early nineteenth century. This trade is often described as being triangular because it connected (1) port cities in England and Europe with (2) Africa's western and central Atlantic coasts with (3) the Atlantic seaboards of southern North America and northern South America, including the Caribbean islands. Slaves were taken from Africa and then exchanged for money and merchandise in the Americas and the Caribbean; the merchandise and money were taken to Europe, where they further fuelled the Atlantic slave economy. It is estimated that in the period of 1440–1880, nearly twelve million slaves were forcibly removed from Africa, with about two million of these dying during the 'middle passage' across the Atlantic to the Americas and the Caribbean (Chapter 7 discusses this further). This Atlantic slave trade not only created a very particular globalised world over this period, but the legacies of this past have also left their mark upon the contemporary globalised world.

in the slave trade as well as financial reparations for slavery, and the High Commissioner of St Lucia, who argued that the bones should be interred in Heroes Park, Castries, the island's capital. At the time of writing, the bones were held at Barnstaple Museum, wrapped in plastic and kept in cardboard boxes. The museum would not release them until their origin could be proved. In August 2004, while saying that it was happy to share the history of the wreck, St Lucia threatened legal action if the bones were not returned.

Activity 6.6

1   Given the uncertainty surrounding the 'slaves' of Rapparee Cove, how would you choose to commemorate the dead? Remember, irrespective of origin and circumstance, more than forty people lost their lives on that stormy October night in 1796.

2   As importantly, what would you do with the bones that were unearthed?

On 1 August 1997, the national African Remembrance Day was celebrated at Rapparee Cove (see Figure 6.10). At the ceremony, members of the Africa Reparations Movement held an African prayer ceremony and observed three minutes of silence for the dead. The day itself is intended to be an occasion for both remembrance and healing, yet unsettling questions remained. These questions were concerned not only with how to commemorate the dead, and which wrongs of a globalised past to recognise, but also with where the bones should

Figure 6.10   Members of the Africa Reparations Movement visiting Rapparee Cove for a commemoration service, 1 August 1997

finally rest. Should the bones be repatriated to St Lucia, or not? The unresolved question remains: whose bones were they? There is, today, a plaque on the cliffs recalling the loss of *The London* (see Figure 6.11). After what you have just read, you may feel the inscription does not quite do justice to those who died.

The north Devon coast is haunted by the events of 9 October 1796. It is not just that the bones of the dead emerged into daylight after centuries of lying buried and forgotten. It is more that these bones knot together both far off times and the present, and the far off places of St Lucia and north Devon; of France and England; of Africa and Europe in a tight binding of there and here. As Vron Ware observes, 'Rapparee Cove can be seen as a point on a circuit that linked the three continents of Africa, North America, and Europe' (Ware, 2002, p.215).

Sometimes the slave trade can be forgotten, or thought to be *absent* from the history and geography of much of the Atlantic world but, as Ware argues, finds such as those at Rapparee Cove reveal how even tiny, out of the way places are knotted into – sometimes unsettling, sometimes haunting – globalised pasts (2002, p.218). The debate about the bones in Rapparee Cove, rather than clouding the features of a globalised world created by the slave trade, highlighted the ways in which specific places were entangled in it. These knots of history and geography involve slavery, certainly, and global military adventures by emergent powers such as France and Britain, but they also remember the long distances travelled by Devon fisher folk.

Figure 6.11   The Rapparee memorial, 2004

The bones of slavery haunt contemporary politics on a world scale, as justice – or at least proper remembrance – is sought for its victims. Indeed, the bones of Rapparee Cove serve as a solemn reminder that Britain was heavily involved in, and profited from, the slave economy. Furthermore, importantly, this past has not completely disappeared; its legacies linger, and it is not always easy to shrug off a globalised past simply by saying it is long gone. Alas, the globalised world is haunted by more than bones.

4.2 '... bound for damnation': what to do with a toxic past?

Hidden for centuries, the bones of Rapparee Cove showed that Ilfracombe was still haunted by histories and geographies of slavery. Threads of history and geography connected the bones to the Caribbean, to Africa, to Europe. However, the bones themselves had not moved for years. In this section, we will look at how the globalised world can become haunted by ghosts that move, by pasts that arrive from far away. In particular, we will examine the political storm, from late 2003 onwards, that surrounded a fleet of ships. Why? Because this was a 'ghost fleet', containing toxic substances that threatened the marine environment. The harmful materials on board the ghost ships included, for example:

- oils and oily ballast, which could damage the marine environment;
- asbestos, which is a known carcinogen;
- polychlorinated biphenyl, which is the name for several toxic compounds (usually known as PCBs) commonly formed as waste in industrial processes: they are probably carcinogens and have also been linked with neurological and developmental problems in humans;
- mercury, lead, chromium and cadmium, which are highly toxic (for the marine environment and human beings).

The ships were part of a fleet of thirteen Second World War supply vessels belonging to the US Navy. They were moored on the James River in Virginia, and were all in a serious state of deterioration. The US Navy concluded that they had to be scrapped. Nonetheless, the dangerous materials, buried within the ships, created a problem of disposal. It was estimated that the fleet contained, for example, almost 100 tons of PCBs, which are difficult to destroy, and almost 3000 tons of fuel oils. The US Navy decided to contract out the problem to a firm capable of disposing of the toxins safely. In July 2003, the US

Navy decided that the ships should be dismantled by Able UK, located in Hartlepool in England. This would mean sailing the frail, toxic ships from Virginia to Teesside.

Immediately, two US environmental groups (the Basel Action Network and the Sierra Club), represented by Earthjustice, instigated legal action to prevent the fleet from entering international waters. They argued that the ships were a threat to the global marine environment, especially if they should sink on the difficult journey across the Atlantic. On 20 October 2003, the action failed, and the ships set sail shortly after. In the UK, Phil Michaels of Friends of the Earth (FoE) expressed his disappointment that the departure of the 'toxic ghost fleet' had not been prevented.

Figure 6.12   In 2003 one of the US naval 'ghost ships' is towed to Hartlepool to be broken up. By mid 2005, the work had not yet begun, delayed by objections from environmental protestors about hazardous PCBs and other materials

Activity 6.7

Initially, the British press were calling the ships the 'toxic fleet', but very quickly they became known as the 'ghost fleet'. Soon, they were simply described as the 'ghost ships'.

1   Why do you think it is 'ghost' rather than 'toxic' that stuck as a description?

2   What difference do you think it makes (emotionally and politically) to describe the fleet as 'ghostly' rather than 'toxic'?

3   Do you think that something more neutral such as 'rusty' or 'obsolete', or something positive such as 'recyclable', would have been a better expression for the ships? Why?

By calling the ships 'ghosts', the British press seemed to be saying several things at once:

1   That there was something deadly about these ships (for which the term 'toxic' would have done equally well).

2   That there was something 'wrong' about the ships (again, toxic would have done).

3   That the ships had unexpectedly come back from a globalised past to haunt the present. Long forgotten, the Second World War ships

had suddenly become hazardous. This hazard was not going to be handled by the Americans, however. Instead, they were going to export it.

4   That there was something sinister and creepy about the ships: abandoned, forgotten, silently decaying, unsafe, seemingly malignant, yet now suddenly all too present. They seemed to evoke an emotional kind of revulsion.

It is these last two aspects of the ships that seem to have made the expression 'ghost' stick. The ships not only posed a technical problem of disposal, they seemed to have come back from the past to harm the oceans. In truth, the older the ships got, the deadlier they became. Navy ships, it seems, do not fade away like old soldiers. And it was not simply the case that these ships were 'over there', out of harm's way, for they were on the move. By moving, moreover, the ghost fleet drew attention to its own globalised world, comprised of old ships and deadly toxins, and also of the global economics of ship-breaking.

Once the ships were at sea, the USA had effectively succeeded in exporting the problem of its polluted toxic vessels to the UK. An intense political debate was, in fact, already underway in the UK, with many environmental groups voicing their objections to the arrival of the fleet on Teesside. Bob Pendlebury, chair of Northumbria Tourist Board in 2003, a local councillor and also chair of County Durham Environmental Partnership, said:

> I am very suspicious of the Americans, who should not be shipping this out to other countries, when they are capable of carrying out any work over there. There is a distinct danger to the North East coast in that these ships could break up while being towed here. There is also a danger that materials inside these ships could escape while they are being stripped down or when they are laying offshore. We have had a history in the North East of dirt and dereliction and this will only emphasise this. It will damage the efforts we have made to attract investment and tourism.
>
> (Anon., 2003a)

Similarly, Peter Goodwin of the Middlesbrough Green Party asked this vital question: 'Why should anybody need to bring rotting ships 4000 miles across the Atlantic from the richest country in the world which should be equipped to deal with its own waste?' (Anon., 2003b). Peter Stephenson, managing director of Able UK, believed he had the answer. He defended its contract for the disposal of the ghost fleet by arguing that there was very little waste and asbestos on the ships. He thought that the firm, which also operates the Teesside Environmental

Reclamation and Recycling Centre, was perfectly capable of handling the fleet successfully – and of doing so with as little environmental damage as possible, or risk of environmental harm. Further, the £16 million deal to dispose of the vessels represented 200 jobs in a competitive global market for recycling ships (Anon., 2003b). It was better to have the ghost ships dealt with on Teesside, it was argued, than in the USA – or India, which is often Teesside's main competitor for this kind of contract. A few even suggested that only a fool would consider it better to send the ships elsewhere. Teesside had world-class facilities for handling toxic vessels and it was good for job security in the region.

Meanwhile, Margaret Beckett (then Secretary of State at the Department for the Environment, Food and Rural Affairs) announced that the UK government would monitor the situation. If the ghost ships represented a significant environmental threat, the Maritime and Coastguard Agency promised it would prevent the vessels from entering UK waters. However, the Environment Agency argued that the ships coming to the UK was 'a better solution for the environment than disposing of vessels in under-developed countries [such as India]' (Anon., 2003c).

As a result of this vacillation, FoE sought a judicial review over the ships, saying that the failure of the Environment Agency, English Nature and the Maritime and Coastguard Agency to prevent the ghost fleet from entering UK waters might come back to haunt them. On 12 and 13 November 2003, the first two ships – the USS Canisteo and USS Caloosahatchee – arrived on Teesside, after making the 7384-km voyage across the ocean; as the master of The London might have observed, 'from hell, bound for damnation'. These ghost ships had, like The London, made it across the Atlantic. One globalised past had been rotting away in the USA, geographically and historically far away from Teesside, yet it had now become a problem for the north-east of England – and, in reality, for the world. These ghosts came from the Second World War and from the USA, but Teesside was far from the only place where these ghosts could have been exorcised.

Debates over the environmental consequences of the ghost ships, and over how best to deal with them, raged. The UK government was urged to set up a Ship Recycling Centre, perhaps on Teesside, as part of a national policy on ship recycling; others, meanwhile, wanted the ships returned to the USA. Throughout 2004, the UK government insisted that the Teeside facility was the best place to handle the ghost ships, while Able UK promised that the estimated 200 new jobs created would go to local people. By the middle of 2004, many – including environmental groups such as Greenpeace – were warning of the even greater dangers presented by disposing of the fleet elsewhere, and especially in India.

Activity 6.8

Look back at Chapter 1 to remind yourself of the debates about whether bad jobs are better than no jobs (Section 2.2). Turn now to Reading 6C by Randeep Ramesh (2004) entitled 'Toiling in India's ship graveyard for £1 a day', which you will find at the end of this chapter. Once you have read the piece, consider this question: where do you think the ghost ships should have been disposed of?

Summary

- Ghosts can travel across geographical space as well as historical time: from the time of empires, via St Lucia to north Devon; from the Second World War, via Virginia to Teesside.

- The globalised past can suddenly become uncomfortably present, whether it turns up from the past or from far away (or both).

- The globalised past comes to haunt the present when something about it remains unresolved, for example, the proper way to bury the dead or to dispose of toxins.

- Demands over what to do with the ghosts of a globalised past are difficult to adjudicate. Ghosts are awkward not simply because they return from the past to make their demands, but because they also reach out to other places. Thus, the problems are posed: how, and where, should the bones of *The London* be appropriately honoured; how, and where, should the ghost ships' toxins be disposed of?

5   Conclusion: the haunting demands of a globalised past

In this chapter, we have explored some of the ways that the globalised past can come back to haunt the present. By focusing on the haunted world, we have been able to highlight specific aspects of the return of the past. To begin with, we have seen that haunting can take various forms and have different consequences, emotionally and politically. For example, after the fall of communism, Hungary was haunted by the monuments and statues erected by the old regime. It wasn't simply their presence in the landscape that haunted Hungary, but the problem of how to deal fairly and properly with these ghosts of a globalised past. Meanwhile, in Morrison's (1987a) novel, Beloved returns to haunt her mother, Sethe, casting light upon the horror and tragedy of slavery. People's responses to the return of the past are often emotionally charged. Indeed, the idea of haunting has proved useful in highlighting the emotional qualities bound up in political demands for justice and restitution for past wrongs.

Ideas of proximity and distance, and presence and absence, have been helpful for thinking about how places are embedded in, or disconnected from, their globalised pasts. For instance, some places are deliberately constructed to keep the past proximate and present: places such as cemeteries, sites of memorials, museums, archives and so forth. Yet, on the other hand, buildings or monuments or even whole neighbourhoods that are associated with unwanted memories can be quickly erased by sledgehammers and bulldozers: the past, thought too close for comfort, is made absent. But, remember, absences can also haunt. Think, for example, about Budapest's Statue Park and the gaps left behind by the removed statues.

Through haunting, and even ghosts, it has been possible to show that elements of the past are uncertain, obscure and, ultimately, undecidable. The past can unexpectedly arrive on the scene, as if from nowhere. In other words, something that is seemingly absent or distant can suddenly become both present and proximate. One example of this was the sinking of *The London*. The bones of Rapparee Cove exposed the threads of history and geography that connected a seemingly innocuous part of the north Devon coastline with the violence and tyranny not only of the slave trade but also of British imperial adventures. Here were the bones of a globalised past: enslaved, subjugated, colonised. And yet the bones had lain undiscovered for centuries. Even seemingly absent pasts – pasts considered long gone or far away, or both – can return to haunt the present. The buried geographies of a globalised past are not always gone for good. More than this, it is not always certain what these globalised pasts stand for: whose bones were they in Rapparee Cove, and why did Sethe kill her beloved in *Beloved* (Morrison, 1987a)?

In a globalised world, it is possible to be haunted by events that happened long ago and seemingly far away. This raises the questions of how to deal with the legacies of a globalised past, and of where to deal with them. Thus, the US Navy's ghost ships came back to haunt the oceans and the marine environment – and not just in US waters. The USA was able to export the problems set by its ghost fleet by employing a British company to deal with its toxic products. However, moving the ghost fleet raised questions about how the globalised world is haunted by pollution. This question extended as far as India. And returned to the USA: why did the ships have to move at all? This introduces the issue of whether the past should be kept close (in north Devon or Teesside for example?) or pushed away (in these examples as far as India or St Lucia?).

Figure 6.13
A monument in central Liverpool memorialising William Gladstone (1809–98), four times prime minister of Great Britain

Figure 6.14   The base of the Gladstone statue in central Liverpool

The statue in Figures 6.13 and 6.14 commemorates the former British prime minister, William Gladstone (1809–98). On one side of the memorial sits Justice with her sword and scales, mourning the loss of her champion. The statue may make us think about the long-standing demand for justice, and also the ways in which the legacies of the past are drawn into those demands.

Yet, above the plaque on the statue's base, which proclaims the word 'Justice' (see Figure 6.14), someone has scrawled 'Ready Steady', to which someone else has added 'Cook', thereby reminding us that the legacies and demands of the past are not always taken seriously.

Moreover, from *Beloved* (Morrison, 1987a), we learned that the demands of the past are not always clearly articulated as, for example, they usually are in political demands. Sometimes, the demands of the past are inarticulate, emotional in their appeal, and simply demanding. There is a sense that some injustice or tragedy has befallen people, but it is not always clear what those people want, nor how these injustices might be appeased. A globalised past returns often unexpectedly and in unexpected forms, and this can make the demands of a globalised past difficult to discern or to redress. This problem is difficult to resolve, especially in terms of the legacies of the Atlantic slave trade, which we will explore in greater detail in Chapter 7.

References

Anon. (2003a) '"Ghost fleet" threat to coastline', http://news.bbc.co.uk/1/hi/england/3095786.stm (accessed 21 April 2005).

Anon. (2003b) 'Atlantic trip for "ghost" fleet', http://news.bbc.co.uk/1/hi/england/tees/3103549.stm (accessed 21 April 2005).

Anon. (2003c) 'Four toxic ships free to sail', http://news.bbc.co.uk/1/hi/world/america/3160342.stm (accessed 21 April 2005).

Baros, G. (2002) *Statue Park,* Budapest, Our Budapest.

Barrow, P. (1998) *Slaves of Rapparee (The Wreck of the* London*)*, Bideford, Edward Gaskell Publishers.

Benjamin, W. (1969) *Illuminations* (trans. H. Zohn, ed. H. Arendt), New York, Schocken.

Chakrabarty, D. (2000) *Provincializing Europe: Postcolonial Thought and Historical Difference*, Princeton, NJ, Princeton University Press.

Clemons, W. (1987) 'A gravestone of memories', *Newsweek*, 28 September, pp.74–5.

Coffin, L. (1876, 1968) *Reminiscences of Levi Coffin: The Reputed President of the Underground Railroad*, New York, Augustus M. Kelley.

Devaux, R.J. (1997) *They Called Us Brigands: The Saga of St Lucia's Freedom Fighters*, Castries, St Lucia, Optimum Printers.

Gerő, A. and Pető, I. (1999) *Unfinished Socialism: Pictures from the Kádár Era*, Budapest, Central European University Press.

Gordon, A. (1997) *Ghostly Matters: Haunting and the Sociological Imagination*, Minneapolis, Minn., University of Minnesota Press.

Hawthorne, N. (1850, 1978) *The Scarlet Letter* (2nd edn) (ed. S. Bradley), New York, Norton.

James, C.L.R. (1938) *The Black Jacobins: Toussaint L'Ouverture and the San Domingo Revolution*, 1980 edn, London, Allison & Busby.

Morrison, T. (1987a) *Beloved*, London, Picador.

Morrison, T. (1987b) '"Five years of terror": a conversation with Miriam Horn', *US News and World Report*, 19 October 1975.

Nadkarni, M. (2003) 'The death of socialism and the afterlife of its monuments: making and marketing the past in Budapest's Statue Park' in Hodgkin, K. and Radstone, S. (eds) *Contested Pasts: The Politics of Memory*, London, Routledge, pp.193–207.

Ramesh, R. (2004) 'Toiling in India's ship graveyard for £1 a day', *The Guardian*, 22 June, p.15.

Till, K. (2005) *The New Berlin: Memory, Politics, Place*, Minneapolis, Minn., University of Minnesota Press.

Ware, V. (2002) 'Ghosts, trails, and bones: circuits of memory and traditions of resistance' in Ware, V. and Back, L., *Out of Whiteness: Color, Politics, and Culture*, Chicago, Ill., Chicago University Press, pp.196–226.

Reading 6A

Avery Gordon, 'Ghostly matters: haunting and the sociological imagination'

The Failure of the Explanation

> Somewhere between ... the Actual and the Imaginary ... ghosts might
> enter ... without affrighting us. It would be too much in keeping with the
> scene to excite surprise, were we to look about us and discover a
> form, beloved, but gone hence, now sitting quietly in a streak of this
> magic moonshine, with an aspect that would make us doubt whether it
> had returned from afar, or had never once stirred from our fireside.
>
> Nathaniel Hawthorne, *The Scarlet Letter*

'The Modern Medea – The Story of Margaret Garner' (wood engraving of
Thomas Satterwhite Noble's painting *Margaret Garner*, 1867, published in
Harper's Weekly, 18 May 1867)

*Somewhere between the Actual and the Imaginary ghosts might enter
without affrighting us.* Or at least without scaring us so much that we take off
running, away from the reckoning, but still without adequate preparation, into
the tangle of the historical fault lines that remain. This [extract] is about the
lingering inheritance of racial slavery [...] and the compulsions and forces
that all of us inevitably experience in the face of slavery's having even once

existed in our nation. Slavery has ended, but something of it continues to live on, in the social geography of where peoples reside, in the authority of collective wisdom and shared benightedness, in the veins of the contradictory formation we call New World modernity, propelling, as it always has, a something to be done. Such endings that are not over is what haunting is about. This [extract] continues my consideration of ghostly matters with Toni Morrison's novel *Beloved*, a work I take to be one of the most significant contributions to the understanding of haunting, a work whose monumental importance goes well beyond, although clearly through the very medium of, its literary achievements. As we will see, the full weight of Morrison's contribution will rest on the exceptional premise of the book. The ghost enters, all fleshy and real, with wants, and a fierce hunger, and she speaks, barely, of course, and in pictures and a coded language. This ghost, Beloved, forces a reckoning: she makes those who have contact with her, who love and need her, confront an event in their past that loiters in the present. But Beloved, the ghost, is haunted too, and therein lies the challenge Morrison poses. *Somewhere between the Actual and the Imaginary ghosts might enter without affrighting us.*

Opening in 1873 [...] *Beloved* retells quietly and extravagantly the chronicle of Margaret Garner, the 'slave mother, who killed her child rather than see it taken back to slavery' (Coffin, [1876] 1968: 557). Not just the story, but recurrent and varied versions of the account of a slave woman, Sethe, who runs from Kentucky across the frozen Ohio River, giving birth along the way to a daughter named Denver. Arriving just outside Cincinnati, she spends twenty-eight days with her three other children, her mother-in-law, Baby Suggs, and the community before her owners attempt to capture and return her to Sweet Home in Kentucky under the terms of the 1850 Fugitive Slave Act. Faced with this prospect, she attempts to kill all her children and successfully murders one. This one is unnamed, but her headstone bears one affordable word – Beloved. In 1873, when the novel begins, the two boys are long gone, run off by handprints in cakes and a putatively crazy mother. Denver is growing up but has yet to venture out of the yard; Baby Suggs is contemplating colors, ready to die; and Stamp Paid, an underground railroad operator, loyally keeps history alive and the community in communication. Two arrivals set the story in motion. Paul D, one of the men from Sweet Home, makes his way to town and rids the haunted house, 'with a table and a loud male voice,' of its 'claim to local fame' [Morrison, 1987a, p.37]. And a ghostly young woman walks out of the water and moves into 124 Bluestone Road. Her name is Beloved. A stranger, she arrives with a name and no history she can provide, despite Paul D's persistent request for one. Yet the name she has chosen, which poses a crucial question for us – just who is the beloved? – Sethe and Denver recognise as that of the 'already crawling' baby Sethe has killed.

While ghosts are not foreign to the residents of 124 Bluestone Road or their neighbors, they are rarely so visible or demanding as Beloved. Indeed, all of the characters in the novel weave their pleasures, pains, losses, and desires

into the embellished crevices of Beloved's words and unspeakable
biography. What Beloved cannot or will not say, they fill in with their
simultaneously grand and subtle projections; from bits and pieces, fragments
and portentous signs, they all make Beloved their beloved. *You are mine You
are mine You are mine* [Morrison, 1987a, p.127]. Yet, what they see or think
they see can never quite grasp what Toni Morrison asks us as readers today
to comprehend: that Beloved the ghost herself barely possesses a story of
loss, which structures the very possibility of enslavement, emancipation, and
freedom in which the Reconstructive history of *Beloved* traffics.

And thus Beloved the ghost's double voice speaks not only of Sethe's dead
child but also of an unnamed African girl lost at sea, not yet become an
African-American. (The book's memorial dedication reads simply 'Sixty Million
and more.') However, neither Sethe nor the others can perceive that the ghost
that is haunting them is haunted herself. This would be impossible – too much
– within the complicated mode of production Morrison elaborates for
envisioning history or a totality and its articulations and disarticulations, in time
and across time. Indeed, one major theme of the novel is this question: What
is too much? What is too much self (pride) when you were not supposed to
have one? What is too much to remember when there is yet more? What is
too much violence (slavery)? What is too much to tell, to pass on, when
'remembering seem[s] unwise' [Morrison, 1987a, p.274], but necessary? The
double voice of the ghost will do its work, but it passes itself on as our
haunting burden. *were we to look about us and discover a form, beloved, but
gone hence, now sitting quietly in a streak of this magic moonshine.*

In the latter part of January 1856, Margaret Garner, the slave mother, killed
her child rather than see her taken back to slavery. *Beloved, she my
daughter. She mine. See. She come back to me of her own free will and I
don't have to explain a thing. I didn't have time to explain before because it
had to be done quick. Quick. She had to be safe and I put her where she
would be* [Morrison, 1987a, p.200]. Two moments of traumatic violence and
injury are evoked in this statement: a slave mother's killing of her child and
slavery. 'Rather than' suggests a causal explanatory relation between these
two moments, one seemingly individual and private – a mother kills her child
– and the other systemic and public – Slavery. *I won't never let her go. I'll
explain to her, even though I don't have to. Why I did it. How if I hadn't killed
her she would have died and that is something I could not bear to happen to
her. When I explain it she'll understand, because she understands everything
already* [Morrison, 1987a, p.200]. The elaboration of the explanation that
bridges these two moments of violence, like Sethe's own language, is
struggling to articulate a story that exceeds such a rationalistic and objective
explanation. *I don't have to explain a thing* and yet all those things of which
Sethe speaks in a rush of words that claim her relation to the child she
murdered and the place she knows she cannot return herself or her children
to represent the failure of explanation. *it had to be done quick. ... She had to
be safe. ... Milk that belonged to my baby. ... I was the one she didn't throw*

away. ... Before I could check for the sign. ... I looked everywhere for that hat. Stuttered. ... After the shed, I stopped. ... I don't believe she wanted to get to red. ... Matter of fact, that and her pinkish headstone was the last color I recall. Now I'll be on the lookout. ... Funny how you lose sight of some things and memory others. ... Called me 'Jenny' when she was babbling. ... Somebody had to know it. Hear it. Somebody. ... Schoolteacher wouldn't treat her the way he treated me. ... I stood by her bed waiting for her to finish with the slop jar. ... Good God, I'm going to eat myself up. ... She hates anything about Sweet Home except how she was born. ... The grape arbour. ... Otherwise I would have seen my fingernail prints right there ... the earrings. ... Too thick, he said ... like a daughter which is what I wanted to be. ... I never saw her own smile. ... Running, you think?. ... When I come out of jail I saw them plain. ... I got close. I got close. ... I couldn't lay down with you then. ... Now I can. I can sleep like the drowned. ... She is mine [Morrison, 1987a, pp.200–4].

The failure of the explanation, the cultivated yet vulnerable interval between 'Slavery with a capital S' and the story of a slave mother who killed her child, is the enabling moment of the analysis: 'The book was not about the institution – Slavery with a capital S. It was about these anonymous people called slaves. ... When I say *Beloved* is not about slavery, I mean that the *story* is not slavery. The story is these people – these people who don't know they're in an era of historical interest. They just know they have to get through the day' [Morrison, 1987b, p.75]. The story is not Slavery with a capital S. The story is about haunting and about the crucial way in which it mediates between institution and person, creating the possibility of making a life, of becoming something else, in the present and for the future. The work and the power of the story devolve from beginning with this asymmetry, beginning with a relationship whose evocation requires precisely refusing to reduce these two moments to cause and effect, as if this story of history could be told simply as a 'sequence of events like the beads of a rosary' (Benjamin 1969: 263). The work and the power of the story lie in giving all the reasons why the reasons are never quite enough, why they cannot close the breach between two interrelated but distinct affairs, why haunting rather than 'history' (or historicism) best captures the constellation of connections that charges any 'time of the now' (ibid.) with the debts of the past and the expense of the present, why one woman killed her child and another was haunted by the event. 'I started out wanting to write a story about ... the clipping about Margaret Garner stuck in my head. I had to deal with this nurturing instinct that expressed itself in murder' (Morrison in Clemons 1987: 75). *The clipping about Margaret Garner stuck in my head. with an aspect that would make us doubt whether it had returned from afar, or had never once stirred from our fireside.*

(Gordon, 1997, pp.138–42)

Reading 6B

Toni Morrison, 'Beloved'

Beloved sat around, ate, went from bed to bed. Sometimes she screamed, 'Rain! Rain!' and clawed her throat until rubies of blood opened there, made brighter by her midnight skin. Then Sethe shouted, 'No!' and knocked over chairs to get to her and wipe the jewels away. Other times Beloved curled up on the floor, her wrists between her knees, and stayed there for hours. Or she would go to the creek, stick her feet in the water and whoosh it up her legs. Afterward she would go to Sethe, run her fingers over the woman's teeth while tears slid from her wide black eyes. Then it seemed to Denver the thing was done: Beloved bending over Sethe looked the mother, Sethe the teething child, for other than those times when Beloved needed her, Sethe confined herself to a corner chair. The bigger Beloved got, the smaller Sethe became; the brighter Beloved's eyes, the more those eyes that used never to look away became slits of sleeplessness. Sethe no longer combed her hair or splashed her face with water. She sat in the chair licking her lips like a chastised child while Beloved ate up her life, took it, swelled up with it, grew taller on it. And the older woman yielded it up without a murmur.

Denver served them both. Washing, cooking, forcing, cajoling her mother to eat a little now and then, providing sweet things for Beloved as often as she could to calm her down. It was hard to know what she would do from minute to minute. When the heat got hot, she might walk around the house naked or wrapped in a sheet, her belly protruding like a winning watermelon.

Denver thought she understood the connection between her mother and Beloved: Sethe was trying to make up for the handsaw; Beloved was making her pay for it. But there would never be an end to that, and seeing her mother diminished shamed and infuriated her. Yet she knew Sethe's greatest fear was the same one Denver had in the beginning – that Beloved might leave. That before Sethe could make her understand what it meant – what it took to drag the teeth of that saw under the little chin; to feel the baby blood pump like oil in her hands; to hold her face so her head would stay on; to squeeze her so she could absorb, still, the death spasms that shot through that adored body, plump and sweet with life – Beloved might leave. Leave before Sethe could make her realize that worse than that – far worse – was what Baby Suggs died of, what Ella knew, what Stamp saw and what made Paul D tremble. That anybody white could take your whole self for anything that came to mind. Not just work, kill, or maim you, but dirty you. Dirty you so bad you couldn't like yourself anymore. Dirty you so bad you forgot who you were and couldn't think it up. And though she and others lived through and got over it, she could never let it happen to her own. The best thing she was, was her children. Whites might dirty *her* alright, but not her best thing, her beautiful, magical best thing – the part of her that was clean. No undreamable dreams about whether the headless, feetless torso hanging in the tree with a sign on it was her husband or Paul A; whether the bubbling-hot girls in the colored-school fire set by patriots included her daughter; whether a gang of whites invaded her daughter's private parts, soiled her daughter's thighs and threw her daughter out of the wagon. *She* might have to work the slaughterhouse yard, but not her daughter.

And no one, nobody on this earth, would list her daughter's characteristics on the animal side of the paper. No. Oh no. Maybe Baby Suggs could worry about it, live with the likelihood of it; Sethe had refused – and refused still.

This and much more Denver heard her say from her corner chair, trying to persuade Beloved, the one and only person she felt she had to convince, that what she had done was right because it came from true love.

Beloved, her fat new feet propped on the seat of a chair in front of the one she sat in, her unlined hands resting on her stomach, looked at her. Uncomprehending everything except that Sethe was the woman who took her face away, leaving her crouching in a dark, dark place, forgetting to smile.

Her father's daughter after all, Denver decided to do the necessary. Decided to stop relying on kindness to leave something on the stump. She would hire herself out somewhere, and although she was afraid to leave Sethe and Beloved alone all day not knowing what calamity either one of them would create, she came to realize that her presence in that house had no influence on what either woman did. She kept them alive and they ignored her. Growled when they chose; sulked, explained, demanded, strutted, cowered, cried and provoked each other to the edge of violence, then over. She had begun to notice that even when Beloved was quiet, dreamy, minding her own business, Sethe got her going again. Whispering, muttering some justification, some bit of clarifying information to Beloved to explain what it had been like, and why, and how come. It was as though Sethe didn't really want forgiveness given; she wanted it refused. And Beloved helped her out.

Somebody had to be saved, but unless Denver got work, there would be no one to save, no one to come home to, and no Denver either. It was a new thought, having a self to look out for and preserve. And it might not have occurred to her if she hadn't met Nelson Lord leaving his grandmother's house as Denver entered it to pay a thank you for half a pie. All he did was smile and say, 'Take care of yourself, Denver,' but she heard it as though it were what language was made for. The last time he spoke to her his words blocked up her ears. Now they opened her mind. Weeding the garden, pulling vegetables, cooking, washing, she plotted what to do and how. The Bodwins were most likely to help since they had done it twice. Once for Baby Suggs and once for her mother. Why not the third generation as well?

She got lost so many times in the streets of Cincinnati it was noon before she arrived, though she started out at sunrise. The house sat back from the sidewalk with large windows looking out on a noisy, busy street. The Negro woman who answered the front door said, 'Yes?'

'May I come in?'

'What you want?'

'I want to see Mr. and Mrs. Bodwin.'

'Miss Bodwin. They brother and sister.'

'Oh.'

'What you want em for?'

'I'm looking for work. I was thinking they might know of some.'

'You Baby Suggs' kin, ain't you?'

'Yes, ma'am.'

'Come on in. You letting in flies.' She led Denver toward the kitchen, saying, 'First thing you have to know is what door to knock on.' But Denver only half heard her because she was stepping on something soft and blue. All around her was thick, soft and blue. Glass cases crammed full of glistening things. Books on tables and shelves. Pearl-white lamps with shiny metal bottoms. And a smell like the cologne she poured in the emerald house, only better.

'Sit down,' the woman said. 'You know my name?'

'No, ma'am.'

'Janey. Janey Wagon.'

'How do you do?'

'Fairly. I heard your mother took sick, that so?'

'Yes, ma'am.'

'Who's looking after her?'

'I am. But I have to find work.'

Janey laughed. 'You know what? I've been here since I was fourteen, and I remember like yesterday when Baby Suggs, holy, came here and sat right there where you are. Whiteman brought her. That's how she got that house you all live in. Other things, too.'

'Yes, ma'am.'

'What's the trouble with Sethe?' Janey leaned against an indoor sink and folded her arms.

It was a little thing to pay, but it seemed big to Denver. Nobody was going to help her unless she told it – told all of it. It was clear Janey wouldn't and wouldn't let her see the Bodwins otherwise. So Denver told this stranger what she hadn't told Lady Jones, in return for which Janey admitted the Bodwins needed help, although they didn't know it. She was alone there, and now that her employers were getting older, she couldn't take care of them like she used to. More and more she was required to sleep the night there. Maybe she could talk them into letting Denver do the night shift, come right after supper, say, maybe get the breakfast. That way Denver could care for Sethe in the day and earn a little something at night, how's that?

Denver had explained the girl in her house who plagued her mother as a cousin come to visit, who got sick too and bothered them both. Janey seemed more interested in Sethe's condition, and from what Denver told her it seemed the woman had lost her mind. That wasn't the Sethe she remembered. This Sethe had lost her wits, finally, as Janey knew she would – trying to do it all alone with her nose in the air. Denver squirmed under the criticism of her mother, shifting in the chair and keeping her eyes on the inside sink. Janey Wagon went on about pride until she got to Baby Suggs, for whom she had nothing but sweet words. 'I never went to those woodland services she had, but she was always nice to me. Always. Never be another like her.'

'I miss her too,' said Denver.

'Bet you do. Everybody miss her. That was a good woman.'

Denver didn't say anything else and Janey looked at her face for a while. 'Neither one of your brothers ever come back to see how you all was?'

'No, ma'am.'

'Ever hear from them?'

'No, ma'am. Nothing.'

'Guess they had a rough time in that house. Tell me, this here woman in your house. The cousin. She got any lines in her hands?'

'No,' said Denver.

'Well,' said Janey. 'I guess there's a God after all.'

The interview ended with Janey telling her to come back in a few days. She needed time to convince her employers what they needed: night help because Janey's own family needed her. 'I don't want to quit these people, but they can't have all my days and nights too.'

What did Denver have to do at night?

'Be here. In case.'

In case what?

Janey shrugged. 'In case the house burn down.' She smiled then. 'Or bad weather slop the roads so bad I can't get here early enough for them. Case late guests need serving or cleaning up after. Anything. Don't ask me what whitefolks need at night.'

'They used to be good whitefolks.'

'Oh, yeah. They good. Can't say they ain't good. I wouldn't trade them for another pair, tell you that.'

With those assurances, Denver left, but not before she had seen, sitting on a shelf by the back door, a blackboy's mouth full of money. His head was thrown back farther than a head could go, his hands were shoved in his pockets. Bulging like moons, two eyes were all the face he had above the gaping red mouth. His hair was a cluster of raised, widely spaced dots made of nail heads. And he was on his knees. His mouth, wide as a cup, held the coins needed to pay for a delivery or some other small service, but could just as well have held buttons, pins or crab-apple jelly. Painted across the pedestal he knelt on were the word 'At Yo Service.'

The news that Janey got hold of she spread among the other coloredwomen. Sethe's dead daughter, the one whose throat she cut, had come back to fix her. Sethe was worn down, speckled, dying, spinning, changing shapes and generally bedeviled. That this daughter beat her, tied her to the bed and pulled out all her hair. It took them days to get the story properly blown up and themselves agitated and then to calm down and assess the situation. They fell into three groups: those that believed the worst; those that believed none of it; and those, like Ella, who thought it through.

'Ella. What's all this I'm hearing about Sethe?'

'Tell me it's in there with her. That's all I know.'

'The daughter? The killed one?'

'That's what they tell me.'

'How they know that's her?'

'It's sitting there. Sleeps, eats and raises hell. Whipping Sethe every day.'

'I'll be. A baby?'

'No. Grown. The age it would have been had it lived.'

'You talking about flesh?'

'I'm talking about flesh.'

'Whipping her?'

'Like she was batter.'

'Guess she had it coming.'

'Nobody got that coming.'

'But, Ella – '

'But nothing. What's fair ain't necessarily right.'

'You can't just up and kill your children.'

'No, and the children can't just up and kill the mama.'

It was Ella more than anyone who convinced the others that rescue was in order. She was a practical woman who believed there was a root either to chew or avoid for every ailment. Cogitation, as she called it, clouded things and prevented action. Nobody loved her and she wouldn't have liked it if they had, for she considered love a serious disability.

[...]

Whatever Sethe had done, Ella didn't like the idea of past errors taking possession of the present. Sethe's crime was staggering and her pride outstripped even that; but she could not countenance the possibility of sin moving on in the house, unleashed and sassy. Daily life took as much as she had. The future was sunset; the past something to leave behind. And if it didn't stay behind, well, you might have to stomp it out. Slave life; freed life – every day was a test and a trial. Nothing could be counted on in a world where even when you were a solution you were a problem. 'Sufficient unto the day is the evil thereof,' and nobody needed more; nobody needed a grown-up evil sitting at the table with a grudge. As long as the ghost showed out from its ghostly place – shaking stuff, crying, smashing and such – Ella respected it. But if it took flesh and came in her world, well, the shoe was on the other foot. She didn't mind a little communication between the two worlds, but this was an invasion.

(Morrison, 1987a, pp.250–7)

Toiling in India's ship graveyard for £1 a day

Alang's critics call it a local version of Victorian Britain's dark satanic mills. Shipbreaking bosses say it is a green industry fighting for its life

Randeep Ramesh in Alang

Workers cut up steel at Alang

Monir Chauhan takes off his gumboots and wriggles two stumps at the end of his feet where his big toes should be. 'I went to work even when I lost these. If you do not, you lose your job here,' he says. 'Here' is Alang, a six-mile stretch of shoreline in Gujarat, largely obscured from view by dozens of rusting tankers and cruise liners in various stages of dismemberment. On the oily, grimy coast lie the steel carcasses of vessels brought from as far as Brazil and as close as Iraq.

The biggest hulk belongs to Britain's 400,000 tonne supertanker Hellespont Grand.

Situated off the Arabian Sea coast on India's western flank, Alang is where the world's ships come to die.

Shipbreaking is one of India's economic success stories, a £270m business that provides steel for the country's booming industry and much-needed jobs.

Its critics say Alang is a modern Indian version of Victorian Britain's dark satanic mills: an engine of industrial growth which provides poorly paid jobs to destitute people in inhumane conditions.

Around the ships swarm 40,000 migrant workers, prepared to toil in the 190 'plots' that line the coast. The work is dangerous, backbreaking and by western standards cheap – a 10-hour shift pays as little as £1.

Mr Chauhan, 38, says he earns a little more as he is a 'gas cutter', a person who slices ships up with an oxyacetylene torch.

Eight years of inhaling hot paint fumes have left him with persistent coughing and frequent bouts of breathlessness. 'The doctors have told me that I have gases and poisons inside me,' he says.

But he says competition for jobs is so intense that workers can lose their jobs for being ill. 'If you fall sick and take leave, there will be no job for you when you come back.'

At plot V4, the beach is littered with steel plates from the Hellespont Grand's hull and engine parts cut by blowtorch and saw. The work began last November and it will take a year to finish. While hard hats and goggles are worn by most labourers, masks, gloves and boots are not. This is an improvement on the past, when workers went about barefoot and bare-headed.

Last year, workers say, 25 people were blown up when a torch cut through a Greek tanker containing unreleased gas.

Naveen Singh, the supervisor for the Hellespont, admits that workers might be killed or injured, but adds: 'You have risks in every industry in India. Alang is no different.'

Most workers are migrants who live in slums opposite the shipbreaking yards, with no toilets or electricity. Yet despite the conditions, workers say it is better to work and die than to starve and die.

Burnt shoulder

Almost all come from northern India's poorest states, Orissa, Bihar and Uttar Pradesh.

'I came here five months ago, because I have a family to feed,' says Shivram Pradhan. 'I was a farmer, but I could not make enough from my two acres. Here I can make 80 rupees [£1] a day.' But he cannot work at present because he has burnt his shoulder carrying hot steel plates.

There is a hospital in Alang, but most workers travel the hour's drive to the nearest big town, Bhavnagar, for serious complaints. Malaria is rife and a study estimated last year that one in 20 workers in Alang are HIV positive.

A little more than 20 years ago, Alang was a small poverty-stricken village. Three factors have helped it to become the world's biggest shipbreaking yard.

First, the heavy tides and sloping beaches meant there was no need to build expensive dry docks and piers. Second, environmental and safety regulations that had made shipbreaking unviable in the west were ignored and unenforced in places like Alang. Third was the apparently limitless supply of cheap labour.

But Greenpeace has waged a six-year campaign against perceived abuses, with some notable successes.

In 1998, the US, which once dominated the shipbreaking trade, banned the export of its navy ships to developing countries. It was that order that eight months ago saw the warships towed to Teesside shipbreaking yards in Britain.

Last November, Greenpeace reported how shipowners were flouting international regulations on the subcontinent. Greenpeace found that none of the 145 vessels it surveyed, including the Hellespont Grand, had an inventory of hazardous materials when they arrived at shipbreaking yards.

The environmentalists argue that the rusting hulks landed on Alang contain health hazards such as asbestos, used to insulate pipes, and tributyltin, used as a weather-guard in ship paint.

'These have been proven to be dangerous,' Ramapatty Kumar, a Greenpeace spokesman, says. 'Our aim is to make someone responsible for such hazards.'

Less than 12 miles along the coast from Alang, the ecological price is all too visible. In the village of Gopanath, three generations of fisherman are convinced that the black slick that coats the rocks is the reason for their declining catches.

'I have been fishing for 40 years and when I began you could go half a kilometre from the beach and catch 100kg of big fat fish,' says Gushabhai Chudasma, the 70-year-old patriarch of the extended family. 'Since Alang started we have had to go further and further out, and we catch smaller and smaller amounts.'

Green industry

The industry claims that it has been miscast by environmentalists and human rights activists. Shipbreaking is a green industry, say its supporters, as almost all the reusable materials are recovered. Alang alone produces 2.5m tonnes of steel a year for India's rolling mills.

Everything that could be removed from a ship is sold at Alang: shops and market stands offer diesel generators, lifejackets and kitchen sinks. The most prized items are the ships' bells, which are used in local Hindu temples.

'We do not just break ships up, we recycle them,' says Pravin Nagarsheth, president of the Iron Steel Scrap and Shipbreakers Association.

The industry claims that India's growing environmental and safety laws are increasingly prompting many shipowners to find alternative markets for their vessels in shipbreaking yards in Pakistan, Bangladesh and China, where regulations are even more lightly policed.

'We lost the number one slot last year to China,' says Mr Nagarsheth. 'The problem is that we are increasing the regulatory burden in India, but not in other countries.' Both Mr Nagarsheth and Greenpeace agree that the roots of the problem lie with the global nature of the shipping business.

About 40,000 ships ply the oceans, most of them crewed by the world's poor, owned by shadowy offshore companies and flying flags of convenience.

'The only way of ensuring a level playing field is for every shipowner to clean the ships [of toxic materials] before they bring them here,' says Mr Nagarsheth.

(*The Guardian*, 22 June 2004, p.15)

Chapter 7

Making the past present: historical wrongs and demands for reparation

David Lambert

Contents

1 Introduction

In Chapter 6, Steve Pile discussed how the ghosts of past injustices, such as the Atlantic slave trade and slavery, continue to haunt the world. Seemingly absent pasts can return in unsettling ways. Such reappearances are not always unexpected, however. Sometimes deliberate attempts are made to bring the past back through conscious, organised, political campaigns. Although explicit demands to right past wrongs – demands, that is, for reparations – are being made in today's world, there is no guarantee that they will receive any more attention than the ghosts that haunt us. For while some try to make such wrongs present, others deny them by ignoring and erasing history and making the past absent from contemporary concerns.

'They Stole Us, They Sold Us, They Owe Us! Reparations Now'. With this slogan, the US-based organisation, Millions for Reparations, demands restitution for the descendants of those who were enslaved in the USA between the sixteenth and nineteenth centuries. The campaign is spearheaded by African-Americans as it was African people who were forcibly transported across the Atlantic to work in the USA, and they and their descendants who suffered slavery. Nevertheless, neither this historical form of slavery nor today's demands for reparations is limited to one national context. Millions for Reparations is just one of many campaigns across North and South America, the Caribbean, Europe and Africa. Together they are part of an emerging worldwide reparations movement that is an increasingly significant feature of a globalised world.

Defining slavery

A socio-economic system in which the labourers ('slaves') are owned or controlled by a 'slaveholder' and are forced to work, usually through mental or physical abuse or threatened abuse. The labourers are dehumanised, treated as commodities or bought and sold as 'property', and physically constrained with restrictions placed on freedom of movement. Some find 'enslaved person' to be a more appropriate term than 'slave' as the former recognises the humanity of those bought and sold for their labour.

International recognition of particular past wrongs has been important in sustaining the demands that are made for reparations. For instance, the United Nations (UN) declared 2004 the 'International Year to Commemorate the Struggle against Slavery and its Abolition'. This message from Koïchiro Matsuura, the Director-General of the UN Educational, Scientific and Cultural Organization (UNESCO), makes clear what was being commemorated:

> The slave trade and slavery constitute one of the darkest chapters in the history of the world. This dehumanizing

enterprise, challenging the very basis of the Universal Declaration of Human Rights and roundly condemned by the international community, in particular at the Durban World Conference against Racism, Racial Discrimination, Xenophobia and Related Intolerance [in 2001] which labelled it a 'crime against humanity', gives us all cause for thought and requires each and every one of us to exercise due vigilance ... Aside from looking at the past, the intention is to sound the alarm about all forms of contemporary racism, discrimination and intolerance, and thus to set the stage for a greater awareness of the need to respect human beings ... By institutionalizing memory, resisting the onset of oblivion, recalling the memory of a tragedy that for long years remained hidden or unrecognized, and by assigning it its proper place in the human conscience, we respond to our duty to remember ... As a matter of urgency this major episode in the history of humanity, whose consequences are permanently imprinted in the world's geography and economy, should take its full place in the school textbooks and curricula of every country in the world.

(Matsuura, 2004)

Slavery has existed in many forms and in many places throughout human history, and forms persist to this day despite slavery being banned in most countries and prohibited by the 1948 Universal Declaration of Human Rights. What was remembered in 2004, however, was a specific form of slavery, namely the Atlantic slave trade from Africa across the Atlantic, and the systems of slavery it supplied, mainly in North, South and Central America and the Caribbean. Those enslaved were African and people of African descent, and most were forced to work in colonies and states established by European settlers and their descendants. This form of slavery existed between the sixteenth and nineteenth centuries. Despite being only one type of slavery, it was a 'crime against humanity' (Matsuura, 2004) in terms of its duration, extensiveness and effects.

Although this 'darkest' of chapters in human history occurred in the past, many people and organisations – including the UN – believe it is important to remember this wrong, not only because it serves as a warning about forms of racism and injustice that exist today, but also because its 'consequences are permanently imprinted in the world's geography and economy' (Matsuura, 2004). In other words, the slave trade and slavery have shaped today's world, and their legacies are still apparent in patterns of global inequality (between Africa and the West), as well as in racial inequalities within many societies (between black and white people, for example). The global significance does not end here, though, as the following statement in support of the global reparations movement makes clear:

> Globalization has provided great benefits for US and multi-national corporations and great misery and exploitation for the vast majority of the world. Globalization is a new word for an old concept. Globalization in its infancy kidnapped millions of Africans to bring us to the so-called Western Hemisphere to be enslaved ... [Today] we, the victims of globalization, are making it work for us. My law firm, Thomas, Wareham & Richards, is part of a legal team which brought the first case suing private corporations for reparations for the blood money they made during the Trans-Atlantic Slave Trade and Slavery. This week, the same legal team filed suit against three of the multi-national corporations which profiteered during the Apartheid era in South Africa. What these cases have in common are multi-national corporate defendants; African Continental and Diasporic Plaintiffs. This is a new form of globalization – where the victims strike back. Globalization has indeed shrunk the world – the perpetrators of crimes against humanity have lost their impunity and have nowhere to hide.
>
> (Wareham, 2002)

The description of a 'new form of globalization – where the victims strike back' (Wareham, 2002) emphasises how a global reparations movement is emerging out of the possibility of forging connections between different national campaigns and using the opportunities presented by international recognition to make demands. In addition, the argument that 'Globalization is a new word for an old concept' (Wareham, 2002) places the slave trade and slavery within a history of globalisation that is longer than we might commonly think. By connecting parts of the globe (Africa, Europe and the Americas) together in new relationships, resulting in the mass movement of people (enslaved Africans) and fostering the accumulation of wealth in some parts of the world (notably Europe), slavery was crucial to the development of today's world. Moreover, it is, in part, because of the role of this 'crime against humanity' (Matsuura, 2004) in contributing to the creation of a globalised world that current movements for reparations have a similarly global character, demands bringing together different parts of the world that were first connected by the slave trade. For all these reasons, a past wrong like slavery is of considerable consequence for life in a globalised world today.

In Chapter 1, John Allen discussed Iris Marion Young's (2003) argument that complex structural processes connect groups of people and institutions in distant geographical places. The slavery reparations movement claims that such processes also connect today's world to distant historical periods because processes operating in the past continue to have effects now. Young also argues that responsibility for others does not stop with those who are directly to blame for the conditions in sweatshops, and that distant consumers and others are politically responsible through their participation in ordinary economic transactions. Young's argument is also helpful for thinking about the past wrong of the slave trade and slavery because their sheer scale and complexity, as well as the fact that they occurred long ago, make it unhelpful to focus on direct relationships between guilty perpetrators and their specific victims. Those demanding reparations argue that the responsibility of those in the West for past wrongs rests not only with their direct connections to them, but also to the wider injustices in the world that have stemmed, in part, from the globalised past. So, just as Chapter 1 showed that life in a globalised world involves demands that seek to bring distant places – like sweatshops – close, we will see in this chapter that demands are also raised that seek to make absent pasts present.

Chapter aims

◆ To explore the kinds of demands that are made when reparations for past wrongs are sought.

◆ To consider the specific past wrong of the Atlantic slave trade and slavery, the kinds of demands made for reparations and the types of response they receive.

◆ To examine how reparation demands for historical wrongs work by making absent pasts present.

2   Reparations to right past wrongs

Imagine that I were to collide with you on the street and knock you over. That is something that could be called a 'wrong'. We could call me the 'perpetrator' (of the wrong) and you the 'victim'. Let us say that you then asked me to apologise for knocking you over. We can describe that as a 'demand' for reparations – the form of reparation being an apology. When you make this demand, you are asserting my responsibility for the wrong and we can think of you as the 'claimant' and me as the 'respondent'. Although this is a trivial example, it does help to illustrate what we mean by a simple demand to right a past wrong. We can represent our exchange as shown in Figure 7.1.

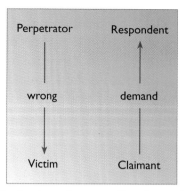

Figure 7.1   The basic structure of a reparation demand

Figure 7.1 shows the structure of a reparation demand for a past wrong in terms of four 'roles' taken by those involved (perpetrator, victim, claimant and respondent) and two 'actions' (the wrong and the demand). This is necessarily a simplification of what actually happens, and to understand reparation demands for past wrongs we need to add detail and context from real case studies. While you are reading and thinking about the specific examples that follow, however, bear in mind this more abstract way of thinking about reparation demands.

Real and infinitely more serious demands for reparations have become particularly common since the end of the Second World War. During the war, the Nazi regime in Germany was responsible for genocide against the Jewish people. Six million people were murdered in the Holocaust, most in concentration camps. When the war was over, the new West German Government offered to pay reparations to Jewish Holocaust survivors and to the state of Israel. In 1952, West Germany signed an agreement to pay US$715 million in goods and services to Israel as compensation for taking in survivors, US$110 million for programmes to finance the relief and resettlement of Holocaust survivors, and direct reparations to selected individuals over a twelve-year period. The payment of reparations for the Holocaust has encouraged other groups of people to demand reparations for past wrongs inflicted upon them. Here are two examples of other claims:

▪ *Compensation for the internment of Japanese-Americans during the Second World War.* Following the Japanese attack on Pearl Harbor in December 1941, the USA was gripped by war hysteria, especially along its Pacific coast where residents feared Japanese attacks on their cities, homes and businesses. Political leaders in the western states of California, Oregon and Washington demanded that residents of Japanese ancestry be removed from their homes and relocated in isolated inland areas. The result of this pressure was the internment of people for no other reason than their ancestry.

Beginning in 1942, 120,000 people were forcibly confined in camps. After the war, the last of the camps was closed in March 1946. After decades of lobbying by Japanese-American institutions such as the Japanese American Citizens League (JACL), the US Government made a formal apology for the internment in 1989. It also provided monetary funds as compensation and the restitution of confiscated property.

■ *Aboriginal claims for land and recognition.* From the sixteenth century until well into the twentieth century, European settlers and those of European descent established colonies across large parts of the world. In the process, land was seized and the indigenous populations were often devastated or seriously reduced in number because of the introduction of diseases, the destruction of agricultural and economic systems, or through deliberate policies of extermination. Although many parts of the world that had been colonised became independent countries after the Second World War, there were places such as Canada, the USA, Australia and New Zealand where pre-colonial populations remained marginalised. Since the 1960s, many of these 'aboriginal' populations have begun to make demands on the states in which they reside for full political recognition, the return of traditional lands and artefacts, and apologies for past policies. For example, individuals and institutions representing the aboriginal or 'First Nations' peoples of Canada, have demanded recognition of certain historical facts such as 'the physical and sexual abuse in residential schools and the assimilationist agendas pursued there; the forced relocations of aboriginal communities and the consequences thereof ... and the cultural aggression ... which forbade certain customs and provided the legislative framework for a system of internal colonialism' (cited in Cairns, 2003).

One of the things that should be clear from these examples is that different forms of reparations have been demanded for past wrongs. For example, the JACL demanded:

■ a formal apology;

■ monetary compensation;

■ restitution of property.

Consequently, the term 'reparations' encompasses both demands for material recompense that relate directly to the wrong, such as the return of property, and more diffuse, immaterial demands, for example for an apology. Figure 7.2 conceptualises the various types of demands for reparations.

Figure 7.2   Different forms of reparations
Source: Torpey, 2003, p.6

At the centre of Figure 7.2 is the phrase 'transitional justice'.
Transitional justice involves the punishment of an identifiable group of
perpetrators through criminal trials and truth commissions. The South
African Truth and Reconciliation Commission, which was established
in 1995 to help deal with the human rights abuses that had occurred
under apartheid, is one such organisation that is involved in
transitional justice. The 'transition' in question is usually from
authoritarian to democratic forms of government. The first ring out
from the centre of Figure 7.2 shows restitutions. These are commonly
of a material kind. Monetary compensation is the most obvious form,
such as that paid by West Germany to Holocaust survivors and the
state of Israel. Restitution may also involve the return of territory, as in
the demands made by aboriginal claims for the restoration of
traditional lands, or other forms of cultural property with particular
meaning for the claimants. The next ring out in Figure 7.2 shows
apologies, which can include statements of regret. These involve
exchanges between respondents and claimants, such as the US
Government's apology in 1989 for the internment of Japanese
Americans. Apologies are usually more symbolic than restitutions,
though even monetary compensation may be symbolic. How
meaningful apologies really are, especially for descendants of the
original victims, is a moot point. Finally, the outermost ring of
Figure 7.2 shows concerns with the remembrance of past wrongs and
giving them due recognition. Such forms of reparations involve
rewriting historical narratives by and from the perspective of those
groups that are most directly affected by the history in question. The
message from the UNESCO Director-General in Section 1 captures
this in the case of the slave trade and slavery when it refers to the
importance of 'institutionalizing memory, resisting the onset of

oblivion, recalling the memory of a tragedy that for long years remained hidden or unrecognized, and ... assigning it its proper place in the human conscience' (Matsuura, 2004).

Why represent the different types of reparations that might be demanded as a series of concentric rings and a central circle? One reason is that the demands closer to the centre in Figure 7.2 focus on material or legal matters, while those further out are more symbolic in character. Another reason is that the demands shown further out from the centre tend to be less focused on directly punishing those responsible or repairing the wrong and more concerned with the effects and legacies of the wrong. For example, transitional justice typically focuses on the specific politicians or officials with direct responsibility for perpetrating the wrong. If, however, the wrong was committed in the distant past, then attempts to punish individuals might become less important than providing restitution to those who live with the consequences. This is the case in the example of aboriginal land claims, where the settlers and colonial officials who perpetrated the original wrong are long dead, as are their victims. Instead, the focus is on the return of traditional lands and artefacts to current aboriginal peoples. Moreover, some wrongs are just so great and have such widespread and complex effects that it is very difficult to identify the individual perpetrators who are responsible. For this reason, something like the slave trade and slavery may not even be easy to identify as a particular wrong, but rather be seen by some as part of the taken-for-granted course of global events. It is almost as though such wrongs are too large to comprehend. In these cases, more diffuse demands for recognition and remembrance (shown in the outer ring of Figure 7.2) may be all that is possible at first, and a crucial prerequisite for later, more focused demands (closer to the centre).

We can also say that the forms of reparations that are further from the centre in Figure 7.2 are often concerned with wrongs that are more distant in the past. In such cases, however, it can be difficult for claimants to make their demands. Let us return to our simple example of when I collided into you and knocked you over (see Figure 7.1). In this case, it would be straightforward to identify who was responsible because the wrong and the demand were almost instantaneous. To make a demand, the claimant has only to establish that a wrong has been committed – that he or she is the victim – although this does not guarantee that the perpetrator/respondent will provide reparations, such as an apology. Yet just as John Allen showed in Chapter 1 that the antisweatshop campaign has to work to bring distant victims and perpetrators closer together to change consumer behaviour, so in this chapter we will see that if a long period of time has passed between the wrong and the demand, it becomes less straightforward to establish responsibility. In the case of our imaginary scenario, perhaps I might respond by claiming that I do not remember bumping into you or insist that you 'get over it', even though you are still feeling hurt or upset.

Recognising that wrongs and demands may be distant from each other in time, because the wrong took place in the past, serves to complicate how we think of the structure of demands for reparation. Figure 7.3 offers a way to represent this.

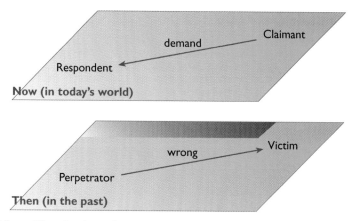

Figure 7.3   The structure of a reparation demand for a past wrong
Source: Trouillot, 2000, p.175

Like Figure 7.1, the schematic representation in Figure 7.3 shows four roles or positions of those involved in reparation demands and two actions. The big difference in Figure 7.3 is that the 'wrong' and the 'demand' are shown in different temporal 'planes' – *then* and *now* – representing the time that has passed between the two. This means that the perpetrator and victim are not present in same period of time as the respondent and claimant. This creates distinct problems for making a reparation demand for a past wrong:

1   Demands for reparations must establish that a past wrong occurred.

This, of course, is exactly the same as in the case of the simple demand we considered in Figure 7.1 but, in addition:

2   Demands for reparations must show that the past wrong continues to matter in some way – that the past wrong is *present* in today's world.

Making a past wrong present for current generations may involve universal arguments about violations of human rights and human dignity. For example, the UNESCO statement condemned slavery as a challenge to 'the very basis of the Universal Declaration of Human Rights' (Matsuura, 2004). Another way of making a past wrong present may be by identifying its impact in shaping today's world. To explain this, let us return to the scenario when I collided with you and knocked you over. Imagine that this occurred because we were both running to get to a station in order to catch a train. It was important for each of us to do so because we were both trying to get to the same job interview. To make things worse, I got the job, while you did not even make the interview. Now this scenario is all a little far-fetched, but it does indicate that a past wrong may have subsequent consequences that are beneficial for the perpetrator and detrimental for the victim. To put it another way, a wrong might shape the course of subsequent events (I got the job, you did not). Consequently, wrongs do not just happen *then*; they may continue to have effects *now*. In our scenario, your subsequent demand for reparations might not be for the original wrong alone, but also for its later consequences. You might want more than an apology; you might want some form of monetary restitution to compensate for the fact that you did not get the job. The sum you demand could be based on what you would have earned if you had. It is this idea, that the effects of the past wrong of the slave trade and slavery are still present in today's world, that is evident in the UNESCO reference to it as a 'major episode in the history of humanity, whose consequences are permanently imprinted in the world's geography and economy' (Matsuura, 2004).

Nevertheless, making it clear that a past wrong has present consequences is likely to be more difficult if the wrong occurred in the distant past. Of course, the predicament that may be caused by the passing of time is not at all unusual. Indeed, most cases of reparations involve some kind of temporal distance, and the wrong is unlikely to be 'instantaneous' with the demand. If you look back at the case studies of reparation demands in Section 1, you will notice that years, even centuries, passed between the wrongs being committed and demands being made for reparations. So, in addition to the two points raised above about reparation demands for past wrongs:

3   Demands must also establish a relationship of identity between past perpetrator and present respondent, and between past victim and present claimant.

This is not necessarily about determining direct (perhaps individual or familial) connections in terms of blame and victimhood; it often involves arguments about collective responsibilities and entitlements. In the case of many demands for reparations, establishing connections between then and now is complicated because it is not individuals who are involved – as it was when I knocked you over – but groups of people. Using the terms 'the victim/claimant' and 'the perpetrator/respondent' may imply that we are talking about individuals here, but usually reparation claims involve groups of people, and institutions, such as national governments or campaigning organisations, that represent these groups. For example, in the case of compensation for the internment of Japanese-Americans, 'the victim' was the 120,000 or so Japanese-Americans and 'the perpetrator' was the US authorities. The demands for reparations were made mostly by Japanese-American institutions, such as the JACL, which represented the claimants; the respondent was the US Government. Sometimes when groups of people or institutions are making demands of other groups or institutions, it is less clear who has the right to make demands and who should respond. This is particularly true when all the direct victims and perpetrators are long dead, as in the case of the slave trade and slavery, and it is the descendants of the victims, or others who identify with them, who are making the reparation demands. The following sections explore this case in more detail.

Summary

- Demands for reparations for past wrongs have become more common since the end of the Second World War.

- Demands are made for different types of reparations, ranging from contemporaneous demands for transitional justice and material restitutions to more symbolic forms, such as apologies or the remembrance and recognition of the past wrong.

- Making a reparation demand can be more difficult if the wrong is in the distant past and/or if groups of people are involved. The claimants must try to connect 'then' and 'now' to show the wrong present in today's world and to demonstrate that claimants and respondents in the present correspond to victims and perpetrators in the past.

3   The past wrongs of the slave trade and slavery

Organisations like Millions for Reparations are making demands about the specific past wrong of the Atlantic slave trade and slavery. Definitions of this wrong give some idea of what enslaved people faced, but it still might seem a little abstract and unreal. In Chapter 6, you came across a more personal exploration of the terror and injustice of slavery in the American South through the novel *Beloved* (Morrison, 1987). A sense of what the slave trade and slavery entailed for the individuals involved is also conveyed by the life story of an African man, Olaudah Equiano, who was born in what is now Nigeria and enslaved when he was young (see Figure 7.4).

Figure 7.4   Olaudah Equiano

Activity 7.1

Turn now to Reading 7A by Olaudah Equiano (1789) entitled 'The interesting narrative of the life of Olaudah Equiano, or Gustavus Vassa the African. Written by himself', which you will find at the end of the chapter. While you read, note down who appear to be the victims of slavery and who appear to be the perpetrators of the victims' enslavement.

In the narrative of Reading 7A, which he wrote later in his life, Equiano describes how he and other enslaved African people were transported aboard a slave ship crewed by white people that was taking them to the 'white people's country to work for them'. His account is of being taken from West Africa, the ocean journey across the Atlantic (the so-called 'Middle Passage'), and the arrival at the Caribbean island of Barbados. This was a common route for enslaved African people as Barbados was both a major destination for enslaved workers itself and a port of call for their re-export to other parts of the Americas. Equiano himself was sold on to a plantation owner in Virginia, in what is now the USA. Note that Equiano also refers to those African people who had 'brought me on board, and had been receiving their pay' from the white slave traders. In other words, although Equiano and some other African people were the clear victims here, those responsible for their enslavement included some Africans as well as white slave traders (and those who bought the enslaved people in the Americas). What is also clear from Equiano's writing is the horror and bewilderment of the slave trade. There is a strong sense of the dislocation that Equiano felt at being taken from Africa to the unfamiliar 'white people's country' and we also witness something of violence when one enslaved person is flogged for attempting to commit suicide.

A personal narrative account provides one representation of the history of slavery. A more general view is provided in Figure 7.5, which shows part of the route that Equiano took during his life, and the forced movement of enslaved Africans that made up the trans-Atlantic slave trade. Equiano was just one of the millions of African people with similar experiences.

Perhaps twelve million people were deported, and the life stories of most will never be known. It has been estimated that about two million did not survive the Middle Passage (Curtin, 1969; Richardson, 1998). Those that did, and their descendants, formed part of the 'African' or 'black' diaspora (see Chapter 4, Section 2.2 for a definition of 'diaspora'). The phenomenal demand for enslaved labour that was supplied by the slave trade was fuelled by the colonisation of the Americas by Europeans from the fifteenth century onwards, and the establishment of colonies. The geographer Miles Ogborn (2000, p.43) notes that by 1800 parts of Africa, Europe and the Americas (as well as Asia) were 'tied together into a new set of relationships' that can be seen as part of the long process of globalisation. This globalised past involved, among other things, the forced traffic of millions of people like Equiano to work on plantations; the transportation of the goods produced in the plantations, such as sugar and cotton, to markets in Europe; and movement of profits and revenues from the colonies to those countries that financed them. Although these networks were largely organised for the benefit of Europeans and colonists of European descent, the slave trade could not function without the involvement of some Africans (and Arabs) who sold enslaved people

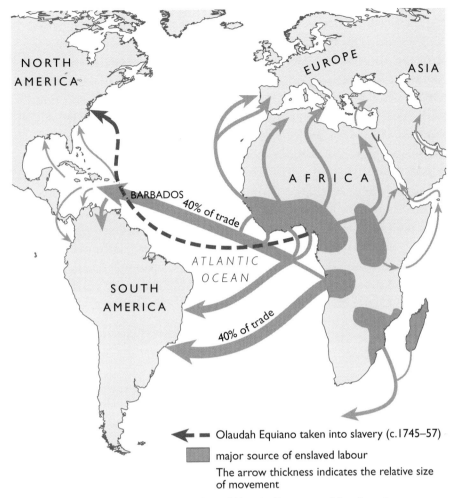

Figure 7.5   Major slaving routes from Africa to Europe and the Americas, including that taken by Olaudah Equiano
Source: Finkelman and Miller, 1998, vol.1, p.xvii

to the Europeans. Various forms of slavery did exist in Africa prior to the growth in the demand from European colonies (what Equiano (1789) refers to as 'my former slavery') and, before the sixteenth century, most enslaved people exported from Africa went to the Arabian Peninsula. Nevertheless, it was the development of European overseas empires that drove the expansion of the slave trade, which peaked in the late eighteenth century. It was also European colonisation in the Americas that transformed the system of slavery into part of an emerging set of global relations.

Slavery was driven by the economic demands of plantation owners, but it was also bound up with cultural assumptions about the inferiority of the people who were enslaved. The association of blackness with sin and evil was an aspect of European culture before the fifteenth century. Such connotations were reinforced and applied wholesale to African people during the expansion of slavery in the Americas. As a result, African people came to be seen as naturally inferior. By the nineteenth century, the idea that there were absolute racial differences between 'white' and 'black' had become commonly accepted in the societies of Europe and their overseas colonies and settlements. The commonplace division of people by race is therefore, in part, a product of the Atlantic slave trade and of slavery (Chaplin, 2002), and its legacies are still apparent to this day in various forms of racism. You will remember that one of the reasons the UN declared 2004 the International Year to Commemorate the Struggle against Slavery and its Abolition was in order to 'sound the alarm about all forms of contemporary racism, discrimination and intolerance, and thus to set the stage for a greater awareness of the need to respect human beings' (Matsuura, 2004). The slave trade and slavery were not only responsible for creating an African diaspora across North and South America, the Caribbean, Europe and beyond, but also contributed to the development and dissemination of ideas of racial difference.

Despite the brutality and inhumanity involved, the morality of the slave trade and slavery did not begin to be questioned by substantial numbers of Europeans and people of European descent until the end of the eighteenth century. With the enslaved people themselves this was a different matter, of course, and there had been many rebellions and revolts, as well as other smaller scale, more frequent acts of resistance, since the sixteenth century. Although white abolitionists were important in the various campaigns that eventually resulted in the abolition of the slave trade and slavery during the nineteenth century, the role of people of African descent cannot be underestimated. Equiano's narrative (1789), for instance, was an anti-slavery bestseller, and its account of the horrors involved furthered the campaign of those who sought to end the slave trade and slavery.

Defining racism

An ideology that makes value judgements about the physical and mental capacity, social status or moral worth of people on the basis of the biological differences that supposedly exist between different 'racial types' of human beings, as well as discrimination or unequal treatment on this ideological basis. Such beliefs about the inferiority of some human groups and the superiority of others are often based on observations about physical characteristics such as skin colour, hair type and nose shape.

The experiences of Equiano and millions of other Africans help to explain why the slave trade has been recognised as a 'crime against humanity' (Matsuura, 2004) and it would seem that this is just the sort of past wrong that demands some form of redress. Indeed, when Britain became the first European state permanently to abolish slavery in its overseas empire between 1833 and 1838, compensation was paid – £20 million in total, which was an enormous sum of money at the time. However, this money did not go to the newly freed people of African descent for all their unpaid labour and mistreatment in the British colonies. Instead, the money went to the people who had formerly owned the enslaved workers and to others involved in slavery. The money paid was not reparation for a past wrong; it was compensation for the loss of property – human property. When slavery was abolished in the USA between 1863 and 1865, there was some talk of providing each of the ex-enslaved people with 'forty acres and a mule' as restitution (see Conley, 2003). This came to nothing and, again, the victims received no financial redress. According to the African-American campaigner against slavery, Frederick Douglass, they were sent away 'empty-handed, without money', left at the mercy of former slaveholders and without any kind of material aid to help them in their new lives (Douglass, 1881, p.514). Douglass's criticism of the absence of restitution for newly freed black Americans amounted to one of the first demands for slavery reparations. Even as the struggle for emancipation from slavery was ending in different parts of the world, the struggle to right this past wrong was already beginning.

Summary

- The enslavement of Africans and people of African descent involved coerced work, ownership or control by a 'slaveholder', dehumanising treatment and violence, and restrictions on movement. It provoked resistance from enslaved people and, later, opposition from anti-slavery campaigners.

- The slave trade that connected distant places on both sides of the Atlantic, and the systems of slavery it supplied in the Americas from the sixteenth to the nineteenth centuries, as well as the forms of opposition it spawned, form part of a globalised past.

- When Atlantic slavery was abolished during the nineteenth century, there was an absence of compensation for the former enslaved people.

4   Demanding reparations for slavery

In Section 3, we saw something of the past wrong of the Atlantic slave trade and slavery. In this section, we will turn to the reparation demands that have been made in relation to it and the types of responses that they have received. It was in the USA in the late 1960s and early 1970s that the current campaign for reparations for the slave trade and slavery began as an organised movement. It was related to the US Civil Rights Movement which came to prominence after the Second World War and sought to challenge the discrimination and institutional racism faced by African-Americans. Such discrimination itself had much to do with how the effects of slavery were still present in US society. The campaign for reparations was given new impetus in the late 1980s and early 1990s by the decision of the US Government to compensate surviving Japanese Americans interned during the Second World War. The campaign is ongoing and headed by organisations such as Millions for Reparations and the National Coalition of Blacks for Reparations in America (N'COBRA). Robert Brock (cited in Barkan, 2000, p.289), a leading restitution activist in the USA, identifies the goals of the campaign as follows:

- To punish the white community for the sins of slavery committed by its ancestors and oblige it to render retribution to the descendants of the slaves;

- To provide the black population with restitution for the unpaid labor of its slave ancestors;

- To redirect to blacks that portion of the national income which has been diverted from blacks to whites as a result of slavery and post-Emancipation racial discrimination;

- To provide the black community with the share of the national wealth and income which it would by now have had if it had been treated as other immigrant communities were, rather than enslaved.

(cited in Barkan, 2000, p.289)

Activity 7.2

Look back at Figure 7.3. It shows in a generalised manner the different elements that make up the structure of a reparation demand for a past wrong ('perpetrator', 'wrong', 'victim', 'claimant', 'demand' and 'respondent'). Using Robert Brock's summary of the goals of the US reparations movement, try to identify the different groups of people and institutions that fit into these abstract concepts.

The goals expressed by Brock (cited in Barkan, 2000, p.289) are a demand for reparations for the enslavement (the wrong) of the ancestors of African Americans (the victim – although 'the victim' is a reference to large numbers of people). While it does not say so explicitly, the perpetrator is the white American community that held enslaved people until the 1860s. The demand is for material restitution in the form of a share of national income, which is made for the African-American community by individuals such as Brock and through institutions such as N'COBRA (the claimant). These are directed towards white society in the USA, including the US Government (the respondent).

4.1   The global reparations movement

Although the campaign in the USA has probably been the most organised, demands for reparations are not limited to this country. There has been a globalisation of the movement, especially since the end of the Cold War. For instance, the Black Consciousness Centre at the University of São Paulo in Brazil, the country with the second highest proportion of black people in the world after Nigeria, submitted demands for reparations to the country's parliament in 1987 and again in 1995. In the UK, the Africa Reparations Movement (ARM-UK) was founded in 1993, inspired by, and seeing itself as part of, the reparations movement that had developed in Africa a couple of years earlier (see Figure 7.6).

It is the African reparations movement that is the most global in its agenda. In 1992, the Organization of African Unity (OAU) began to investigate the possibility of demanding restitution from countries with a moral obligation to restitute the crimes of slavery. This resulted a year later in the Abuja Proclamation, which set out the aims and demands of the African reparations movement.

Africa Reparations Movement

Figure 7.6   Main logo from ARM-UK's website

Source: Africa Reparations Movement (UK), 2005

Activity 7.3

I would like you to turn to Reading 7B, the 1993 Abuja Proclamation, which appears in Ali Mazrui and Alamin Mazrui's book *Black Reparations in the Era of Globalization* (2002). You will find the reading at the end of the chapter. You should be able to identify the different groups of people and organisations that represent the perpetrator, victim, claimant and respondent as shown in Figure 7.3. How convincing do you find the argument made here concerning the present consequences of the past system of slavery?

At first sight, it may seem that the perpetrator in Reading 7B refers to countries involved in the slave trade and slavery, and that the victim is the continent of Africa that had its population enslaved and the African people forced into slavery. Yet you will notice that the Abuja Proclamation refers not only to the 'damage done to Africa and its Diaspora by enslavement' but also to 'the damage done ... by ... colonization, and neo-colonization' (Mazrui and Mazrui, 2002).

African proponents of reparations, like the Kenyan-born intellectual and activist Ali Mazrui, see the slave trade as just the first aspect of a long-standing relationship between Africa and the West (especially Europe) that was to the detriment of the former. As he puts it: 'The long-term effects of slave raids and colonization are part of the brutal legacy of the present day' (Mazrui and Mazrui, 2002, p.90). The abolition of the slave trade and slavery by European countries in the nineteenth century did not end their involvement in Africa. Britain, for example, abolished its slave trade in 1807 and fully ended slavery in its colonies by 1838. It then began to extend its influence into other parts of Africa in an effort to abolish slavery there – which some might see as a little ironic, given how much Britain had profited from slavery in the past. This was the beginning of the colonisation of the continent by European powers and was facilitated, in some measure, by the impoverishment of Africa and the enrichment of some European states. The latter's enrichment had been at least partly due to the slave trade and slavery. This colonisation was also driven by the anti-African racial attitudes that had become embedded in European culture, again partly a product of slavery. Between about 1880 and 1914, many European countries seized parts of the continent in what has been called the 'Scramble for Africa' (see Figure 7.7).

Defining neo-colonialism

A form of political and economic domination by more developed countries over less developed countries in the absence of direct or formal rule. Neo-colonialism developed after former colonies became independent, and resulted in the continued control of their political and economic systems from outside. This stemmed from such things as the continuing political influence of the former colonial power, the presence of foreign business interests, dependence on former imperial markets or reliance on aid. Critics of neo-colonialism argue that it prevents the full realisation of the economic and political independence of the post-colonial state.

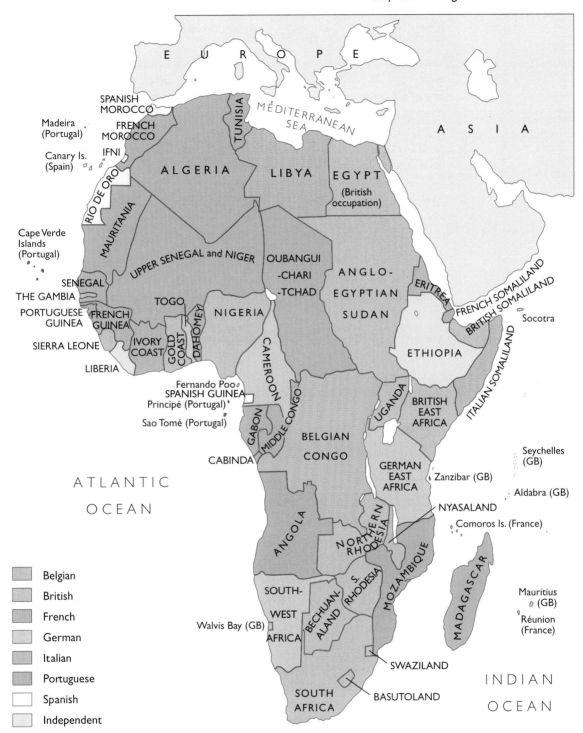

Figure 7.7   Colonial Africa in 1914, showing the partition of the continent by European powers
Source: Knox and Agnew, 1998, p.267, Figure B

Africa remained colonised by European powers until after the Second World War, and some parts did not become independent until the 1960s and 1970s. As a result, the reparations campaign, particularly in Africa, is concerned with more than slavery; it is also involved with the forms of exploitation that came later and which continue to occur. We can see this from the refrain in the Abuja Proclamation which says that 'the damage sustained by the African peoples is not a "thing of the past" but is painfully manifest in the damaged lives of contemporary Africans' (Mazrui and Mazrui, 2002). For reparations campaigners, the wrong was not merely something that happened 'in the past', but rather had effects that are clearly present in today's globalised world. We will return to the way in which reparation demands seek to make the past present in Section 5.

As far as the claimant goes, the Abuja Proclamation articulates a reparation demand by the OAU, a regional body that sought to promote the unity and solidarity of African states and act as a collective voice for the continent (it was replaced by the African Union in 2002). Following the Abuja Proclamation, a twelve-member Group of Eminent Persons (GEP) was sworn in to lead the African reparations movement, and included members such as Ali Mazrui. Their demands are made on behalf of 'the African peoples' across 'Global Africa' (Mazrui and Mazrui, 2002). The latter term is used by Ali Mazrui to describe the people of the African continent *and* the black diaspora together. The black diaspora was, to a large extent, produced by the slave trade, slavery and colonialism. In effect, 'Global Africa' refers to all people in the world who could be identified, or would identify themselves, as of black African descent.

This perspective gives the African reparations movement a global dimension, as is evident from the list of countries represented at the first international conference that focused on reparations for slavery (see Figure 7.8).

Just as the Atlantic slave trade and slavery played an important part in creating a globalised world between the sixteenth and nineteenth centuries, so the current reparations movement has brought together many individuals, institutions and states across Global Africa in the role of claimant. Indeed, these demands for reparations are seen as being 'a learning experience in self-discovery' (Mazrui and Mazrui, 2002) that will help to unite Global Africa.

The Abuja Proclamation makes apparent that although the reparations movement initially started in the black diaspora – especially in the USA – it has spread to involve campaigns across Global Africa.

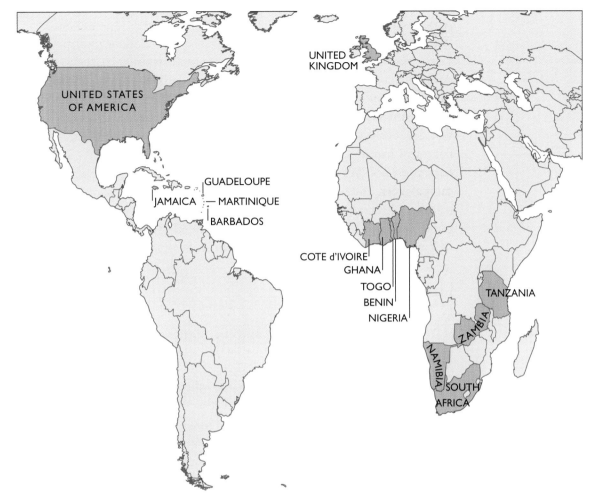

Figure 7.8   The participating countries at the African World Reparations and Repatriation Truth Commission (AWRRTC) based in Ghana and held in 1999

Yet, Global Africa may not be as unified as it first seems, and there is the potential for real tensions between different parts of the worldwide reparations campaign. After all, who are the greater victims: African people *in* Africa or those of African descent *across* the diaspora, many of whom may be the actual descendants of enslaved people? Indeed, many critics point out that the slave trade would not have been possible without some African (and Arab) involvement, and yet the demands are directed solely towards 'states in Europe and the Americas' (Mazrui and Mazrui, 2002). The demand for slavery reparations is less straightforward than it seems in terms of who is to be held responsible, and exactly what sorts of reparations are to be sought.

4.2 What is being demanded?

Demands for reparations are being made by organisations and individuals across Global Africa. For them, the past wrong of the slave trade and slavery is clearly present in today's world, having created and maintained inequalities and injustices that shape life in a globalised world. However, what kinds of demands are they making? One of the common features of the earliest demands was for territory. You will remember that there was some discussion in the USA of providing each former enslaved person with 'forty acres and a mule' as restitution. The idea was that this would allow those who had suffered under slavery to make a living. Other demands for territory have been of a much larger scale and aimed at allowing people of African descent to make their own lives, not only as individuals but as a separate people. For example, since the 1960s some African-American campaigners have called for the US states of South Carolina, Georgia, Alabama, Mississippi and Louisiana to be given to the descendants of enslaved people and united in a separate nation called the Republic of New Africa (see Figure 7.9).

If you look back at the UNESCO message in Section 1, you will recall its statement about how the consequences of slavery 'are permanently imprinted in the world's geography and economy' (Matsuura, 2004). Those who campaign for the creation of the Republic of New Africa argue that as the present geography of the USA has been made through slavery, it needs to be *re-made*.

Figure 7.9   The proposed Republic of New Africa

The most predominant and persistent reparation demand has been for monetary restitution, often based on calculations of what enslaved people would have earned if they had been paid for their labour (we will return to this idea of asking 'what if ...?' in Section 5.1). Many of the proposed figures have been huge. People of African descent in Brazil demanded US$100,000 for each of the country's citizens descended from an enslaved person. In total, this amounted to US $600 billion (US$600,000,000,000) in restitution or twelve times the annual gross national product (GNP) of Brazil (Barkan, 2000, p.285). On an even greater scale, African campaigners demanded US$77,700 billion (US$77,700,000,000,000) in monetary compensation from governments in North and South America, and Europe, as well as from those institutions that participated in and benefited from the slave trade and colonialism, including private companies and religious organisations in these countries. Such monetary demands have come to nothing and many critics scoff at the enormous sums involved. Yet, while the figures may seem fantastic, they do point to the scale of the slave trade and slavery, and the problem of trying to value centuries of unpaid labour and mistreatment that involved millions of people across large parts of the world.

Moreover, many of these figures are not simply plucked out of the air. For instance, one demand in the USA was for US$198,149 for every descendant of an enslaved person, this being based on the estimated value of 'forty acres and a mule' at today's prices. Such claims are not only about money; they often involve demands for other things like tax relief, the creation of training funds and educational scholarships, and the handover of fixed capital like factories, buildings, ships and planes. In a similar way, but on an international scale, the African-based GEP wants 'capital transfer, skill transfer and power sharing based on global structural reform' (Mazrui and Mazrui, 2002, p.24). This relates to part of the Abuja Proclamation, namely that slavery has resulted in 'the damaged economies of the Black World from Guinea to Guyana, from Somalia to Surinam' (Mazrui and Mazrui, 2002) – not least through the removal of twelve million African people from the continent through the slave trade. The demands to make up for these stolen people and the effects of their absence on the continent go beyond the more straightforward issue of compensation, and are part of an attempt at establishing social justice by altering the conditions of life in a globalised world for people of African descent.

Other reparation demands, like that from ARM-UK, combine claims for financial compensation with calls for an admission of guilt and a formal apology from the UK Government. The perspective of ARM-UK is more orientated towards Global Africa than the nationally focused demands of the US campaign, and one of its more symbolic demands is for the restitution to Africa of artefacts taken by Europeans in the past. Among these are the Benin bronzes and ivories that currently reside in a number of British museums. The following letter from ARM-UK relates to a demand for such artefacts to be returned:

Letter from Bernie Grant, MP, Chair of ARM-UK, to the Director of the Glasgow Art Gallery and Museum, 10 December 1996

I write on behalf of the Oba of Benin, Oma n'Oba, Uku Akpolokpolo, Oba Erediauwa, and on behalf of the Africa Reparations Movement (UK) of which I am the Chair. The subject of this letter is the Benin Bronzes, Ivories and other cultural and religious objects contained in the Glasgow Art Gallery and Museum, about which I understand you have recently spoken to Mr Edward Wood of the House of Commons Library.

As you are aware, most of the Benin religious and cultural objects currently in British museums and other institutions, were looted in February 1897 from Benin City. The context of this was the battle for trade in the carve up of Africa, into 'spheres of influence', by the European powers, and the launching of a military expedition by the British in 1897, to depose the King of Benin who insisted on preserving the independence and sovereignty of his kingdom.

The Benin religious and cultural objects belong to a living culture and have deep historic and social value, which go far beyond the aesthetic and monetary value which they hold in exile ... Moreover, the objects have come to symbolise the intense sense of injustice widely felt in Africa, and indeed amongst many people of African origin in Britain, about the mis-appropriation of African art, cultural and religious objects, arising from the period of European colonisation.

There has for many years now, been a demand for these religious and cultural objects to be returned to Benin, and as the centenary of their looting approaches in February 1997, the strength of feeling around this has intensified. Formal requests for their return have been made in the past by the Nigerian Government, and by the Obas of Benin themselves, but have been met with refusal ... The denial and destruction of the history of the Benin people were acts of appalling racism, which need urgently to be rectified. These are indeed some of the most distasteful and abiding injustices arising out of the period of European colonisation of Africa.

(Africa Reparations Movement (UK), 1996)

This letter articulates a particular demand for the restitution of cultural property, relating to the express wrong of its removal by the British during the so-called 'Scramble for Africa'. The respondent to which the demand is addressed is quite distinct – the Glasgow Art Gallery and Museum. As this shows, not all demands are financial; some are for more symbolic acts of restitution of cultural property. As with many of those emanating from Africa, such as the Abuja Proclamation, or directed towards Africa, as in the case of ARM-UK, such demands go beyond reparations for the slave trade and slavery, and into the wider field of Africa's relationship with the rest of the world. Thus, colonialism looms large in such claims, and the forms of reparations demanded are wider than for the specific injustice of slavery. This is not the unexpected return of a haunting past, as we saw in Chapter 6, but a deliberate, political effort to make the past present by recalling historical wrongs and demanding the return of absent artefacts to redress those wrongs.

4.3   Responses to reparation demands

Despite the efforts of claimants on both sides of the Atlantic in campaigning for reparations for the slave trade, slavery and related wrongs, there has been an absence of positive responses, and much resistance. Let us consider some of the most commonly cited arguments against slavery reparations:

1   We recognise that slavery is a bad thing *nowadays*, but people thought differently in the past.

It might be suggested that slavery was acceptable then – during the sixteenth, seventeenth, eighteenth and nineteenth centuries – and that it is wrong to judge the past by today's standards. A more extreme version of this response is a straightforward denial that the slave trade and slavery is a 'crime against humanity' (Mazrui and Mazrui, 2002) as the UN and other international bodies have asserted. In other words, this sort of response asserts that there was no past wrong to answer for in the first place.

2   Okay, so slavery was bad, but it all happened a *long* time ago. We should let bygones be bygones.

Whereas the Holocaust and the internment of Japanese Americans occurred during the Second World War – within living memory – some people object to reparations for slavery on the grounds that it has been abolished for over a century in Brazil and longer elsewhere. None of the victims or perpetrators is alive today. Given this absence, maybe we should stop raking up the past.

3   I wasn't alive then and had nothing to do with slavery.

People might say that they had nothing to do with slavery, and so ask why they should pay for reparations through their taxes. They might say this not only because they were not alive then, but perhaps because they have no direct connection to slavery – after all, not everyone's ancestors were slaveholders. Some people might argue that their ancestors were not living in a country that was involved in slavery in the past, and only migrated to the USA or the UK later. A similar argument focuses on the claimants:

4   'The reparations argument is based on the unfounded claim that all
    ... descendants of slaves suffer from the economic consequences of
    slavery and discrimination' (Horowitz, 2001).

This response comes from a US critic of reparations, David Horowitz (2001), who insists that during the slavery era in the USA, 'many blacks were free men or slaveowners themselves, yet the reparations claimants make no distinction between the roles blacks played in the injustice itself'. Horowitz goes so far as to argue that demands for slavery reparations are 'racist' because they cast all white people as perpetrators and all black people as victims. The argument that demands for reparations are flawed because some African people acted as slave traders themselves is related to this.

If you look back at Figure 7.3 and the discussion of the difficulties involved in making demands for reparations for past wrongs, you may see that these four objections to slavery reparations relate to the different conditions that were necessary for such demands to be made:

1   We saw that demands for reparations must establish that a past
    wrong occurred. Arguing that we should not judge the past by
    today's standards amounts to questioning whether the wrong still
    matters in today's world. This negative response seeks to excuse
    the past because the temporal distance between 'now' and 'then'
    makes the wrong acceptable.

2   We also saw that demands for reparations must show that the past
    wrong continues to matter in some way – that the past wrong is
    present in today's world. Saying that it all happened a long time
    ago serves to deny this by saying that 'that was then' and 'this is
    now', and that the two are unrelated. In effect, this is an attempt
    to deny or erase the relevance of history today or, to put it another
    way, to refuse to make the past present.

3   Finally, we saw that demands must also establish identity between
    perpetrator and respondent, and between victim and claimant. This
    is where the third and fourth objections to slavery reparations come

in. The third objection ('I wasn't alive then and had nothing to do with slavery') denies the link between the historical perpetrators (that is, slaveholders in the past) and contemporary respondents. The argument here, quite simply, is that the purported respondent was absent from the 'scene of the crime', perhaps because slavery happened 'over there' in the colonies or because their ancestors were from 'somewhere else'. The fourth objection ('The reparations argument is based on the unfounded claim that all ... descendants of slaves suffer from the economic consequences of slavery and discrimination' (Horowitz, 2001)) challenges the link made between historical victims (that is, those who were enslaved) and the contemporary claimants who are making the reparation demands. The logic here is that the absence of a *direct* victim today, means that the claimants have no right to make demands.

These negative responses to reparation demands involve making the past distant – pushing it away – and denying its significance or any responsibility for it. The more distant in time the wrong, the easier it becomes for respondents to reject reparation demands made upon them by saying such things as, 'It's time we all moved on', 'It's nothing to do with me', and so on. As we saw earlier in Section 2, it is more difficult for the claimant when the wrong and the demand are not temporally (and spatially) proximate.

Summary

- Although it had its origins in the African diaspora, the movement for reparations for the slave trade and slavery now extends across Global Africa.

- The focus of the movement for reparations often moves beyond the immediate effects of the Atlantic slave trade and slavery, into the wider consequences of the relationship between Global Africa and the rest of the world. Demands are made for material restitution, including monetary compensation, apologies and the return of material artefacts.

- The demands for restitution are made through conscious political actions, such as proclamations produced at international conferences, letters to museums, and in the goals set out by campaigning groups.

- Many respondents have rejected demands for restitution, attempting to make the past wrong distant from, and absent in, today's globalised world.

5   Making the past present

Positive responses to reparation demands for the slave trade and slavery have been conspicuous by their absence. Those campaigning for reparations keep on persevering though, even in the face of negative responses that make slavery and the slave trade distant and absent. The campaigners have adopted a number of strategies to make this past wrong present today, and to make stronger links between past victims and present claimants, past perpetrators and present respondents. We explore two of these strategies below.

5.1   Counterfactual claims

One of the most important arguments to support claims for reparations, especially for campaigners in Africa, was laid out by Walter Rodney in his book *How Europe Underdeveloped Africa* (1974). Rodney was born in Guyana but his intellectual and political activism and outlook extended to the whole of Global Africa. In his writing, he showed how the enslavement of African people had started the continent's economic decline and political marginalisation in global affairs, and that this continued when Africa was colonised. Rodney made his argument by showing that the slave trade was a basic factor in African underdevelopment and that this form of European involvement in Africa had prevented it from developing. It is this argument that is made in the Abuja Proclamation when it refers to 'the damage done to Africa and its Diaspora by enslavement, colonization, and neo-colonization' (Mazrui and Mazrui, 2002).

Activity 7.4

Turn now to Reading 7C by Walter Rodney (1974) entitled 'How Europe underdeveloped Africa', which you will find at the end of the chapter. In the light of what we have learned about the effects of the slave trade and slavery, take a little time to reflect on Rodney's question: 'What would have been Britain's level of development had millions of them been put to work as slaves outside of their homelands over a period of four centuries?'

Clearly this is a very difficult question, but one fictional answer is suggested by the US author Steven Barnes:

> Late at night, when the children were asleep and the adults of the crannog gathered around the fire, some of the Druids and the older folk told stories of the Northmen and how they raided villages,

stealing women and children to sell to dark people they called
'Moors.' A very few of those had escaped and found their way
home, with tales of a fabulous land of unbelievable wealth and
power. But they also whispered that many were sent across the sea
to another world, from which no one had ever returned at all.

(Barnes, 2002, p.60)

Barnes's book, *Lion's Blood* (2002), is set in a world in which Europe has
been devastated by war and disease, and no powerful Christian states have
emerged in the continent. As a result, the 'New World' has been
colonised by African Muslims who buy enslaved Europeans from
Northmen (Viking) slave traders to work on their plantations in
'Bilalistan', which is part of what we call North America (see Figure 7.10).

Figure 7.10   Map of the fictional 'Bilalistan'
Source: Barnes, 2002

The islands of Britain and Eire are the source of many of the enslaved workers. The constant slaving raids by Northmen, and the resultant loss of people and the disruption to trade and agriculture this causes, has kept the local populations small and their societies impoverished. Although Barnes's account is fictional, it does suggest some answers to Rodney's (1974) question. If hundreds of thousands of British people had been taken and enslaved elsewhere in the world for hundreds of years, it would be almost impossible to imagine the country being as commercially and industrially successful as it has been for much of the last three centuries. Of course, not all of Africa was affected directly by the slave trade, but we could also speculate on the probable effects on the development of Britain if its population had remained free – as did large parts of Africa – while other parts of Europe were affected by slavery. Rodney suggests that had this been the case, Britain would not have been able to trade fully with mainland Europe and its economic prosperity would have been damaged indirectly.

Considering what might have happened and asking 'what if ...?' is called 'counterfactual history'. Counterfactual approaches to the past are controversial, and some people dismiss them as an exercise in fantasy: what might have happened if Napoleon Bonaparte had won the Battle of Waterloo in 1815? Would there have been a Second World War if Adolf Hitler had never been born? Yet these approaches can also provide a powerful way of thinking about the past by helping us to identify the important factors or key individuals that led to events playing out one way rather than another.

Drawing on Rodney's arguments (1974), many supporters of reparations in Africa relate contemporary levels of poverty, poor health and political instability to slavery and colonialism. They demand reparations for the problems caused by arguing that if Africa had been left alone, it would be a more prosperous continent. They insist, in other words, that the global past has served to create a fundamentally unequal world today by enriching Europe and the states that their descendants founded in the Americas, while impoverishing or 'underdeveloping' Africa. Such claims rely on the idea that Africa would have developed in similar ways to the West if its people had not been enslaved and if its land had not been colonised. It is not just the reparations campaign in Africa that makes use of such counterfactual arguments. If you look back at Robert Brock's goals for the US reparations movement campaign in Section 4, you will see that one goal is: 'To provide the black community with the share of the national wealth and income which it would by now have had if it had been treated as other immigrant communities were, rather than enslaved' (cited in Barkan, 2000, p.289). Counterfactual arguments can help put a figure on demands for restitution by asking the question: if enslaved people had been paid as waged workers for their labour, how much would they have earned?

By emphasising how events, relationships and processes occurring *then* have shaped circumstances *now*, counterfactual claims make the past present. They show that we cannot dismiss what occurred in the past as things that just happened 'a long time ago' because these things have fundamentally shaped the globalised world in which we live today. As the Abuja Proclamation puts it: 'the damage sustained by the African peoples is not a "thing of the past" but is painfully manifest in the damaged lives of contemporary Africans from Harlem to Harare, in the damaged economies of the Black World from Guinea to Guyana, from Somalia to Surinam' (Mazrui and Mazrui, 2002). Moreover, by asking 'what if ...?', counterfactual claims call forth absent worlds – even fictional worlds like Barnes's Bilalistan (2002) (see Figure 7.10) – that never were, but could have been. The claims demand that we consider what the world might have been like if particular past wrongs had not been committed, calling upon us to repair the damage caused. In this way, counterfactual claims provide one way in which distant places and distant times can be made present in today's world, and reparations can be demanded in respect of past wrongs.

5.2 Collective, shared identities

So asking 'what if ...?' is one means of making past wrongs present by highlighting their impact on today's world. However, what about the other aspect of connecting the then and now in Figure 7.3 – establishing identity between claimants and victims, and between respondents and perpetrators? As all those actually involved in the slave trade and slavery are long dead – are, in other words, absent – it is very difficult to establish direct relationships between those who are entitled to demand reparations for slavery and those with responsibilities to react. In fact, most demands for reparations for slavery do not attempt to establish individual or familial blame and victimhood, and are more concerned with issues of collective identity.

Robert Brock, for instance, states that one of the purposes of reparations is: 'To redirect to *blacks* that portion of the national income which has been diverted from *blacks* to *whites* as a result of slavery and post-Emancipation racial discrimination' (cited in Barkan, 2000, p.289, emphasis added). The issue here is the relationship between white people and black people. By highlighting the issue of 'race', the connection is made between victims and claimants, perpetrators and respondents as collective groups of people. Not all black people agree with this, however. The following contrasting statements are from prominent African-Americans, the first from Walter Williams, a columnist and professor of economics at George Mason University in Virginia who is opposed to reparations, and the second from John Conyers Jnr, a politician who has been a leading figure in the reparations campaign within the US Congress.

> It's perverse to say that some poor white kid who's the son of a coal miner in West Virginia owes me – someone in the top 1 per cent or 2 per cent of income earners in the US – money.

> Just as white Americans have benefited from education, life experiences, and wealth that was handed down to them by their ancestors, so too have African Americans been harmed by the institution of slavery.

> (cited in Barkan, 2000, pp.292–3)

These commentators take opposing perspectives on the issue of reparations, demonstrating that there is no consensus on reparations even within the African-American community. Like some other African-Americans, Walter Williams is opposed to reparations because he sees them as unnecessary and racially divisive. He asks why a poor white American, perhaps the descendant of someone who migrated to the USA after slavery was abolished, should have to pay reparations to a rich African-American like him. One response to Williams's argument, however, is that because it is often impossible to connect the situations of particular individuals to the harmful outcomes of past wrongs, 'there is no point in seeking to exact compensation or redress from some isolatable perpetrators' (Young, 2003, p.4). Or to put it another way, demands for slavery reparations are collective demands and it makes no sense to personalise responsibility as Williams does when he talks about his relationship to 'some poor white kid' (cited in Barkan, 2000, p.292). This is the point made by John Conyers Jnr in the second quotation above, who points to the continuing effects of slavery on the life chances of African-Americans as a group. Similar arguments are made by African campaigners for reparations in the Abuja Proclamation. Thus, issues of collective social justice are brought to the fore and the pursuit of reparations relies on claims about the foreshortened opportunities available to African people and people of African descent as a whole, and about the legacies of the slavery apparent in the 'underdevelopment' of Africa. This is why reparation demands link the experience of Africa and people of African descent under slavery to the issues of continuing Western dominance in Africa, and institutionalised and embedded racism in the West. By emphasising the continuing effects of the slave trade and slavery on groups of people defined by their racial identity, demands for reparations make the connections between victims and claimants, perpetrators and respondents. In a sense, those victims and perpetrators who were present when the past wrong was committed but are absent now, are made present again through shared racial identities that transcend historical distance. The victims and perpetrators then and the claimants and respondents now are clearly different individuals and collections of individuals, but they share the same racial identities, and the relationships between them (between white people and black people) remain unequal and sometimes exploitative.

The evocation in reparation demands of collective, shared racial identities to make the past wrong present is not coincidental. In Section 3, we saw that the commonplace division of people into different racial 'types', such as 'black' or 'African-American' and 'white', is partly a product of the history of the slave trade and slavery. It was part of that past wrong. Furthermore, and again as Conyers argues above, one of the legacies has been to disadvantage black people – *even if they were not the direct descendants of enslaved people* – and advantage white people – *even if they were not the direct descendants of those responsible for the slave trade and slavery.* Some of the descendants of enslaved people today have widened the relevance of this racially-based 'black'/'white' division by using it to articulate their demands for reparations from various institutions that they associate with 'white' wealth and authority, such as Western European and US governments.

The use of collective racial identities to make reparation demands is another way in which the temporal distance between then and now can be bridged, and past wrongs made present. Yet problems remain with such a use of collective, shared racial identities. For instance, some critics of reparations believe that campaigners are deliberately downplaying the role of African (and Arab) people in slavery in order to portray all black people as victims/claimants and white people as the sole perpetrators/respondents. For critics such as David Horowitz, this 'whitewashing' of the African and Arabic role in slavery is symptomatic of the campaign's anti-Western political motives and relates to the fourth objection to reparations that we discussed in Section 4.2: that not all 'descendants of slaves suffer from the economic consequences of slavery and discrimination' (Horowitz, 2001).

The challenge of claiming reparations for slavery, demonstrating the contemporary relevance of these past injustices, and finding a clear identity between past victims and perpetrators and present groups or institutions, remains.

Summary

- Considering what might have happened and asking 'what if ...?' is called 'counterfactual history'. Articulating demands for reparations through counterfactual histories is an important way in which past wrongs are made present in today's world.

- Asking 'what if ...?' questions makes present an absent world that does not actually exist, but shows how today's world has been shaped by the past (and how it might have turned out differently), and can provide a basis for calculating the cost of the wrongs.

- Demands to right wrongs committed in the distant past can also make links between claimant and victim, respondent and perpetrator by focusing on the collective entitlements and responsibilities of groups of people who share an identity, such as that based on race.

- Arguments about collective, shared identities are another way in which past wrongs are made present. They acknowledge that the original victims and perpetrators are absent, but that their descendants still suffer or benefit.

6   Conclusion

By focusing on the example of the Atlantic slave trade and slavery, this chapter has considered the kinds of demands that are made when reparations for past wrongs are sought. We have also considered the serious obstacles these demands face which partly explain the absence of reparations. These obstacles stem from the difficulty of making the globalised past present in today's world, specifically because of the temporal distance between the wrong then and the demand now, and the fact that the absence of distinct victims and perpetrators makes it impossible to attribute individual responsibility. In Section 5, we examined two ways in which reparation demands are made in the face of this: counterfactual claims and an emphasis on collective, shared identities. The work required to make absent wrongs present is represented in Figure 7.11.

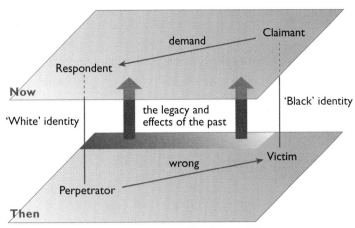

Figure 7.11   Modified structure of a reparation demand for a past wrong
Source: Trouillot, 2000, p.175

Figure 7.11 is a modified version of Figure 7.3. The thick, vertical
arrows pointing from *then* to *now* represent the legacy and effects of
the globalised past: specifically the institutionalised inequalities resulting
from the slave trade and slavery. This is the impact of the past wrong
on today's world that counterfactual claims make present and seek to
calculate. The thin, vertical lines that connect perpetrator to
respondent and victim to claimant represent the continuity in the
identities of those involved in the past wrong and the demand today. It
is these connections that are asserted through the emphasis on
collective, shared black and white identities.

On the whole, however, those respondents called upon to provide
reparations for the slave trade and slavery have sought to keep the
past at a distance, and assert the absence of its effects today.
Nonetheless, claimants across Global Africa have challenged this by
calling forth the past in campaigns that bring it close and make it
present. Unlike in Chapter 6, where Steve Pile showed how the
horrors, traumas and injustices of past wrongs continue to haunt life in
a globalised world, perhaps returning when we least expect them to, in
this chapter we have seen that the past can also be made to return
through distinct political campaigns that involve articulate
representations, financial calculations and the use of historical
knowledge to draw connections between then and now. Such
campaigns are part of the demands made upon us to remember and
respond to the past. As Koïchiro Matsuura, the Director-General of
UNESCO, noted in 2004: 'By ... recalling the memory of a tragedy that
for long years remained hidden or unrecognized, and by assigning it its
proper place in the human conscience, we respond to our duty to
remember'. In Chapter 8 we will see that demands are also made to
prevent wrongs from occurring in the first place.

References

Africa Reparations Movement (UK) (ARM-UK) (1996), 'Letter from Bernie Grant, MP, Chair of ARM-UK, to the Director of the Glasgow Art Gallery and Museum, 10 December 1996', http://www.arm.arc.co.uk/CRBBletter1.html (accessed 22 June 2005).

Africa Reparations Movement (UK) (ARM-UK) (2005), http://www.arm.arc.co.uk (accessed 22 June 2005).

Barkan, E. (2000) *The Guilt of Nations: Restitution and Negotiating Historical Injustices*, London, W.W. Norton.

Barnes, S. (2002) *Lion's Blood*, New York, Warner Books.

Cairns, A. (2003) 'Coming to terms with the past' in Torpey, J. (ed.) *Politics and the Past: On Repairing Historical Injustices*, Oxford, Rowman & Littlefield.

Carretta, V. (ed.) (1995) *'The Interesting Narrative' and Other Writings*, New York, Penguin.

Chaplin, J.E. (2002) 'Race' in Armitage, D. and Braddick, M.J. (eds) *The British Atlantic World, 1500–1800*, Basingstoke, Palgrave Macmillan.

Conley, D. (2003) 'Calculating slavery reparations: theory, numbers, and implications' in Torpey, J. (ed.) *Politics and the Past: On Repairing Historical Injustices*, Oxford, Rowman & Littlefield, pp.117–25.

Curtin, P.D. (1969) *The Atlantic Slave Trade: A Census*, Madison, University of Wisconsin Press.

Douglass, F. (1881) *Life and Times of Frederick Douglass: His Early Life as a Slave, His Escape from Bondage, and His Complete History to the Present Time*, Hartford, Conn, Park.

Finkelman, P. and Miller, J. (eds) (1998) *Macmillan Encyclopaedia of World Slavery*, New York, Macmillan, vol.1.

Horowitz, D. (2001) 'Ten reasons why reparations for blacks is a bad idea for blacks – and racist too', *Front Page Magazine*, http://www.frontpagemag.com/Articles/ReadArticle.asp?ID=1153 (accessed 22 June 2005).

Knox, P. and Agnew, J. (1998) *The Geography of the World Economy: An Introduction to Economic Geography* (3rd edn), London, Arnold.

Matsuura, K. (2004) 'Message of the Director-General of UNESCO on the occasion of the International Day for the Remembrance of the Slave Trade and its Abolition 2004', http://portal.unesco.org/en/ (accessed 22 June 2005).

Mazrui, A.A. and Mazrui, A.M. (2002) *Black Reparations in the Era of Globalization*, New York, Institute of Global Cultural Studies.

Morrison, T. (1987) *Beloved*, London, Picador.

Ogborn, M. (2000) 'Historical geographies of globalisation, c.1500–1800' in Graham, B. and Nash, C. (eds) *Modern Historical Geographies*, Harlow, Prentice-Hall.

Richardson, D. (1998) 'The British Empire and the Atlantic slave trade, 1660–1807' in Marshall, P.J. (ed.) *The Oxford History of the British Empire Vol. 2: The Eighteenth Century*, Oxford, Oxford University Press, pp.440–64.

Rodney, W. (1974) *How Europe Underdeveloped Africa*, Washington, DC, Howard University Press.

Torpey, J. (2003) *Politics and the Past: On Repairing Historical Injustices*, Oxford, Rowman & Littlefield.

Trouillot, M.-R. (2000) 'Abortive rituals: historical apologies in the global era', *Interventions*, vol.2, pp.171–86.

Wareham, R.S. (2002) 'Testimony of Roger S. Wareham, at the City Council Committee on governmental operations concerning Councilman Barrow's resolution on reparations', http://www.millionsforreparations.com/news.html (accessed 22 June 2005).

Young, I.M. (2003) 'From guilt to solidarity: sweatshops and political responsibility', *Dissent*, Spring, pp.39–44.

Reading 7A

Olaudah Equiano, 'The interesting narrative of the life of Olaudah Equiano, or Gustavus Vassa the African. Written by himself'

The first object which saluted my eyes when I arrived on the coast was the sea, and a slave-ship, which was then riding at anchor, and waiting for its cargo. These filled me with astonishment, which was soon converted into terror, which I am yet at a loss to describe, nor the then feelings of my mind. ... When I looked round the ship too, and saw a large furnace of copper boiling, and a multitude of black people of every description chained together, every one of their countenances expressing dejection and sorrow, I no longer doubted of my fate, and, quite overpowered with horror and anguish, I fell motionless on the deck and fainted. When I recovered a little, I found some black people about me, who I believed were some of those who brought me on board, and had been receiving their pay; they talked to me in order to cheer me, but all in vain. ... I now saw myself deprived of all chance of returning to my native country, or even the least glimpse of hope of gaining the shore, which I now considered as friendly: and I even wished for my former slavery in preference to my present situation, which was filled with horrors of every kind, still heightened by my ignorance of what I was to undergo. ... In a little time after, amongst the poor chained men, I found some of my own nation, which in a small degree gave ease to my mind. I inquired of these what was to be done with us? They gave me to understand we were to be carried to these white people's country to work for them. ... At last, when the ship we were in had got in all her cargo, they made ready with many fearful noises, and we were all put under deck, so that we could not see how they managed the vessel. But this disappointment was the least of my sorrow. The stench of the hold while we were on the coast was so intolerably loathsome, that it was dangerous to remain there for any time, and some of us had been permitted to stay on the deck for the fresh air; but now that the whole ship's cargo were confined together, it became absolutely pestilential. The closeness of the place, and the heat of the climate, added to the number in the ship, which was so crowded that each had scarcely room to turn himself, almost suffocated us. This produced copious perspirations, so that the air soon became unfit for respiration, from a variety of loathsome smells, and brought on a sickness among the slaves, of which many died, thus falling victims to the improvident avarice, as I may call it, of their purchasers. This wretched situation was again aggravated by the galling of the chains, now become insupportable; and the filth of the necessary tubs, into which the children often fell, and were almost suffocated. The shrieks of the women, and the groans of the dying, rendered the whole a scene of horror almost inconceivable.

...

One day, when we had a smooth sea, and a moderate wind, two of my wearied countrymen, who were chained together (I was near them at the time), preferring death to such a life of misery, somehow made through the nettings, and jumped into the sea: immediately another quite dejected fellow, who, on account of his illness, was suffered to be out of irons, also followed their example; and I believe many more would soon have done the same, if they had not been prevented by the ship's crew, who were instantly alarmed. Those of us that were the most active were, in a moment, put down under the deck; and there was such a noise and confusion amongst the people of the ship as I never heard before, to stop her, and get the boat to go out after the slaves. However, two of the wretches were drowned, but they got the other, and afterwards flogged him unmercifully, for thus attempting to prefer death to slavery. In this manner we continued to undergo more hardships than I can now relate; hardships which are inseparable from this accursed trade. – Many a time we were near suffocation, from the want of fresh air, which we were often without for whole days together ... At last we came in sight of the island of Barbadoes, at which the whites on board gave a great shout, and made many signs of joy to us.

(Equiano, 1789, in Carretta, 1995, vol.1, pp.55, 56, 58, 59, 60)

Reading 7B

The Abuja Proclamation 1993

This First Pan-African Conference on Reparations held in Abuja, Nigeria, April 27–29, 1993, sponsored by the Group of Eminent Persons (GEP) and the Commission for Reparations of the Organization of African Unity, and the Federal Government of the Republic of Nigeria

Recalling the Organization of African Unity's establishment of a machinery, the Group of Eminent Persons, for appraising the issue of reparations in relation to the damage done to Africa and its Diaspora by enslavement, colonization, and neo-colonization

Convinced that the issue of reparations is an important question requiring the united action of Africa and its Diaspora and worthy of the active support of the rest of the international community

Fully persuaded that the damage sustained by the African peoples is not a 'thing of the past' but is painfully manifest in the damaged lives of contemporary Africans from Harlem to Harare, in the damaged economies of the Black World from Guinea to Guyana, from Somalia to Surinam

Respectfully aware of historic precedents in reparations, ranging from German payment of restitution to the Jews for the enormous tragedy of the Nazi Holocaust to the question of compensating Japanese-Americans for the injustice of internment by the Roosevelt Administration in the United States during the World War II

Cognizant of the fact that compensation for injustice need not necessarily be paid only in capital transfer but could include service to the victims or other forms of restitution and readjustment of the relationship agreeable to both parties

Emphatically convinced that what matters is not the guilt but the responsibility of those states and nations whose economic evolution once depended on slave labor and colonialism, and whose forebears participated either in selling and buying Africans, or in owning them, or in colonizing them

Convinced that the pursuit of reparations by the African peoples in the continent and in the Diaspora will itself be a learning experience in self-discovery and a uniting experience politically and psychologically

Convinced that numerous looting, theft and larceny have been committed on the African people, calls upon those in possession of their stolen goods, artefacts and other traditional treasuries to restore them to their rightful owners, the African people

Calls upon the international community to recognize that there is a unique and unprecedented moral debt owed to the African peoples which has yet to be paid – the debt of compensation to the Africans as the most humiliated and exploited people of the last four centuries of modern history

Calls upon Heads of States and Governments in Africa and the Diaspora itself to set up National Committees for the purpose of studying the damaged Black experience, disseminating information and encouraging educational courses on the impact of enslavement, colonization and neo-colonization on present-day Africa and its Diaspora

Urges the Organization of African Unity to grant observer status to select organizations from the African Diaspora in order to facilitate consultations between Africa and its Diaspora on reparations and related issues

Further urges the OAU to call for full monetary payment of repayments through capital transfer and debt cancellation

Convinced that the claim for reparations is well grounded in International Law

Urges on the OAU to establish a legal Committee on the issue of reparations

Also calls upon African and Diaspora groups already working on reparations to communicate with the Organization of African Unity and establish continuing liaison

Encourages such groups to send this declaration to various countries to obtain their official support for the movement

Serves notice on all states in Europe and the Americas which had participated in the enslavement and colonization of the African peoples, and which may still be engaged in racism and neo-colonialism, to desist from any further damage and start building bridges of conciliation, co-operation, and through reparation

Exhorts all African states to grant entrance as of right to all persons of African descent and right to obtain residence in those African states, if there is no disqualifying element on the African claiming the 'right to return' to his ancestral home, Africa

Urges those countries which were enriched by slavery and the slave trade to give total relief from Foreign Debt, and allow the debtor countries of the Diaspora to become free for self-development and from immediate and direct economic domination

Calls upon the countries largely characterized as profiteers from the slave trade to support proper and reasonable representation of African peoples in the political and economic areas of the highest decision-making bodies

Requests the OAU to intensify its efforts in restructuring the international system in pursuit of justice with special reference to a permanent African seat on the Security Council of the UN.

April 29, 1993.

(Mazrui and Mazrui, 2002, pp.135–8)

Reading 7C

Walter Rodney, 'How Europe underdeveloped Africa'

To achieve economic development, one essential condition is to make the maximum use of the country's labour and natural resources. Usually, that demands peaceful conditions, but there have been times in history when social groups have grown stronger by raiding their neighbours for women, cattle and goods, because they then used the 'booty' from the raids for the benefit of their own community. Slaving in Africa did not even have that redeeming value. Captives were shipped outside instead of being utilised within any given African community for creating wealth from nature. It was only as an accidental by-product that in some areas Africans who recruited captives for Europeans realised that they were better off keeping some captives for themselves. In any case, slaving prevented the remaining population from effectively engaging in agriculture and industry, and it employed professional slave hunters and warriors to destroy rather than build. Quite apart from the moral aspect and the immense suffering that it caused, the European slave trade was economically totally irrational from the viewpoint of African development.

For certain purposes, it is necessary to be more specific and to speak of the trade in slaves not in general continent-wide terms but rather with reference to the varying impact on several regions. The relative intensity of slave-raiding in different areas is fairly well known. Some South African peoples were enslaved by the Boers and some North African Muslims by Christian Europeans, but those were minor episodes. The zones most notorious for human exports were, first, West Africa from Senegal to Angola along a belt extending about 200 miles inland and, secondly, that part of East Central Africa which today covers Tanzania, Mozambique, Malawi, Northern Zambia and Eastern Congo. Furthermore, within each of those broad areas, finer distinctions can be drawn.

It might therefore appear that [the] slave trade did not adversely affect the development of some parts of Africa, simply because exports were non-existent or at a low level. However, the contention that [the] European slave trade was an underdeveloping factor for the continent as a whole must be upheld, because it does not follow that an African district which did not trade with Europe was entirely free from whatever influences were exerted by Europe. European trade goods percolated into the deepest interior, and (most significantly) the orientation of large areas of the continent towards human exports meant that other positive interactions were thereby ruled out.

The above proposition may be more fully grasped by making some comparisons. In any given economy, the various components reflect the well-being of others. Therefore, when there is depression in one sector, that depression invariably transfers itself to others to some extent. Similarly, when there is buoyancy in one sector then others benefit. Turning to biological sciences, it will be found that students of ecology recognise that a single change, such as the disappearance of a snail species could trigger off negative or positive reactions in spheres that superficially appear unconnected. Parts of Africa left 'free' by export trends in captives must have been affected by the tremendous dislocation – in ways that are not easy to comprehend, because it is so much a question of what *might* have happened.

Hypothetical questions such as 'What might have happened if ... ?' sometimes lead to absurd speculations. But it is entirely legitimate and very necessary to ask 'What might have happened in Barotseland (southern Zambia) if there were not generalised slave-trading across the whole belt of central Africa which lay immediately north of Barotseland?' 'What would have happened in Buganda if the Katangese were concentrating on selling copper to the Baganda instead of captives to Europeans?'

During the colonial epoch, the British forced Africans to sing

Rule Britannia, Britannia rule the waves
Britons never never never shall be slaves.

The British themselves started singing the tune in the early 18th century, at the height of using Africans as slaves. 'What would have been Britain's level of development had millions of them been put to work as slaves outside of their homelands over a period of four centuries?' Furthermore, assuming that those wonderful fellows could never never never have been slaves, one could speculate further on the probable effects on their development had continental Europe been enslaved. Had that been the case, its nearest neighbours would have been removed from the ambit of fruitful trade with Britain. After all, trade between the British Isles and places like the Baltic and the Mediterranean is unanimously considered by scholars to have been the earliest stimulus to the English economy in the late feudal and early capitalist period, even before the era of overseas expansion.

(Rodney, 1974, pp.108–10)

Chapter 8

The geopolitics of intervention: presence and power in global politics

Jennifer Robinson

Contents

1 Introduction

In a globalised world, communications and information flows often make dramatic events in distant places viscerally present, especially those involving disasters and suffering. The direct connections between such events and the viewers' circumstances may be opaque and difficult to trace, as we noted with market relations in Chapter 1 and historical forms of injustice in Chapter 7. Yet many people are moved by images and stories about the suffering of others, wherever they may be (as described in Chapter 5), and make strong demands for their governments, powerful states and other organisations to respond with assistance.

People caught up in emergencies and conflict situations regularly make their demands for assistance known to powerful agents and to what is often a global audience through the media. In many situations, non-governmental organisations (NGOs) and campaigning organisations do mobilise resources to offer assistance; citizens' lobbying spurs governments to action. Nevertheless, alongside sometimes spectacular examples of generosity – as with responses to the tsunami of December 2004 in Asia – the history of global assistance in situations of disaster is littered with examples of inaction or tales of failure. Despite the opportunities offered by transport technologies and communications and information links, attempts to influence events in different parts of the world have often been non-existent or subject to failure and substantial criticism. Regardless of popular calls to 'do something!' in response to extreme human suffering, often nothing at all, or very little, is done, especially when conflict and war are the causes of the emergency.

This chapter looks at the situations where human suffering, particularly arising from conflict and war, has led to demands for international bodies and powerful states to intervene to bring an end to the conflict, or to bring relief to those affected. It asks who might be expected to intervene, explores whether they respond to these demands and considers what happens when they do so.

Activity 8.1

Take a look at both Table 8.1 and Figure 8.1 below. They show the personnel that a selection of different countries contributed to United Nations (UN) intervention forces in humanitarian emergencies around the world during 2004, and where these emergencies were. Bearing in mind that the UN is frequently the organisation tasked with responding to emergencies on behalf of the international community, note down any thoughts you might have about this information.

Table 8.1   Country contributions of personnel to UN peacekeeping forces as at December 2004

Country	Civilian police	Military observers	Troops	Total
Argentina	135	5	963	1103
Australia	32	14	94	140
Austria	29	12	377	418
Bangladesh	108	78	7838	8024
Belgium	0	11	5	16
Brazil	10	8	1349	1367
Canada	106	12	196	314
China	194	55	787	1036
Denmark	20	34	1	55
Egypt	50	50	15	115
Ethiopia	0	22	3410	3432
Germany	270	15	11	296
Ghana	107	61	3154	3322
India	343	54	3515	3912
Japan	0	0	30	30
Jordan	832	66	2052	2950
Kenya	48	66	2116	2230
Nepal	440	44	2967	3451
New Zealand	0	14	1	15
Nigeria	226	78	2586	2890
Pakistan	482	79	7579	8140
Russia	149	98	114	361
Senegal	151	19	1398	1568
Sweden	41	30	234	305
Switzerland	14	18	2	34
UK	102	16	424	542
Ukraine	225	34	946	1205
Uruguay	22	56	2414	2492
USA	404	17	8	429

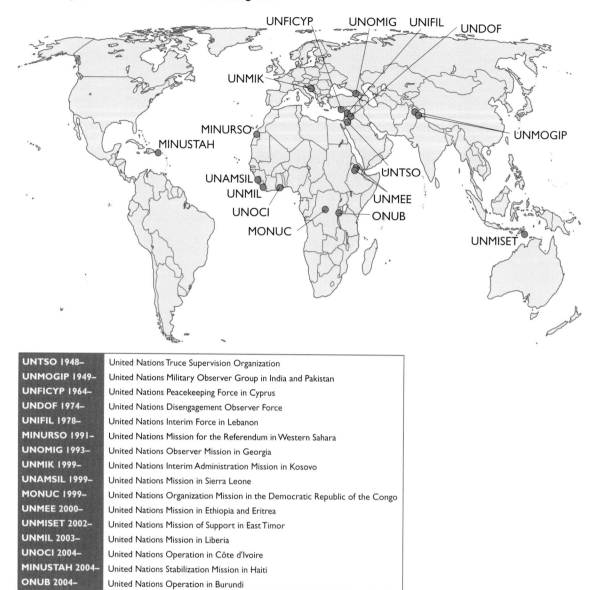

UNTSO 1948–	United Nations Truce Supervision Organization
UNMOGIP 1949–	United Nations Military Observer Group in India and Pakistan
UNFICYP 1964–	United Nations Peacekeeping Force in Cyprus
UNDOF 1974–	United Nations Disengagement Observer Force
UNIFIL 1978–	United Nations Interim Force in Lebanon
MINURSO 1991–	United Nations Mission for the Referendum in Western Sahara
UNOMIG 1993–	United Nations Observer Mission in Georgia
UNMIK 1999–	United Nations Interim Administration Mission in Kosovo
UNAMSIL 1999–	United Nations Mission in Sierra Leone
MONUC 1999–	United Nations Organization Mission in the Democratic Republic of the Congo
UNMEE 2000–	United Nations Mission in Ethiopia and Eritrea
UNMISET 2002–	United Nations Mission of Support in East Timor
UNMIL 2003–	United Nations Mission in Liberia
UNOCI 2004–	United Nations Operation in Côte d'Ivoire
MINUSTAH 2004–	United Nations Stabilization Mission in Haiti
ONUB 2004–	United Nations Operation in Burundi

Figure 8.1   UN peacekeeping operations, December 2004
Source: United Nations Peacekeeping, 2004

Table 8.1 is striking. Some of the world's poorest nations are making the largest contribution of personnel to international peacekeeping, while the richest are either absent or contribute trivial numbers of troops. Equally striking is that the humanitarian emergencies shown in Figure 8.1 seem to be taking place primarily in poorer country contexts. Table 8.1 does not show that even when a decision is made by the UN to assist in a situation of humanitarian disaster, it can take the

Secretary-General and the UN staff months to secure even the small contributions of forces and equipment needed to staff the mission – months in which the humanitarian disasters continue to claim victims. However, all financial contributions to the UN are based on an assessment of the capacity of countries to pay, giving wealthier countries an important role in funding its operations as well as considerable influence within the organisation. For poorer countries, volunteering forces for peacekeeping duty can earn valuable foreign exchange but can involve putting large numbers of troops into dangerous situations for long periods of time.

The UN, which aims to address global questions of peace, security and humanitarian disasters, faces a vast challenge. Large numbers of civilians in different parts of the world get caught up in violent conflicts and civil wars, and have become the targets of genocidal campaigns, aiming to eliminate entire populations – such as the Jewish people in the Nazi Holocaust, Serbs in Kosovo, Tutsis in Rwanda, and indigenous populations in many parts of the world. These are obviously enormous tragedies for the people involved, for their countries and for survivors. However, in a globalised world, many of these conflicts and disasters have an impact on quite distant places. As shown throughout this book, in a globalised world even places far apart are often profoundly interconnected. The Canadian government, in its document about international security, *Freedom from Fear*, observed that:

> Events in recent years have reconfirmed that, in an increasingly interdependent world, the safety and security of Canadians at home are inextricably linked to the safety of those living beyond our borders. ... A globalizing world brings new promises and new threats. Transnational phenomena, including terrorism, international crime and trafficking in small arms, drugs, women and children increase the risks to us all. For all its promise, globalization has a dark underside that requires a broadened understanding of security and new approaches.
>
> (Canada, Department of Foreign Affairs and International Trade, 2002, pp.1–2)

Defining the United Nations

The organisation officially came into existence on 24 October 1945 when the United Nations Charter was ratified by China, France, the Soviet Union, the UK, the USA and a majority of other countries. The purposes of the UN are to maintain international peace and security; to develop friendly relations among nations; to cooperate in solving international economic, social, cultural and humanitarian problems and in promoting respect for human rights and fundamental freedoms; and to be a centre for harmonising the actions of nations in attaining these ends. The UN executive body is the Security Council, comprised of five permanent members with a veto on all decisions (USA, UK, France, Russia and China) and nine ordinary members, serving for two years. The General Assembly is made up of representatives from all member countries.

Source: United Nations, 2004

It is not simply, as the Canadian government seems to fear, that violence and poverty might reach out and affect its citizens' lives 'at home'. It is also, as Carolyn Nordstrom notes in her study of war zones in Africa, that 'a large and well-developed set of networks stretch across the globe and into the most remote battlefield localities to provide everything required by militaries, from weapons to training manuals, food, medicines, tools, and state-of-the-art computers' (Nordstrom, 2004, p.10). Wealthier nations selling military hardware, the sweatshops that produce basic consumer goods and the local people whose produce is traded in informal networks are all linked to the pursuit of war.

If battlefields are so well connected to the rest of the world, why is it so hard for actors like the UN or powerful nations to intervene, to become present in such places, in ways that might end conflict and suffering? This chapter sets out to understand why, in a world in which vast information flows make events in distant places present to many observers often in raw and immediate ways, action to assist people in situations of conflict and violence is frequently so tardy, sometimes very ineffectual, and generally controversial.

Section 2 explores a well-known example of horrifying violence where it seemed as if the whole world was doing nothing. The genocide in Rwanda (April–July 1994) was a controversial, even defining, moment in the history of international humanitarianism. It stands as a touchstone for ongoing discussions in international forums about whether or not and how to act in situations of disaster and conflict. Events there played a major role in reshaping international strategies around aid and assistance in emergencies. We will ask how and why, in this famous case, demands for intervention and assistance were deflected by states, international organisations and audiences of news reports. The demand to 'do something' was widely ignored: instead of using their resources and capacities to help, powerful actors in the world chose to do nothing. After exploring the details of this specific case, Section 3 looks more closely at the global context in which decisions are made to intervene or not in situations of conflict and disaster. It explores the political, cultural and economic processes that shape the capacities of powerful international agents to make their presence felt in distant places, and their willingness to do so in different contexts.

Alongside states and international bodies like the UN, NGOs and public opinion in wealthier countries have also played an important role in shaping international responses to disasters and emergencies. Section 4 considers how the nature of such responses has been changed through the humanitarian concerns of non-state actors. It looks at some new ways in which wealthy nations have made their presence felt in distant places, especially through the emergence of transnational networks among NGOs, states, and private commercial and military enterprises. Taking responsibility though, is itself a highly politicised process and contributes to shaping a wider geopolitics. Section 5 returns to post-genocide Rwanda to consider the ways in which a range of different actors – powerful states and international organisations but also NGOs and ordinary people – became involved in the aftermath of the genocide. It returns to a question we have been considering throughout this book: who should take responsibility in the face of demands to address situations of injustice and suffering?

Defining humanitarianism

Concern for the well-being of people around the world is often referred to as 'humanitarianism'. The foundations of humanitarian concern are diverse, including a belief in the basic human rights of all people, as well as a particular concern for those whose lives are intertwined with our own which, in many Western contexts, can be traced to the emergence of colonial networks of exchange and exploitation, including the slave trade. Many religions advocate concern for others, and support global networks of assistance. Questions are raised by some about the assumption that universal human rights might apply across different cultures, and about limiting humanitarian concern to human beings.

Chapter aims

- To consider who takes responsibility in the case of demands to assist with humanitarian disasters.

- To explore how the capacity to intervene is constructed. How are certain organisations able to achieve a presence in distant places so that they can respond to demands to end conflict or maintain peace? And what influences agents with the capacity to intervene to do so?

- To understand the global politics that arise from taking responsibility for the suffering of other people, often at a distance.

2   A failure to intervene

What is involved here is, as I have said, a bitter failure, not only for the UN, but for the international community as a whole. We are all responsible for this failure, whoever we may be – international organisations, the great powers and NGOs, as well as the African countries themselves.

(Boutros Boutros-Ghali, at the OAU Annual Summit, June 1994, cited in United Nations, 1996, p.52)

Between March and July 1994, 800,000 to 1 million people, mainly but not all thought of as Tutsi, were massacred by Hutu militia and civilians in the small central African country of Rwanda (see Figures 8.2 and 8.3). This was not the first time that political conflict between Tutsi and Hutu people had led to mass killings there. In 1959, Tutsi leaders were targeted in attacks associated with the handover of Belgian colonial power to the Hutu majority, and more than 10,000 Tutsis fled the country. When these refugees staged an armed incursion in 1963, widespread massacres of Tutsis took place; some estimates place the numbers killed between December 1963 and January 1964 at 10,000–14,000. There have also been reports of intermittent violence against Tutsis on other occasions (Eltringham, 2004, p.42). Yet in 1994 it was the first time that this had occurred across the entire country as part of a determined political project by some Hutu leaders to eliminate the minority Tutsi presence from the country altogether.

The genocide of 1994 took place in the context of a protracted civil war in which exiled Tutsi rebels had invaded, initially from neighbouring Uganda, and progressively occupied parts of northern and eastern Rwanda, hoping to depose the Hutu government. A fragile peace process concluded in 1993 at Arusha, Tanzania, known as the 'Arusha Accord', had hoped to bring the Tutsi rebels and exiles, many of whom had spent long years in the neighbouring state of Uganda, back to the country and to establish a shared government with the existing Hutu rulers.

All of this was taking place against the hopeful backdrop of the first democratic elections in South Africa in April 1994, as the white apartheid government negotiated away its power and ceded to the ANC (African National Congress), a largely black party. Democracy was also on the agenda for Rwanda. By the 1990s, international donors had decided that supporting development in poor countries required the countries to implement more democratic forms of government, and further aid became conditional upon democratisation. So much aid followed from the peace process in Rwanda that through 1990–93 some observers suggest that 'the international development community in Rwanda had essentially substituted itself for the central government with regard to the provision of public services' (Tilly, 2003, p.136). Peter Uvin, a long-time scholar of Rwanda, estimates that aid amounted to US$80 per capita per annum at this time, about the average annual income of Rwandans (Uvin, 2001, p.95).

In nearby countries such as Zambia, democratisation had proceeded relatively peacefully. In Rwanda, however, democratisation was being encouraged and rewarded at a moment when the Hutu government was

Figure 8.2   Africa, showing Rwanda
Source: adapted from Mamdani, 2001

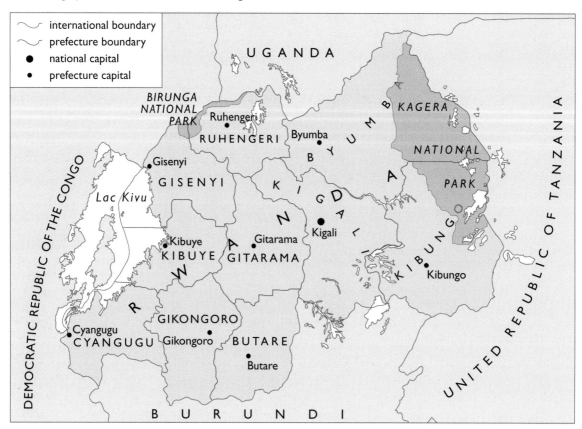

Figure 8.3   Rwanda, showing regions, major centres and neighbouring countries
Source: adapted from Mamdani, 2001

facing a strong military challenge from Tutsi rebels, as well as intense pressure from extremist Hutu power movements within the ruling party who were opposed to sharing power with the Tutsis. The moment of democratic opening and the attempts to impose a peace settlement that was favourable to the Tutsi rebels and more moderate Hutu politicians took place in a situation where the government military forces were slowly being defeated and pushed out of more and more of the countryside, and rising anti-Tutsi sentiment made any implementation of the peace settlement increasingly unlikely. Some commentators feel that the international community's push to establish a multiparty democracy was at least partly to blame for the consequent violence.

A hard-line Hutu constituency strongly opposed the peace settlement and secretly mobilised to defend Hutu dominance and their control of the country. In addition to their existing youth and military wings, these forces within the ruling party drew on local authorities to mobilise Hutu civilians, and started a new station for radio and TV broadcasts

(Radio et Télévision Libres des Milles Collines) to spread their message of Hutu power. Weapons were stored and, as the civil war progressed, preparations were made for implementing what was perceived as a 'final solution' to the conflict, the elimination of the Tutsi population: registers were drawn up of all the Tutsis and the politically moderate Hutus in each locality. The killings, when they started, were carried out not only by the militia, the mobilised youth brigades or militarised wings of political parties; although the massacre was centrally organised and politically motivated, many ordinary Hutu people became involved in killing their Tutsi neighbours, even family members. Eltringham (2004, p.69) notes that some estimates suggest that as many as 10 per cent of ethnic Hutus actively participated in the killings. For many commentators, this was the true horror of this genocide. How could ordinary people take up the humble weapons available to them, like farm implements and clubs, to participate in the centrally organised slaughter of an entire population group? As Mahmood Mamdani, a Ugandan scholar, notes: 'The response and initiative from below involved multitudes and presents the true moral dilemma of the Rwandan genocide' (2001, p.7).

There is another equally important question that continues to haunt people both within Rwanda and around the world: why did no one do anything to stop this genocide? Since the Holocaust in Europe, in which more than six million Jewish people were systematically killed by the Nazi powers, the world has been mobilised behind the slogan, 'Never again'. The UN drew up the Genocide Convention in 1948 to empower nations to intervene to prevent genocide, even when this would mean invading another sovereign state. Yet, in the case of Rwanda, although the killings went on for months, with a UN force already in the country to oversee the peace negotiations, and the world could observe the events on TV, hear about them on radio broadcasts and read about them in the newspapers, still nothing was done by anyone to prevent the killings. The plight of the banyarwanda (people of Rwanda), while made proximate in the living rooms and boardrooms of the powerful Western nations, was kept at a distance. Why?

Defining genocide

Genocide was a term coined in the 1940s by a Polish jurist, Raphäel Lemkin, combining the Greek word *genos* (race, tribe) with the Latin root *cide* (killing of), and used in the UN Genocide Convention of 1948 where it was defined as the intent to destroy 'in whole, or in part, a national, ethnic, racial or religious group'. This clause limits the ability to use the Convention to punish perpetrators or to take decisive preventative action in cases where targeted populations are members of different national, ethnic, racial or religious groups: this makes it difficult to act in cases where the target population is defined in political terms, for example with the mass murder of moderate Hutu people in Rwanda (Hinton, 2002).

Activity 8.2

Take some time to read the chronology of events in Rwanda, from April to July 1994, in Extract 8.1 below. Make a note of the key actors mentioned. This chronology was prepared by a BBC reporter, Fergal Keane, writing about his experiences in Rwanda during the genocide. In his account, which actors are assumed to be in a position to do something about the ongoing events?

Extract 8.1

'Genealogy of inaction'

6 April 1994: President Habyarimana and the president of (neighbouring) Burundi, Cyprien Ntaryamira, are killed when Habyarimana's plane is shot down as it comes in to land at Kigali Airport in Rwanda's capital city. Extremists, suspecting that the president is finally about to implement the Arusha Peace Accords, are believed to be behind the attack. That night the killing begins.

7 April 1994: The Rwandan armed forces and the Interahamwe (the youth militia of the ruling party, MRND – Mouvement Révolutionnaire National pour la Démocratie et le Développement) set up roadblocks and go from house to house killing Tutsis and moderate Hutu politicians. Thousands die on the first day. UN forces stand by while the slaughter goes on. They are forbidden to intervene, as this would breach their 'monitoring' mandate.

8 April 1994: The RPF (the Rwandan Patriotic Front, a Tutsi party and military force founded in 1988 by exiles in Uganda to secure repatriation of Tutsi exiles and power sharing in Rwanda) launches a major offensive to end the genocide and rescue 600 of its troops surrounded in Kigali. The troops had been based in the city as part of the Arusha Accords.

21 April 1994: The UN cuts the level of its forces from 2,500 to 250 following the murder of ten Belgian soldiers assigned to guard the moderate Hutu prime minister, Agathe Uwiliyingimana. The prime minister is killed and the Belgians are disarmed, tortured and shot and hacked to death. They had been told not to resist violently by the UN force commander, as this would have breached the mandate.

30 April 1994: The UN Security Council spends eight hours discussing the Rwandan crisis. The resolution condemning the killing omits the word 'genocide'. Had the term been used, the UN would have been legally obliged to act to 'prevent and punish' the perpetrators. Meanwhile, tens of thousands of refugees flee into Tanzania, Burundi and Zaire. In one day, 250,000 Rwandans, mainly Hutus fleeing the advance of the RPF, cross the border into Tanzania.

17 May 1994: As the slaughter of the Tutsis continues the UN finally agrees to send 6,800 troops and policemen to Rwanda with powers to defend civilians. A fresh Security Council resolution says 'acts of genocide may have been committed'. The United States government forbids its spokespersons to use the word 'genocide'. Deployment of the mainly African UN forces is delayed because of arguments over who will pay the bill and provide the equipment. The United States argues with the UN over the cost of providing heavy armoured vehicles for the peace-keeping forces.

22 June 1994: With still no sign of UN deployment, the Security Council authorizes the deployment of French forces in south-west Rwanda. They create a 'safe area' in territory controlled by the government. Killings of Tutsis continue in the 'safe area', although some are protected by the French. The United States government eventually uses the word 'genocide'.

July 1994: The final defeat of the Rwandan army. The government flees to Zaire, followed by a human tide of refugees. The French end their mission and are replaced by Ethiopian UN troops. The RPF sets up an interim government of national unity in Kigali. A cholera epidemic sweeps the refugee camps in Zaire, killing thousands. Different UN agencies clash over reports that RPF troops have carried out a series of reprisal killings in Rwanda. Several hundred civilians are said to have been executed. Meanwhile the killing of Tutsis continues in refugee camps.

(Keane, 1995, pp.196–8)

There are many different actors in the sequence of events in Extract 8.1. You may have noted, for example, a range of nations, including those of the USA, France, Belgium, Ethiopia, Tanzania, Zaire and Burundi alongside Rwanda. They were mentioned for different reasons – some because they were nearby and Rwandan people escaped there or returned to the country from there; some because, as neighbours, they took more responsibility for trying to shape events in Rwanda; and some, like the French, because they were former colonial powers in the central African region and retained influence and interests in the area, including trading arms and offering support for the Hutu government. The Belgians had direct historical links to Rwanda, stretching back to their colonisation of the region in 1904 and continuing to their overthrow in the revolution of 1959.

Not only did foreign countries fail to assist the Tutsi victims of genocide, but they also helped to lay the foundations for these events. Belgian colonial powers, as well as missionaries and educationalists, played a large role in taking what were trans-ethnic, somewhat malleable identities of 'Hutu' (a term used to define people who had been conquered by the dominant pre-colonial Tutsi state in the region) and 'Tutsi' (a ruling elite, which could include people who had formerly been known as 'Hutu' in their ranks), and turning them into starkly defined races with official documents provided to determine who belonged to which 'race'. They also layered in a racist ascription of Hamitic, or 'civilised', external origins to the dominant Tutsi group, and made use of subordinate rulers from the Tutsi, who received privileged access to education, to dominate Hutu peasants who were excluded from any such benefits. Belgian colonial power was notoriously ruthless, depending on forced labour and violent punishments. When the Tutsi were deposed along with the Belgians in 1959, these hardened oppositional identities of Hutu and Tutsi, largely invented in the colonial era, were transferred into the politics of the post-independence revolutionary government (Mamdani, 2001).

More recently, the 'soft' power of development aid in the 1990s saw foreign countries playing a strong role in initiating peace negotiations by insisting that the Hutu-dominated state democratise and open the country's borders to Tutsi rebels and exiles. In the course of these negotiations, an underestimation of the strength of the Hutu extremists within the government saw the peace process itself become a cause of increasingly entrenched anti-Tutsi politics, and ultimately a cause of the genocide as extremists sought to defend their position of power (Clapham, cited in Wheeler, 2000, p.213). The situation in Rwanda was not simply one of distant non-involvement by the more powerful nations in the world; they were already deeply enmeshed in politics there. In fact, they were very present in shaping the causes of the genocide as well as the international response to the killings.

The USA may have had no colonial ties to Rwanda but, along with other wealthy donor countries, it was also widely expected to respond to the events. However, the USA played a major role in refusing to allow the UN to define the events in Rwanda as genocide, which would have demanded foreign intervention. Moreover, even when this definition was eventually agreed, the USA and other wealthy nations stalled on providing the military resources needed for the UN intervention force.

Repeated appeals to the UN to intervene were made both before and during the period of mass killings by the commander of the UN forces already in Rwanda (General Romeo Dallaire first alerted the UN to the dangers on 11 January 1994), by local aid workers, human rights activists and the media as well as by the Organisation of African Unity. Representatives of two small nations – New Zealand, whose ambassador, Colin Keating, was president of the UN Security Council for the month of April 1994, and Czechoslovakia, whose ambassador, Karel Kovanda, came from a family that had survived the European

Holocaust – made special efforts to bring the events as they unfolded to the attention of the security council and to persuade members to support preventative humanitarian intervention in Rwanda (Wheeler, 2000). African representatives suggested that the lack of response could be taken as a measure of the indifference felt towards the suffering of African people (United Nations, 1996). Why did the powerful, wealthy countries not respond?

One set of reasons why the USA was unwilling to be drawn into an intervention at the time was related to an earlier experience in Somalia in December 1992, when nineteen US troops had been publicly humiliated and killed, and the peacekeeping operation there terminated. There was concern more widely within the UN that another failed intervention so soon after this one could diminish international confidence in UN forces. There was a general air of caution about staging any more militarised interventions. For the USA, domestic opposition to its role as the 'world's policeman' led to a Presidential Decision Directive being issued by President Clinton, to the effect that 'the USA would contribute to operations only where its national interests were engaged and that its soldiers would always remain under national control and command' (Wheeler, 2000, p.224). The US President himself observed on 25 May 1994, after weeks of killing, that 'the USA had no vital interests in Rwanda and that US military personnel could not be sent to every trouble spot where Americans were "offended by human misery"' (Wheeler, 2000, p.229).

The USA, as the dominant military power in the world, and the major European nations who might also have been able to mobilise a sufficiently large force to intervene, refused to get involved. To some extent, they were reluctant to set a precedent for usurping the sovereign power of states elsewhere. Members of the Security Council steadfastly refused to send in further troops until domestic popular opinion in many countries and growing calls from human rights groups made some form of action unavoidable. Since using the term 'genocide' would require firm action, Security Council resolutions continued to describe the situation as one of chaos and disorder as a result of the civil war, rather than one of systematic slaughter of one ethnic group. On 17 May 1994, agreement was finally reached to send a small UN task force to the area, and the Secretary-General was at last publicly describing the events as 'genocide'.

Nonetheless, equipping the forces was a stumbling block because Western refusal to engage meant that it was left to African countries concerned with regional stability to provide the military staff for the operation. Table 8.2 shows the actual country contributions to the

Table 8.2   Country contributions to the Rwanda Assistance Mission

Country	Military personnel			Civilian police	Grand total
	troops	observers	total		
Argentina	0	1	1	0	1
Australia	302	0	302	0	302
Austria	0	15	15	0	15
Bangladesh	1	33	34	0	34
Canada	105	20	125	0	125
Chad	2	0	2	0	2
Djibouti	0	0	0	7	7
Ethiopia	811	0	811	0	811
Fiji	0	1	1	0	1
Germany	0	0	0	9	9
Ghana	842	35	877	10	887
Guinea	0	17	17	0	17
Guinea-Bissau	0	0	0	5	5
India	833	17	850	0	850
Jordan	0	0	0	3	3
Malawi	185	14	199	0	199
Mali	199	31	230	10	240
Nigeria	333	17	350	10	360
Poland	0	2	2	0	2
Russian Federation	0	17	17	0	17
Senegal	241	0	241	0	241
Tunisia	840	10	850	0	850
UK	2	0	2	0	2
Uruguay	0	23	23	0	23
Zambia	833	20	853	4	857
Zimbabwe	0	24	24	0	24
Total	5529	297	5826	58	5884

Source: United Nations, 1996

Rwanda mission. With little in the way of necessary military hardware available to these troops, debates over resources delayed the intervention. The French then agreed to send a small force to establish a safe haven in the south until the African troops could get there. Controversially, this safe haven protected the remaining troops of the government, allowed killings of Tutsis to continue in the area (although some received protection), and effectively prevented the advance of the Tutsi Rwandan Patriotic Front (RPF) forces, thereby changing the balance of power in the civil war. When refugee camps were set up here and in the border regions of neighbouring countries (see Figure 8.4(a) and (b)), once again extremist Hutu politicians and perpetrators of the genocide found a safe haven and, as Keane (1995) notes in Extract 8.1, some Tutsis continued to be killed.

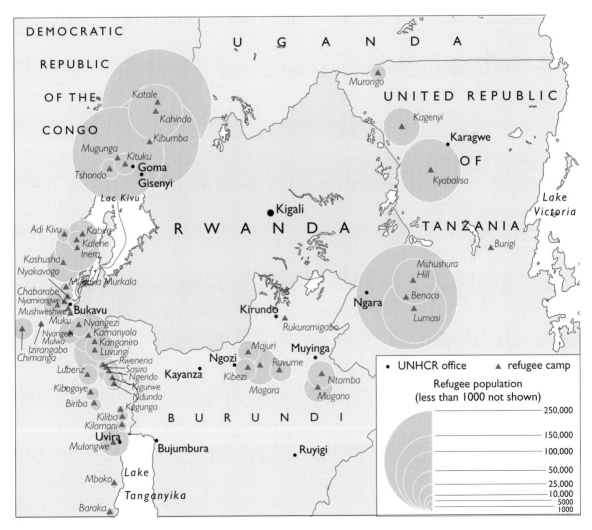

Figure 8.4(a)   Safe havens and refugee camps in Rwanda and surrounding countries, December 1994
Source: United Nations, 1996

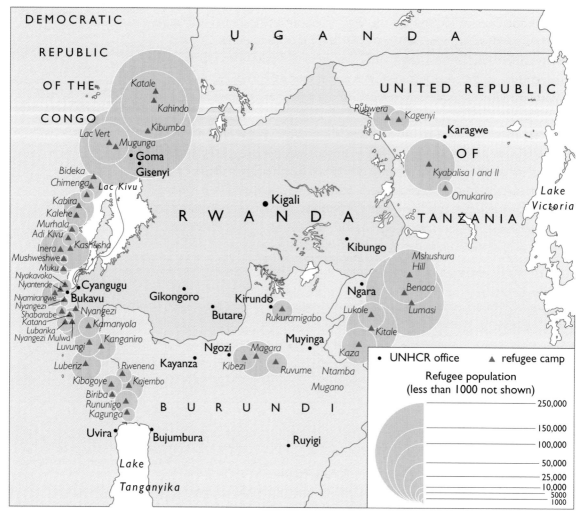

Figure 8.4(b)   Safe havens and refugee camps in Rwanda and surrounding countries, May 1996
Source: United Nations, 1996

The ambiguous intervention of the French, the delays in international decisions to intervene and the reluctance of wealthy nations to pay for the operation or to supply troops all raise questions about the reasons for doing nothing, for remaining absent from the situation in Rwanda despite plenty of evidence concerning the genocide and popular concern about the atrocities being reported. As Section 3 will explore further, the reasons for intervening or not were bound up with the perceived national interests of the countries concerned (as in the contrasting cases of the USA and the French), as well as wider calculations about the relative importance of a place like Rwanda in world politics. From the perspective of the UN, there were also serious political concerns about respecting the sovereign rights of member-states, which prevented its early intervention.

The Genocide Convention of the UN offers an institutional and legal framework to justify international intervention in situations like this. Yet members of the Security Council were unwilling to condone intervention in Rwanda partly because it might open up the possibility for intervention by powerful nations in other more controversial situations or, in the future, perhaps even in their own countries. The principle of the sovereign independence of states, a founding element of the UN as an interstate body, limited the inclination of the Security Council to strengthen the mandate of the UN mission in Rwanda from monitoring and peacekeeping, under the auspices of a sovereign government, to preventing killings perpetrated by that government on other parties.

The discourses of humanitarian concern reinforced by the memories of the Holocaust fell foul of wider international politics, in which Africa was no longer of any strategic interest to the USA and other world powers, and where setting precedents for intervening in the affairs of sovereign states could shift delicate political agreements about interventions which were far more strategic, such as in the oil-rich Middle East. Section 3 considers these wider geopolitical dynamics of intervention in more detail.

Summary

- Atrocities, like the genocide in Rwanda, can come quickly to the attention of international observers, the general public and organisations like the UN. They are brought close through various forms of media, reporting and observer missions.

- Powerful agents do not always respond to atrocities with assistance; they can choose to keep their distance from such events.

- Although social and political dynamics specific to the context in question are an important determinant of violence and conflict, external influences can also play a significant role including, as in the case of Rwanda, aid contributions, political influence, arms trading and even peace initiatives.

3   The geopolitics of intervention: near and far in global politics

Defining geopolitics

Geopolitics is a term used since the beginning of the twentieth century to refer to the dynamics of international politics, especially as related to the significance of territory, the relative location of countries and the distribution of strategic resources. More recently it has also come to include a critique of ways of understanding the geographies of world politics, including how different places are perceived by powerful countries as well as more popular preconceptions about different places and people (Dodds, 2000).

It has been widely suggested that in Rwanda early and substantial intervention from UN forces, already on the ground, could have prevented atrocities on the scale on which they happened. However, many of the different actors who were in some way involved in, connected to or called on to respond to the Rwandan genocide all chose not to respond, at least not initially. We have seen a little of the different motivations for their action, or inaction. Yet it was noticeable that only some actors were the target of demands to intervene, mostly powerful governments and international agencies. Furthermore, while smaller African nations seemed more ready to go to the aid of people in Rwanda, they apparently lacked the means to fund such a mission.

This section establishes some of the broader context for the international response to the Rwandan genocide as well as other examples of responses to demands for intervention. It will consider in general how some actors on the world stage have the capacity to respond – how they build the capacity and have the organisational reach to make their presence felt in distant places. The section will also ask why, even if agents have the capacity, decisions to intervene – to become present in different situations – are made selectively. What motivates action in some cases, and inaction in others? How do we explain, for example, the failure of powerful states to intervene to stop the genocide in Rwanda and, on the other hand, the decision almost ten years later by some of these same states, the USA and the UK in particular, to invade Iraq despite the lack of agreement of the UN Security Council, making their presence felt with a spectacular show of force? The wider geopolitics of decisions to intervene or not can help us to appreciate the reasons for these differences.

3.1   The international reach of states: the capacity to intervene

The ability to reach out and broadcast power across the globe – to attain a presence and influence events in distant parts of the planet – has depended on a changing set of technologies. At different times this might have involved long journeys by sailing ship, navigating with charts and sextants, delivering letters of introduction to distant rulers or, by the early twentieth century, communicating through intercontinental cables, telegrams and telephones, which made contact at a distance almost immediate. As we saw in Chapter 2, recent communications technologies allow for interaction to take place in near instantaneous time. Nevertheless, the ability to reach out and influence events at a distance, as we discussed in Chapter 3, more often involves 'a succession of practices bridging the gap between here and there in a more mediated fashion' (Allen, 2003, p.64). The ability to transmit information or influence opinions is rather different from the capacity to dispatch census enumerators or, in the examples in this chapter, the goods, troops and munitions to try to secure peace through military interventions. This requires complex logistical organisation across long distances and usually a delay between decision and action.

The range of techniques for reaching out to influence events in distant places forms the foundation of any actor's ability to respond to demands to intervene in situations of disaster and emergency. In the context of a globalised world, technologies for communication and transport offer increasingly effective means to achieve presence and influence around the world. However, not all actors have the capacity to make use of them.

For the last few centuries, one of the core dynamics shaping global interactions has been that of state-building (see Chapter 3). States, in relationship with one another, have been key agents of intervention at a distance. Establishing international trading relations, fighting wars, extracting taxes or plunder from new territories, creating the conditions to support business ventures across the globe – historically, states have been involved in all these and more. Yet among states, unequal power relations have meant that relations of influence and the capacity to intervene at a distance have been varied. The most fundamental requirement for influence and intervention at a distance in the world system of states is sufficient resources to sustain the communications networks, logistical capabilities, person power and military hardware on which global influence depends. Historically, the uneven nature of economic development across the world has meant that states in some parts of the world have had substantially more resources to influence and intervene in distant places than others. It is instructive to consider the example of one of the most powerful states in the world today, the USA.

For most of the twentieth century, and notably since the First World War, the USA assumed dominance on the world political stage, supported by the largest economy in the world and substantially more investment in the military capacity required to support its ambitions to be a global power than any other country (see Table 8.3). Its capacity to intervene across the world vastly exceeds that of other countries, especially since the decline of the Soviet Union from the late 1980s. Nonetheless, the USA is the first world power to attain dominance without seeking actually to conquer territory – partly because by the time it came to power all territory had already been claimed within the international system of states. Some commentators have described the USA's military interventions in places like Panama, Nicaragua, Kosovo, Afghanistan and Iraq, for example, as 'Empire Lite' (Ignatieff, cited in Harvey, 2003, pp.3–4), hinting at the characteristic US ambition to influence politics and open areas to economic trade and investment without investing in the costly infrastructure of rule or settlement. This is quite different from earlier global powers, particularly in the late nineteenth century, when at the height of European colonial ambition they occupied and ruled territories across large areas of the globe.

Table 8.3   Global military expenditure, 2002

Country	$US billion (in constant 2000 $)	Global military expenditure (%)
USA	335.7	42.80
Japan	46.7	5.95
UK	36.0	4.58
France	33.6	4.28
China	31.1	3.96
Germany	27.7	3.53
Saudi Arabia	21.6	2.75
Italy	21.1	2.68
Iran (2001 figures)	17.5	2.23
South Korea	13.5	1.72
India	12.9	1.64
Russia	11.4	1.45
Turkey	10.1	1.28
Brazil	10.0	1.27
Israel	9.8	1.24

Source: Gregory, 2004, p.193

Coming late to global ambitions and power, the USA confronted a world which had already been carved up among existing colonising powers, and created a distinctive style of being a superpower without territorialising ambitions, but with a strong interest in influencing and trading with as much of the world as possible. While former colonial powers remained influential in the countries and regions they had previously dominated, and often continue to protect their privileged relationship with these places (as with France and Belgium in central Africa), for the USA, other kinds of geographies have been important. Open borders that encourage free trade have been crucial components of twentieth-century US dominance and international policy (Smith, 2003). The influence of the USA across the globe, and the substantial resources it has accumulated to reach out to distant places, mean that demands for assistance and intervention are directed its way from all over the world, whereas for former colonial powers there might be stronger expectations of assistance in areas where they have historically been influential.

The USA may have more resources than other nations to pursue its dominance of the world system, but not all commentators believe that this dominance is very secure. Although a group of 'new imperialist' policy makers in the USA hope to ensure this dominance for the twenty-first century, Michael Mann (2003) suggests that its dominance of the world political system might be coming to an end. He outlines four different sources of US power which he argues are unlikely to support dominance in the long term. Mann suggests that the sources of international power available to states in general are:

1   Economic – the relative wealth of a country.

2   Military – the state's accumulation of a large force, both in terms of military hardware and personnel.

3   Political – the state's ability to influence leadership and political stability in different parts of the world.

4   Ideological – the state's ability to shape the beliefs and understandings of people in distant places.

On these four fronts, Mann (2003) suggests that the USA is not going to hold on to its position of global dominance for much longer. He advises that US economic capacities are declining relative to its competitors (for example, China, the European Union (EU) and smaller nations in Southeast Asia), and are in any case not within the direct control of the state. In general the resources to support the logistical capabilities for global intervention are becoming relatively less concentrated in US hands. The military ambitions of the US government, then, could be expanding beyond affordability. More than this, Mann claims that US ability to shape actual political outcomes is limited, both by the powers of international institutions like the UN and other international bodies, and specifically in many local situations because of the US government's unwillingness to commit resources to the day-to-day rule of distant places. Unlike former colonial powers, the USA wants to avoid assuming political control of distant territories. So, while it may be able to effect change in places like Afghanistan and Iraq through military intervention, it seems unable to sustain that change while maintaining its arm's-length approach to political rule in these places. In addition, Mann notes that perhaps the strongest source of US power, that of ideological influence, is wielded by agents like corporations and the media which are beyond the control of the state, the formal agent of US power in the world. Unlike military and political power, which are under the direct control of the state, these very diffuse forms of power are difficult to marshal in any direct way to the ambitions of global influence (Allen, 2003). Mann concludes that current US dominance is at best an 'Incoherent Empire':

> I do not see the demise of the [USA] as coming from the rise of another power or from general imperial over-stretch, but from extremely uneven power resources. These lead not to general collapse but to imperial incoherence and foreign policy failure. ... The American Empire will turn out to be a military giant, a back-seat economic driver, a political schizophrenic and an ideological phantom. The result is a disturbed, misshapen monster stumbling clumsily across the world. It means well. It intends to spread order and benevolence, but instead it creates more disorder and violence.

> ... In response to their limitations, the new imperialists [in the USA] are grasping ever more firmly on to the one power they do possess in abundance – offensive military devastation. My conclusion will be that in reality the new American imperialism is becoming the new American militarism.

> (Mann, 2003, pp.13, 16)

Mann also points out that in terms of US ambitions for global influence, Russia and China, past and future competitors on the world stage, 'are much too big and powerful to be messed with' (2003, p.14). Consequently, the USA maintains a wary military presence near these countries' borders, with little likelihood of intervention, but with a strong focus on increasing trade links and fostering ideological influence. Thus, even for this most powerful of contemporary states, the business of reaching out to influence events at a distance is fraught with difficulties and has some definite limitations.

Differential distribution of resources among states and over time provides a backdrop to explaining whether different actors might have the capacities to assist in situations of conflict and disaster. Also of importance, however, is whether these actors have the will to intervene.

3.2 Geopolitical imaginations: the will to intervene

States have different resources to draw upon to influence places and people beyond their borders. Yet, as the Rwanda case most clearly demonstrated, simply having the capacity to intervene does not mean that action will follow. An important reason for this is that while at some moments places can come to seem very close to the interests of powerful states, at others they might seem quite distant, or indeed irrelevant. One way of understanding this is to consider the geopolitical imaginations of states – how do governments and policy makers see the relative significance of different parts of the world?

Let us consider first the situation of Africa in the geopolitical imagination of those Western countries that had the capacity to respond to the pleas for intervention in the Rwandan genocide.

During the Cold War, a number of Western countries became heavily involved in supporting regional conflicts in different parts of Africa, for example in Ethiopia, Angola and Mozambique. Military assistance and financial support were given to governments and armed groups that were fighting against communist-supported states or militia. The USA and other Western powers saw the Soviet Union and its ambitions for global influence as the major geopolitical threat, and used their capacities to influence distant events to try and contain the Soviet Union and its allies.

However, after the end of the Cold War in the late 1980s, these strategic interests changed. Africa's relative place in the world in geopolitical terms, from the point of view of the USA or Europe, Russia or China, became rather remote. With weak markets and few crucial resources and a large proportion of the population living in poverty in Africa, the strategic and self-interested motivations for influence or intervention have been very slight for most powerful nations.

Supporting this strategic uninterest are the long histories of imaginative constructions of Africa as, for example, inferior and prone to violence as was discussed in Chapter 5.

Sub-Saharan Africa, economically weak and playing only a minor role in supplying strategic resources, has been generally 'off-limits' to US military and political intervention since the end of the Cold War and is mostly engaged by the USA through diffuse economic and ideological sources of influence. However, for some other world powers, for example France and the UK, colonial legacies mean that stronger relations of influence and political presence, as well as ongoing economic connections, have been maintained, as we observed in the case of France and the events surrounding the Rwandan genocide. Moreover, of course, for many African countries, events in the region are of crucial concern, and Section 4 will explore this in more detail.

Therefore, a combination of the changing strategic interests of Western countries in the post-Cold War era and cultural imaginations about Africa help to explain the inaction of many countries in response to the Rwandan crisis in 1994. Since these events though, the geopolitical imaginations of powerful states have once again been shifting. Do these changes indicate any greater propensity on the part of wealthier nations to assist in situations of humanitarian crisis?

In the early part of the twenty-first century the US government has been inspired by the thinking of a group of neo-conservative policy makers, the Project for a New American Century, which is eager to ensure the USA's place on the global stage for the next century. The group's influential 2000 report asks whether the USA 'has the resolve to shape a new century favourable to American principles and interests?' (Project for a New American Century, 2000). Facing no global rival since the break-up of the Soviet Union, the Project for a New American Century suggests that US foreign policies should aim to 'preserve and extend this advantageous position as far into the future as possible' (ibid., p.i). Whereas during the Cold War the ambition had been to contain the Soviet Union, the demise of this bipolar world order means that the USA's strategic goal is simply to 'preserve an international security environment conducive to American interests and ideals' (ibid., p.2). This, the group advises, can be achieved through expanding 'zones of democratic peace' around the world – zones in which the USA's trade and influence can thrive – and defending strategically important regions (such as the Middle East, East Asia and Europe), while ensuring the USA's continued military dominance compared with other countries. The Project for a New American Century proposes that this requires a military preparedness to operate across the globe in what it sees as a 'more complex and chaotic world', in order to preserve the 'American peace' (ibid., pp.8, iv).

The geopolitical imagination of these 'new imperialists', as Michael
Mann has called them, has been captured by one of their advocates in
a map in which the world is divided into two zones: the 'non-
integrating gap' and the 'functioning core' (see Figure 8.5). Areas in
the first zone are characterised as sources of danger because they are
seen to be relatively disconnected from the global system and because
ongoing conflicts in some regions (for example, compare Figures 8.1
and 8.5) have been very destabilising: 'disconnection defines danger',
writes the creator of this map (cited in Roberts et al., 2003, p.889).
The solution for these policy makers is to shrink this gap aggressively,
drawing dangerous places into relationship with the core areas of the
globe and establishing peace. It is a geopolitical imagination of
integration and interdependency – a one-world vision of security
orchestrated and dominated, however, by the USA and its allies.

This is a very different imagination of the world from that which was
at work during the decades of the Cold War, for example. Then, the
world had been imagined as divided between East and West, with the
two superpowers, the USA and the USSR, each dominating within one
sphere. Many wars were fought in smaller countries in regions where
one of the superpowers tried to initiate dominance or to stem the
influence of the other power – these regional wars were 'proxies' which
stood in for the ongoing battle between the superpowers for influence

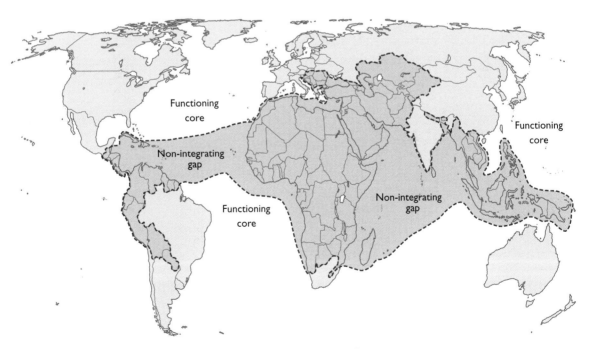

Figure 8.5   The geopolitical imagination of US 'new imperialists'
Source: Roberts et al., 2003, p.891

across the globe. Today, the ambition of most wealthy countries is to tie all places across the globe into a network of trade and ideological influence, which favours their interests and operates within a broad policy framework often known as neo-liberalism, encouraging open borders and privileging private investment.

For the 'new imperialists' facing the twenty-first century, the world has been reconfigured from the array of strategic sites for Cold War conflict into a world in which some places are seen as disconnected from the dominant economic system and others come into view as vitally important in order to protect strategic resources. In 'disconnected' regions, this geopolitical imagination could lead to more support for interventions that seek to end conflicts and stimulate trading relations. However, in those regions with significant resources, the motivations for intervention remain much stronger. Some observers suggest that the demand for oil has come to be particularly important in shaping the strategic interests of powerful countries. The geographer David Harvey notes that:

> The only oilfields that look set to last fifty years or more are those in Iran, Iraq, Saudi Arabia, the United Arab Emirates, and Kuwait. While new discoveries could change this picture, most strategic thinkers have to confront the increasing significance of the Middle East as the key provider of oil over time.
>
> (Harvey, 2003, p.23)

Harvey updates the observations of a nineteenth-century geopolitician, Halford MacKinder, who had noted the strategic significance of the Russian heartland at that time, and suggested that command of this region could bring control of the entire world. In applying his insights to the early twenty-first century, MacKinder's 'geographical pivot of history' has been relocated from the Russian heartland to the Middle East. As Harvey quips, following MacKinder, 'whoever controls the Middle East controls the global oil spigot and whoever controls the global oil spigot can control the global economy, at least for the near future' (Harvey, 2003, p.19). Through its ironic reference to the Iraq War, the Oxfam campaign image in Figure 8.6 observes that Africa might receive more attention from the rest of the world if alleviating poverty was as crucial for wealthy countries as securing their supplies of oil.

Some places, like the Middle East, may be half a planet away from the USA, but they have been brought very close to the concerns and interests of this and other powerful economies across the globe. As we saw in Chapters 2 and 5, through direct military presence, incessant

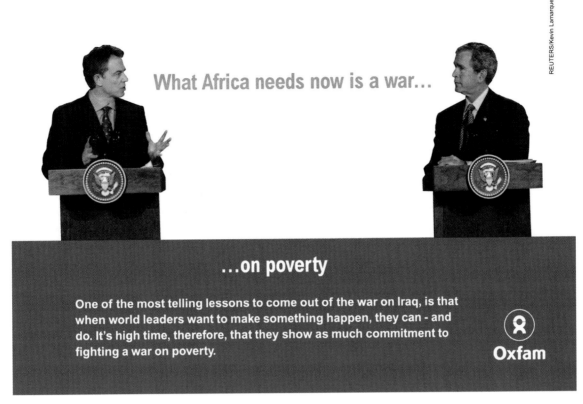

Figure 8.6   Make war on poverty, Oxfam campaign image
Source: Oxfam, *c.*2003

news coverage and even close personal connections, the two gulf wars brought events in Iraq, for example, into the daily lives of citizens of the USA, the UK and other countries that participated in the invasion of the country.

Other parts of the globe continue to have considerably less prominence in the geopolitical imaginations of the USA and other wealthy countries. Moreover, as we have already hinted in the case of Africa, geopolitical imaginations are made up of more than just strategic interests. Popular opinions and background cultural assumptions about different places and people also play an important role in shaping the actions of states.

One way of appreciating this intersection between popular culture and geopolitical imaginations is to notice how popular media, like magazines or films, articulate but in turn can also shape the cultural assumptions that underpin more strategic geopolitical approaches to different places. During the Cold War era, through numerous articles and commentaries, the *Reader's Digest* constructed for its readers a picture of US freedom and democracy, whereas the Soviet Union was portrayed as forcing individuals to be subject to the whims of the bureaucracy and its attendant inequities of nepotism and favouritism. From these and other images, the Soviet Union emerged as the 'ultimate alter ego' of the USA, implacably opposed to all its values, and this reinforced in the cultural realm the political divisions of the Cold War (Sharp, 1993).

Through a range of different cultural practices, layers of popular cultural meanings have accrued to different places, especially through the process of colonialism, as Chapters 5 and 7 discussed. In the case of Africa, for instance, deep-rooted and often racist historical representations of this large and diverse continent as primordial, uncivilised and economically backward continue to shape US and European responses to events there. During the Rwandan crisis, this evoked a popular perception in some circles that the killings were a simple product of age-old tribal animosities rather than the determined outcome of a modern state and an elite eager to retain political power.

Geopolitical imaginations are produced within a broader cultural environment, shaped by cultural norms and understandings from outside of the state. In this context, popular opinion can play an important role in shaping the geopolitical ambitions of states.

Humanitarian concerns among the public in wealthier countries, particularly about famine in the 1980s, genocide and conflicts through the 1990s, and increasingly about the persistence of poverty in the first decade of the twenty-first century, have been important in reconfiguring the geopolitical strategies of governments in these countries, notably in relation to Africa. Section 4 explores how such popular opinion has changed the geopolitical landscape, bringing places which had been kept at a cultural and political distance more to the forefront of global political imaginations. The Rwandan experience has played an important role in this.

Summary

- States have varying capacities to intervene in distant parts of the world. The international reach of states is influenced by the uneven distribution of resources, especially national income and military capacity.

- Different parts of the world are brought closer, or made more distant, through the geopolitical interests and imaginations that shape the strategic viewpoints of states.

- The shift from a bipolar world order in the Cold War to the dominance of one major power, the USA, has led to a substantial shift in the significance of different parts of the world in the geopolitical imaginations of wealthier countries.

- The variable responses of states to calls to intervene in crises and disasters can be explained by their different capacities, by strategic interests and by popular cultural imaginations about different places.

4   Remaking global presence after Rwanda

So far, we have at least part of the answer to the question we have posed in this chapter: why did powerful nations in the world do nothing to stop the genocide in Rwanda, when patently their combined military and logistical capacity might have been mobilised to save people's lives? The range of geopolitical interests that influences the actions of major powers across the globe marks out places like Rwanda as lacking in strategic significance, and the cultural geopolitical imaginations about some of the poorest places in the world make assumptions about people and events there that have tended to place the blame firmly in their court. As a result, the governments most powerful states do not feel responsible for events in places like Rwanda, and have tended to keep them imaginatively and strategically at a distance.

Nevertheless, as Section 3.2 noted, geopolitical imaginations are also shaped by popular media and public opinion. These brought Rwanda very close to home for many citizens in other countries, and demands for intervention were aired in various forums at the time. In this section, we will consider how popular demands for humanitarian intervention have reshaped global geopolitics since the Rwanda crisis and initiated new ways for different agents to make their presence felt in distant contexts.

4.1   Do something!

Activity 8.3

Take a look at the two letters to newspaper editors from directors of major international aid agencies reproduced below in Extract 8.2.

1   On what basis were the authors calling for action in relation to the violence in Rwanda in 1994?

2   Who was targeted as being responsible for taking action?

Extract 8.2

'Letters to the editor'

A dangerous and deadly myopia

It is apt that Drs Peter Hall and Andrew Carney quote Swift when writing about genocide in Rwanda (Letters, October 24). The response of the international community has been of Lilliputian proportions.

The international community has already failed the people of Rwanda, both in supplying the perpetrators of genocide with the means to carry out the killings and by an abject failure of will and nerve to intervene once the killings had started. The complacency and inaction of the most powerful member states of the UN in failing to heed the warning signs contributed to the slaughter.

These same nations are in danger of failing the people of Rwanda once again. It is crucial to establish a judicial process to prosecute individuals suspected of crimes against humanity. This will require the establishment of an international tribunal and a new legal and judicial system. It is also important to send UN human rights monitors to every commune in the country, which would also deter revenge killings. All these initiatives are in danger of failing because governments are apathetic towards or politically opposed to such initiatives. It is reported that the French, for example, have blocked EU assistance to the UN Human Rights operation and reconstruction aid to the new Rwandan administration.

By their failure the international community is condoning a further cycle of brutality. It is vital that nations act consistently to uphold the basic rights of human beings wherever they are threatened, strengthen the UN's ability to undertake preventive diplomacy and action and reduce the flow of arms to areas where they are likely to result in civilian suffering.

Stewart Wallis, Overseas Director, Oxfam.

(*The Guardian*, 1994a)

Moral dilemmas of aid to Rwanda

The withdrawal of Médecins Sans Frontières from camps in Tanzania highlights the growing dilemmas and pressures faced by aid agencies working on the Rwandan refugee crisis.

While UNHCR [United Nations High Commissioner for Refugees] has provided invaluable co-ordination of the relief operation in Rwanda and neighbouring countries, the UN Security Council and individual UN member states have repeatedly failed to support the work of aid agencies on the ground. Instead, now Rwanda has disappeared from the headlines, they have reverted to an 'out of sight, out of mind' policy of inaction.

Agencies such as Actionaid/Assist know only too well the growing problems faced by aid workers on the ground. In recent months, in addition to the dilemma of providing relief to some of the perpetrators of the massacres, the security situation in the refugee camps has deteriorated severely. The Hutu militias are increasingly in control, often diverting aid from those in greatest need and intimidating refugees wishing to return home. In the midst of this chaos, some aid workers have received death threats and many face daily intimidation.

While aid workers are on the frontline, the international community is standing by and watching. Over a month ago, the UN Secretary General proposed to the Security Council that a 5,000-strong security force – with a strict humanitarian mandate – be sent to the camps in Zaire.

To date, however, this proposal has been met with deafening silence from UN member states, including Britain, and there is growing evidence from New York, Geneva and London that security assistance will not be supported in any shape or form.

This is despite the fact that the lessons of inaction are all too plain to see. In April, the UN's failure to respond to the emerging crisis in Rwanda set the scene for the massacres which claimed over 500,000 lives. In 1994, the international community failed the people of Rwanda. As the year nears an end, it is also failing the aid agencies. It is to be hoped that, in 1995, lessons will be learned – and that it will be a year of action rather than words.

Nigel Twose, International Director, ACTIONAID, London N19.

(*The Guardian*, 1994b)

Media coverage of the Rwandan genocide provoked a strong and vociferous outpouring of humanitarian concern from many countries across the globe. In Extract 8.2, the authors are partly concerned about the role that international actors had played in fuelling the violence (supplying arms, for example), but much of their argument for action rests on feelings of compassion for the suffering of other people, and a desire to protect basic human rights, rather than on the existence of historical or immediate connections between themselves and the events in Rwanda.

As the Rwandan crisis unfolded, humanitarian concerns dominated the news and public debates in a number of places around the world as some states and many NGOs, development organisations, human rights groups and individuals expressed their demand that those who had the capacity to respond – wealthy countries and the UN especially – should, clearly, do something about the situation. Eventually, and very belatedly in terms of the killings, international organisations and donor countries made their presence felt in Rwanda, managing aid and refugee camps for those who had fled, trying to orchestrate their return to a safe environment, and devoting funds to reconstruction and the search for justice.

Activity 8.4

I would now like you to turn to Reading 8A by Mark Duffield (2001) entitled 'Global governance and the new wars: the merging of development and security', which you will find at the end of the chapter. Make some notes for yourself about how Duffield considers that humanitarian concerns have changed the face of global politics, but also how more strategic security concerns have subsequently been woven into humanitarian interventions. In your opinion, are these changes likely to lead to more effective interventions in conflicts and disasters?

According to Mark Duffield (2001), a groundswell of popular opinion in the 1980s made humanitarian concerns a much more prominent part of global politics, and a range of humanitarian organisations – linked to the UN or independent NGOs – have become important agents in shaping international interventions. How states and international agencies make themselves present in distant situations has shifted from direct interventions, using the capacities and personnel of states, to a more networked form of intervention in association with humanitarian NGOs and private sector agents. All these agents have also shifted from attempting to deliver assistance in impartial ways, independent of the political situation, to a stronger awareness of the political effects of humanitarian interventions themselves. The following section considers how these changes have had an impact on the kinds of interventions that powerful global agents are willing to make.

4.2   Networked forms of global presence

In a number of different contexts, NGOs and donor countries have become increasingly aware that attempts to deliver purely humanitarian assistance can become part of the problem, fuelling conflicts and sustaining armies. In the case of Rwanda, NGOs were unable to prevent the Hutu perpetrators of the genocide from regrouping and maintain their militia in the refugee camps in the neighbouring Democratic Republic of the Congo (formerly Zaire). NGOs have consequently become more concerned with actively engaging with the politics of conflicts, being alert to the political consequences of their actions, getting involved in attempting to resolve conflicts, establish and maintain peace, and using development interventions to promote peaceful reconstruction in post-conflict situations. Since the difficulties of purely impartial 'prophetic' humanitarian responses became apparent through the 1990s (Duffield, 2001), complex new networks have been formed to facilitate interventions and governance in conflict and disaster zones.

These networks embed NGOs in the strategic and political ambitions of the donor governments that largely fund the NGOs' work. Here, the broader strategic hope of realising a liberal or democratic peace that could facilitate economic growth and stability across 'dangerous' zones of destabilisation (as articulated by US, Canadian and British policy makers, as well as some regional powers in Africa (see African Union, 2004)) has drawn together popular humanitarian responses to the suffering of others with the strategic goals of wealthy and poor states to form new and complex relationships. As Duffield observes,

> The blurring of humanitarian action and politics is a reflection of the general merger of development and security. Moreover, within the new humanitarianism, with its emphasis on using humanitarian action to help resolve conflicts and reconstruct war-torn societies, the politicisation of aid is made complete. ... aid is no substitute for political action because it is the political action. It is now a tool of international regulation and is embedded in the networks and strategic complexes that make up liberal peace.
>
> (Duffield, 2001, p.88)

Defining governance

Whereas government refers to the particular activities of states, dependent upon formal authority and usually hierarchical forms of organisation, governance refers to a wider distribution of political power, including non-state agents, in organising and coordinating aspects of social, political and economic life. State and non-state agents work together normally in non-hierarchical partnerships, or other forms of association, that might require more informal interactions dependent on shared values and goals rather than the formal decision-making structures of the state.

Some of the mechanisms by which powerful nations become present in distant places have altered somewhat within the context of a globalised world. Instead of interventions that rely purely on individual state-directed actions, drawing on the personnel and resources of the state, forms of networked governance now dominate the geopolitics of intervention. States support and work with large NGOs, subcontract military activities to private firms, and rely on these agents and their contacts with military groupings and traders within the countries concerned to deliver humanitarian aid or work towards peace and reconstruction.

Wealthier nations have increasingly come to define international security in more than a purely military sense, including economic, social and environmental security. The meshing of developmental, security and humanitarian agendas through the 1990s and 2000s has represented a major shift in the geopolitical landscape. In those regions where the more obvious strategic interests of countries are not relevant, foreign policy has come to be defined by development aid policy, and where such aid is not deemed worthwhile because of conflict or the breakdown of governance, the presence and influence of wealthier countries has come to be defined by humanitarian and emergency aid (Humanitarian Policy Group, 2000).

According to commentators like Mark Duffield (2001) and the Humanitarian Policy Group (HPG) (2000), there has been a differentiation of the geopolitical landscape between places with strategic and economic relevance to powerful countries, and those where such interests are much weaker, and conflict is perhaps endemic. The latter are drawn into geopolitical relations through aid and humanitarian support, rather than through more conventional foreign policy relations. Not without justification, there is concern that the search for security and 'liberal peace' in these poorer contexts, although perhaps desired by local people, reflects a Western agenda, and depends upon criteria that are imposed unilaterally by powerful countries. As we saw in the Rwanda case, imposing external conditions on volatile situations can have serious and unforeseen consequences.

Alongside the strategic objectives of powerful states, the geopolitical landscape has come to include a new set of relations between wealthier countries and poor, more insecure parts of the world, defined by the politicised implementation of humanitarian relief and development objectives.

The making present of distant events and the bringing proximate of the plight of distant others can mobilise a sense of responsibility for fellow human beings. Humanitarian responses to emergencies as well as an awareness of the implication of distant people and governments in the broad structures or background conditions that make conflict, hunger and displacement possible can follow. However, state-led humanitarian responses to these situations are also motivated by more strategic concerns. The highly politicised nature of the new connections that are produced through interventions, in the name of both humanitarianism and security, make it clear that taking responsibility can in its turn introduce new forms of political relationship between different people and places.

Furthermore, while demands to take responsibility for humanitarian emergencies are often directed at powerful states, international agencies and NGOs (as the letters in Extract 8.2 illustrate), it is clear from the case of Rwanda that who should take responsibility in any particular conflict situation is rather more complicated, and needs to consider local and regional actors too. Section 5 returns to the example of Rwanda to reflect on the wider politics of taking responsibility.

Summary

- Partly as a result of experiences in Rwanda, responses to humanitarian disasters have arguably become more important in the international arena, but political and humanitarian concerns have also been more closely tied together. The desire to establish a liberal peace across conflict-ridden areas has become a core security ambition of many countries.

- Maintaining a presence in situations of conflict and disaster provokes dilemmas and difficulties for military and humanitarian agents alike, and generates a new set of operational and political issues. It highlights that there are inevitably political consequences to taking responsibility.

5 Taking responsibility

During the course of the genocide in Rwanda, and at times since then, Rwanda's position in the geopolitical imaginations of powerful political actors relegated events there to relative insignificance. Far away from wealthy Western countries in terms of time required to deploy troops, Rwanda was perhaps even further away in the strategic geopolitical imaginations of these places. In fact, for a range of political and self-interested reasons, the dreadful events in Rwanda came to be denied, literally made absent from the calculations of powerful actors.

Yet, in the longer term, repressing this knowledge and choosing to ignore these events has not been possible. As the true enormity of the Rwandan genocide became apparent to the world, finding appropriate ways to respond in a time of peace, given the lack of action in the time of killing, has become an imperative. In retrospect, many commentators note the shame felt by the international community – by the NGOs that campaigned and set up refugee camps, by the public that was both outraged and reluctant to act, by the states and international organisations that, despite their vast resources, did not choose to assist Tutsi victims. In a way, like the Holocaust, the memories of these events continue to haunt people around the world – whether they are far away, or close up as, for example, the neighbouring countries or the banyarwanda themselves who continue to feel the personal, political and military reverberations of the genocide. These events, once distant, are now a very present part of global political experiences and, as mentioned in Section 4, have played an important role in reshaping international politics.

As the example of Rwanda demonstrates, mapping the geopolitics of intervention and considering who might be best placed to take responsibility for atrocities in an interconnected world are very complex processes.

Activity 8.5

Reflect on what you have read in this chapter so far, and consider some of the issues raised by holding people responsible for the genocide.

1   What might be the pros and cons of meting out justice to individual perpetrators of the genocide? Think especially about how the genocide was organised and the wider political context in which it took place.

2   What might be the difficulties of holding 'Hutu' people collectively responsible for the genocide?

3   To what extent can the international community be held responsible for its role in these events?

Many individual perpetrators of violence – the ordinary men and women who participated in the massacre – have indeed been held responsible for their actions. Post-genocide judicial processes, including a genocide tribunal, formal judicial processes as well as more informal and traditional forums (gacaca), have seen many thousands of people imprisoned and punished, and some pardoned and freed after confessing (Uvin and Mironko, 2003). Many, though, have already spent years, or died, awaiting trial in hopelessly overcrowded jails.

However, Mamdani (2001) argues that for peace in the future it is not the vengeful justice of victims that this situation requires, but the justice of coexisting survivors, on both sides of the conflict. He notes that:

> One needs to recognize that it was not greed – not even hatred – but fear which was the reason why the multitude responded to the call of Hutu Power the closer the war came to home ... FEAR – not as a relatively timeless cultural reflex but as a much more time-bound response to a rapidly shifting political and social context.
>
> (Mamdani, 2001, p.191)

In this sense, holding individuals responsible for these events might be quite complicated. Relevant aspects of the wider political context of the genocide include the encroaching civil war and the history of brutal colonial conquest that Hutu civilians often recalled as they recounted their fears of the Tutsi forces, the RPF. They feared these forces might reinstate colonial forms of rule if they won the civil war raging through the northern regions of Rwanda during 1993 and 1994. The genocide was a political response to the looming loss of power by the Hutu government, as a result of negotiations with the RPF, and the process was strongly centrally organised. Hutu people who refused to participate were often killed themselves, and even brave people, who risked their lives to save Tutsi friends and neighbours in one context, were found to be involved in killings in other parts of the country. Mamdani's (2001) argument is that any long-term peaceful resolution of the Rwandan situation will need a new political order, one that does not simply reproduce the cycle of violence by stigmatising all Hutus as perpetrators and all surviving Tutsis as victims. Indeed, it is estimated that some 60,000 Hutus lost their lives in the genocide for refusing to participate in killings or because they supported political parties that were prepared to share power with the RPF. A de-ethnicised state in which all residents are equal citizens is Mamdani's hope for a stable future for Rwanda and many other post-colonial conflict situations.

Many Rwandan people have had to take responsibility for the events of their past and try to build a new kind of future for the country and for the many displaced people living in an extensive banyarwandan diaspora, although conflict between the post-genocide government and Hutu militia has continued in neighbouring Democratic Republic of the Congo. The new government was formed as a coalition between RPF and other political parties, and included both Tutsis and Hutus in senior positions. Broadly, it has been committed to multiparty democracy and to discontinuing forms of ethnic classification. However, the post-genocide political order in Rwanda continues to be characterised by fear and hostility, in spite of many efforts to build a lasting peace (Uvin, 2001).

Nevertheless, as was discussed in Section 2, the demand for assistance during the genocide of 1994, for peacekeeping and preventative humanitarian intervention, was made to people and governments who were physically distant from the events but were closely connected historically and politically. Responsibilities for peace also rest with them.

The UN embarked on a substantial number of initiatives around peacekeeping, monitoring of human rights, and post-conflict justice and development in view of this sense of responsibility among the international community (see Figure 8.7). Commemoration of the event has been facilitated by international funds and local efforts – a national memorial has been built in Kigali, for example, along with many others across the country, where the memories, bones and possessions of thousands of victims are preserved.

The Organisation of African Unity, frustrated by the lack of commitment from the international community to addressing African crises such as the Rwandan genocide, has, in its new guise as the African Union, implemented an ambitious programme to have a regional peacekeeping force on standby, ready to intervene. The plan is to work with donor organisations and governments to secure advance

Figure 8.7   In July 1995, UN Secretary-General, Boutros Boutros-Ghali, travelled to Nyarubuye, Rwanda. He is shown placing a flower wreath next to a shed, where lie the remains of Rwandan civilians massacred the year before in the genocide

funding and support for well-trained troops, able to be mobilised at short notice for duty across the continent (Malan, 2003; African Union, 2004).

Within Rwanda many aid organisations and local groups have tried to contribute to rebuilding a desperately traumatised and poor society by working with women survivors of rape, many now with HIV/AIDS, with orphans and with those suffering the emotional after-effects of violence.

The question of who is responsible in the aftermath of an event like the genocide in Rwanda highlights that some individual perpetrators, especially political and military leaders, can be held responsible for their actions. A small group of people (about twenty) have been formally judged guilty of genocide by the International Tribunal for their individual actions in orchestrating the genocide. Yet political responsibility for the genocide has also been tracked to the broader historical and social structures that created the background conditions in which ethnically-based fears, privilege and power gave rise to the political ambition to eradicate one group of people (Uvin, 2001). These broader structural conditions incorporate relations of interdependence and inequality in the global economy as well as the asymmetrical power relations that shape decisions taken at international forums like the UN, the distribution of aid and political conditionality, and the consequences of long colonial histories as discussed in Section 2 above.

While we can trace a range of historical and structural connections from the Rwanda conflict to other places and to distant observers, we have seen that there are also other dynamics of responsibility at work here: those that owe more to the traditions of humanitarian concern, which provoke us to identify with distant people and to mobilise in some way to assist with alleviating their suffering and plight. These relations of generosity, care and concern do not necessarily depend on being structurally implicated in or connected to distant events, although they can be provoked by a sense of sharing a common world, a common past or perhaps common experiences as much as by a sense of being embroiled in the wider social relations that shape events. Forging communities of responsibility at a distance, through these processes of identification and concern, may be one starting point for a forward looking and collective politics of responsibility (as discussed by Iris Marion Young in Reading 1A, Chapter 1) that is interested in changing some of the wider power relations that have contributed to the international community's failure to respond in situations like Rwanda.

Summary

- The example of Rwanda highlights that the answer to the question of who takes responsibility for situations of disaster and conflict can include those immediately embroiled in the situation as well as those more distant from it, both those who are structurally connected to events there and those who are moved to become involved on more humanitarian grounds.

- Forging communities of responsibility at a distance can involve bringing individual perpetrators to justice, acts of commemoration, building new political relations, making better preparations for responding to future events or attempting to change wider circumstances that can lead to denial or indifference.

6   Conclusion

The geopolitical order that shapes forms of intervention in humanitarian disasters and conflict situations is constantly changing: its terms are contested not only between states but by popular opinion and non-state agents like NGOs. In the post-Cold War era, and in association with an upsurge in humanitarian concern throughout the 1980s, new kinds of priorities have emerged for powerful states which have led to a stronger interest on their part in securing peace and stability in different parts of the world. However, other factors continue to shape the geopolitical landscape in which interventions take place. Differential state capacities, but also strategically informed understandings of the relevance and importance of different places to the interests and concerns of powerful states, determine the nature of states' involvement in situations of conflict and disaster.

Geopolitical relations of proximity and presence are constantly being reworked in the face of demands for intervention, demands for humanitarian assistance and demands to take responsibility for the needs of distant strangers. Different contexts have been drawn closer to the concerns of powerful states, partly through changing strategic interests and geopolitical imaginations, but also through the operation of the global media bringing events and experiences in distant places close to decision makers and ordinary people who are able to lobby their governments for action. Yet, as we have seen, distant observers and powerful governments are often already involved in the events that have led to conflict or disaster. They might be thought of as responsible by virtue of their being implicated in the wider structures and connections of a globalised world that have contributed to these events, for example colonial histories, the arms trade or global inequality.

Throughout this book we have seen the potential for different kinds of communities of responsibility to emerge, stretching across the boundaries of nation-states. Decisions to take responsibility can draw on an awareness of the structural interconnectedness of a globalised world, or involve responses to the presence of mediated distant events in our daily lives. Although the strategic interests and uneven capacities of nation-states will remain influential in shaping the geopolitics of intervention, in this chapter we have seen that wider political action to take responsibility has brought new issues, such as peace, humanitarian assistance and alleviating poverty, onto the international agenda.

However, even if those actors with the capabilities and will choose to take responsibility and act to assist in situations of disaster and conflict, securing a presence in distant arenas in order to offer assistance is in itself a complex and highly political issue. Furthermore, taking responsibility can introduce a new round of power-laden geopolitical relationships. Expensive and difficult logistical capabilities are required to deploy forces, deliver food supplies and arrange the munitions and hardware required to prevent violent conflict, often in dangerous situations. The politics of responsibility are established in the interface between state, NGO and private sector agents willing to offer assistance, the local political groupings they need to interact with to achieve this and the wider networks that sustain both conflicts and life in conflict zones.

Consequently, while the geographies of connection and care that we have outlined throughout this book do sometimes lead to actors – individuals or organisations – taking responsibility in the face of demands, these actions of responsibility can themselves entrain new forms of political contestation. In conflict situations, the very resources being offered as assistance can sometimes fuel further violence. Moreover, as we have seen, taking responsibility can set in place new kinds of unequal geopolitical relationships between wealthier and poorer countries. In a demanding world, taking responsibility is itself politically contested.

References

African Union (2004) 'Solemn declaration on a common African defence and security policy', Sirte, Libya, 28 February 2004, http://www.africa-union.org (accessed 24 January 2005).

Allen, J. (2003) *Lost Geographies of Power*, Oxford, Blackwell.

Canada, Department of Foreign Affairs and International Trade (2002) *Freedom from Fear: Canada's Foreign Policy for Human Security*, Ottawa, Canadian Government.

Dodds, K. (2000) *Geopolitics in a Changing World*, London, Prentice-Hall.

Duffield, M. (2001) *Global Governance and the New Wars: The Merging of Development and Security*, London, Zed Books.

Eltringham, N. (2004) *Accounting for Horror: Post-genocide Debates in Rwanda*, London, Pluto.

Gregory, D. (2004) *The Colonial Present*, Oxford, Blackwell.

Harvey, D. (2003) *The New Imperialism*, Oxford, Oxford University Press.

Hinton, A.L. (2002) 'The dark side of modernity: toward an anthropology of genocide' in Hinton, A. (ed.) *Annihilating Difference: The Anthropology of Genocide*, Berkeley, CA, University of California Press, pp.1–42.

Humanitarian Policy Group (2000) *HPG Briefing: The Politics of Coherence: Humanitarianism and Foreign Policy in the Post-Cold War Era*, London, ODI (Overseas Development Institute).

Keane, F. (1995) *Season of Blood: a Rwandan Journey*, London, Penguin.

Malan, M. (2003) 'New tools in the box?: towards a standby force for the AU' in Field, S. (ed.) *Peace in Africa: Towards a Collaborative Security Regime*, Johannesburg, Institute for Global Dialogue, pp.193–224.

Mamdani, M. (2001) *When Victims Become Killers: Colonialism, Nativism, and the Genocide in Rwanda*, Princeton, NJ, Princeton University Press.

Mann, M. (2003) *Incoherent Empire*, London, Verso.

Nordstrom, C. (2004) *Shadows of War: Violence, Power and International Profiteering in the Twenty-first Century*, Berkeley, CA, University of California Press.

Project for a New American Century (2000) *Rebuilding America's Defences: Strategy, Forces and Resources for a New Century*, Washington, DC, Project for a New American Century.

Roberts, S., Secor, A. and Sparke, M. (2003) 'Neoliberal geopolitics', *Antipode*, vol.35, no.5, pp.886–97.

Sharp, J. (1993) 'Publishing American identity: popular geopolitics, myth and the Reader's Digest', *Political Geography*, vol.12, pp.491–504.

Smith, N. (2003) *American Empire: Roosevelt's Geographer and the Prelude to Globalisation*, Berkeley, CA, University of California Press.

The Guardian (1994a) 'A dangerous and deadly myopia', Letter to the editor, 31 October, p.19.

The Guardian (1994b) 'Moral dilemmas of aid to Rwanda', Letter to the editor, 24 December, p.22.

Tilly, C. (2003) *The Politics of Collective Violence*, Cambridge, Cambridge University Press.

United Nations (1996) *The UN and Rwanda, 1993–1996*, UN Blue Book Series, vol.x, New York, United Nations.

United Nations (2004) 'The United Nations: organisation', http://www.un.org/aboutun/basicfacts/unorg.htm (accessed 26 July 2005).

United Nations Peacekeeping (2004) 'United Nations peacekeeping operations', http://www.un.org/depts/dpko/dpko/bnote.htm (accessed 25 January 2005).

Uvin, P. (2001) 'Reading the Rwandan genocide', *International Studies Review*, vol.3, no.3, pp.75–99.

Uvin, P. and Mironko, C. (2003) 'Western and local approaches to justice in Rwanda', *Global Governance*, vol.9, pp.219–29.

Wheeler, N.J. (2000) *Saving Strangers: Humanitarian Intervention in International Society*, Oxford, Oxford University Press.

Reading 8A

Mark Duffield, 'Global governance and the new wars: the merging of development and security'

Requiem for the prophets

In 1984 the harrowing TV pictures of famine in Ethiopia unleashed an unprecedented surge of humanitarian concern and popular mobilisation throughout Europe. In Britain, through the efforts of media celebrities such as Bob Geldof, the Band Aid trust was formed. By raising public awareness through popular songs and international music events, Band Aid eventually raised £174 million for famine relief in Africa before its closure in 1987. With the rigidities of the Cold War beginning to wane, it represented a populist form of anti-establishment politics. The public mood that it caught was that politicians, bureaucrats and official aid programmes were a major part of the problem. Reflecting this feeling, Geldof made the 'Sayings of the Week' spot in the *Observer* when he railed against delays: 'I'm not interested in the bloody system! Why has he no food? Why is he starving to death?' (Geldof 1985). In a world of plenty, public opinion in Europe was morally affronted by the images of death and want coming out of Ethiopia and Sudan. Moreover, many ordinary people were mobilised to do something about it. Besides making unprecedented donations to famine relief organisations, EU food mountains and milk lakes were picketed; public vigils were held; newspaper columns vented their outrage; politicians were bombarded with protest letters; and radio and TV programmes echoed with expressions of concern. Famine not only highlighted gross inequalities in global wealth and affluence, it also demonstrated the seeming indifference of governments and UN agencies. Using its publicly donated funds, when red tape threatened to hold up famine relief, Band Aid rented its own trucks and chartered its own aircraft. Such actions not only shamed donor governments but also gave substance to the view that humanitarian assistance was a universal and unconditional right.

In discussing humanitarian action, Hugo Slim (Slim 1998), using the analogy of religion, makes the useful distinction between prophecy and priesthood; the difference between the two lies in the tension between faith and organisation. The prophet 'confronts society with a truth and is concerned with personal, social and political transformation' (*ibid.*: 29). The priesthood, however, is more concerned with maintaining the truth through enshrined ritual, standards of purity, membership and worship. In terms of humanitarian action, the priesthood is embodied in the International Committee of the Red

Cross. As for the prophets, the public reaction in Europe to the famines in Ethiopia and Sudan during the mid-1980s gave a great moral and financial boost to aid agencies delivering emergency relief. A period of rapid growth and increasing influence of NGOs engaged in emergency operations began. During the latter part of the 1980s, such NGOs found themselves at the forefront of a movement that put the saving of lives above any political consideration or bureaucratic constraint. Not only was humanitarian aid a universal right, its neutrality placed it beyond politics. Indeed, politics both caused wars and famines and, at the same time, created delays and bureaucratic difficulties that hampered the relief of suffering. In retrospect, this mood was very much in tune with the rapidly approaching end of the Cold War. In the war-torn Horn of Africa, for example, international respect for Ethiopian and Sudanese sovereignty had been sufficient to dissuade the UN and most international NGOs from working in rebel areas where human suffering also existed (Duffield and Prendergast 1994). Placing humanitarianism above politics, as a right in itself, became a compelling critique of the inhumanity of the rigidities of the Cold War and of its suffocating political etiquette. For this reason, apart from saving lives, a neutral humanitarianism appeared radical and progressive; at the same time, it had widespread public support.

The growing pressure by increasingly influential NGOs for cross-line relief interventions helped shape developments immediately following the end of the Cold War. As early as April 1989, with the formation of the UN-led Operational Lifeline Sudan (OLS), a new phase of neutral, negotiated-access relief programmes working across the lines in ongoing conflicts emerged. These system-wide programmes not only brought UN organisations and NGOs together in new ways, they were based on the UN securing the agreement of warring parties to allow impartial aid agencies to provide humanitarian assistance to war-affected populations, irrespective of their location. This represented a major opportunity for the expansion of relief agencies. Taking a lead from OLS, in 1990 similar UN-led negotiated-access programmes were established in Ethiopia and Angola. Following the Gulf War in 1991, these neutral humanitarian operations were increasingly seen as a graphic expression of the changing priority accorded sovereignty within the new international system. Not only were military establishments joining the strategic complexes of an emerging global governance, a New World Order that included a right to humanitarian assistance for a while appeared to be in the realm of the possible. International intervention under UN auspices in Bosnia and Somalia in 1992 and the creation of the UN's Department of Humanitarian Affairs (DHA) strengthened such convictions.

As the mid-1990s approached, however, following the setbacks in Somalia and the increasing difficulties in Bosnia, a different view began to take shape. The insistence that humanitarian intervention was good in itself and required little, if any, justification began to be questioned. In many respects, while attempting to hold itself above politics, the prophetic movement to save lives at all costs had become a victim of its own political success. It started as a radical opposition that gathered its strength in relation to the political rigidities of the Cold War. In this respect, initially the UN system was seen as the epitome of all that was unacceptable and corrupt. This did not prevent the same system quickly incorporating the principles of a neutral humanitarianism as soon as the international climate was conducive. Although powerless to end wars, during the early part of the 1990s, through negotiated access and establishing new strategic relations with aid agencies and military establishments, the UN attempted to develop new ways of providing humanitarian assistance to all war-affected populations (Duffield 1997). The ill-fated 'safe area' policies of the time were part of this attempt. At the same time, whereas politicians had been placed on the defensive by the populism of the mid-1980s, by the early 1990s they had learnt how to harness the humanitarian juggernaut together with the media exposure and influence that it brought. When President Mitterand travelled to Sarajevo in June 1992 and publicly declared the lifting of the Serb siege with the opening of the airport for UN relief flights, it was a piece of political theatre that well reflected the prevailing accommodation. Many European politicians, such as Bernard Kouchner (France), Jan Pronk (Netherlands), and David Owen (UK), together with international figures like ex-US President Jimmy Carter, placed their names and careers in the service of humanitarian intervention. At the same time, a number of European aid departments, including Britain's Overseas Development Administration (ODA), for a while at least, would become more directly involved in humanitarian operations (ODA 1991). When the European Commission Humanitarian Office (ECHO) was established in 1993, its brief was not only to coordinate EU emergency assistance better, but also to develop an operational capacity of its own.

The incorporation of a neutral humanitarianism within a UN-led international relief system during the early 1990s gave it an institutional framework for its realisation. Simultaneously, however, its prophetic values were undermined and compromised. The new post-Cold War UN-led humanitarian operations were very different from those of the past. During the Cold War, the UN rarely intervened in ongoing conflicts. Its preferred mode of operation was to police ceasefires already agreed between warring parties (Goulding 1993). UN-led negotiated-access programmes represented a radical and profound break with tradition. They were radical in that earlier restrictions against working in non-government areas were either overcome or greatly reduced. At the same time, however, and more worryingly, work in unresolved and unstructured wars could also be seen as reflecting a new international system that was now either unable or unwilling to end conflict. Indeed, such a commitment appeared to suggest that Northern governments were now prepared to accept instability and violence as part of a generic Southern predicament (Kaplan 1994). Humanitarian assistance, while still regarded as necessary, was increasingly seen as a substitute for the concerted political action that was the real requirement (Higgins 1993). From being a radical aim, humanitarian assistance began to assume the form of a lowest international common denominator in the context of operations that, through experience, were being redefined as long-term and politically complex. In the absence of a clear political resolve to end conflict, humanitarian assistance could even be seen as counter-productive. For example, in providing transport and shelter, aid agencies in Bosnia were often accused of facilitating the very ethnic cleansing they abhorred.

In the absence of clear and unequivocal international structures working effectively for peace, the idea of a neutral humanitarianism able to stand above politics became increasingly strained in the seemingly intractable conflicts of the 1990s. In this respect, the strategic complexes of liberal governance do not provide such a system. Liberal peace is a contested and regionally differentiated reality that, through its fluid and changing networks, is capable of marked hierarchies of concern. At the same time, through an exposure to ongoing conflict, aid agencies began to deepen their understanding of the interaction between aid and war and the complexities involved. While external assistance is capable of playing many roles (one should not overestimate the effectiveness of aid in this respect), it was increasingly understood as being far from neutral. Humanitarian assistance, while it could help keep people alive, like any other resource inevitably became part of the local political economy (Duffield 1991; Keen 1991) – especially when the new wars have effectively dissolved conventional distinctions between people, army and government. In other words, in today's network wars the traditional distinctions – 'military/civilian', 'combatant/non-combatant', etc. – that a neutral humanitarianism ideally would base itself on, no longer properly exist. While wishing to stand above politics, prophetic humanitarianism inevitably has been drawn in – network war does not countenance neutrality – and been compromised through its encounter. It has fallen victim to a world in which the competence and authority of nation states have changed radically.

Faced with the prospect of long-term relief operations, which many saw as a contradiction in terms, by the mid-1990s certain strategic actors had developed a direct criticism of humanitarian assistance. This criticism tended to avoid the fact that the international community had crossed the Rubicon of undertaking work in ongoing conflicts while, at the same time, failing to develop an effective means of resolving the wars in which it was now enmeshed. Instead, the critical message was that humanitarian assistance itself was part of the problem. Despite its good intentions, it had many unforeseen consequences, some of which entrenched conflict and made it more difficult to resolve. For example, among rural communities, free food aid could lower agricultural prices and so deter farmers from planting. Far from helping them, this would reinforce their dependence on aid agencies. At the same time, through diversion, looting and informal taxing by warring parties, relief supplies themselves could become part of a self-sustaining war economy. In other words, humanitarian assistance was capable of entrenching the modalities of underdevelopment and conflict (UNDP 1994).

As well as doing good, humanitarian aid is also capable of doing harm (Anderson 1996). Such criticisms have been very influential in shaping aid policy since the mid-1990s. Rather than having the saving of life as its overriding and prophetic concern, a new humanitarianism has emerged that bases actions (or inaction) on the assumed good or bad consequences of a given intervention in relation to wider developmental aims (Slim 1998). This new or principled humanitarianism complements the radicalisation of development which now sees the role of aid as altering the balance of power between social groups in the interests of peace and stability. From saving lives, the shift in humanitarian policy has been towards analysing consequences and supporting social processes.

The new humanitarianism is a genuine, if particular, response to the complexity of the new wars. A concern with consequences and processes has to be part of any reappraisal. What is important in understanding its particularity, however, is not so much the practical veracity of the new development-oriented humanitarianism – whether it will be any more successful than the regime it has replaced – as its implications for liberal governance. A concern with limiting harmful consequences while encouraging beneficial processes demands new forms of surveillance, appraisal and monitoring if desired outcomes are to be achieved. If politicians had come to terms with humanitarian assistance in the early 1990s, then very soon the official aid departments they controlled would have begun the task of creating new forms of management and regulation with which to enmesh their subcontracting and implementing partners. While sidestepping the issue that Northern governments have yet to create an international structure that can enforce peace, the view that humanitarian aid entrenches underdevelopment and conflict has motivated a thickening of the governance relations linking donors and aid agencies. Gathering momentum with the debate on relief and development, more detailed and demanding contractual agreements have emerged highlighting the need to avoid harmful consequences; the number of social advisers within official aid departments has increased, allowing donors to be more closely involved with NGOs in project design and policy implementation; more rigorous forms of project monitoring and appraisal have emerged; the number of consultative mechanisms and joint policy fora has increased; finally, since the consequences of assistance are important, new forms of surveillance and aid impact assessment are being created (Pankhurst 1999). Through the deepening of such governance relations, Northern donors have regained the policy initiative that was lacking during the latter part of the 1980s and early 1990s. In other words, compared to the prophetic years of humanitarian action, they have learnt how to consolidate and project their authority through the non-territorial and differentiated networks of global liberal governance.

The aftermath of the 1994 genocide in Rwanda and, especially, the controversy surrounding the Hutu refugee camps in what is now Eastern Congo and their eventual fate, are seen by many aid agencies as the nadir of a neutral and universal humanitarianism (Fox 1999). If the sentiments that lay behind the formation of Band Aid coalesced in the arid highlands of Ethiopia, in little over a decade they unravelled in the rainforests of the Congo. Paying little heed to what UNHCR and NGOs had been saying and trying to do, many strategic actors concluded that the aid agencies' response to the plight of the Hutu refugees crystallised everything that was wrong with humanitarian assistance. By helping to feed and shelter the refugees, NGOs and the UN were also supporting the vicious killers that lived among them and, at the same time, allowing their destabilisation of Rwanda to continue. Whereas over 150 NGOs had flocked to the sprawling and unsanitary refugee camp at Goma in 1994, a year later their number had dropped to five following a barrage of international criticism and the collapse of donor confidence. When an alliance of regional forces exacted its own violent retribution on the Hutu refugees in 1997, despite the evidence of serious human rights abuse and appeals by aid agencies, the international community was in no mood to intervene. These events set the tone for the present period of humanitarian conditionality and regionally differentiated patterns of intervention. They also mark the great distance that has been travelled since the mid-1980s.

Where once relatively independent aid agencies were able to mobilise public concern through the media and put politicians on the spot, we now have a situation in which Northern governments have regained initiative and control of the humanitarian agenda. Through a complex transition involving the professionalisation of aid and the emergence of new forms of regulation, politicians are able to argue that the excesses of the past are no longer acceptable or necessary. At the same time, public opinion, while never to be underestimated, appears more disengaged. Not only has an interest in things international declined in the media, but politicians have shown themselves increasingly adept at managing the news from disaster zones (Hilsum 1997). Indeed, since Bosnia, rather than simply having to react to the next emergency, they have shown that, if necessary, they can sit it out (Hurd 1993). This is the political environment of the new humanitarianism. While prophetic humanitarianism may have been naïve and the agencies involved made many mistakes, one cannot help feeling uneasy about the new accommodation and its willingness to sacrifice lives today on the promise of development tomorrow.

References

Anderson, Mary B. *Do No Harm: Supporting Local Capacities for Peace Through Aid*. Cambridge, MA: Local Capacities for Peace Project, The Collaborative for Development Action, Inc.; 1996.

Duffield, Mark. *War and Famine in Africa*. Oxfam Research Paper No. 5. Oxford: Oxfam Publications; 1991.

—. NGO Relief in War Zones: Toward an Analysis of the New Aid Paradigm. *Third World Quarterly*, 1997; 18(3): 527–42.

Duffield, Mark and Prendergast, John. *Without Troops or Tanks: Humanitarian Intervention in Eritrea and Ethiopia*. Trenton, NJ: Africa World Press Inc./Red Sea Press Inc; 1994.

Fox, Fiona. *The Politicisation of Humanitarian Aid: A Discussion Paper for Caritas Europa – November 1999*. London: CAFOD; 1999 November.

Geldof, Bob. Sayings of the Week. *The Observer*. 1985 October 27.

Goulding, M. The Evolution of United Nations Peacekeeping. *International Affairs*. 1993 July; 69(3): 451–64.

Higgins, R. The New United Nations and the Former Yugoslavia. *International Affairs*. 1993 July; 69(3): 465–83.

Hilsum, Lindsey. In the Land of the Lion King. *The Times Literary Supplement*. 1997 May 23: 9.

Hurd, D. Extract From Travellers Club Speech, *The Guardian 2*. 1993 September 17: 3.

Kaplan, Robert D. The Coming Anarchy: How Scarcity, Crime, Overpopulation, and Disease are Rapidly Destroying the Social Fabric of Our Planet. *Atlantic Monthly*. 1994 February: 44–76.

Keen, David. A Disaster for Whom?: Local Interests and International Donors During Famine Among the Dinka of Sudan. *Disasters*. 1991; 15(2): 58–73.

ODA. News Release. *Immediate Help for Disaster Victims*. London. Overseas Development Administration; 1991 August 14.

Pankhurst, Dona. Report Prepared for OXFAM. *Conflict Impact and Monitoring Assessment: Does It Exist? Can It Work?* University of Bradford: Department of Peace Studies; 1999 April.

Slim, Hugo. Doing the Right Thing: Relief Agencies, Moral Dilemmas and Moral Responsibility in Political Emergencies and War. Studies on Emergencies and Disaster Relief, Report No. 6 Uppsala, Sweden: The Nordic Africa Institute; 1997. *Journal of Human Rights.* 1998 Winter; 2 (4): 28–48.

UNDP. Draft. *Position Paper of the Working Group on Operational Aspects of the Relief to Development Continuum.* New York: UNDP; 1994 January 12.

(Duffield, 2001, pp.76–82)

Conclusion

Clive Barnett, Jennifer Robinson and Gillian Rose

Living in a globalised world brings all sorts of demands into our daily lives. As we have seen, demands to be in touch, for fair wages, for justice and for assistance are all able to travel from place to place. Sometimes, these demands solicit responses which, in turn, bring different people and places close together; at other times, demands can be pushed away, creating new distances.

Globalisation itself generates a number of the demands that this book has investigated. Often this is because the consequences of globalisation involve increasing economic inequality and social injustice. We saw this in Chapter 1, which looked at how the transnational production of various commodities has created a highly unequal world in terms of wages and working conditions. This has produced demands for companies and consumers to take action to improve the conditions of sweatshop labour in poorer countries. Or, to take another example, in Chapter 3 we noted how a globalised oil industry is implicated in environmental destruction. In both these cases, the globalisation of economic activity generates demands that corporations, governments or consumers do something to reduce these environmental impacts or to improve working conditions.

However, globalisation does not just generate demands; it also enables all sorts of demands to be addressed to audiences in different parts of the globe. Mediated forms of communication can make humanitarian crises, as discussed in Chapter 8, very present in the lives of distant observers, raising demands for action. Moreover, in Chapter 5 we saw how visual images can be very important in producing the sense of presence that can move people to action. Therefore, globalisation both produces and enables the proliferation of demands, and it is in this sense that living in a globalised world also means living in a demanding world.

Throughout this book, we have been exploring ways to understand the nature of life in a globalised world by taking a closer look at how the process of levying demands – and responding to demands – works. In particular, focusing on demands has enabled us to see how globalisation involves a range of processes that can draw people, places and things close together, or push them away, or enable actors to reach out over distance. Demands are one way of throwing light on the dynamic relationships between proximity and distance that shape the globalised world. The circulation of demands can span geographical distance, bringing events or people close together in new ways, but it can also provoke new experiences of distance. In some circumstances, demands can encourage people to take action and strengthen relationships of proximity, or to acquire a presence in distant places. Sometimes, though, demands can just as easily lead to indifference or denial, to a sense that there is nothing that can be done or perhaps that nothing should be done about, say, poverty or war on the other side of the world.

In Chapter 2, we looked at one of the most powerful means through which this process of bringing close and opening up distances works in a globalised world – the media and communications technologies. One important thing we noted was that the new personal and social proximities that communications can enable – the speed with which one can stay in touch by mobile phone or email, for example – are closely related to the emergence of new forms of distance. We explored how new communications technologies also enable people to switch off, to limit and manage the communications coming at them. Those places not linked into these new communications networks can seem further and further away as others become more closely connected.

This last point is worth reflecting upon a little more. It suggests that as well as things being distant, which one may or may not take notice of, there are people, places and events that we may never hear about, about which we know very little, or that make no claims on our attention at all. Some people, places and events are not just far away, they are entirely absent from our lives. This is a theme that became more explicit in Chapters 5–8. There we saw that some types of demands relate not just to things that are brought close together, which are here, or which remain far away, over there, but relate instead to things that are, at various moments, not here at all. For example, Chapter 5 explored how part of the visceral impact that some photographs have comes from the way in which they depict people and things that have disappeared, either because they happened in the past or because they have been lost to us, perhaps traumatically. Furthermore, Chapter 6 investigated how absent pasts can suddenly emerge into the present and demand our attention, sometimes with an intense haunting quality, indicating that the often unjust consequences of past events have yet to be addressed.

The theme of presence and absence adds another dimension to understanding the nature of globalisation. On the one hand, it highlights some of the intense, emotional dynamics that frame the range of communications and interactions that we associate with globalisation. People and events can seem present to us in raw and powerful ways, even though they are actually many kilometres away. Chapter 2 examined how some technologies of communication produce a sense of 'simultaneous presence', bringing faraway places within reach instantaneously (Allen, 2003, p.135). These communication technologies can enable forms of attachment and belonging to emerge beyond our immediate localities. New, imagined communities have been formed, whether through radio and television, creating a sometimes strongly felt sense of national identity, or through the internet, allowing more centripetal relationships to form among communities of interest.

Various kinds of interactions at a distance have been especially important in the kinds of entanglements between near and faraway places that shape the forms of belonging of transnational migrant communities, as Chapter 4 noted. For many people, feelings of presence, of being a part of events that are otherwise quite distant, are an important part of living in a globalised world.

We have also considered how something from the past can be made present to us in the here and now. This is an aspect of presence that geographer Rob Shields (1992) has pointed out. Thus, relationships of presence are also about time, memory and history, and suggest that to understand life in this globalised world we need to keep in mind the globalised past. This includes the legacies of past globalisations, like the slave trade, which, as Chapters 6 and 7 showed, has yet to receive the political and emotional attention that its consequences for individuals and societies warrant. These past injustices can be made present to us today either in surprising ways through their haunting qualities or through the conscious political action of campaigns for reparations. In addition, the globalised past involves the ways in which the histories of different places come to be entangled in shaping contemporary experiences as these pasts are mobilised in, or travel to, new contexts. The toxic 'ghost' ships in Chapter 6, for example, made US naval history very present for the residents of northern England; in Chapter 4, the past cultural experiences of East Asian migrants travelled with them as they sought to make a home in new contexts.

Consequently, in a globalised world we are exposed to the possibility of an ever widening range of relationships with faraway people and places, and even with past times, that makes all sorts of demands upon our attention, our consciences, our time and our energy. In the process, the nature of life in a globalised world is remade as new kinds of proximity and distance are produced, along with a new sense of what is present in our lives and even a new awareness of things that seem to be absent.

Throughout the book, we have noticed that the demands which circulate in and shape life in a globalised world usually involve the desire for some sort of response – from ordinary people, from states or from other actors. As we have seen in the different chapters, these responses may vary – they might take the form of acknowledging someone's grievance or just noticing them in the street; they might consist of joining an organisation, voting or signing a petition; they might involve some form of redress; or they might simply involve remembering to phone friends or family once in a while. Nevertheless, these demands for action, for a response, may not be acted upon. People or institutions may not be able to respond in the ways demanded of them. They may not have the money to do so, for example, or they may not want to respond for any number of reasons, including a judgement that this might be the best thing to do, as we saw in the case of sweatshops in Chapter 1. Yet one thing should be clear: globalisation enables demands to be articulated in new ways to larger and more dispersed audiences, and it also enables responses to be made to this proliferation of demands. Just as demands are involved in making the geographies of the globalised world, producing new kinds of proximity and distance, so too are the responses to those demands.

The different sorts of actions that individual or collective actors make in response to demands – whether these are positive responses, negative refusals or denials – involve geographical processes of drawing close, pushing away, reaching out, becoming present. If making demands involves the spanning of distance and the drawing together of people and places, then so too does responding to these demands. Deciding to boycott Nike or Gap, for example, is a way of showing one's allegiance with workers far away. Donating money to a development charity is a way of directly reaching out across distance to offer aid and assistance.

Geographies have been central to our understanding of the responses that are made to demands. In particular, we have seen how communities of *responsibility* can be forged at a distance. As geographer Ash Amin observes, in a globalised world 'there is no compelling reason to assume that "community" implies local community, or that local ties are stronger than interaction at a distance' (Amin, 2003, p.124). We have seen many instances of the emergence of communities of responsibility: the communities of national and transnational citizenship that form in response to the demands of the state discussed in Chapter 3; or the transnational communities of belonging that keep diasporic connections alive as shown in Chapter 4;

or the communities of concern that facilitate collective responses to injustice or misfortune in distant contexts explored in Chapter 8. In discussing these sorts of responses, we have focused on two broad ways in which communities of responsibility can be forged in response to demands.

First, we have examined responses where the demands identify some type of pre-existing relationship between events or people in one place or time and those in another place or time, suggesting that they are already proximate in some way, perhaps bound up in the same processes. In the case of sweatshops, for example, in Chapter 1 the argument was made by antisweatshop campaigners that consumers help to sustain the exploitative system that leads to poor working conditions. Sometimes the relationship can be identified through assessing who benefits from connections. This is the case, for instance, in the argument that Western nations should pay reparations for past systems of slavery because their economies benefited from the slave trade (Chapter 7). Alternatively, the connection may be based on a sense of self-interest. For example, the types of claim made by Friends of the Earth discussed in Chapter 5 make demands on people on the grounds that their connection to environmentally destructive systems of production and consumption implicates them in future risks to their own health, livelihood or security. It is worth noting that in each of these cases, people may be connected to wider patterns or systems quite unintentionally, but this does not undermine the claims that they have some responsibility to take action.

This type of understanding of responsibility involves tracking the routes and networks through which our own actions are linked to actions and events elsewhere, in the past or, indeed, in the future. This connection model of responsibility is one aspect of the argument made by Iris Marion Young (2003) which was discussed in Chapter 1 and which has been referred to throughout the book.

Second, communities of responsibility can also be formed on a decision to take responsibility even if there is no direct connection to the demand or to its causes. If we were to look only at connections, we could reasonably suppose that it is possible to decide on the scope of responsibility simply by mapping which things we are related to and in which processes we are implicated. However, often enough, people decide that they should take some action in support of distant people or events out of a sense of compassion, sympathy or solidarity – a sense of being in the same boat, sharing the same interests or simply caring about the fate of others less fortunate. Sometimes, the decision to take responsibility, to take action of some sort, might be based on a sense of shared humanity that acknowledges and identifies with similarities among people, as Chapter 5 discusses in relation to the use of family photos in political campaigns. The decision to respond might also be based on an appreciation of some of the vast differences between different places – action may be motivated by compassion for those caught up in situations of violent conflict, as illustrated in Chapter 8. In all of these cases, communities of responsibility are forged on the basis of a desire to respond to demands which have made distant people and places feel very present.

In both of the types of communities of responsibility explored in this book, taking responsibility is seldom simply an individual action taken by a person or an organisation; it often involves joining up with others and feeding into wider networks of cooperation which reach out and influence actors and events elsewhere. In fact, demands to act may often leave us feeling relatively powerless as individuals in the face of the enormous challenges presented by living in this globalised world.

We can now return to Young's (2003) account of political responsibility. As we saw in Chapter 1, rather than focusing on who is to blame for certain outcomes, Young argues that people who benefit from processes and patterns for which they are not to blame do, nonetheless, bear some responsibility to act to alleviate these harms. She suggests that questions of *power* and *privilege* are most important in helping us to address the question of who has the ability or the capacity to respond to various demands or to change a situation. This is a theme taken up in the companion volume to this book **(Clark et al., 2008)**.

Therefore, responsibility is differentiated according to the power one can bring to bear on changing things. Chapter 8 showed that many people were motivated to assist in ending the Rwandan genocide in 1994, but relatively few had the resources or the capacity to take action. Yet, as Young notes, 'Because the agents with the greatest power in social structures often have a vested interest in maintaining them as they are ... external pressure on the powerful is often necessary to move these agents to action' (Young, 2003). Consequently, collective action – for example, the movement for a stronger humanitarian approach in international politics – can help to shift the priorities of the powerful towards appropriate action. In the different examples examined in this book, people with a strong interest in the outcome, perhaps African countries, sweatshop workers or citizens affected by environmental pollution, can play a crucial role in mobilising for change.

If one is not powerful or particularly personally invested in the issues around which demands are being posed, Young (2003) suggests that there is still the question of relative privilege. Even if you cannot really be thought of as causally responsible for historical wrongs like slavery or the affairs of the state you live in, nonetheless you may recognise that some groups of people benefit or derive privileges from these conditions and practices. This, then, may be another source of responsibility in a globalised world: to consider the ways in which one is privileged or benefits from distant or past events.

Thus, responses to demands build on the geographies of proximity and presence to create new kinds of relationships in a globalised world. These could be relations of distancing, pushing people and their demands further away, or they could be relationships that build new kinds of networks of interaction or communities of responsibility in order to address the issues which give rise to demands.

By exploring the circulation of demands and the different kinds of responses that people and organisations have to demands, this book has opened some windows into appreciating the nature of life in a globalised world. We have shown how new kinds of geographical relationships are being created, drawing some people and places into closer proximity, and keeping others at a distance. We have observed how some events or places can come to seem a very present part of our lives, and how even apparently absent places and pasts have the potential to shape the patterns of life in a globalised world. We have considered some of the demands of living in a globalised world, and we have also seen the many different ways in which this world is constantly being remade through the responses and actions of individuals and organisations to these demands. In the broadest sense, we have suggested that understanding globalisation needs a subtle geographical imagination, one attuned to the myriad ways in which different people and places are drawn into interactions with one another or, for many different reasons, continue to be kept apart. Living with globalisation certainly involves a creative responsiveness to its demands; it also requires an agile appreciation of its constantly changing geographies.

References

Allen, J. (2003) *Lost Geographies of Power*, Oxford, Blackwell.

Amin, A. (2003) 'Spaces of corporate learning' in Peck, J. and Wai-Chung Yeung, H. (eds) *Remaking the Global Economy*, London, Sage, pp.114–29.

Clark, N., Massey, D. and Sarre, P. (2008) *Material Geographies: A World in the Making*, London, Sage/Milton Keynes, The Open University.

Shields, R. (1992) 'A truant proximity: presence and absence in the space of modernity', *Society and Space*, vol.10, pp.181–98.

Young, I.M. (2003) 'From guilt to solidarity: sweatshops and political responsibility', *Dissent*, Spring, pp.39–44.

Acknowledgements

Grateful acknowledgement is made to the following sources for permission to reproduce material within this book.

Chapter 1

Text

Extract 1.1: Oxfam Community Aid Abroad www.oxfam.org.au; Reading 1A: Young, I. (2003) 'From guilt to solidarity: sweatshops and political responsibility', *Dissent*, Spring 2003. By permission of Dissent Magazine.

Table

Table 1.1: Castree, N. et al. (2004) *Spaces of Work: Global Capitalism and the Geographics of Labour*, Sage Publications Ltd.

Figures

Figure 1.2: copyright © AP Photo/Richard Vogel/Empics; Figure 1.3: copyright © Clean Clothes Campaign www.cleanclothes.org; Figure 1.4: copyright © AP Photo/Le Thanh Hiep/Empics; Figure 1.5: copyright © Clean Clothes Campaign www.cleanclothes.org; Figure 1.6: Dicken, P. (2003) *Global Shift*. Copyright © Sage Publications 2003; Figure 1.7: copyright © Julio Etchart/Panos; Figure 1.8: copyright © Irene Slegt/Panos; Figure 1.11: copyright © Clean Clothes Campaign www.cleanclothes.org; Figure 1.12: Dicken, P. (2003) *Global Shift*. Copyright © Sage Publications 2003; Figure 1.13: copyright © No Sweat www.nosweat.org.uk.

Chapter 2

Text

Reading 2A: Thompson, J.B. (1995) *The Media and Modernity*, Polity Press.

Table

Table 2.1: Thompson, J.B. (1995) *The Media and Modernity*, p.85, Polity Press.

Figures

Figure 2.1: courtesy of John Frost Newspapers; Figure 2.2: Wallsten, S. (2003) *Regulation and Internet Use in Developing Countries*. AEI-Brookings Joint Center for Regulatory Studies; Figure 2.4: copyright © Radio Times; Figure 2.5 (top left): copyright © Thomas Kienzle/AP/Empics;

Chapter 3

Text

Table

Figures

Chapter 4

Text

Tables

United Nations. Reprinted with the permission of the publisher; Table
4.2: from THE PENGUIN ATLAS OF DIASPORAS by Gerard
Chaliand and Jean-Pierre Rageau, translated by A.M. Berrett, copyright
© 1995 by Gerard Chaliand and Jean-Pierre Rageau. Used by
permission of Viking Penguin, a division of Penguin Group (USA) Inc.

Figures

Figure 4.1: courtesy of Karim Murji; Figure 4.2: Castles, S. and Miller,
M. (2003) *The Age of Migration*, Guilford Publications, Inc; Figure 4.3:
courtesy of Jatinder Verma; Figure 4.4: copyright © Peter
Macdiarmid/Rex Features; Figures 4.5 and 4.6: 'Indian Diaspora
Today', 'Transport of Indian Workers in the 19th Century' by Catherine
Petit, from THE PENGUIN ATLAS OF DIASPORAS by Gerard
Chaliand and Jean-Pierre Rageau, translated by A.M. Berrett, copyright
© 1995 by Gerard Chaliand and Jean-Pierre Rageau. Used by
permission of Viking Penguin, a division of Penguin Group (USA) Inc.

Chapter 5

Figures

Figure 5.1: the leaflet shown on p.193 was published by Oxfam GB,
and is reproduced with the permission of Oxfam GB, 274 Banbury
Road, Oxford OX2 7DZ, UK www.oxfam.org.uk/publications; Figure
5.2: copyright © Friends of the Earth; Figure 5.2 (photo centre right):
copyright © DigitalVision Ltd; Figure 5.2 (photo right): copyright ©
Ingram Publishing; Figure 5.4: copyright © Owen Logan; Figure 5.5:
copyright © Enrique Marcarian/Reuters; Figure 5.6: courtesy of the
Financial Times; Figure 5.7: copyright © Seamus Murphy; Figure 5.8:
copyright © William Thomas Cain/Getty; Figure 5.9: Refugee
Council; Figure 5.10: courtesy of Jo-Anne Driessens.

Illustrations

p.226: copyright © Josep Renau; pp.229–35: all photographs in the
photographic essay courtesy of Owen Logan.

Chapter 6

Text

Reading 6A: Gordon, A.F. (1997) *Ghostly Matters: Haunting and the
Sociological Imagination*, University of Minnesota Press. Copyright 1997 by
the Regents of the University of Minnesota; Reading 6B: Morrison, T.
(1987) *Beloved*, Picador; Reading 6C: Ramesh, R. (2004) 'Toiling in
India's ship graveyard for £1 a day', *The Guardian*, 22 June 2004.
Copyright © Guardian Newspapers Limited 2004.

Figures

Figures 6.1, 6.4, 6.5, 6.6. 6.9, 6.11, 6.13 and 6.14: courtesy of Steve Pile; Figure 6.2: copyright © Hansi Krauss/AP Photo/Empics; Figure 6.3: copyright © MTI; Figure 6.7: courtesy of Ilfracombe Museum; Figure 6.8: copyright © Ilfracombe Museum. By kind permission; Figure 6.10: copyright © Paul Slater/Apex Photo Agency Ltd; Figure 6.12: copyright © Martin Godwin.

Illustrations

p.275: Library of Congress, Prints & Photographic Division, reproduction number LC-USZ62–84545; p.285: copyright © A. Mukesh.

Chapter 7

Text

p.314: copyright © Bernie Grant Trust; Reading 7B: Mazrui, A.A. (2002) *Black Reparations in the Era of Globalization*, Global Academic Publishing; Reading 7C: Rodney, W. (1972) *How Europe Underdeveloped Africa*, Bogle l'Overture Publications Ltd.

Figures

Figure 7.4: courtesy of Bridgeman Art Library; Figure 7.5: from MACMILLAN ENCYCLOPAEDIA OF WORLD SLAVERY, Vol.1, by (eds) Paul Finkelman and Joseph C. Miller, Macmillan Reference USA, © 1998, Macmillan Reference USA. Reprinted by permission of The Gale Group; Figure 7.6: copyright © African Reparations Movement (ARC). By permission of the African Reparations Movement; Figure 7.10: from LION'S BLOOD by STEVEN BARNES. Copyright © 2002 by Steven Barnes. By permission of Warner Books, Inc.

Chapter 8

Text

Extract 8.1: from SEASON OF BLOOD: A RWANDAN JOURNEY by Fergal Keane (Viking, 1995). Copyright © Fergal Keene, 1995; Extract 8.2 (first item): Wallis, S. (1994) 'A dangerous and deadly myopia', Letter to the Editor, *The Guardian*, 31 October 1994. Copyright © Stewart Wallis; Extract 8.2 (second item): Twose, N. (1994) 'Moral dilemmas of aid to Rwanda', Letter to the Editor, *The Guardian*, 24 December 1994. Copyright © Nigel Twose; Reading 8A: Duffield, M. (2001) *Global Governance and the New Wars*, Zed Books Ltd.

Tables

Table 8.1: from www.un.org/depts/dpko/dpko/contributors/ 2004/ December2004_1.pdf. Copyright © 2004 United Nations.; Table 8.2: from The United Nations and Rwanda 1993–1996 by the Department of Public Information, United Nations. Copyright © 1996 United Nations. Reprinted with the permission of the publisher; Table 8.3: Gregory, D. (2004) *The Colonial Present: Afghanistan, Palestine, Iraq*, Blackwell Publishing Ltd.

Figures

Figure 8.4(a) and (b): from The United Nations and Rwanda 1993–1996 by the Department of Public Information, United Nations. Copyright © 1996 United Nations. Reprinted with the permission of the publisher; Figure 8.5: courtesy of Dick Galbreath, University of Kentucky Cartography Lab.; Figure 8.6: the advertisement on p.363 was published by Oxfam GB, 2004, and is produced with the permission of Oxfam GB, 274 Banbury Road, Oxford, OX2 7DZ, UK www.oxfam.org.uk/publications; Figure 8.7: copyright © DPI/UN Photo.

Cover illustration

Copyright © Patricia & Angus Macdonald/Aerographica.

Every effort has been made to contact copyright holders. If any have been inadvertently overlooked the publishers will be pleased to make the necessary arrangements at the first opportunity.

Index

Page numbers in **bold** refer to definitions of terms.